THE CAUSE THAT FAILED

THE
CAUSE THAT
FAILED

Communism in American Political Life

Guenter Lewy

New York   Oxford
OXFORD UNIVERSITY PRESS   1990

Oxford University Press

Oxford   New York   Toronto
Delhi   Bombay   Calcutta   Madras   Karachi
Petaling Jaya   Singapore   Hong Kong   Tokyo
Nairobi   Das es Salaam   Cape Town
Melbourne   Auckland

and associated companies in
Berlin   Ibadan

Library of Congress Cataloging-in-Publication Data
Lewy, Guenter, 1923–
The cause that failed : Communism in American political life
Guenter Lewy.
p.   cm.
Includes bibliographical references.
ISBN 0–19–505748–1
1. Communist Party of the United States of America—History—20th century.
2. Communism—United States—History—20th century.
3. United States—Politics and government—20th century.   I. Title.
JK2391.C5L48   1990
324.273′75′08—dc20   89–26653

9 8 7 6 5 4 3 2 1
Printed in the United States of America
on acid-free paper

For Ilse

Preface

A spectre is haunting Europe—the spectre of the demise of Communism. Only this paraphrase of the *Communist Manifesto* of 1848 seems appropriate to describe the extraordinary and momentous events of the year 1989 which have transformed the political landscape of the European continent. Together with the bloody suppression of the student-led democracy movement in China, the decisive repudiation of Communism by the people of Eastern Europe has shaken the world Communist movement to its core, and even the American Communist party, long a stronghold of Stalinism, is unlikely to escape the turmoil that has ensued. A look backward at Communism's past should enable us to see these stunning developments in the proper historical perspective and help us better understand the dilemmas for the future of American Communism in particular that have arisen.

"The most confused and controversial problem of the age"—this is how Clinton Rossiter, the editor of a series of books dealing with the impact of Communism on American life, characterized the Communist problem in America during the 1950s. Since then, almost forty years later, the waning of the Cold War and other public controversies like the Vietnam conflict have pushed the issue of domestic Communism into the background. Decimated in strength by the Smith Act prosecutions and the impact of Khrushchev's speech in 1956 denouncing the crimes of the Stalin era, the American Communist party today plays a rather insignificant role in the political life of the nation. Justifiably, it is no longer seen as a threat to the country's national security. Indeed, the notion, adhered to by some segments of the Right, that the Communist party would attempt, let alone succeed, by force to overthrow the government of the United States was always a paranoid fantasy.

There was a time when the American Communist party represented a political force to be reckoned with. In the late 1930s, the Party had close to 100,000 members, and its circle of supporters in various allied organizations was larger still. The Communists claimed that for every party member there were twenty sympathizers, but even if we halve this figure we arrive at possibly one million Americans who more or less followed the party line during those years. At the end of World War II, membership was down to 80,000, but the unfolding Cold War, the Soviet Union's domination of Eastern Europe, the ascension of Communist regimes in China and Czechoslovakia, the discovery of several highly placed Communist spies, as well as the dramatic rise in Communist strength in Western Europe made concern about the threat of Communism more than an idle fear. The American Communist party, being party of a powerful worldwide movement, was seen not only as a radical domestic political organization but as an important element in a fateful international power struggle.

And yet just a few years later, by 1957, the American Communist party was reduced to a paid-up membership of just above 3,000. Rarely have political parties experienced such a swift and drastic decline in strength and influence. At that point in time, when the Party appeared to be about to disappear for good from the American political scene, it was rescued from oblivion by a significant change in the attitude toward American Communism on the party of an influential segment of the intellectual community. These repeated and striking shifts that have taken place in the political fortunes of the American Communist movement call for examination and explanation.

The new political climate which has benefited American Communism as of late involves another radical about-face that demands explication. For much of its history the American Communist party was regarded as a disloyal and generally distrusted political entity. Opposition to communism, i.e. anticommunism, was widespread and, among most liberals, was seen as a litmus test of political and moral integrity. Since the emergence of the New Left in the 1960s, on the other hand, and as a belated reaction to the demagogic antics of Senator Joseph McCarthy and his supporters in the 1950s, a substantial part of the American intellectual community has adopted a self-conscious anti-anticommunism that appears to be no less reflexive than the often unthinking anticommunism of the 1950s it has replaced. In these circles it is considered bad form to refer to anyone as a Communist. Even Angela Davis, a highly placed Party functionary and twice the Party's candidate for vice-president of the

United States, is usually called by the media a "black activist" rather than a Communist. These new attitudes, it should be stressed, came to the fore many years before the appearance of Mikhail Gorbachev as a radical reformer of Soviet Communism and well before the emergence of more benevolent views towards the Soviet Union that have developed in this country as a reaction to these reforms and as a result of the improved international climate.

Other manifestations of anti-anticommunism can be found in recent scholarship dealing with the Communist party. During the last decade, young scholars who are graduates of the student New Left of the 1960s, have produced a large volume of writings on the history of American Communism. This new body of scholarship is not uncritical of the Party, yet, in the words of one of its practitioners, it also "emphasizes the genuine achievements of Communists in labor and political life during the 1930s and 1940s." Moreover, most of these scholars go out of their way to reject what they call "cold war liberalism" and its associated attitude of anticommunism. This preoccupation with avoiding anticommunism, as we will have occasion to note, often leads to a new bias and results in strained, if not distorted, interpretations of the past. Just as during the 1930s the liberal community experienced sharp divisions in its reaction to communism, the attitude of liberals toward the Communist problem in the 1950s was far from monolithic. The pejorative label "cold war liberalism," a more careful and dispassionate examination of the historical record makes clear, is inaccurate and misleading.

The literature on American Communism is enormous. An annotated bibliography, *Communism in the United States,* compiled by Joel I. Seidman of the University of Chicago and published by Cornell University Press in 1969, included almost 7,000 items. To this must be added the large number of books and articles published during the recent renaissance of scholarship dealing with the American Communist party. Between 1979 and 1984 alone, there appeared thirty-five books, twenty-three dissertations, and fifty-eight articles concerned with the history of American Communism. Also, during the last twenty years, a considerable number of former members and sympathizers of the Party have published their memoirs. This large volume of writings on American Communism throws new light on many aspects of the Communist issue; it calls for an attempt to evaluate and synthesize the new materials that have been produced so that scholars and general readers alike can share in the current state of knowledge.

During much of human history, intellectuals—individuals concerned with ideas and ideals—have functioned as guardians and defenders of traditional values. In modern times on the other hand, it is generally agreed,

intellectuals have exhibited a pronounced tendency to criticize the established order of things. One of the main themes of the first part of this
book is the relationship of the American intellectual community and the
American Communist party. (No attempt has been made to include the
history of the Trotzkyist movement or other communist sects.) This relationship has gone through many different phases ranging all the way from
principled rejection to the granting of political legitimacy during the days
of the Popular Front and the last two decades. In the process of tracing
this changing relationship and taking into account the new sources that
have become available, we will re-examine questions such as the following: Why did the Party attract so little support from intellectuals during
its first decade? What accounts for the widespread support of liberals for
the Popular Front of the 1930s? What made it so difficult for some intellectuals to acknowledge the true nature of Stalin's dictatorial regime?
Why did some liberals during the late 1940s refuse to accept the possibility that men like Alger Hiss could have committed espionage? What
caused the divisions in the intellectual community over the inroads of
McCarthyism? How important was the Vietnam war in creating the new
mood of anti-anticommunism? To find answers to questions such as these
is not an easy task; they involve the subtle interplay between objective
circumstances and the complex dynamics of the human personality which
shapes the course of human history and often defies generalization and
explanation.

Part II of this study takes up the issue of political cooperation with the
Communist party by way of a series of case studies of organizations and
their dealings with the Party. Here, too, we encounter far-reaching changes
during the last twenty years. Until the late 1960s liberal organizations like
the American Civil Liberties Union and the Committee for a Sane Nuclear Policy adhered to a policy of excluding Communists from positions
of leadership and generally refused political cooperation with the Party
and its fronts. These policies had been adopted in order to prevent Communist infiltration as well as to safeguard the political standing of these
organizations during a strongly anticommunist political climate. The
manner in which during recent years these exclusionary policies have
been repealed or tacitly ignored is not generally known and indeed involves an intricate and often fascinating tale. Part III seeks to assess the
current status of organized Communism in America.

This book is not a history of the American Communist party, and it
therefore does not offer an exhaustive account of the Party's manifold activities during its seventy-year existence. Neither does the book discuss
all the many individuals and organizations that came in contact with
the Party. Some readers will find certain topics as treated too briefly while

others will consider some sections as already familiar ground. In a book addressed not only to the specialist but also to the general reader, such dilemmas are unavoidable. There also exist obvious generational differences in knowledge of American Communism. Today most people in this country have neither seen nor heard a live American Communist, and not a few of them appear to consider this particular political species an invention of the late Senator Joe McCarthy. If during the 1950s Americans suspected a Communist under every bed, many of them now are equally firmly convinced that there are no Communists under any bed. Both views, this book argues, are erroneous. If nothing else, just the fact, disclosed a few months ago by a Communist party official, that 80 percent of American Communists keep their membership secret, would seem to indicate the need for more attention than this problem has received in recent years.

The debt which a work of the scope undertaken here owes to the writings of earlier scholars is considerable. In discussing the first two decades of the Party's history, I have benefited especially from the valuable spade work done by Theodore Draper and Harvey Klehr, who had access to important unpublished materials. For the chapters on organizational responses, I have drawn on minutes and other internal papers of the groups examined. Some of these materials I acquired while serving as a local officer of the ACLU and SANE. Additional materials on the ACLU were made available to me by Associate Director Alan Reitman, for which I express my gratitude. I consulted still other archival sources at the Swarthmore College Peace Collection, whose curators and staff proved ever-courteous and helpful. In the notes to this book I have listed the most important sources. To include a critical bibliography would have required another book.

A final word of thanks is due colleagues and friends who have given me the benefit of their criticism. They include Abraham Ascher, Harvey Klehr, Rita Simon, and Hans Tütsch. As is customary, I should add that the opinions and conclusions reached in this book remain, for better or for worse, my own responsibility.

Washington, D.C.   G.L.
February 1990

Contents

I
History of an Encounter

1. Early Years: Isolation and Internal Strife, 3
2. Progressives, Socialists, and the United Front, 13
3. The Theory and Practice of Front Organizations, 25
4. The "Red Decade," 41
5. World War II: Demise and Rebirth of the Popular Front, 60
6. Liberal Anticommunism During the Cold War Era, 76
7. The Revival of Anti-anticommunism, 115

II
Organizational Responses: Cooperation with, Acceptance or Exclusion of Communists

8. The American Civil Liberties Union Through Changing Times, 141
9. The Peace Movement: The Difficulty of Learning from Experience, 166
10. The Travail of Progressivism, 198
11. The Committee for a Sane Nuclear Policy: From Center to Left, 224
12. The Nonexclusionary Policy Triumphant: SDS and the Movement Against the Vietnam War, 250

III
American Communism Today

13. The Old Left-New Left Nexus, 279
14. Retrospect and Outlook, 294

Appendix, 307   Notes, 309

Appendix: Communist Party Membership, 1919–1988, 345

Index, 347

I

History of an Encounter

1

Early Years: Isolation and Internal Strife

Origins

The American Communist party developed out of American socialism. Formed in 1901, the Socialist party by 1912 had gained a membership of 150,000. It was led by Eugene Victor Debs, an inspiring figure, whose call to brotherhood and revolt found a ready echo in a time of questioning and unrest. Muckrakers like Lincoln Steffens were exposing graft and corruption. Upton Sinclair's novel *The Jungle* described and castigated life in the Chicago stockyards and helped bring about food inspection laws. Both Sinclair and his contemporary Jack London, another writer of realistic fiction, considered themselves socialists.

The Socialist party was divided into several rival factions. A right wing identified with the conservative American Federation of Labor (AFL) and generally was suspicious of "revolutionary phrase mongering." The left, in turn, was split into two factions. One group was sympathetic to or active in the Industrial Workers of the World (IWW), or Wobblies, as they were called. The Wobblies were syndicalists, self-declared radicals given to verbal violence, who sought to build industrial unions through militant labor struggle. Their contempt for politics and social reform was to have a strong influence on the early history of American Communism. A smaller faction of the Socialist party's left wing was Marxist. Many of the early Communist leaders came from this group.[1]

The divisions within the party continued during World War I, though formally all segments went on record as opposing American involvement. Once the United States entered the war, the Socialists, like other antiwar groups, were subjected to vicious attacks from both the government and mobs of patriots. Their publications were banned from the mails, their offices were raided, and strikers were beaten up. Many of their leaders were indicted and convicted under the Espionage Act of 1917. Still, the Socialist party grew.

The outbreak of the Russian Revolution had a galvanizing effect on the American radical movement. Almost everyone hailed the overthrow of the Tsar and the Bolshevik revolution that followed several months later. Intellectuals in particular were inspired by what presented itself as the world's first workers' state, the realization of the socialist dream. Even a right-wing Socialist like Louis Waldman called the Bolshevik upheaval an "awakening to freedom and to self-government." Eugene Debs declared: "From the crown of my head to the soles of my feet I am a Bolshevik, and proud of it."[2] The lesson seemed to be that even a small proletarian party could seize power if it only had enough revolutionary zeal and purity of doctrine. "It was the Russian Revolution—the Bolshevik Revolution of November 7, 1917—which created the American Communist movement," proclaimed one of the American Communist leaders, Charles E. Ruthenberg, in 1922.[3]

There followed revolutions in Hungary, Austria, and Germany. Italian workers seized factories. This upsurge of the European working class encouraged American radicals and further contributed to the strengthening of the left wing of the Socialist party. A wave of strikes during the year 1919 increased revolutionary expectations. More workers were involved in labor disputes in 1919 than the total number during the following six years. The foreign-language federations, semiautonomous organizations of non-English-speaking workers affiliated with the Socialist party, were especially caught up in revolutionary fervor and sought to shape themselves in the image of Bolshevism. "A great deal in the early history of the American Communist movement that was sectarian to the point of stupidity, and much that was downright absurd," note Irving Howe and Lewis Coser in their history of the Party, "can be traced back to the 'Russian fever' which beset the left-wingers."[4]

Pressure was mounting for the creation of a new revolutionary party built upon the Leninist model. In April 1919, the left wing of the Socialist party began publishing the *New York Communist*. It was edited by the journalist John Reed, one of the first Americans actually to have been to Russia and to have seen the revolution at first hand. Party leaders, primarily right-wingers, reacted to the rapidly growing left wing with strong-arm methods. Entire branches were expelled; the Russian, Polish, and other foreign language federations were suspended. These measures enabled the right wing to maintain its control of the party machinery, but it also led to a large loss of membership. In January 1919, the Socialist party had reached its second highest point in membership with a total of 109,589 members. By July, membership was down to 39,750.[5] The purge persuaded the last hold-outs on the left that the time had indeed arrived to organize an independent Communist party.

In early September 1919, two Communist parties came into being at conventions held in Chicago—the Communist Party of America and the Communist Labor Party of America. The differences between them involved previous disagreements over whether to try to take over the Socialist party, rival claims of doctrinal orthodoxy, as well as tensions between the English-speaking "Americans" and the far more numerous "foreigners" in the foreign-language federations. Internal bickering and factional infighting continued to be a hallmark of American Communism for much of its early history. It was not until May 1921 that the rival groups, pressured by the Comintern in Moscow, agreed to form a united party. First known as the Communist Party of America, it adopted its present name, Communist Party, USA (CPUSA), in 1929.

During the First World War, American radicals had drawn the enmity of patriots because of their opposition to the war. After the end of hostilities, the desire of conservatives that radicals be held accountable for their wartime disloyalty, fear of the Bolshevik Revolution, and the open identification of the Left with that revolution led to a wave of repression known as the "Red Scare." Under the direction of Attorney General A. Mitchell Palmer, mass indictments under criminal syndicalism laws and the deportation of alien radicals seriously weakened the entire Left. The new Communist movement was driven underground.

A report issued in May 1920 by twelve distinguished lawyers, including such constitutional authorities as Dean Roscoe Pound, Zechariah Chafee, and Felix Frankfurter, described and denounced the repressive measures:

> Under the guise of a campaign for the suppression of radical activities, the office of the Attorney General, acting by its local agents throughout the country, and giving express instructions from Washington, has committed continual illegal acts. Wholesale arrests both of aliens and citizens have been made without warrant or any process of law; men and women have been jailed and held *incommunicado* without access of friends or counsel; homes have been entered without search warrant and property seized and removed; other property has been wantonly destroyed; working men and women suspected of radical views have been shamefully abused and maltreated. . . . Agents of the Department of Justice have been introduced into radical organizations for the purpose of informing upon their members or inciting them to activities; these agents have even been instructed from Washington to arrange meetings upon certain dates for the express object of facilitating wholesale raids and arrests.[6]

Sources of Weakness

By the end of 1920, the tide of fear had ebbed, and the Communists emerged into the open. Development of a legal party had been urged by the Communist Third International in Moscow, the center of the world Communist movement established in 1919 and known as the Comintern. However, also on orders of Moscow, an underground apparatus continued to provide leadership. Altogether, the American Communists, seeking to emulate their Russian counterparts, delighted in secrecy, which became a veritable mystique adhered to beyond all objective needs. Together with the Party's tactic of infiltrating and taking over other organizations, this compulsive adherence to secrecy and deception soon earned the Communists a reputation of being intriguers and manipulators and diminished their political influence.

Another source of weakness was the foreign image projected by the Communist party. A twenty-one-point statement of principles issued by the Comintern in 1920 imposed upon all member parties a system of strict discipline and subservience to the decisions of the Comintern. The Comintern saw itself as the single Communist party of the entire world. The national parties in the various countries were to be but separate sections of a worldwide revolutionary army led by a general staff in Moscow, authorized to chart strategy and impose discipline to implement that strategy. American Communist leaders took pride in their faithful adherence to instructions coming to them from the ideological and organizational center of the Communist movement. "I am for the Comintern from start to finish," declared William Z. Foster in 1925. "I want to work with the Comintern, and if the Comintern finds itself criss-cross with my opinions there is only one thing to do, and that is to change my opinions and fit the policy of the Comintern."[7] Since the Comintern in turn was dominated by the leadership of the Russian Communist party, this dependence inevitably created a picture of a party more loyal to its Russian masters than to the homeland of its members. As an unidentified wit at the time put it, the Communist party, like the Brooklyn Bridge, was suspended on cables—from Moscow.

The fact that a large majority of the membership was foreign-born and composed of relatively recent immigrants still speaking their native tongue further reinforced the Party's foreign appearance. During the first years of its history, when the Party included numerous foreign-language groups in addition to an English-speaking section, probably only one in ten of the members was American-born. In 1925 the Party underwent a process of restructuring which abolished the foreign language branch as the basic unit of organization. As a result of this "Bolshevization" the Party lost half of its membership—dropping from 14,037 to 7,215 members within one month. Yet the predominance of the foreign-born continued. As late as 1929 only one-third of the membership was English-speaking.[8] Not until October 1936 was the Party able to claim that a majority of members were American-born. In New York State this did not happen until September 1938.[9]

The Communist party's endeavor to appear as a truly Bolshevik party, affiliated with the leading edge of the world revolutionary movement, attracted radicals. But the Party's mindless imitation of rhetoric developed in the Russian environment also alienated many would-be followers. There is the well-known story of Israel Amter, a leading Communist functionary, who opened a meeting in New York City with the greeting: "Workers and Peasants of Brooklyn!"[10]

The slavish adherence to the ever-changing directives of the Comintern created other problems, for the leadership in Moscow developed its strategy with little reference to the realities of American society. At best the Comintern laid down a line on the basis of a perspective that was predominantly European. A right or left turn in Europe led inevitably to a right or left turn in America. At its worst, Comintern policies reflected internal rivalries and factional struggles in the Russian Communist party. "Whichever it was," concludes Theodore Draper, "the Comintern could not be challenged; it was the repository of the infallible doctrine and the supreme court of political orthodoxy."[11] For example, as we will see in more detail in the next chapter, between 1922 and 1924 the American party had managed to gain influence in the Farmer-Labor movement in Minnesota. But in 1924 Foster returned from Moscow with the news that the Comintern regarded this alliance as an impermissible "united front from above," and the Party quickly reversed direction and repudiated Senator Robert LaFollette, the popular leader of the Progressive party. The result was the loss of whatever tenuous link to an authentic American radical movement the American Communist party had been able to develop. "The rest of the twenties," recalled Earl Browder years later, "was spent in isolation and destructive inner factionalism."[12] At the end of its first decade, the Party had less than ten thousand members. Turnover in membership was high.

Unable to establish any real rapport with the masses of American workers, the Party turned its best energies inward and exhausted itself in internal feuds and factional strife. On the grounds of being insufficiently Bolshevik, the Ludwig Lore faction was expelled in 1925; the Cannon-Shachtman group in 1928. The expulsion of the Cannonites marked the beginning of the American Trotskyist movement, but the ideological differences involved in other struggles were often murky, and their relevance to the situation of the American Communist party was hard to discern. When Jay Lovestone and his followers were forced out in 1929 the key factor in their demise was the fact that for too long they had sided with a loser in a power struggle inside the Russian party— with Bukharin rather than Stalin.[13]

A Rebuff to Intellectuals

The ouster of Lovestone, one of the founders of the American Communist party, was in part the ouster of a college-educated individual who had refused to accept party discipline. Tension between the "professional proletarians" and the "college boys" was indeed a constant problem in the American party. In the factional struggles that beset the Party, a college education was a definite handicap. The rigidly authoritarian structure of the Party and its suspicion and even disdain for intellectuals explain why few intellectuals joined or supported the Party during the twenties. Writers like Lincoln Steffens, John Reed, and Max Eastman felt that the Bolshevik revolution had opened a new age of freedom for mankind, but many of them at times were less than enthusiastic about the American branch of the world communist movement.

Although he took a strong stand for the Comintern Eastman did not take out a membership in the American party. By 1921 his growing opposition to the churchlike features of the Party and its opéra-bouffe imitation of Russian precedents led him to go public with his criticism. In an article published in the *Liberator,* Eastman called upon the Party to give up its infantile leftism and its infatuation with conspiracy. The Party had been stressing the idea of party discipline to a degree that would seem sensible only on the eve of battle, yet no such violent struggle faced the American party. "To make that idea an essential part of the general propaganda of communism in a country as complacent of its democracy, and as far from a conscious struggle of classes as the United States," Eastman argued, "is to ignore the essential difference between the two situations." The Party, he concluded, had to get rid of those "pure and perfect theologians of Bolshevism, whose only purpose is to establish in this country a secret brotherhood of revolutionary saints."[14]

The young radical economist, Scott Nearing, did join the Communist party in 1927, but he soon ran afoul of the Party's system of censorship. His book *Dollar Diplomacy,* which appeared in 1925, had been well received, but a new manuscript, *The Twilight of Empire,* completed in 1929, was found unorthodox by Moscow and the Party denied permission to publish. Rather than agree to the suppression of his work Nearing resigned from the Party, though he expressed the wish to continue to uphold its principles and to support its work. But the Party did not agree to his voluntary departure and expelled him with a stinging denunciation. The revolutionary party, declared the *Daily Worker,* cannot be satisfied with sympathy: "It must demand subordination of the individual to the line and to the activities of the Party and the revolutionary working class. For the working class, a disciplined advance guard is the question of victory or defeat." And Earl Browder added: "To be a friend of the Party is to be a soldier in its lines. Outside the ranks of the Party, the 'friend' ceases to be a positive factor on the side of the working class in the revolutionary struggle and therefore strengthens the enemy of the proletariat."[15]

For much of its history, the Party followed the same policy of refusing to accept or recognize the resignation of important members. Dissidents were commonly expelled amidst charges of treason, adherence to Trotskyism, or lack of a stable personality. A few writers swallowed their distaste for the Party's rigid system of discipline and became Communists. Mike Gold and Joseph Freeman were Jewish radicals who joined the Party in the early twenties and who assumed a leading role in editing a literary journal, the *New Masses,* which appeared in 1926. At first, the magazine was controlled by liberals and radicals who wanted a commitment to art and aesthetic freedom rather than to politics. After Mike Gold became editor in 1928, the *New Masses* began to move closer to the Party, though for a while it continued to publish non-Communist writers. Eventually, both Gold and Freeman convinced themselves that their intellectual independence had been a mistake, that the Party was more important than any single individual, and that art and politics had to become one enterprise. There was need to produce a proletarian literature, dedicated to the creation of a new and better America. "Neither of us was aware," Freeman recalled in his autobiography published in 1936, "to what extent our moods, undisciplined by Marxist analysis, fluid and contradictory in the bohemian tradition which cried anathema on will and worshiped sensibility, were the result of the historic period in which we lived."[16]

In October 1929, the Party organized the John Reed Clubs, designed to appeal to intellectuals and to help create a "proletarian culture." The purpose of revolutionary art was said to be to inspire the workers to greater militancy in the class struggle. The first club, in New York City, had fifty members. By the time of the first national congress of John Reed Clubs held in Chicago at the end of May 1932, there were 642 members in ten different cities.

Among those who joined the Communist party by way of the John

Reed Clubs was the aspiring black writer Richard Wright in Chicago. Wright was impressed by the Communists in his club. He found them to be "fervent, democratic, restless, eager and self-sacrificing." At the same time, Wright was struck by the anti-intellectualism of his new comrades. "He talks like a book," Wright recalled one comment about himself. "And that was enough to condemn me for ever as bourgeois." Another black Communist told him that intellectuals don't fit well into the Party, that the Party had had lots of trouble with them in the past, and he obliquely warned Wright against showing too much independent thinking. Unable to function as a writer in this oppressive atmosphere, Wright eventually tried to leave the Party, only to be branded a traitor and one whose faith had failed. His comrades, he related in his contribution to *The God That Failed,* "had never been able to conquer their fear of the individual way in which I acted and lived, an individuality which life had seared into my bones."[17]

Created as a party auxiliary, the John Reed Clubs soon succeeded in branching out and spawning other groups designed to attract non-Communists to the Party's cause. It was of vital importance, Mike Gold wrote in the *New Masses,* to bring all friendly intellectuals into the ranks of the revolution. "Every door must be opened wide to the fellow travelers." At that time, the term "fellow traveler" still had a positive and laudatory meaning. It was meant to describe, Freeman explained, "artists and writers who are not members of the Communist Party but who sympathize with the revolution and assist in their capacity as artists and writers."[18]

By the end of the twenties, a growing number of American intellectuals were willing to listen to what the Communist party had to offer. The collapse of the stock market in 1929 and the sense that American capitalism was failing raised the reputation of the Soviet Union, the world's first socialist country. In March 1930, the John Reed Clubs and the Friends of the Soviet Union rallied 3,000 people to a meeting to protest anti-Soviet propaganda. Eighty-two intellectuals signed an appeal defending the "workers' fatherland."

In late 1930 the John Reed Clubs succeeded in getting two non-Communist writers, Theodore Dreiser and John Dos Passos, to agree to serve as chairman and treasurer respectively of a newly created Emergency Committee for Southern Political Prisoners. By May 1931 other intellectuals such as Malcolm Cowley, Henry Newman, Franz Boas, and Suzanne LaFollette had joined the newly created National Committee for the Defense of Political Prisoners. The fact that the committee operated under the control of the Party did not yet trouble its non-Communist members eager to advance civil liberties. After the committee had sent a well-publicized delegation to Harlan County in Pennsylvania, where a Communist-led strike by mine workers had been accompanied by much violence, Theodore Dreiser urged a vote for the Communist party in the 1931 elections: "Without insisting upon my agreement with the larger aims of the Communist party, I feel that its candidates and program represent the only current political value worth supporting."[19]

A similarly complementary view of Communism was articulated by Edmund Wilson, a literary critic and an editor of the liberal *New Republic*, in early 1931. In an article entitled "An Appeal to Progressives," Wilson argued that the time had come for liberals to reconsider their belief in a benevolent capitalism and the usefulness of gradual change. Nine million men were out of work, and American cities were scenes of unprecedented misery. The capitalist system had experienced a full-scale disaster and the machinery of representative government appeared unable to deal with the unfolding Depression. The Communist party, Wilson reminded his readers, hoped to benefit from a final collapse of capitalism; such an outcome no longer seemed unthinkable. To prevent this from happening Americans might have "to put their traditional idealism and their genius for organization behind a radical social experiment." Only social control and a planned society such as existed in the Soviet Union could bring meaningful change.

> I believe that if the American radicals and progressives who repudiate the Marxist dogma and the strategy of the Communist party still hope to accomplish anything valuable, they must take Communism away from the Communists, and take it without ambiguities, asserting that their ultimate goal is the ownership by the government of the means of production. If we want to prove the Communists wrong, if we want to demonstrate that the virtue has not gone out of American democracy, if we want to confute the Marxist cynicism implied by "economic laws" the catastrophic outcome of which is, after all, predicted only on an assumption of the incurable swinishness and inertia of human nature—if we seriously want to do this, an American opposition must not be afraid to dynamite old conceptions and shibboleths and to substitute new ones as shocking as necessary.[20]

Norman Thomas, the leader of the Socialist party, reminded readers of the *New Republic* that the Socialists sought the very same collective ownership of the means of production favored by Wilson. Those who supported this position therefore should join the Socialist party. John Dos Passos spoke for many intellectuals of his time, for whom only the most radical solution appeared to be attractive, when he rejected this invitation out of hand: Socialists and other radicals have their usefulness, he wrote in the summer of 1932, "but I should think that becoming a Socialist right now would have just about the same effect on anybody as drinking a bottle of near-beer."[21]

The Communist party, in turn, highly suspicious of all independent intellectuals, denounced Wilson as a social fascist. His favorable view of Communism and the Soviet Union counted as nothing. Several more years were to pass before the Comintern would switch its line and actively seek out radicals like Wilson.

2

Progressives, Socialists, and the United Front

The early Communist movement had hoped to supplant the Socialists and to become the main voice of the working class, but by the early 1920s this hope had been disappointed not only in the United States but in the rest of the world as well. European capitalism had begun to recover from the wave of revolutionary unrest that had followed the end of World War I. The newly formed and inexperienced Communist parties were under attack for having split the existing organizations of the working class. In order to gain access to the masses of workers who remained loyal to the Socialist parties, the Comintern developed the slogan of the "united front."

The Comintern distinguished between two main forms of the united front tactic—"from above" and "from below." The united front from above signified an alliance between the Communist party and the leaders of other workers' organizations. Since the main purpose of the united front was to capture the masses and take them away from the influence of the Socialist leadership, this form of united front was used only sporadically. The united front from below, on the other hand, involved the attempt to reach the rank and file of the Socialist parties and the unions connected with them by going over the heads of the leaders of these organizations. The belligerent edge of this strategy was openly acknowledged. "We entered upon this road," declared Karl Radek at the Fourth Congress of the Comintern in 1922, "not because we want to merge with the social democrats, but in the knowledge that we shall stifle them in our embrace."[1]

The Farmer-Labor Movement

The issue of the united front arose in the American context first in connection with the Farmer-Labor movement. Several such parties did spring up during the postwar Depression, most of them developed by local trade unions. A Labor party organized in Chicago in November 1919 changed its name the following year to the Farmer-Labor party. In February 1922, the Conference for Progressive Political Action (CPPA) convened in Chicago, attended by the Farmer-Labor party, the Socialist party, and several large unions. The conference decided to support progressive candidates in the 1922 primaries pledged to the principles of "genuine democracy" in agriculture, industry, and government. The Communists were not invited, and undoubtedly would have refused the invitation anyway. Preoccupied with their own internal problems, they looked upon the Farmer-Laborites as "reformists," worse than the Socialists.[2]

By the time the CPPA met for its second conference in December 1922 in Cleveland, the Comintern had started encouraging member parties to make overtures to other working-class organizations. The Communists, therefore, without even waiting for an invitation, sought admission to the Cleveland gathering. They were rebuffed by the credentials committee, controlled by the conservative railroad unions, who maintained that the Communists' belief in dictatorship was incompatible with the conference's commitment to democracy. Only the delegates of the Chicago Farmer-Labor party voted for seating the Communists. When the conference also refused to agree to the immediate formation of a national third party, the Farmer-Laborites pulled out and resolved to go ahead on their own.

In March 1923, the Farmer-Labor party, led by John Fitzpatrick, decided to call a convention to organize a national party of workers and farmers. Fitzpatrick was a militant trade unionist who looked upon the Communists as fellow radicals. The Communists, therefore, received an invitation for the convention set for July 3 in Chicago. But by June it had become clear that most unions and the Socialist party would not come. Fitzpatrick was warned that the Communists would seek to "pack" the convention, and he consequently developed second thoughts about the idea of forming a new party. His concerns, it turned out, were well founded.

The Farmer-Labor convention opened on July 3, 1923, with some 500 delegates claiming to represent 600,000 workers and farmers. The Communists, with a national membership of less than 14,000, had been allotted ten delegates, but they actually controlled almost half of the delegates in attendance. Some were there as delegates from local trade unions; others belonged to a variety of party fronts such as the Lithuanian Workers' Literature Society, the Rumanian Progressive Club, and the United Workingmen Singers. Strategically placed throughout the convention floor and with captains to keep the delegates in line, the Communists overwhelmed the unorganized members of the convention. At the end of the second day, they pushed through a resolution calling for the immediate organization of a new party—the Federated Farmer-Labor party (FFLP). It was called a federated party because it was to be based on organizational affiliations rather than individual membership. Fitzpatrick denounced the Communists for killing the Farmer-Labor party and destroying "the possibility of uniting the forces of independent political action in America," but by now it was too late. On the third and last day of the convention, a bitter Fitzpatrick and his supporters walked out.[3]

The Communists were jubilant and boasted that they had assumed the leadership of a genuine mass movement. But their triumph was short-lived. Their superior organization and discipline had enabled them to take control of a convention, but the hundreds of thousands of affiliated members represented in Chicago began to fade away just as soon as Communist control of the new party became obvious. A few months after the Chicago convention it became clear that the Communists essentially had captured themselves. The FFLP, admitted one Communist leader in December 1924, consisted of "ourselves and our nearest relatives."[4]

The break with the Farmer-Labor party cost the Communists dearly. There followed a wave of expulsions in the trade unions which wiped out hard-won gains. The Communists were themselves sharply divided over what had gone wrong. A letter from the Comintern received at the Party's convention held in late December 1923 congratulated them for correctly applying the united front policy and for "an achievement of prime importance." The letter called for a larger "United Front of all proletarian and farmers' parties and organizations."[5] But this bombast could hardly hide the setback that had occurred.

The Communists got a second chance to play the united front card in connection with the Minnesota Farmer-Labor party, which had recently scored some impressive electoral gains. Complicating this new endeavor, which became known as the "third party alliance" tactic, was the possibility that Republican Senator Robert M. LaFollette of Wisconsin, the favorite spokesman of liberals and progressives, might start a third party that would swallow up the Farmer-Laborites and in which the Communists could not possibly hope to play any significant role. In the Minnesota Farmer-Labor party the Communists had the cooperation of William Mahoney, a former Socialist, and together the two groups organized the Farmer-Labor Federation, an electoral coalition. Problems arose when Mahoney wanted to postpone any commitment on nominating a candidate for the 1924 presidential election until LaFollette's plans had become clear. LaFollette's backers, organized in the Conference for Progressive Political Action, wanted to await the outcome of the Republican contest and had scheduled a convention in Cleveland, Ohio, on July 4, 1924.

For the Communists the question was whether to stick with the wavering Mahoney or whether, once again, they should try to take over a Farmer-Labor organization. The candidacy of the "bourgeois" LaFollette presented additional complications for them. Unable to resolve the issue, the Party decided to send a delegation to Moscow. Meanwhile, the Communists and Mahoney agreed to convene on June 17 in St. Paul in order to nominate their candidate.

The Americans arrived in Moscow in the midst of the turmoil that followed the death of Lenin in January 1924. The struggle for power pitted Zinoviev, Kamenev, and Stalin on one side against Trotsky on the other. The latter was attacking the Comintern, headed by Zinoviev, for being too conciliatory and opportunistic, and he singled out the American party's proposed alliance with LaFollette as an example of this mistaken course. To undercut Trotsky, Zinoviev resolved on a "Left Turn" and issued an order for all Communist parties to cease any cooperation with liberal or Social Democratic parties.

The American delegation was back in New York on June 1 and reported what the Comintern had decided. The consternation that ensued was described by party leader Alexander Bittelman in an article published in the *Daily Worker* a year later:

> All our tactics, all our literature, all our slogans formulated during the months of January to May were based on this general idea of the third party alliance and then at a certain moment the Communist International said to our party, you cannot do it. . . . We were confronted with the necessity of completely reorienting ourselves practically within 24 hours, and comrades, a reorientation which was to take place [not] in the close study of our library, not in your own room, a reorientation of a political party on the open political arena, under the very fire of the enemy, because you must remember that at about the same time LaFollette and Gompers opened their attack on the June 17 convention and the Communists.[6]

The Comintern's decision to forbid Communist support for LaFollette was a secret, but meanwhile the projected alliance came apart at the other end. On May 29, the *New York Times* carried a letter from La-Follette in which he denounced the Communists as "the mortal enemies of the progressive movement and democratic ideals" and urged progressives to refuse to make any common cause with them. The result of this move was to persuade most Farmer-Labor delegates to shun the St. Paul meeting.

Over 500 delegates assembled in St. Paul on June 17. The Communists once again had excelled in creating paper organizations in order to give them the maximum number of delegates. There were counterfeit Farmer-Labor parties as well as new "mass organizations" such as the Red Eye Farmers Club, the Illinois Self-Advancement Club, and the People's Voice Culture Club. Their control of the convention thus assured, the Communists pushed through a resolution which accepted the candidacy of LaFollette on the condition that he submitted his campaign to the control of the Farmer-Labor party. This, of course, was merely a maneuver to prevent the non-Communist delegates from bolting the convention. LaFollette, after all, had already made clear his feelings about the Communists and there was no chance in the world that he would accept this arrangement. The alternative slate nominated by the convention in case LaFollette turned down the Farmer-Labor nomination was thus the real slate of candidates.

The Conference for Progressive Political Action met on July 4 and nominated Senators Robert LaFollette of Wisconsin and Burton K. Wheeler of Montana for President and Vice President on a third-party ticket. The unhappy Mahoney was punished for his dealings with the Communists by being excluded from the convention, but the gathering had strong support from many unions, cooperative societies, the original Farmer-Labor party, and the Socialists. The Communists quickly adjusted their line and on July 8 announced their own candidates for the presidential election. Soon thereafter, the ghost of the Federated Farmer-Labor party was laid to rest.

In conformity with the new Comintern policy, the Communists now turned all their fury against LaFollette. He was denounced as a "reactionary," a "tool of big business," an "enemy of labor," and the "candidate of political gangsters." The LaFollette movement was described as the most dangerous enemy of America's toiling masses and as future fascists. Predictably, the masses failed to listen to this counsel. When the votes were counted it turned out that LaFollette had received almost five million votes to the Communists' William Z. Foster's 33,300.

To the Progressives behind LaFollette the outcome was a big disappointment. Their candidate had received a mere 13 electoral votes to Calvin Coolidge's 382. LaFollette died the following year and his idea of a third party died with him. The Communists took pride in how faithfully they had executed the Comintern's orders. "The quick change in tactics," wrote Bittelman, proved that "we are well on the road to become a Leninist party."[7] Only many years later did some of them admit that their manipulative handling of the Farmer-Labor movement had squandered one of their best opportunities to break out of political isolation.

Socialists and Communists

Unperturbed by the American fiasco, the Comintern continued to use the idea of the united front as a ram against the Socialists. A resolution adopted at the Fifth Congress of the Comintern in 1925 stated: "The main purpose of the united front tactic consists in the struggle *against* the leaders of counter-revolutionary social democracy and in emancipating social-democratic workers from their influence."[8]

During the years that followed, the American Communist party followed this strategy to the letter. "The united front," argued the Party's general secretary, Earl Browder, at a party conference held in July 1933, "is not a peace pact with the reformists. The united front is a method of struggle against the reformists, against the social fascists, for the possession of the masses." If the Party concentrates upon the basic work "from below," Browder explained in his report to the central committee in September 1934, "we do not have to worry as to whether the Socialist party leadership ever agrees to the united front or not." The Party would win over the membership of the Socialist party and could disregard what the Socialist leaders thought about this maneuver.[9] Not surprisingly, this kind of offer of cooperation found few takers. The "famous 'united front from below,'" wrote Bertram D. Wolfe, who had been expelled from the Party in 1929, "is an invitation to the non-Communist workers to support the Communist Party! That is all! In short, the 'united front from below' is no united front at all." What it means is that the Communist party "will actually permit Socialists and members of the A.F. of L. unions to vote for Foster and call it a united front!"[10]

Until Hitler's assumption of power in Germany in January 1933, the Comintern had vigorously rejected the idea of any united front from above. Those members of the German party who sought to rally the anti-fascist forces in order to stem the rising menace of Nazism were purged. During the so-called "Third Period," which began with the Sixth Congress of the Comintern in 1928, the Communist International and its affiliated Communist parties orchestrated a chorus of hatred which denounced the Socialists as "social fascists" and declared them to be a greater threat to the interests of the working class than the fascists themselves. When during the election campaign of 1928 some California Communists challenged the Socialists to a debate in a letter addressed to "Dear Comrades," they were rebuked by the national party leadership for sending a communication to the ever "more fascist" Socialist leaders.[11] The chief enemy in the workers' movement, wrote a Comintern functionary in October 1932, is not fascism but social fascism (social democracy). In order "to win over the majority of the proletariat, i.e. to prepare the *basic* condition for the proletarian revolution, it is necessary to direct the chief blows against Social Fascism."[12] The victory of fascism was held to be a prelude to the victory of the Communists.

A half-turn in the Communist line took place after Hitler's appointment as chancellor in January 1933. As it became clear that the Nazi regime was no transitory episode and that a rearmed Nazi Germany could become a serious threat to the security of the Soviet Union, the Comintern began to shift. Two more years were to pass before the Comintern would fully accept the idea of a united front from above and embrace the slogan of the Popular Front. Meanwhile, however, Communist parties were encouraged to make overtures to the Socialists—to pursue the united front from above as well as from below.

The new Comintern line was well received by a faction of the American Socialist party known as the "Militants," headed by the leader of the party, Norman Thomas. Many younger Socialists, in particular, looked upon the Communists as fighters in a common cause, and they opposed the Communism-hating "Old Guard," a largely Jewish faction centered in New York and led by Morris Hillquit. Throughout the twenties, Thomas had expressed the hope that the Soviet Union would abandon its dictatorial features and that the Communists would return to the fold of democratic socialism. During this time the Communist party had poured its venom upon Thomas as a soft-headed bourgeois afraid of violence and had scorned his commitment to evolutionary change. Yet Thomas had refrained from denouncing the Communists. Under the impact of Hitler's victory in Germany, the militant faction of the Socialists now began to favor some kind of united action between Socialists and Communists in order to save America from the fate of Germany.

In a book published in 1934, *The Choice Before Us,* Norman Thomas gave his qualified support to the idea of an alliance with the Communists.

Short of organic unity or a general coalition, Communist and Socialist parties might logically be expected to work out a united front to achieve certain immediate ends upon which both sides are agreed. . . . I happen to belong to that group of Socialists, at present in a minority internationally, who believe that the urgency of the situation and the chances of success make it worth while to try boldly and carefully for a united front with Communists upon certain specific issues, especially if and when that united front includes elements which are neither Socialist nor Communist.

Thomas acknowledged the difficulty of developing a united front with a party which boasted openly that good faith is a "bourgeois virtue" and which had repeatedly stated that the purpose of a united front was to undermine the Socialist parties and destroy their leadership. Moreover, in order to win the workers away from Socialist influence the Communists resorted to "all manner of slander and falsehood." He himself, Thomas complained, had been subjected to numerous gratuitous lies and slanders, "made up out of whole cloth or out of deliberate distortions of statements and facts." Still, sheer necessity required "that Socialists and Communists act together in certain matters unless they wish to be destroyed separately."[13]

To the Old Guard in the Socialist party all this was anathema. In their view there existed a basic incompatibility between socialism and communism. For years they had experienced the disruptive tactics of the Communists. Time and again Socialist meetings had been invaded by organized bands of Communists who had shouted down speakers and broken up gatherings. Over the protest of the American Civil Liberties Union, the Communist party had defended such actions as justified violence "used by the workers against the oppressors."[14] The resentment of these Communist tactics by the Old Guard reached a new high when on February 16, 1934, a band of 5,000 Communists provoked a riot that wrecked a Socialist rally at Madison Square Garden in New York City convened in order to protest the bloody suppression of the Austrian Socialists by Chancellor Engelbert Dollfuss. Many in the Socialist party and outside its ranks saw a united front with an organization resorting to such tactics as completely unacceptable and self-defeating.

For a time, the Madison Square Garden riot put all talk about Socialist-Communist cooperation on ice. At its November 1934 meeting, the national executive committee of the Socialist party made all "sporadic and spontaneous local united front agreements" subject to approval by state and national executive committees.[15] Still, the Old Guard continued to think that Norman Thomas and his followers had not given up their support of the united front idea. An event that further increased tension within the divided Socialist party was the decision of Thomas to engage in a public debate with Earl Browder. In a press release prior to the debate held in Madison Square Garden on the evening of November 28, 1935, Thomas explained why a continuation of the Socialist-Communist dialogue was important: "Communists and Socialists, however sharp their past and present differences, recognize that they are in common danger from Fascism in America and if it is by any means possible intelligent Socialists and Communists do not want to have to learn to get along only in a concentration camp here in America."[16]

Thomas was far from wanting a general united front with the Communists. He was still thinking primarily in terms of joint actions and cooperation on specific issues such as civil rights cases and unemployment protests. But in the eyes of the Old Guard the debate with Browder represented a "love feast." The fact that Thomas during the debate had referred to the Soviet Union as a bright pillar in a turbulent and confused world, one of mankind's great hopes, added fuel to the fire. In a statement on the debate, Louis Waldman, the official spokesman for the Old Guard, criticized Thomas for engaging in a united front activity without first obtaining the consent of the party local to which he belonged. More basically, Waldman rejected the very idea of cooperation with the Communist party:

> We regard unity with the Communists, either on specific or general issues, as suicidal from a tactical standpoint and as thoroughly dishonest as a matter of principle. The Socialist Party has traditionally and constantly adhered to the principles of democracy and freedom. The Communist Party believes in dictatorship and the suppression of civil rights. Between the two there is an unbridgeable gulf.[17]

Critics of the Old Guard accused them of developing their own theory of social fascism. To the Old Guard, wrote Haim Kantorovitch in the *American Socialist Monthly,* the fight against communism is more important than the struggle against capitalism.

> This is a point of view that cannot of course be accepted by a revolutionary socialist. Communism is, for the revolutionary socialist, not the chief enemy. It is part of the revolutionary movement of the working class. Communism represents a theory, a point of view, which the revolutionary socialist believes to be wrong. The road proposed by communists does not, in the opinion of the revolutionary socialist, lead to socialism but away from it. It is the duty of the revolutionary socialist to use every opportunity to explain to the working class that the communist way is wrong, that it does not lead to socialism, but it is not the duty of the revolutionary socialists to drive the communists out of the labor movement. They cannot be driven out because they are part of it.[18]

Meanwhile, as the real meaning of Hitler's assumption of power sank in, Russian foreign policy had begun to adjust to the new constellation of forces in Europe. Soviet foreign minister Maxim Litvinov scurried around seeking security pacts with the much maligned Western democracies. In September 1934 the Soviet Union joined the previously despised League of Nations. The Comintern, too, was enlisted in the new drive for unity against the fascist menace. At its Seventh Congress held in July-August 1935, Georgi Dimitroff called not only for a broad united front of all working-class organizations but for a Popular Front of all progressive forces against fascism. This meant that the Communists now could accept a united front from above—could enter into negotiations for an alliance with Socialist leaders and even with bourgeois elements like the Radical party in France.

Following the 1935 Comintern Congress, the change in Communist tactics and rhetoric was striking. American Communists stopped referring to President Franklin D. Roosevelt as "the leading organizer and inspirer of Fascism" and as the agent through whom bankers and industrialists were "exercising their hidden dictatorship." Earlier the Communists had rebuked Norman Thomas, who had seen the fascist danger in private gangs, and they had insisted that "it is the White House that is the central headquarters of the advance of fascism." All this vilification was now forgotten. The New Deal ceased to be a "step in the direction of fascism," and by 1938 the Communists proclaimed that "Communism is 20th Century Americanism." Browder told the Party's Tenth Convention in September 1938 that only a judicious updating of Jefferson's principles was needed to ensure the "complete amalgamation of Jefferson's teachings with those of Marx, Engels, Lenin and Stalin." President Roosevelt was now "the chief figure in the progressive or liberal camp . . . the symbol which unites the broadest masses of the progressive majority of the people."[19]

While the Communist party moved toward the right, the Socialist party drifted to the left. As a result, the kind of united front sought by the Communists became less and less attractive even to the Militants in the Socialist party. Norman Thomas continued to favor cooperative action on specific issues. In the spring of 1936 he agreed to a joint May Day meeting with the Communist party in Union Square in New York City. In protest the Old Guard left the Socialist party and formed the Social-Democratic Federation. But even after being free from the restraining influence of the Old Guard, Thomas continued to reject the idea of "organic unity" with the Communists:

> The differences between us preclude organic unity. We do not accept control from Moscow, the old Communist accent on inevitable violence and party dictatorship, or the new accent on the possible good war against Fascism, and the new Communist opportunism. We assert genuine civil liberty in opposition to communist theory and practice in Russia.[20]

The Communists' acceptance of the New Deal and the idea of collective security ended all hope for a real alliance between the Communist and Socialist parties. Thomas and his followers were convinced that the New Deal was no answer either to the economic and social ills of capitalism or to the threat of fascism; they opposed collective security as leading to American involvement in a European war. By February 1937, the Socialist leadership had abandoned any further interest in cooperation with the Communists. In a book published in 1938, Norman Thomas came out against a Popular Front in America. Revising his earlier fear of an impending American fascism, he now wrote: "There is as yet no such fascist emergency as would justify or excuse it."[21]

Moreover, Thomas was becoming increasingly disillusioned with the Soviet Union. After a visit in the spring of 1937 and under the impact of the purge trials that took place there between 1936 and 1938, Thomas began to speak of the "degeneration of socialism" in Russia, and he started referring to both fascism and communism as totalitarian. Thomas served as a leading member of the Committee for the Defense of Trotsky, a decision he defended in a letter to the *New York World Telegram:*

I am not a Communist neither a Trotskyist nor a Stalinist. I believe that behind the present tragic situation lies the initial failure of the Communist Party to provide within its own party structure and within the structure of the government which it controls in Russia any proper means of discussion or protection for what we commonly regard as civil liberty.[22]

The American Communists' lip service to democracy in unions and in the state, Thomas pointed out in 1938, had to invite suspicion as long as the Communists praised Stalin's Russia where no real democracy was allowed to exist. "Either they do not know what words mean, or their faith in democracy in bourgeois lands is only a tactic . . . to be abandoned without notice if and when they no longer feel any need for, or hope in, 'collective security' and the Popular Front."[23]

Also, by the late 1930s, Norman Thomas and his followers had finally had enough of the Communists' manipulative tactics, including the use of the united front slogan to capture organizations close to the Socialist party such as the Workers' Alliance and the Student League for Industrial Democracy. Accompanied by appeals for unity, the Communists had resumed the old practice of making vicious attacks upon the Socialist party and some of its members. Norman Thomas was slow to realize that Communists could be as bad as or worse than Democrats and Republicans, whom he considered callous and indifferent to the fate of the poor and downtrodden. When it dawned on him that the Old Guard's vehement opposition to any cooperation with the Communists had been right after all, the impact was strong. One of Thomas's biographers writes:

His discovery that his honesty had been repaid by fraud, that his anti-Fascism and his support of the Spanish Loyalists and his dream of an "inclusive party" had all been used by the Communists to exterminate him politically and to advance a Russian regime that was itself as evil as Fascism, was a thunderclap that reverberated in his mind for years.[24]

In May 1939 the Communists again invited the Socialists to participate in a joint May Day parade. But Thomas was no longer interested in such a cooperative venture and instead joined the Social Democratic Federation's May Day gathering. There, to the satisfaction of the Old Guard, he gave a ringing denunciation of the Communists. The final straw was the Hitler-Stalin Pact of August 3, 1939. Thomas wrote in the Socialist party's *Socialist Call:* "Stalin's Agreement with Hitler becomes a piece of infamy besides which Munich was an adventure in ethics, and the hypocritical nonintervention in Spain a model of international good faith."[25]

Thus ended Norman Thomas's hope that it might prove possible to restore the unity of the working-class movement and his wish, adhered to in the face of all adverse information, that the Soviet Union would provide the shining inspiration for a new world of social justice. Eventually Thomas conceded that the Old Guard—men like Morris Hillquit, Sidney Hillman, and David Dubinsky—had been more nearly right than he in their appraisal of Communism,[26] and he became an ardent foe of any cooperation with the Communists. We will return to the Popular Front in a subsequent chapter.

3

The Theory and Practice of Front Organizations

The decade of the 1930s was a time of unprecedented social upheaval and distress in America. With the help of its Popular Front strategy, by the end of this period the American Communist party had become a significant force in American political life. The Party had achieved this role less as a result of a growth in membership—its core of moderately active members probably never was greater than 50,000[1]—but on account of its ability to reach, mobilize, and manipulate for the Party's advantage a large number of non-Communists. The primary instrument for this broadening of the Party's political influence was and remains the front organization.

The Communist party demanded strict discipline and complete adherence to all aspects of its program. Relatively few men and women were prepared to make this kind of total commitment. In order to extend its influence beyond its own members, the Party created "auxiliary organizations," also called "formally non-Party mass organizations," which transmitted the Party's voice to the masses and therefore were referred to as "transmission belts." These organizations became known as Communist fronts because they fronted for the Party—they hid control by the Party and their pro-Communist outlook behind innocent-sounding names such as American Slav Congress, Civil Rights Congress, and International Workers Order. Under the guise of honorable activities like promoting brotherhood, social justice, and peace these organizations could attract "useful idiots"[2] who did the Party's work. The task of these groups, writes a French student of Communist tactics, consisted in "transposing the music of Moscow into the different registers of trade unionists, philosophers, pacifists, Christians, etc., while giving them the impression that what they play is not a transposition but an original work."[3]

Most of the members of these fronts accepted one or more of the Party's aims, but were not yet prepared to take the final step of joining the Party. However, eventually many members of these "auxiliary organizations," as the Party in its internal communications usually referred to these fronts, came to embrace the entire Communist program. Those who accepted the leadership of the Party in one area frequently extended this acceptance to other areas. The Party, therefore, used its fronts as an all-important recruiting ground.[4]

Front organizations also proved useful in battles for the control of other organizations not yet under the domination of the Party. In order to take over a meeting or conference, the Party needed a large number of delegates, and the attendance of delegates from front organizations could provide the winning margin. Thus, for example, by mobilizing every front available the Party increased the number of Communist delegates attending the Farmer Labor Conference of July 3, 1923, in Chicago from ten to about two hundred. The same tactic, as we will see later, assured control of the American League Against War and Fascism and the American Youth Congress. As Draper observes, "the more organizations the Communists controlled, the easier it became for them to seize control of other organizations."[5]

Front organizations at times could also be used as a source of finance for the Party's other activities. The Friends of the Soviet Union, established in 1921 and soon to become the largest of early membership fronts, maintained a goodly number of party functionaries on its payroll. An American Party functionary boasted in 1931 that his district had "succeeded in making the fraternal organizations pay the Party 10% of the income on affairs."[6] During the 1940s, the Anti-Fascist Refugee Committee, a well-known Communist auxiliary, diverted funds raised for the orphans and widows of anti-fascist refugees to pay for the salary of Gerhard Eisler, the Comintern's representative in the United States.[7] Not all fronts were lucrative, however, and the Party had to depend on various sources of funds, including direct subsidies from the Soviet Union.[8] Nevertheless, at least some fronts could be tapped to help support the Party's manifold activities.

The idea of forming party fronts goes back to Lenin during the early days of the Comintern. "In all organizations without exception," Lenin wrote in 1920, "(political, industrial, military, co-operative, educational, sports etc. etc.), groups or nuclei of Communists should be formed— mainly open groups, but also secret groups."[9] Communists, Lenin insisted, had to be where the masses were. This meant joining associations and societies even if they were not wanted. The most important such mass organizations of the working class were trade unions, and Lenin heaped his scorn upon "leftists" within the German Communist party who refused to work within the German trade union movement on the grounds that it was too "reactionary."

The leaders of these opportunistic unions, Lenin conceded, would make every effort to keep Communists out or make their work as unpleasant as possible. Nevertheless, he insisted,

> We must be able to withstand all this, to agree to all and every sacrifice, and even—if need be—to resort to various stratagems, artifices, illegal methods, to evasions and subterfuges, only so as to get into the trade unions, to remain in them, and to carry on communist work within them at all costs.[10]

Lenin saw no moral issue in such tactics of deceit because, he argued, "morality is what serves to destroy the old exploiting society and to unite all the toilers around the proletariat." Communist morality, Lenin explained in an address to the Russian Young Communist League in October 1920, is the morality which serves the class struggle. "We repudiate all morality taken apart from human society and classes. . . . We say that our morality is entirely subordinated to the interests of the class struggle of the proletariat."[11]

The Comintern continued to follow this line of thinking after Lenin's death. Communist functionary Ottomar V. Kuusinen told the sixth plenum of the executive committee of the Communist International in March 1926 that, to extend their influence, Communist parties had to "create a whole solar system of organizations and smaller committees around the Communist Party so to speak, smaller organizations working actually under the influence of our Party."[12] Following Kuusinen's recommendations, the executive committee approved a resolution that called on all Communist parties to organize "sympathizing mass organizations" which had to be under the control of "the more or less invisible Communist fraction" within them.[13] The German Communist Willi Münzenberg, a master in the creation of such fronts, referred to them as "Innocents' Clubs."[14]

Clarence A. Hathaway, a Communist party leader from Minnesota and editor of *The Daily Worker,* applied this tactic to American conditions. It was not enough, he wrote in 1931, to build the Communist party and recruit new members for it.

> We must learn to set up and work through a whole series of mass organizations . . . , to systematically utilize mass organizations . . . as transmission belts to the broad masses of non-Party workers. The Communist Party is necessarily composed of the most conscious and self-sacrificing elements

among the workers. These mass organizations, on the contrary, with a correct political line, can be made to reach many thousands of workers not yet prepared for Party membership. Through these organizations, led by well-functioning Party fractions, the Party must necessarily find its best training and recruiting ground.[15]

The mode of operation of the fraction or caucus was described by Josef Peters, another Communist leader, in an organizational manual authored by him. The fraction's task was to insure Party control of the front. It "meets regularly before the meeting of the organization. At this meeting the members of the Party fraction discuss and decide how to apply the policy of the Party in the organization." No Party member had the right to speak or act against the decisions of the fraction. "The Party members must always act as a solid unit."[16]

During the 1920s, the leaders of fronts frequently were top-ranking Party officials. During the Popular Front of the 1930s, on the other hand, the Party maintained its control in a more surreptitious manner and used for this task secret Communists* who became known as "submarines."[17] The large number of such members who hid their affiliation with the Party gave rise to many liberals and labor leaders who were accused of being Communists. Some superpatriots in the American Legion and the Daughters of the American Revolution called anyone left of center agents of the Kremlin. Such indiscriminate charges, in turn, notes one observer, protected actual Communists. "A kind of Gresham's law operated: the more non-Communists who were branded Communists—whether from malice, confusion, or error—the greater the tendency to discount anyone named as a Communist."[18]

Then as now, the membership of Communist front organizations can be divided into four distinct groups. The first two groups are relatively small and consist of open and secret members of the Party respectively. The third and much larger group is made up of sympathizers under the control of the Party who for various reasons refrain from formally joining the Party. Lastly, there are the "innocents" for whom the front is set up. Well-known public figures among the innocents typically are given a prominent, though usually largely ceremonial role in the front in order

---

* The existence of secret Communists is not questioned by anyone. The Party's national organizational secretary recently acknowledged that 80 percent of the members continue to keep their membership secret (*Political Affairs*, August 1989, p. 17). Controversy has arisen occasionally in regard to specific individuals alleged to be or to have been secret members of the Party. In this book I have accepted the allegation of secret membership only in the case of a belated acknowledgment by the Party itself (as in an obituary) or when based on the testimony of several reliable individuals in a consensus of informed opinion.

to lend it respectability. Both sympathizers and innocents are generally known as "fellow travelers."[19]

There is some question about the real number of innocents among the fellow travelers of the Popular Front period in particular. "Even if some proverbial innocents were sucked in without any inkling of what they were getting into," notes one student of the subject, "they would have had to be deaf, dumb and blind not to realize in short order that they had blundered into a Communist auxiliary of some kind."[20] The far larger contingent among the fellow travelers was made up of sympathizers of the Party who were not deceived at all. Irving Howe and Lewis Coser, in their history of the Party, give a good description of these individuals:

> They were people who acquiesced in and winked at the process of deception that made them its apparent victims. They were people whose sympathies lay essentially with the Communists but whose personal situations or characters kept them from assuming the burdens of party membership, and who felt that the least they could do was to help the party build and smoothly control the front organizations. As their "contribution" they would often assume a variety of roles, from that of the professed near-Communist to that of the honest worker or utterly non-political citizen who simply wanted to lend his mite to the struggle against fascism. And it gave these people a vicarious delight to see the party spin its web of manipulation and to feel that, in however modest a way, they too helped with the spinning—that they too labored for a vast movement extending from Shanghai to Havana, from the Urals to Brooklyn Heights. Nor did the party have to coach these actors in the mock drama of the front organization: they came to each performance with their lines rehearsed and parts prepared. They were Good Volunteers.[21]

There were many different kinds of fronts. Some consisted of no more than a name on a letterhead capable of winning outside support and a small staff; others were membership organizations that accepted both group and individual affiliations, held conventions, and established local branches. Some, such as the Civil Rights Congress, were more or less permanent; others, like the National Scottsboro Action Committee, were temporary. Some, like the Veterans of the Abraham Lincoln Brigade, were created by the Party; others, like the American Youth Congress discussed below, were organizations established by non-Communists and subsequently captured by the Communists. In many instances, organizations were able to repel Communist infiltration or to minimize Communist influence. But on the whole, the Popular Front period saw Communist influence reach an all-time high. There were never more than 100,000 Party members at any one time. Yet the Party, benefiting from the sense of crisis created by the Great Depression and using the organizational device of the front organization, was able to dominate a vast array of labor unions, youth groups, peace and civil rights organizations, and other clubs and associations.[22] In a report to the eighth convention of the American Communist party held in April 1934, Browder bragged:

> If we make a conservative estimate of the total membership of mass organizations around the Party, and under its influence, allowing for possible duplication of membership, we will see that we have approximately 500,000 individual supporters in these organizations.[23]

Browder may have overstated the success of the Party at that time, but there can be no doubt that the use of front organizations proved highly productive. We will look at two examples.

The American Youth Congress

What has been called the most successful Communist front organization of the 1930s, the American Youth Congress (AYC), was started by a young woman who in her subsequent autobiography called herself a "political virgin." Impressed by similar organizations in Europe, Viola Ilma in August 1934 convened a meeting on the campus of New York University to which she invited all manner of youth groups. There were the Boy Scouts, the Girl Scouts, young Methodists, young Zionists, and many more, seventy-nine groups in all. Also invited and present were the Young Communist League and the National Student League, the Party's student branch. With the help of sympathetic young Socialists, Ilma writes, the Communists engineered a coup which left them in control of the organization.[24]

"The fraud began," recalled James Wechsler, then a leading member of the Young Communist League and later editor of the *New York Post*, "when members of the communist fraction posed as simple peasants from the hinterland to obtain top posts in the structure of the organization." Ilma had invited not only organizations but also unaffiliated individuals, and a large number of those who came as "unaffiliated" were in reality associated with the Young Communist League and the Young People's Socialist League. We were persuaded, writes Wechsler, "that Miss Ilma was a potential tool of American reaction and the very vagueness of her thoughts was regarded as sufficient proof that she was dangerous. Our coup, we were certain, had halted fascism on its own five-yard line."[25]

After Ilma and her supporters had walked out of the meeting of which she had lost control, the remaining delegates elected a fifteen-member continuations committee dominated by the Communists and their Socialist allies. From that point on, it was smooth sailing for the Communists. What facilitated their hold over the AYC was the fact that the organization had no individual members but functioned as a clearinghouse for other youth organizations. It was easier to deal with and manipulate the single delegate of a youth group than to confront an entire organization with its many members of diverse political orientation, some of whom might be distinctly hostile to Communism. When, as often turned out to be the case, the delegate of an organization was himself a fellow traveler the task of domination was eased even more.[26]

The leaders of the Communist party were delighted by the exploits of their young comrades and bragged about the leading role of the Young Communist League in the AYC. Browder observed that its "political center of gravity is work of the YCL [Young Communist League]" and that "practically all the basic proposals and policies came from us and from those influenced by us."[27] The umbrella of the AYC helped young Communist cadres gain entry into religious and black youth groups. "The YCL," the *Daily Worker* noted with approval on September 2, 1935, "has gone directly into the Y's, settlements, churches, and there reached the masses of youth that are not yet organized into unions and sport organizations."[28] At the Sixth Young Communist International Congress, the work of the Communists in the AYC was singled out as a model. "This is an example of how to influence the masses of youth instead of commanding them in a bureaucratic way."[29]

After the Party had embraced the New Deal and collective security, the AYC followed, achieving respectability and acceptance by important New Dealers in Washington. Mrs. Eleanor Roosevelt developed a warm relationship with these young people whose "earnestness" and idealism she admired. Warnings that the AYC was not simply the liberal assembly she supposed it to be were disregarded. On one occasion, she recalled years later, she had asked the AYC leaders whether any of them were Communists and that "in every case they said they had no connection with the Communists, had never belonged to any Communist organization, and had no interest in Communist ideas. I decided to accept their word, realizing that sooner or later the truth would come out."[30] Unfortunately, in this case as in many others, the truth came out rather belatedly. "The ability of the AYC to ingratiate itself in Washington circles," write Howe and Coser in their history of American Communism, "was only one of the ways by which the Communists worked themselves into the government apparatus during the Popular Front period."[31] Some of these men and women used their positions to influence government policy; others were drawn into espionage networks.

A successful front like the AYC enabled the Communists to recruit members from other youth organizations and to gain access to official Washington. Together with other such fronts, the AYC also contributed to the development and spread of the Popular Front atmosphere which made wide inroads in the labor movement and among the country's cultural elites. The impact of the Depression and the growing threat of fascism made many Americans embrace a naïve social utopianism and to regard the Communists as mere "progressives in a hurry." These attitudes, in turn, predisposed many well-meaning people to accept other far less innocuous aspects of Communism.

By the time the Fifth American Youth Congress convened in July 1939, the AYC had lost almost all outward vestiges of radicalism and, like its mentor the Communist party, surrounded itself with the halo of the New Deal. It claimed to represent groups with a total of 4.7 million members. Yet the organization's machinery was securely in Communist hands. As John Gates, former editor of the *Daily Worker,* recalls in his memoirs written after his exit from the Party, a Communist majority at the Congress was again secured by using the time-tested device of loading the meeting with delegates from "neutral" organizations who actually were members of the Young Communist League.[32] To allay the doubts of liberals a resolution was passed expressing the opposition of the Youth Congress "to all forms of dictatorship, regardless of whether they be Communist, Fascist, or Nazi, or any other type." The delegates of the Young Communist League voted for it; this bit of deception was seen as a small price to keep the organization above suspicion.[33]

Like many other Communist fronts of the Popular Front era, the AYC self-destructed as a result of the Hitler-Stalin Pact. Ever-faithful to their Russian masters, the Communists now abandoned their support of collective security and assailed President Roosevelt as "the political leader of the warmongers" whose task it was "to lead the country as far and as fast into the war as the financial oligarchs deem necessary."[34] When the Party started to use the AYC to assail U.S. foreign policy using similar rhetoric, even Mrs. Roosevelt had had enough and dissociated herself from the organization. Many of AYC's constituent groups now also dropped their membership, and the Communists soon found themselves running a front with few other members. After the German invasion of the Soviet Union in June of 1941, requiring yet another switch in the Communist line, the AYC disappeared from the scene.

The National Negro Congress

During the early years of its existence, the American Communist party, preoccupied with factional conflicts, did not pay much attention to blacks. In 1925, the Party was ordered by Moscow to establish the American Negro Labor Congress (ANLC). The national organizer of this organization was Lovett Fort-Whiteman, one of the first blacks to become a Communist and subsequently sent to Russia for training. Writing in a Comintern organ in August of that year, Fort-Whiteman described the purpose of the Congress with exemplary candor:

> The fundamental aim in calling the American Negro Labor Congress is to establish in the life of the American Negro working class an organization which may serve as a medium through which the American Communist Party may reach and influence the Nego working class, and at the same time constitute something of a recruiting ground for the Party.[35]

In actual fact, the ANLC never attained much influence in the black working class and it never succeeded in doing much recruiting. At the end of the Communist party's first decade, no more than 200 blacks were said to be party members.

In 1928 the Comintern adopted a new approach committing the Party to the principle of "Self-Determination for Negroes in the Black Belt." Southern blacks were defined as an oppressed group entitled to secede from the United States and to create a separate black nation. But the League of Struggle for Negro Rights, an auxiliary set up to implement the new line, failed to get off the ground. Not only were Communist organizers in the South met with much physical brutality, but the slogan of a separate black republic failed to gain support among blacks. Many of them were antagonized by the Party's attack upon the black churches. "For most Negroes," writes a student of black radicalism during that period, "the gospel according to Matthew continued to have more appeal than the gospel according to Marx."[36]

Communist agitation among blacks achieved an uplift when in 1931 another Party auxiliary, the International Labor Defense (ILD), appropriated the Scottsboro case for the Communist cause. In its appeals for funds the ILD claimed to be an organization whose members belonged to many different parties. At the same time, the secretary of the ILD, a highly placed Communist functionary, noted in his reports to the Party how important it was for the Communist party, the vanguard of the working class, to lead and coordinate the activities of all non-Party mass organizations. "Therefore the Party must guide the ILD, both locally and nationally."[37] Communist control meant that the ILD excluded or expelled anyone critical of the role of the Party in the organization. It also meant that the ILD agreed to handle only those cases which provided some political benefit.

The Scottsboro case involved nine young blacks in Alabama who in a travesty of a trial had been sentenced to die for raping two white women on a freight train. From the beginning it was clear to unprejudiced observers that the nine blacks, ranging in age from thirteen to twenty, had been framed, and the case soon attracted wide attention as an example of Southern bigotry and legal injustice. At that point there ensued a tug-of-war between the National Association for the Advancement of Colored People (NAACP) and the ILD over who should represent the defendants during their appeals. The Communist party and its auxiliary the ILD were determined to use the case for their own political purposes, and they initiated a campaign of mass protests in which they accused the NAACP of being "bourgeois reformists" who followed "legalistic tactics" and were helping to "lead the boys to the electric chair."

It was futile, wrote a Communist functionary in 1932, to rely upon the capitalist system of justice. Any appeal to the high courts of Alabama and the United States had to be subordinated to the "development of revolutionary mass action outside of courts and bourgeois legislative bodies." Bourgeois liberals, warned the *Daily Worker* in June 1932, would use the legal appeals to disrupt the "mass defense by fostering illusions as to the 'fairness' and 'justice' of the bosses' courts."[38] Small wonder that in the eyes of many blacks and whites at the time the agitation of the Communists did the nine boys more harm than good.

As in earlier such cases, for the Communists these tactics carried little risk. If they lost the case they could charge that defeat was due to the injustice and fraud of the capitalist court system. If they won they could claim credit for the Communist tactic of mass pressure. For a time, the mobilization of American and world opinion in support of the Scottsboro boys gained the Party new support among both blacks and whites. But the Communists' doctrinal rigidity failed to translate this temporary success into lasting gains. During 1931, the year of greatest effort at recruitment, only 1,300 blacks joined the Party and many of these soon drifted away again.[39]

The doctrine of Negro self-determination in the black belt was an albatross that isolated the Party from the black masses. There was also the damaging revelation in September 1935 that the Soviet Union, which claimed to oppose the Italian aggression against black Ethiopia, was shipping large quantities of oil, coal tar, and wheat to Mussolini. Some of these supplies, the *New York Times* reported, went directly to Africa for use in the Ethiopian campaign.[40] The gradual abandonment of the doctrine of self-determination and the switch to the tactic of the Popular Front eventually enabled the Party to escape its own self-imposed ghetto.

In February 1936, the Party helped convene the National Negro Congress (NNC) which brought together a broad coalition of Negro groups—more than 800 delegates from 550 organizations claiming to represent 33 million members.[41] A. Philip Randolph, the prominent head of the Brotherhood of Sleeping Car Porters, was elected president. Other acknowledged leaders in the black community were given positions of prestige, but as usual, the Communists controlled the organization through the office of the executive secretary. From the beginning, note Howe and Coser, the Communists' "ability to provide organizational forces, experienced personnel, and a variety of skills assured them a powerful role. The non-Communists might show up for meetings and congresses, *but the Communists were there every day.*"[42]

For a time, the NNC gave the Party an extensive network of friendly relations with important black and white individuals and groups. Some local branches of the NAACP were successfully infiltrated, and in a few places the NNC overshadowed the NAACP. After traveling through the country in 1938 and 1939, the Swedish sociologist Gunnar Myrdal reported that "the local councils of the National Negro Congress were the most important Negro organizations in some Western cities."[43] This was an exaggeration, but it was not far off the mark. The NNC never became a mass movement, but it helped the Party reach a wide audience.

Like the American Youth Congress and other fronts, the NNC completely lost its effectiveness in the wake of the Hitler-Stalin Pact. At the Third National Negro Congress held in Washington in April 1940, the Communists denounced Roosevelt and his foreign policy. In response, Randolph refused reelection as president, and membership in the NNC was quickly reduced to a handful of Party hacks and their followers. The high-handed tactics used by the Communists in imposing the new anti-imperialist-war line on the NNC is said to have taught Randolph and other black leaders a lesson about Communist deception they never forgot.[44]

An articulate and influential anticommunist bloc now emerged in the black community. The Brotherhood of Sleeping Car Porters passed a resolution barring Communists from office in the union. In 1941 Randolph organized his March on Washington movement to demand jobs for blacks in national defense industries and achieve the placement of blacks as soldiers and officers in all ranks of the armed forces. The Communists at first ignored the proposed march, but when they saw how effectively Randolph's call to action galvanized the black community they called upon their followers to join the march and to turn it into a demonstration "against the administration's entire war program." One Party leader had the nerve to suggest that the idea for the march had really come from the NNC. At that Randolph denounced the Communists as a "definite menace, pestilence and nuisance, as well as a danger to the Negro people" and he insisted that Communists, fellow travelers, and their allies be excluded from local March on Washington committees and from the march itself.[45]

In 1946 the NNC resurfaced, but its Communist composition was well known and fooled few innocents. In December 1947, the NNC merged with several other fronts to form the Civil Rights Congress. However, Communist infiltration continued to be a problem for the NAACP. The NAACP retaliated by barring the Civil Rights Congress and the Communists from participating in the National Civil Rights Mobilization held in Washington in February 1950. That same year the NAACP convention empowered its national office to expel any local affiliate that in the judgment of the board of directors had come under Communist control.[46] In later years, some southern legislatures from time to time charged the NAACP as being Communist, but even the House Committee on Un-American Activities had to acknowledge that such accusations were baseless. A report in 1963 by the FBI's most experienced domestic intelligence officers concluded that there had been "an obvious failure" on the part of the Communists "to appreciably infiltrate, influence, or control large numbers of American Negroes," and that the Communist influence on the civil rights movement was "infinitesimal."[47] FBI Director J. Edgar Hoover refused to accept this assessment and ordered a massive intelligence investigation to uncover Communist influence on civil rights leaders, including Martin Luther King, Jr. There is general agreement today that Hoover's fears here, as in many other areas of Communist subversion, were bordering on the paranoid.[48]

An Assessment of Front Operations

The history of the American Youth Congress and the National Negro Congress illustrates how the American Communist party subordinated its organizational activities to the demands of the changing foreign policy goals of the Soviet Union. Groups allegedly organized to advance the interests of American youth and blacks were destroyed when forced to take positions on issues entirely unrelated to the groups' original mission and purpose. The imperative of providing unflinching support for Soviet realpolitik triumphed over every other goal.

Some recent scholars have questioned this conclusion. The "tiny Communist party," maintain two students of Communist politics in the Hollywood film industry, never dominated the major front organizations of the Popular Front era. Such accusations, made at the time and later, are "intended by the conservatives to unglue a strong liberal-radical alliance, and by the liberals to protect their flanks in troubled times." Sharp changes in the fronts' line as after the Hitler-Stalin Pact allegedly do not prove the Party's domination or manipulation of these organizations. These changes are said to have occurred only after "liberals had jumped ship, leaving the Communists and fellow-travelers alone at the tiller."[49] A similar position is taken in a recent book dealing with the Communist issue in American higher education. The behavior of Communists in front groups, concedes Ellen Schrecker, "often did become manipulative," but the "extent [to which] these groups were, as they were alleged to be, dominated by the CP is unclear."[50]

The question to what extent an organization had become a captive of the Communist party must, of course, be answered on the basis of factual information about the conduct of each and every such organization separately. Such an inquiry would involve seeking answers to questions such as the following: To what extent did the group cooperate with the campaigns and activities of the Party? Did the publications and public positions of the organization follow the changing twists of the party line? Did the group have Communists or reliable fellow travelers in positions of authority? Quite obviously, an individual or group could reach conclusions about various public issues that occasionally paralleled those reached by the Communist party. But when an organization systematically agreed with all positions supported by the Communists and changed them whenever the Party did, this phenomenon exceeded coincidence.

It is also factually incorrect that front groups changed their positions only after liberals had left them. As we have seen from the examples of the American Youth Congress and the National Negro Congress, the time sequence and cause and effect relationship usually were the other way around. In a typical case, liberals abandoned the organization because they had become fed up with the manipulative activities of the Party fraction within it. They left the front because they had found themselves powerless to control the small minority of strategically placed Communists who dominated the group and who adjusted the front's positions to the changing dictates of the Party irrespective of the wishes of the membership.

Some revisionist historians of American Communism have suggested that the Communists' resort to secrecy and subterfuge has been the result of persecution and thus has been a necessary, if regrettable, way for the Party to defend its political role. In point of fact, while the practice of denying membership in the Party had begun during the 1920s when many AFL unions excluded known Communists, the policy was continued later since it was convenient. Because of the strong anticommunism of the American working class, the Party argued, open acknowledgment of Party membership was an obstacle to gaining the confidence of workers. "Even in unions such as the UE [United Electrical Workers]," writes a student of the role of Communists in the labor movement, "where most of the membership came to know that the bureaucracy and leadership were top-heavy with Communists, party members were reluctant to be identified for fear of alienating members."[51] Carl Milton Bernstein, active in the United Public Workers of America during the 1940s, told his son, the journalist Carl Bernstein, that he kept his political affiliation secret in order to protect his political effectiveness,[52] and this was the Party's policy for most of its history. The usual way of handling questions about Party membership was to impugn the motives of the questioners. When in 1935 Wyndham Mortimer, vice president of the United Automobile Workers and a secret party member, was called a Communist by a conservative AFL official, he gave the standard response: "I will not dignify the wild charges made against me . . . by either denying or admitting them. Red-baiting is, and always has been, the employers' most potent weapon against those of us who believe in and fight for industrial unionism."[53] To this day, Communist front organizations fend off charges of pro-Soviet bias with the retort of red-baiting or claim that they are hosts to a wide variety of political viewpoints, with Communists being no more than one of many different groups represented.

The policy of secrecy and deception practiced by the American Communist party was in line with the counsel given by Lenin in 1920, quoted earlier, to use all possible stratagems and evasions in order to gain and maintain a foothold in the trade unions. Conspiracy and duplicity, therefore, soon became the hallmark of Communist parties the world over, and party leaders took pride in living up to the difficult ideal of a professional revolutionary who could not afford to be a practicing moralist. Using the language of Machiavelli, the German Communist writer Bertold Brecht has described the ethos of the Communist functionary in his play *Die Massnahme* with frightful candor:

You are no longer yourself. . . . You are without a name, without a mother, blank sheets on which the Revolution will write its orders. . . . He who fights for Communism must be able to fight and to renounce fighting, to say the truth and not say the truth, to be helpful and unhelpful, to keep a promise and to break a promise, to go into danger and to avoid danger, to be known and to be unknown. He who fights for Communism has of all the virtues only one: that he fights for Communism.[54]

Not surprisingly, this code of conduct, resolutely subordinating means to ends, eventually was adhered to by the Communists not only in their fight against the class enemy but also in the struggles for power within the various national parties and the Communist International. In 1956, after Soviet leader Khrushchev in his speech to the Twentieth Party Congress had revealed Stalin's reign of terror against his own party comrades, many American Communist leaders not only felt deeply disillusioned about the helmsman of world Communism they had come to idealize, they also were shocked by the realization that, had they been in power, they might have committed the same crimes against each other. As one of them, Dorothy Healey, put it many years later: "I was a little Stalin. I'm not talking about anybody else."[55] Another leader who left the Party in 1958, George Charney, has blamed the corrupting influence of the unchecked and unaccountable power wielded by party leaders for giving them a vested interest in the movement "that resulted in total commitment and a gradual loss of independent judgment."[56]

The American Communist party's high-handed tactics, manipulation of democratic procedures, and resort to duplicity and secrecy kept many sympathizers from joining. Lying and evasiveness are generally frowned upon by Americans who admire those who stand up for what they believe. Historian Harvey Levenstein relates that when in 1938 a close associate asked the left-leaning union leader Ralph Rasmussen to join the Communist party, the latter replied that he "did not want to become part of any secret organization that was ashamed of itself."[57] If Americans over time developed a strong animus against Communism, a hostility that often led to persecutions and infringements of the civil liberties of Communists, this was undoubtedly in part the result of the secretive and manipulative character of the Party. Disabilities imposed upon party members by unions, employers or the government, in turn, provided excuses for more secrecy and deceit.

The creation of front organizations run by secret party members or reliable fellow travelers and loyal to the interests of a foreign power was and remains an activity for which Communist parties have developed special expertise. Fritz Kuhn, the leader of the pro-Nazi German American *Volksbund,* during the 1930s formed a considerable number of front organizations, but their ability to deceive was limited. The Socialist party had its League for Industrial Democracy, which functioned as an ally of the Socialists, and American Jews have channeled their support for the state of Israel through special organizations created for that purpose. In neither of these cases, however, is the real sponsorship of these groups in doubt, and no secret machinations are necessary to maintain control. Communist front organizations, on the other hand, in Lenin's classical phraseology, employ stratagems, evasions, and subterfuges in order to hide Communist direction and domination. The opprobrium that has come to be attached to these activities is understandable.

4

The "Red Decade"

During the twenties, dissenting intellectuals had been concerned mainly with the critique of commercialism. They had been rebels against what they regarded as a society of philistines. The Depression of the thirties turned many of these same intellectuals toward Marxism. Men who had always felt isolated from America's business civilization now identified with the working class, another outsider. Passionately eager to get away from their own class, they sought to find a home with the proletariat and to make common cause with the downtrodden suffering from the ravages of the Great Depression.

The Communist party, which claimed to be the spokesman of the dispossessed and promised a radical overhaul of a sick society, provided a strong attraction. Communism was seen as a crusading faith and its total opposition to the seemingly failed capitalist system had a powerful emotional appeal. In the eyes of writers such as Lincoln Steffens, Theodore Dreiser, and Matthew Josephson, the Communists were men of action, and if they did not immediately join the Party it was because as mere intellectuals they did not consider themselves worthy. "I was not a Communist," Steffens recalled a few years later, "because that implied leadership and no ex-liberal was fit to lead the people."[1]

For a majority of the intellectuals who joined the Party or who associated with the Communists in various activities or associations, it was the nature of the times that radicalized them. During what has been called the "red decade," Communism gained considerable influence among American intellectuals not because the Party excelled at manipulating innocents—although it certainly was very good at that—but because it offered a new all-encompassing ideology. For men of little political sophistication communism represented a set of ideas that provided both explanation and emotional assurance. Neither were these intellectuals necessarily all neurotic. "Communism's appeal," writes Daniel Aaron, a close student of the period, "can never be understood if it is considered merely an escape for the sick, the frustrated, and the incompetent or a movement of fools and knaves."[2]

Writers and Artists Turn Left

For the election of 1932, the Communists had chosen William Z. Foster and James W. Ford, the first black to be nominated for national office, as their candidates for President and Vice President. On September 12 several major newspapers carried a statement of support for the Communist ticket that was signed by fifty-three writers, artists, and other intellectuals. Some of the signers were well-known novelists such as Dreiser, Dos Passos, and Waldo Frank; others were younger and aspiring writers and critics such as Erskine Caldwell, Newton Arvin, Edmund Wilson, Malcolm Cowley, and Granville Hicks. Also among the signers was the philosopher Sidney Hook, soon to become one of the sharpest and most articulate critics of the Communists, who, as he recalls, supported the Communist ticket as "an expression of protest, hope and faith nurtured by naïveté, ignorance and illusion."[3]

The statement began: "There is only one issue in the present election. Call it hard times, unemployment, the farm problem, the world crisis, or call it simply hunger—whatever name we use, the issue is the same." The Democrats and the Republicans had no serious proposals to cope with this desperate situation, and the Socialist party was simply "the third party of capitalism." Only the Communist party, the statement continued, stood "for a Socialism of deeds, not words. . . . The Communist Party is the only party which has stood in the forefront of the major struggle of the workers against capitalism and the capitalist state. . . . The Communist party proposes as the real solution of the present crisis the overthrow of the system which is responsible for all crises." A vote for the Communist candidates, the statement urged, was the only effective way to protest against the chaos and indescribable misery inherent in the capitalist system.[4]

The fifty-three signers of the manifesto of support formed the League of Professional Groups for Foster and Ford. Several of them, including Matthew Josephson, Malcolm Cowley, Sidney Hook, Lewis Corey, and James Rorty, authored a pamphlet, *Culture and Crisis: An Open Letter to the Writers, Artists and Other Professional Workers of America,* of which some 40,000 copies were distributed. The pamphlet stated that the only choice for intellectuals was to serve either as the cultural lieutenants of the capitalist class or as allies of the working class. "As responsible intellectual workers, we have aligned ourselves with the frankly revolutionary Communist Party." The pamphlet was edited by Party regulars and, in line with the party line of the day, directed some of its harshest language against the Socialist party. By their insistence on democracy the Socialists were "indirectly helping Fascism."[5]

League members spoke at rallies in support of the Communist ticket, but the results were disappointing. The Socialist party candidates, Norman Thomas and James Hudson Maurer, were supported by a "Committee of Ten Thousand" (eventually renamed "Committee of One Hundred Thousand") which included many prominent intellectuals, including Henry Hazlitt, Stuart Chase, John Dewey, Reinhold Niebuhr, Elmer Davis, and Joseph Wood Krutch. After the ballots had been counted it turned out that the Socialists had received over 880,000 votes, more than seven times as many as the Communists.

Many of those who had supported the Communist ticket were willing to continue to work for an alliance between the Communist party and the intellectual community. The League was renamed the League of Professional Groups and its program committed the organization, by now containing a number of Communists and their close sympathizers, "to propagandiz[e] and activize the professions, to engage in communist activity on the cultural front, to provide technical aid to the Communist Party and its mass organizations." But the Party was suspicious of the intellectual independence shown by some key members of the League, and most of the early founders soon left in disgust. The League, writes Harvey Klehr, "faded into oblivion, a victim of the Party's need to control with an iron fist any organization associated with it."[6]

There were those in the intellectual community who were willing to swallow their discomfort with the Party's high-handed tactics. The Communists were "uncomfortable allies," recalled Granville Hicks years later, "intense, dogmatic, intolerant. But they were against the things we were against." The Socialists were more reasonable, but in the big crisis of capitalism their very reasonableness seemed a liability. Hicks identified with the sentiments of his friend, the literary critic Newton Arvin, who wrote him in 1932:

> It is a bad world in which we live, and so even the revolutionary movement is anything but what (poetically and philosophically speaking) it "ought" to be: God knows, I realize this, as you do, and God knows it makes my heart sick at times. . . . But surely this is what *history* is. It just is not made by

gentlemen and scholars, and "made" only in the bad sense by the Norman Thomases and the Devere Allens and the John Deweys. Lenin must have been . . . a dreadful man; so must John Brown, and Cromwell, and Marat, and Stenka Razin, and Mahomet, and all the others who have destroyed and built up. . . . I believe we can spare ourselves a great deal of pain and disenchantment . . . if we discipline ourselves to accept proletarian and revolutionary leaders and even theorists for what they are and must be: grim fighters in about the most dreadful and desperate struggle in all history—*not* reasonable and "critically minded" and forbearing and infinitely farseeing men.[7]

Writers like Hicks and Arvin had become dazzled by the revolutionary ideas of Marx, Engels, and Lenin. "By giving us the key to history," Hicks writes, "we were convinced, Marxism enabled us to understand science, literature, art, all human activity, and we eagerly launched upon Marxist studies of this, that, and the other thing." Moreover, the Communists could point to the Soviet Union that was showing the world the face of the future. To be sure, the revolution had been bloody and there were no civil liberties in Russia. But, taking into account the backwardness of the country, Communism was seen to have done quite well. "After all, as we kept reminding ourselves, there was no unemployment in Russia, whereas there was plenty in the United States and in the other capitalist countries, and that proved the superiority of a planned socialist economy to an anarchic capitalist economy."[8] By the late 1980s the glaring failure of centrally planned economies had become obvious, and the Communist rulers of China, the Soviet Union, and other East European countries had begun to introduce profit incentives and market mechanisms. In the midst of the Great Depression, on the other hand, the myth of the superiority of socialist planning over the crisis-prone capitalist system was still widely accepted. It provided strong support for the Communist world view.

Despite his strong identification with the Communist cause, Hicks did not join the Party until the Communists, following the switch to the Popular Front at the Seventh Congress of the Comintern in August 1935, started to court writers, artists, and other intellectuals. Party discipline now became more relaxed and Communist tactics for a time were more in tune with American realities. Our relationship to the Party changed, Hicks recalled. Until then, "we knew that we were deficient in the Bolshevik virtues, and the party knew it too and did not encourage us to join. But after the summer of 1935 the party wanted us, and wanted us for what we were, middle-class intellectuals."[9]

Actually, the American Communist party's openness toward the intellectuals had begun even before the formal adoption of the Popular Front line. In the fall of 1934 the Party decided to liquidate the John Reed Clubs, regarded as too sectarian, and to establish a bigger organization that would include the leading writers of the nation. On January 22, 1935, the *New Masses* published a call for the convening of an American Writers' Congress. It was signed by sixty-four persons—practically all of them Party members or close collaborators. The list included Theodore Dreiser, Erskine Caldwell, Malcolm Cowley, Waldo Frank, Granville Hicks, and John Dos Passos, alongside such Party functionaries as Earl Browder, Clarence Hathaway, and Alexander Trachtenberg. American writers who had achieved standing in their field and who had "clearly indicated their sympathy for the revolutionary cause" were called upon to organize in a League of American Writers in order to "fight against imperialist war and fascism, defend the Soviet Union against capitalist aggression; for the development and strengthening of the revolutionary labor movement; against white chauvinism (against all forms of Negro discrimination or persecution)."[10]

Communist control of the congress, which convened in New York City on April 26, 1935, was apparent. Twelve of the sixteen members of the presiding committee were Party members; the seventeen members of the executive committee were all Communists or reliable fellow travelers. Earl Browder's appearance before the 216 delegates during the opening evening session therefore simply confirmed what everyone present recognized and happily accepted—the central role of the Party in the new organization.

Browder began his address by explaining why he, secretary of the Communist party, had been invited to speak to a congress of writers at its opening meeting. The great majority of American writers, he asserted, had become conscious of the unfolding class struggle between capitalists and workers and of the role of the Communist party in this struggle. They had recognized "the necessity of establishing cooperative working relations, a united front, of all enemies of reaction in the cultural field." American writers had taken the side of the working class and, at a time when the decaying capitalist system was breaking up, they stood alongside "the school of Marx" to search for the values of a new society.

> This new society is not yet in existence in America, although we are powerfully affected by its glorious rise in the Soviet Union. The new literature must help to create a new society in America—that is its main function—giving it firm roots in our own traditional cultural life, holding fast to all that is of value in the old, saving it from the destruction threatened by the modern vandals brought forth by a rotting capitalism, the fascists, combining the new with the best of the old world heritage.

These words of revolutionary bombast were followed by some calmer remarks designed to appeal to the hesitant and skeptical. Browder assured the assembled writers that the Party had no wish to control or politicize them. The first demand of the Party upon its writer-members is "that they shall be good writers, constantly better writers, for only so can they really serve the Party. We do not want to take good writers and make bad strike leaders of them." There was no fixed party line to which writers had to conform. The Party sought "to arouse consciousness among all writers of the political problems of the day," but this could not be achieved "by imposing any pre-conceived patterns upon the writer." Browder ended his talk by calling for the unity of all progressive forces in the fight against reaction and fascism. "We are all soldiers, each in our own place, in a common cause. Let our efforts be united in fraternal solidarity."[11]

Most of the other speakers voiced similar views. Waldo Frank told the congress that his premise "and the premise of the majority of writers here assembled is that Communism must come, and must be fought for." The revolutionary writer could no longer simply be a fellow traveler. His "art must be coordinate with, not subordinate to, the political-economic aspects of the re-creation of mankind." Joseph Freeman asked writers to recognize that only the proletariat could create a just society for the people. "The intellectual cannot lead the fight for the new world. He has his own vested interests in the old. He finds it hard to break with the old culture." Malcolm Cowley called for the alliance of writers with the proletariat and the revolutionary movement. The congress ended with the singing of the "International."[12]

One of the few dissenting notes was sounded by John Dos Passos, who, even as a fellow traveler, never trusted the Party's attitude toward writers and artists. A writer, he stressed, "must never, I feel, no matter how much he is carried away by even the noblest political partisanship in the fight for social justice, allow himself to forget that his real political aim, for himself and his fellows, is liberty." In working for a new and better society, the writer must protect and demand "during every minute of the fight the liberties of investigation, speech and discussion that are the greatest parts of the ends of the struggle."[13] Not surprisingly, Dos Passos was to be one of the first of the left-leaning writers to lose his infatuation with the Communists.

The Writers' Congress signified a broader Communist appeal to intellectuals and an end to the notion of "proletarian culture." The party now sought to win over all those intellectuals whom previously it had attacked as insufficiently leftist. At the same time, the League of American Writers created by the congress was no less closely controlled by the Party than the earlier John Reed Clubs. Most of the members were not Communists, but, perhaps out of indifference or preoccupation with more pressing concerns, they did let the Communists run the organization. "If necessary," Hicks recalls, "the Communists relied on parliamentary stratagems and whatever political tricks they could work out, but the occasion seldom arose."[14]

The Second American Writers' Congress met in June 1937. In line with the Popular Front policy now in full force, the Communists in the League were kept in the background. Still, the congress passed the standard party-line resolutions on Spain, antifascism, and the defense of the Soviet Union. A priori agreement was assumed on such potentially divisive subjects as the purge trials and executions in August 1936 of the veteran Bolshevik leaders Zinoviev and Kamenev, found guilty of forming a terrorist bloc with Trotsky. Just prior to the convening of the congress, Waldo Frank, the first president of the League, had had the temerity to question the evidence on the grounds of which the convictions had been based. When Earl Browder addressed the congress he made it clear that such views were unacceptable. The Communists, he maintained, were the last to want to regiment the writers. "But in relation to the two great warring camps, democracy against fascism, they [the writers] will find it necessary to adjust their own work to the higher discipline of the whole struggle for democracy." When democracy faced an open and dangerous enemy "it shall not be attacked from the rear by those who pretend to be part of it."[15] Dwight MacDonald, who openly defended Trotsky, was branded a "Trotskyite wrecker" and disrupter of the congress.[16]

It is indicative of the temper of the times that the League of American Writers could continue to gain members despite its clear alignment with Stalinist policies. By 1938 membership stood at 750. The League had become so respectable that when it offered honorary membership to President Roosevelt inasmuch as "your writings constitute a unique contribution to the body of American letters," Roosevelt accepted the invitation with "hearty appreciation."[17] The Third American Writers' Congress, meeting in June 1939, was addressed by Thomas Mann, Eduard Beneš, the president of Czechoslovakia, and other notables.

Many American artists shared in the spirit of the Popular Front and participated in another Communist auxiliary organization, the American Artists' Congress. The call to the first meeting held in February 1936 in New York City was signed by 378 artists and critics. Among those attending were well-known individuals such as Rockwell Kent, Stuart Davis, and Meyer Shapiro. The presiding officer, Lewis Mumford, began his opening address with the greeting: "Friends, comrades, ladies and gentlemen."[18]

The congress spent relatively little time discussing matters of art. Instead, it stressed political issues like the need for unity in the fight against war and in the struggle against fascism at home and abroad. The speeches lauded the peaceful intentions of the Soviet Union. Rockwell Kent insisted that "artists *should* be active in the movement against war, for artists, of all people in the world, are most concerned with life." The Communists stayed discreetly in the background and issues of possible disagreement were successfully avoided.[19]

Following its first meeting, the American Artists' Congress continued to function as a defender of the key ideas of the Popular Front. It called for lifting the embargo on arms for Republican Spain, for a revision of the neutrality act of 1935 which forbade the shipment of weapons to either aggressor or victim, and for a boycott of trade with Germany, Italy, and Japan. But the organization also addressed the specific concerns of artists. It lobbied for federal support of the arts and it organized campaigns to aid artists whose works had attracted the ire of overzealous administrators or boards of trustees.

By 1938, the purge trials and the banning of modernist art in the Soviet Union had begun to undermine the earlier enthusiasm for a united front with the Communists. In the summer of 1939, Meyer Shapiro and Fairfield Porter, both of whom had signed the original call, protested the failure to condemn the Kremlin dictatorship and the Communists' packing of the executive committee. As all other Communist front organizations of the Popular Front era, the American Artists' Congress suffered a devastating blow from the Hitler-Stalin Pact of the same year. By June 1940, the dissidents had formed their own counterorganization—the Federation of Modern Painters and Sculptors—and the Artists' Congress soon declined into oblivion.[20]

Liberals Confront the Challenge of Communism

The 1930s produced sharp divisions in the liberal camp. Their ranks, Diana Trilling noted in an article written in 1950, "were broken into two profoundly antagonistic groups—those whose only enemy was fascism; and those who had two enemies, both fascism and Communism."[21]

There were, first, the fellow travelers who defended the Soviet Union as the world's first socialist and planned society. These liberals admired the Communists for their dedication and favored working with them in order to prevent the advances of fascism at home and abroad. A typical representative of this group was Malcolm Cowley, the literary editor of the *New Republic*. The editorial stands of this magazine, founded in 1914 by Herbert Croly and labeling itself variously as "progressive" or "liberal," also strongly followed the fellow-traveling impulse. The second group consisted of those liberals who rejected Communism as a philosophy incompatible with individual liberty and who considered the Soviet

Union as dictatorial and oppressive as Nazi Germany or Fascist Italy. The group included philosophers John Dewey, Horace Kallen, and Morris Cohen; historians Carl Becker and Charles Beard; and journalists Elmer Davis, John Chamberlain, and Alfred Bingham. These men opposed cooperation with the Communists on the grounds that the Communists were deceivers who used the united front simply as a prelude to establishing their own dictatorship.

In the eyes of Joseph Wood Krutch, a typical representative of the liberal anticommunists, the Communists' "intense and burning hatred for that urbanity, detachment, and sense of fair play which makes thinking amiable" demonstrated how close they were to the fascist mentality. Both practiced violence and demanded orthodoxy. Communism was not a religion in the usual sense, yet it had its bible and saints and the party-church ruthlessly rooted out the dubious and heterodox.[22]

In a symposium on Communism published in the *Modern Monthly,* a magazine founded and edited by the independent Marxist V. F. Calverton, the philosopher Morris Cohen insisted that liberalism was not dead and that it was "pure fanaticism" to belittle the gains that had come to mankind from the spirit of free inquiry and free discussion.

> [But even] if liberalism were dead, I should still maintain that it deserved to live, that it was not condemned in the court of human reason, but lynched outside of it by the passionate and uncompromisingly ruthless war-spirit, common to both Communists and Fascists. . . . When the communists tell me that I must choose between their dictatorship and fascism I feel that I am offered the choice between being shot or being hanged. It would be suicide for liberal civilization to accept this as exhausting the field of human possibility.[23]

In the eyes of the *New Republic,* on the other hand, the threat of fascism was so serious that a united front of liberals, socialists, and the Communists was imperative. They sharply criticized the Old Guard in the Socialist party, in particular, who refused to make common cause with the Communists. Fascism had engulfed Europe and was threatening America as well. "It was better to win with the aid of people some of whom we don't like," the magazine declared on January 8, 1936, "than to lose and come under the iron-fisted control of people all of whom we dislike a great deal more."[24]

The Moscow trials further deepened the split among the liberals. On the grounds that Trotsky deserved a fair hearing, John Dewey agreed to chair a Commission of Inquiry into the truth of the diabolical charges leveled against the exiled Trotsky at the Moscow show trials. The formation of the commission led to furious attacks on the motives of Dewey and his colleagues by the Communists and their fellow-traveling allies. Eighty-eight prominent intellectuals signed a statement warning "all men of good will" that the American Committee for the Defense of Leon Trotsky, the organization sponsoring the Commission of Inquiry, did not seek justice but was an instrument to attack and defame the Soviet Union. The signers included Newton Arvin, Theodore Dreiser, Lillian Hellman, Granville Hicks, Henry Roth, Louis Fisher, Max Lerner, and many other eminent individuals—"the most distinguished list of names ever gathered on a single document in America in support of the Soviet Union," Browder boasted in *Pravda*.[25]

After taking testimony from Trotsky in Mexico, the commission in September 1937 pronounced him not guilty. This led to a new round of abuse and harassment. One member of the commission told the critic Lionel Abel that for almost a week his telephone rang every ten minutes from midnight until six in the morning.[26] The adulation of the Soviet Union culminated in a statement in support of the sentence of death against Bukharin and other members of Lenin's Politburo handed down at another show trial held in Moscow in March 1938. The innocence of the "Trotskyite-Bukharinite traitors" has since been confirmed by a commission ordered by Mikhail Gorbachev, and the Supreme Court of the USSR has annulled the sentences of Bukharin, Zinoviev, Kamenev, and Radek. But in April 1938, 150 American writers, artists, actors, and academics signed a statement published in the *Daily Worker* which affirmed that the verdicts in the Bukharin trial had been established beyond a doubt and that it had to be supported by American progressives in the interest of American democracy.[27] The signers included Dorothy Parker, Jerome Davis, George Seldes, Irving Shaw, Lillian Hellman, and Malcolm Cowley.[28] John Dewey became so disgusted with the *New Republic*'s continuing support of the Moscow trials that he resigned his post as contributing editor.[29]

By 1939 some liberals had concluded that the multiplicity of Communist fronts and the inroads of the fellow-traveling mentality had begun to dominate the cultural and literary landscape to such an extent that anticommunist authors had a difficult time being published and heard. In the spring of 1939, therefore, a group of liberals, led by John Dewey and Sidney Hook, organized the Committee for Cultural Freedom. The manifesto of the group, signed by more than 140 well-known intellectuals and cultural figures, many of them former sympathizers of the Party, appeared as a letter to the editor in the May issue of the *Nation*. It asserted that "through subsidized propaganda, through energetic agents, through political pressure, the totalitarian states [have] succeeded in infecting other countries with their false doctrines, in intimidating independent artists and scholars, and in spreading panic among the intellectuals." It therefore called for the "clearest differentiation from Stalinism together with its fronts, stooges and innocents." The statement also denounced all forms of totalitarianism, and, in a direct challenge to Popular Front thinking, it condemned both Russian Communism and fascism as equally dangerous to freedom: "Literally thousands of German, Italian, Russian and other victims of cultural dictatorship have been silenced, imprisoned, tortured or hounded into exile."[30]

Both the *Nation* and the *New Republic* reacted negatively. Freda Kirchwey, editor and publisher of the *Nation*, admitted that the statement of the Committee for Cultural Freedom was honest and that unfortunately it was also true that Communist tactics were "invariably provocative and often destructive."

> Not only do Communists try to inject partisan ideas into the program of most organizations in which they are active; not only do they fight ruthlessly and tenaciously to make those ideas prevail; they also have been guilty, in many known instances, of using against their enemies methods of attack that were both unscrupulous and callous. Their verbal technique is evident in the pages of the party press; vituperation and downright slander have been weapons frequently employed, whether against the "social fascists" of yesteryear or the "Trotskyists" of today.

Still, Kirchwey argued, it was wrong "to create a clear division on the left by relegating members of the Communist Party and the vague ranks of its sympathizers to outer totalitarian darkness":

> To advocate a policy of "clearest differentiation" on the left is a counsel of disruption. With all their faults, Communists perform necessary functions in the confused struggle of our time. They have helped to build up and to run a string of organizations known as "fronts" by their opponents—which clearly serve the cause not of "totalitarian doctrine" but of a more workable democracy. And the value of these organizations lies largely in the energy and discipline and zeal of their Communist elements.[31]

The *New Republic* refused to print the statement of the Committee for Cultural Freedom and, in an editorial, accused the committee of having "a regrettable lack of historical perspective." It was not true that both fascism and communism were equally opposed to individual freedom. The suppression of dissent in the Soviet Union, the editorial argued, was "at least 90 percent" due to Russian tradition rather than to socialist theory.[32] In a response, Ferdinand Lundberg, the secretary of the Committee for Cultural Freedom, charged that the *New Republic* was giving "aid and comfort to the agents of Stalinism" in the United States. The magazine had "simply exposed itself completely and thoroughly as a rank apologist for Stalinism in the liberal ranks."[33]

This was not the first time that the *New Republic* had been thus categorized. In December 1937, Max Eastman had called the *New Republic* a "Stalinist organ." At about the same time, Edmund Wilson wrote Malcolm Cowley protesting the way in which the literary editor of the magazine fulfilled his editorial functions: "You have been carrying on in a way that matches the *New Masses* at its worst. . . . You write better than the people on the regular Stalinist press, but what you are writing is simply Stalinist character assassination of the most reckless and libelous sort."[34] A more recent assessment by a generally sympathetic historian of the magazine is hardly less damning. "The editors' estrangement from the United States drove them to project their own dreams and wishes on Soviet culture, and derive a vicarious pleasure from its so-called successes." The *New Republic*'s "unabashed romance with the Soviet Union attached it firmly to the party line in the international sphere. . . . Judged by the magazine's own lofty standards, the editors, on balance, failed to enlighten their readers about one of the crucial issues of the time for liberals: the morality of communism."[35]

In his memoirs published in 1980, Cowley characterized his role in the 1930s as that of an ardent fellow traveler. He did not join the Communist party in 1932, he recalled, because of "literary reservations." By 1935 he "had developed other than literary doubts about what the party was doing in America and in Russia too."[36] And yet, like so many of his generation, Cowley kept these doubts to himself. There was the concern that any criticism of the Communists would disrupt the antifascist alliance necessary to support the Republican cause in Spain. A fascist triumph in Spain was feared to mean the defeat of democracy worldwide. There was also the fear of losing a faith and a vision that gave meaning to life. Hence Cowley continued to function as a highly effective front man for the Party—more effective than many card-carrying Communists because he could honestly say that he was not a member of the Party and therefore was regarded as more detached.

In an earlier essay, entitled "The Sense of Guilt," Cowley showed himself to be somewhat more self-critical about the role he played in the second half of the 1930s. He acknowledged that he kept quiet about some of his beliefs "out of laziness or loyalty. . . . When I add together these various sins of silence, self-protectiveness, inadequacy, and something close to moral cowardice, there appears to be reason for my feeling a sense of guilt about the second half of the decade."[37] In the same essay, Cowley also quoted the words of his contemporary, Philip Rahv, editor of *Partisan Review,* who was even more stern in his judgment of the period:

The Thirties was a period of radicalization, to be sure, but it was mainly a radicalization controlled and manipulated by the Stalinist party-machine. Hence one can scarcely discuss this decade without also characterizing it as a period of ideological vulgarity and opportunism, of double-think and power worship, sustained throughout by a mean and crude and unthinking kind of secular religiosity.[38]

The Anti-Stalinist Left

Philip Rahv and *Partisan Review* had recognized the real intellectual character of the 1930s earlier than most. The magazine had begun in early 1934 as the organ of the John Reed Club in New York City and with the blessing of the Communist party. Its editors, Philip Rahv and William Phillips, were committed Marxists, though Phillips never became a member of the Party. From the beginning, both men were opposed to the "sloganized and inorganic writing" which they detected in the main body of Communist-sponsored literature. The term "proletarian literature" had in fact become a euphemism for Communist party literature. By 1936–37 their doubts about the Party's literary program had grown and they had lost their earlier belief that two young critics with a magazine could meaningfully affect the Party's anti-intellectual stance. Added to this was their gradual disillusionment with the Soviet Union, which reached its high point with the Moscow trials. By the summer of 1937, Rahv and Phillips had decided to break with the Communist party and its Popular Front strategy. In December 1937 appeared the first issue of the new and independent *Partisan Review*.[39]

In addition to Rahv and Phillips, the new editorial board consisted of Dwight MacDonald, Fred Dupee, and Mary McCarthy. The editors declared that the new *Partisan Review* would be at once radical and "unequivocally independent." The magazine would be "aware of its responsibility to the revolutionary movement in general," though it would reject conformity to any particular ideology or to the dictates of any organization. Critical thought had to be directed toward all systems and ideas. "Formerly associated with the Communist Party, *Partisan Review* strove from the first against its drive to equate the interests of literature with those of factional politics." The magazine's new independent status, the editors affirmed, rested on the conviction "that the totalitarian trend is inherent in that movement and that it can no longer be combated from within."[40]

For the rest of the 1930s *Partisan Review* functioned as one of the sharpest critics of American Communism, a center of radical anticommunist intellectuals. The Party and its Popular Front sympathizers were assailed as culturally backward, anti-intellectual and narrowly dogmatic. Still committed to revolutionary Marxism, the editors accused the Party of "throwing overboard the whole theory of scientific socialism" and substituting for revolutionary principle "the stars and stripes of New Deal Marxism." The Popular Front was actually defending the status quo. Stalinism, Rahv wrote in February 1938, represented "blind faith and accommodation." Instead of upholding a "critical, revolutionary consciousness in art" it reflected the attitudes of a bureaucratic regime. "It is impossible for the intellectual to make the moral and political compromises that Stalinism demands of him without betraying himself."[41]

In their criticism of the Soviet Union and their analysis of the world situation, the editors of *Partisan Review* took up a position that leaned heavily toward Trotsky. The Moscow trials, they argued, had demonstrated the perversion of the Russian Revolution and Leninism. Stalinism was the antithesis of true Marxism. During the year 1938, Rahv came out against the idea of collective security and predicted that capitalism would not be able to conduct a major war without coordinating its human and industrial resources along fascist lines. "Only unalterable opposition to capitalism," Rahv maintained, "only the utilization of the imperialist war for revolutionary ends, opens any prospect to humanity and its culture."[42] Not until many years later did the editors of *Partisan Review* move toward an appreciation of American democracy and a gradual abandonment of their adherence to a revolutionary Marxism.

Another center of radical anticommunism, but far more influential, was the *New Leader,* edited by a man of great intellectual force, Sol Levitas. In the pages of this independent socialist magazine, the Russian Menshevik émigrés Boris Nicolayevsky and David Dallin provided American readers with the first comprehensive picture of forced labor and the Gulag in the Soviet Union. Indeed, much of what America learned about Stalin's crimes was first publicized in the *New Leader*. And then there were those who, like *Partisan Review* after 1937, were anti-Stalinist and harsh critics of the American Communist party but were not necessarily opposed to Communism as such.

In the same symposium published in 1934 in the pages of the *Modern Monthly* in which Morris Cohen had written his essay "Why I Am Not a Communist," Sidney Hook authored a piece entitled "Why I Am a Communist: Communism Without Dogmas." Hook explained that he was not a Communist in the sense of accepting the principles and tactics of the Comintern or its affiliated organizations. The American Communist party was insufficiently Marxist in both its slogans and practices—it followed "mistaken theories and tragically sectarian tactics." But Communist principles were more important than Communist organizations, and this meant that every Marxist had to be a Communist. Hook ended his essay with the observation that only Communism could save the world from its present social evils. "The conclusion is, therefore, clear: *the time has come to build a new communist party and a new communist international.*"[43]

In line with this call, Hook joined with the Protestant minister and labor organizer, A. J. Muste, to form the American Workers party, which came into being in late 1933. According to Muste, the American Communist party throughout its existence had thought in terms of Russia and Europe rather than taking into account the special conditions of the American worker. The Comintern was an appendage of the Russian Foreign Office. The American Party had alienated large sections of the working class "by its sectarian and disruptive activities in the unions and other mass organizations." All these mistakes, Muste argued, would be avoided by the American Workers party, which would be a truly American party working for the revolutionary abolition of the capitalist state.[44]

Early in 1935, the American Workers party fused with the Trotskyist Communist League of America, led by James P. Cannon and Max Shachtman. The new party was called Workers Party of the United States and soon, as Hook and others had feared, became clearly Trotskyist in outlook. In 1938 it took the name Socialist Workers party. To anti-Stalinist Communists such as Hook and Muste the Trotskyists were no less authoritarian and sectarian than the Communist party, and they soon lost all interest in the new party. None of these organizations was able to gain significant support from among the working class. The American Workers party for a time was successful in organizing unemployment leagues, and the Trotskyists from time to time made inroads in some unions. But on the whole all of these parties remained primarily sectarian organizations of intellectuals.

Sidney Hook was probably the first of this group of anti-Stalinist radicals to understand the reasons for the failure of these various Communist parties to find a mass following in America. "Our hypothesis," Hook writes in his memoirs, "that the revolutionary attitude toward American institutions was doomed because it lacked a native garb and spoke in a foreign tongue was invalid. It was not the medium or form of the revolutionary message that was wrong. It was the message."[45] The American people were not prepared to accept the message of revolutionary Marxism no matter what its shape or form. Unlike many of the country's intellectuals, who judged capitalism by its performance and communism by its promises, the overwhelming majority of the American workers, even at the height of the depression, were not prepared to embrace the idea of the class struggle and the utopian creed of a stateless and classless society.

Because they were both anticommunist and anticapitalist at the same time, the anticommunist radicals never received as much attention as their conservative counterparts. Conservative anticommunism often relied on name-calling and unsubstantiated charges that, while less reliable, gained publicity and support from the man in the street little concerned with the niceties of Communist doctrine. This kind of vulgar anticommunism found little rapport among the intellectuals. However, as some radical anticommunists, like the group clustered around the *New Leader*, developed a more positive relationship with American society, their political effectiveness increased. From their nucleus grew after World War II a powerful liberal anticommunism. From this tradition sprang organizations such as the Liberal party of New York and Americans for Democratic Action.[46]

How Red Was the "Red Decade"?

During the period of the Popular Front, from 1935 to 1939, the membership of the American Communist party doubled, reaching almost 100,000. Because of its moderation and identification with the American tradition, the Party also attracted a large number of sympathizers. In the country's cultural world, in particular, the Communists were able to achieve a position of considerable influence and power.

The above assessment is generally accepted. But some of those who lived through this period have gone further. In a book entitled *The Red Decade* and published in 1941, the journalist Eugene Lyons argued that during the days of the Popular Front the Communists and their sympathizers were successful in imposing a veritable "intellectual and moral 'red terror' " on their critics. The name-calling and vilification of opponents, Lyons maintained, was most extreme against "renegades," those who had broken away from the Party. Hence many who otherwise would have left the political environs of the Communist party hid their disaffection and stayed the course.

I have known men and women so frightened by the certainty of persecution from the Left that they hid their doubts and disillusionments like criminal secrets. The prospect of being branded, a thousand times over, a fascist, Trotskyite, Franco spy, agent of Hitler and Japan, tool of Hearst, lackey of Wall Street and the Liberty League has kept many hundreds of comrades toeing the party line long after their faith had turned to ashes. . . . They knew—and that was the most efficacious part of the business—that thereafter they would automatically be ostracized not alone by former friends and comrades but by that whole broad social, literary and intellectual periphery. They would become aware of mysterious pressures against them even on the most conservative newspapers, in seemingly uninfected government bureaus, in solid publishing houses, wherever the party had fellow-travelers or outright agents in key positions—which in these hectic years meant approximately everywhere.[47]

Some contemporaries have confirmed this description. Writing in 1938, Philip Rahv observed that during the last few years "the Stalinists and their friends, under multiform disguises, have managed to penetrate into the offices of publishing houses, the editorial staffs of magazines, and the book-review sections of conservative newspapers." The result, he noted, was a kind of "unofficial censorship" that menaced left-wing writers opposed to Moscow and intellectual freedom generally. Rahv related that he personally knew several novelists and journalists, still "friends of the movement," for whom the "impulse to speak out has been checked time and again by careerist calculations."[48]

William Phillips, Rahv's longtime colleague on the editorial board of *Partisan Review*, recalls that he was cut off from writing for a large metropolitan publication, to which he had been a frequent contributor, and was told that the decision was political. During the late thirties, Phillips writes, he and Rahv had been doing reviews for the *Nation* until one day they were informed by Margaret Marshall, the magazine's literary editor, that she had been given orders not to print any Trotskyites—the designation used by the Communists to cover any anticommunists on the Left.[49]

A similar experience is recounted by Max Eastman. Shortly after his essay "The End of Socialism in Russia" had been published in the January 1937 issue of *Harper's* Eastman was informed by the president of Little, Brown & Company that the firm was interested in publishing his essay as a low-priced book. Little, Brown, he was promised, would get behind it with all the sales and marketing expertise at their command. Yet for reasons Eastman was never able to uncover with certainty the book not only was never pushed by Little, Brown but was not even adequately announced and died stillborn. It probably was not coincidental, Eastman surmises, that at that very time a new president took charge of the staid New England firm and that for a while Little, Brown had a seizure of pro-Soviet enthusiasm. The Communists, Eastman recalls in his memoirs, had managed to plant agents in publishing houses, mail-order houses, bookstores, and distributing agencies all over the country.

Not only were *anti-Communist* books mysteriously turned down in manuscript, ill-advertised when accepted, sabotaged in sales departments, and slipped under the counters in bookstores, but nonpolitical books by authors *known to hold anti-Communist opinions* met the same deadly impediment of underground hostility. While the Communists were continuing the old wail about the suppression of their views, we who opposed them saw their views riding to the surface everywhere while ours sank and were drowned.[50]

It was this sense that the Communists and their fellow travelers had achieved a dominating influence in the cultural and literary landscape and in a few eastern colleges that, as we have seen earlier, led a large number of well-known intellectuals in 1939 to organize the Committee for Cultural Freedom. At the time, Granville Hicks was still a member of the Communist party and he, together with other Party faithful and fellow travelers such as Max Lerner, I. F. Stone, George Seldes, and F. O. Mathiessen, was among the signatories of a statement, published in the *Daily Worker,* that denounced the members of the committee as "reactionaries" who sought to disrupt the united front of all progressive forces.[51] But even after Hicks had broken with the Party he expressed disagreement with Eugene Lyons's view of the domineering cultural influence of the Communists during the Popular Front period and he spoke of the "myth of the red decade."[52]

According to Hicks, the Party scarcely made a dent in any of the media that reached the American people—the popular magazines, movies, or radio. "The big magazines, those that paid good money, were notoriously hostile not only to communism and the Soviet Union but to virtually all the ideas advocated by the Popular Front." In the book publishing field, more important than Communist editors was the fact that during the thirties there was a market for left-wing books; publishers, eager for profit, catered to that market. Eugene Lyons, Hicks pointed out, had cited only one attempt to suppress an anticommunist book and that attempt had failed. Alleged victims of the red terror—John Dewey, Max Eastman, Ben Stolberg, John Dos Passos, and others—all found publishers during the decade. In sum, Hicks concluded, while the Communist party had influence disproportionate to its membership, this influence was not unlimited or dominant. "The notion that communism dominated American culture is false."[53]

On the whole, Hicks probably has the better of the argument. There were undoubtedly instances of intimidation and suppression as some of those who lived through the Popular Front period of the 1930s have related. But, as Daniel Aaron points out, the Communists were never able to bowl over all intellectual opposition or exercise complete control over literary organs.[54] The infatuation of commercial publishers with radical causes found its repetition during the 1960s, but the explanation again was not leftist infiltration but the publishers' eagerness to take advantage of a ready market for such wares. During the second half of the 1930s, conclude Irving Howe and Lewis Coser, "cultural Stalinism had become a significant power in the United States, not unchecked or unchallenged, but exerting far greater influence than its numbers might suggest."[55] Well-organized and determined minorities can gain far more influence than one might infer from a mere counting of heads. And the Communists certainly were a coherent minority.

How red was the "red decade"? No precise answer is possible, but there can be little doubt that the years of the Popular Front were indeed tinged with plenty of pink and red. Some anticommunist authors were ignored; many Communists and proto-Communists, benefiting from the respectability of the Party, were petted and praised. Those who today look at some of the famous names that graced the numerous Communist fronts and public statements issued by them in defense of Stalin's brutally repressive rule are likely to experience a sense of embarassment. There was nothing wrong with supporting antifascist causes or collective security, but to do so in the company of and under the guidance of the American Communist party was unnecessary and less than ennobling. For all too many American intellectuals the decade of the 1930s was not their finest hour.

5

World War II:
Demise and Rebirth of the
Popular Front

The Yanks Are Not Coming

On August 23, 1939, the Soviet Union and Nazi Germany signed a treaty of nonaggression. A secret annex assigned eastern Poland, Finland, Estonia, Latvia, as well as the Rumanian province of Bessarabia, to the Soviet orbit. A supplementary secret protocol attached to the Boundary and Friendship Treaty of September 28 extended the Soviet sphere of influence to Lithuania and further refined the lines of demarcation dividing Poland between Germany and the Soviet Union.

The secret agreements did not become public until the end of World War II when the victorious Allies discovered them among the captured German archives. These documents also showed that the Russians had taken a far more active role in bringing about this pact than had hitherto been believed, while at the same time they had deceived the West about their plans. Yet already in 1939 it was clear that the Hitler-Stalin Pact had paved the way for the Nazi seizure of Poland and for the beginning of World War II. The Russo-German agreement protected Hitler against a two-front war, which he could not have fought successfully in 1939, and enabled Hitler to overrun much of Europe. Whether Britain and France might have been able to prevent the German-Soviet rapprochement by showing a stronger interest in a treaty with Russia or by bringing to bear pressure on Poland to acept the entry of Soviet troops upon their territory in case of a German attack none can say with assurance. It is true that the British, in particular, had not yet overcome the temptation to try to appease Hitler, though as the Soviet historian V. Dashichev has recently conceded, the policy of appeasement "was not just dictated by anti-Sovietism; how could they see a reliable military ally in Stalin who had just decapitated the Red Army?"[1]

The historian Gordon A. Craig believes that Stalin always preferred an agreement with Hitler to a pact with Britain and France, whom he considered unreliable allies. For Stalin such an agreement had the advantage of netting Russia half of Poland, the Baltic states, and Bessarabia and Bukovina. The Nazi-Soviet Pact, Craig concludes, was "based on the common interest of the two partners at the time of its signature."[2]

Aided by Mikhail Gorbachev's *glasnost,* the Hitler-Stalin Pact was recently severely criticized by a Soviet military historian. In an article published in *Komsomolskaya Pravda* in August 1988, V. M. Kulish argued that far from gaining a respite for the Soviet Union, the pact assured Hitler's armies a free hand in France and made it possible for Hitler later to throw his full might against Russia. Stalin himself, Kulish charged, made the Russian campaign a one-front war, with all its bloody consequences.[3] In May 1989, a Polish-Soviet historical commission issued a report on "The Genesis and Beginning of World War II," which called the destruction of the independence of Poland agreed upon in the secret protocol "a serious violation of international norms."[4] On August 18, 1989, after years of denial, an article in *Pravda* for the first time acknowledged that on the eve of World War II the Soviet Union and Nazi Germany indeed had secretly and illegally divided Eastern Europe into spheres of influence.[5]

The impact of the Hitler-Stalin Pact on the American Communist party was strong and the blow to its auxiliaries was devastating. Only six weeks earlier Earl Browder had emphatically denounced rumors of a German-Soviet rapprochement: "There is as much chance of [a Russo-German] agreement as of Earl Browder being elected President of the Chamber of Commerce."[6] But now the seemingly impossible had happened.

The first reactions of the Party were marked by confusion. For a few days the Communist press still talked about the need to defeat "fascist aggression" and to support "the struggle of the Polish people for the independence of their country." But by September 12 the antifascist slogans had disappeared, and in late September and early October 1939 Browder received detailed instructions from Georgi Dimitroff, head of the Comintern, concerning the new line to be pursued. The world war that had broken out, Dimitroff told Browder, was not a war of democracy against fascism but an imperialist war between two equally reactionary parties. Poland, too, was a reactionary and oppressive state and the "international working class had no interest in [the] existence of such a parasitic state." The Soviet Union, by coming to the aid of the people of the West Ukraine and Byelorussia who had been suffering under Polish enslavement, had "extricated eleven million people from [the] hell of capitalism." The slogans of the People's Front were now outdated. The main task of the American party was to prevent Roosevelt from helping England and France and to make sure the U.S. would not enter the war in order "to save [the] crumbling capitalist system." The war that had broken out would weaken all of the imperialist nations. Hitler, without knowing it, was actually helping to shatter the bourgeoisie worldwide.[7]

The propaganda apparatus of the Party soon overcame its initial embarrassment and began to push the new line. The unfolding world conflict was described as a struggle between rival imperialisms for world domination; America had to be kept out of this imperialist war. "The previous alignment into democratic and fascist camps loses its former meaning. The democratic camp today consists, first of all, of those who fight against the imperialist war."[8] The *Sunday Worker* of November 5 weighed in with this bit of dialectical wisdom: "By its declaration in favor of the cessation of the war, by its amity and frontier pact with Germany, the Soviet Union has made a new contribution to the cause of peace. . . . Proletarians, working people. . . . *Demand the immediate cessation of the plunderous, unjust imperialist war!*"[9] For the many Americans who had participated in the Popular Front against the fascist menace, on the other hand, this new view of the world siutation was completely unacceptable, and they deserted the Communist orbit by the thousands. Long-time allies of the Party, such as Adam Clayton Powell, Jr., attacked the Communists for betraying the antifascist principles the Party had espoused during the days of the Popular Front. Other black sympathizers issued similar denunciations.[10]

By the summer of 1939, the American Communist party had become an important force in American political life. A few months later—after the Hitler-Stalin Pact, the invasion of Finland, and the annexation of the Baltic countries—the Party's fortunes had taken a drastic turn for the worse and its major front organizations were in a state of collapse. Among those party auxiliaries hardest hit was the League of American Writers. By 1940, a third of the officers and 100 of its 800 members had formally resigned; many others had drifted away. Those lost included most of the League's prominent figures, such as Thomas Mann, Archibald MacLeish, and Matthew Josephson. One of the first to leave was W. H. Auden. In his letter of resignation Auden noted that the Nazi-Soviet Pact had destroyed the Popular Front in the democratic countries. "The American League of Writers was founded, I understand, as a Popular Front body. As in most such oranizations, the Liberals were lazy, while the Communists did all the work and, in consequence, won the executive power they deserved. This did not matter much so long as the Popular Front was a reality: now it does."[11]

Malcolm Cowley resigned from the League in 1940. In a brief statement published in the *New Republic,* Cowley explained that leaving the League had been a hard decision. He had helped organize the organization and, from the beginning, had been one of its vice presidents. Yet he could not accept the League's policy which, following the current Communist line, opposed the "imperialist war" and was bound to weaken America's power of resistance. The League now made common cause with appeasers and reactionaries and did more "to confuse American democracy than to defend it."[12] The *New Republic,* too, by this time, had abandoned its pro-Communist posture. The Hitler-Stalin Pact, writes a historian of the magazine, had demolished most of the *New Republic*'s dreams. "The Soviet occupation of Poland fractured the core of TNR's beliefs and the invasion of Finland broke it."[13] During the following years, the *New Republic* still occasionally printed pro-Soviet propaganda and, in the name of wartime unity, argued for the appeasement of Stalin. As late as March 1944, Daniel Bell characterized the political line of the magazine as an example of "totalitarian liberalism."[14] Still, for the editors of the *New Republic,* as for so many other liberals, the events of 1939–40 represented an important political watershed.

Few Party functionaries resigned. One of the most prominent who did was Granville Hicks. His statement in the *New Republic* on October 4, 1939, noted that the Nazi-Soviet Pact not only had wiped out the Popular Front but also had destroyed the Party's credibility. "When the Party reverses itself overnight, and offers nothing but nonsense in explanation, who is likely to be influenced by a Communist's recommendations?"[15] For the longest time, he wrote a few years later, he had failed to understand the complete subordination of the Party's bureaucrats to the dictates of the Soviet Union. "Moscow cracked the whip; the leaders jumped; and the rank and file did an about-face or got out. Not only because I was still above all else an antifascist, but even more because I saw how mistaken I had been with regard to the party, I had no choice but to quit."[16]

The American Communist party has always had a high rate of turnover in its membership, but the attrition rate after the Hitler-Stalin Pact was far more serious than in earlier years. On the other hand, most Party notables ignored whatever unhappiness they may have felt about the new line and stayed the course. They regarded the crisis as a moment of testing and allayed their doubts by working harder. As a Hollywood Communist recalls, "the disarray meant only that we had more work ahead of us than ever."[17]

And work there was aplenty. One pamphlet, *The Yanks Are Not Coming,* was distributed to an estimated 50,000 people and Yanks-Are-Not-Coming committees were to be established wherever possible. In order to create antiwar sentiment, the Party's publicists revived memories of the slaughter of World War I. The *Daily Worker* serialized a bitter antiwar novel by Dalton Trumbo, *Johnny Got His Gun,* and printed selections from Henri Barbusse's famous novel *Under Fire.* In place of the dissolved American League Against War and Fascism, the Party organized the American Peace Mobilization, which sought to block aid to Britain. As he had been during the years 1933-35, Roosevelt once again became an "enemy of the people." President Roosevelt, a Party statement of September 5, 1940, declared, "has studied well the Hitlerian art and bids fair to outdo the record of his teacher." It was the tragedy of the American people that they were being "tricked into the chains of a gang of military adventurers as surely and as disastrously as were the German people."[18]

The idea that the Western democracies were as evil, if not worse, than the Nazis appeared in other arguments. Much was made of the fact that England and France, after the German attack against Poland, had been the first to declare war. After the fall of Norway to Hitler's forces, the *People's World* declared that the British imperialists, "intent on spreading the war," remained "the greatest danger to Europe and all mankind."[19] In the spring of 1941, the *Jewish Voice,* the monthly newsletter of the National Council of Jewish Communists, described Nazi atrocities against Jews in various European countries but then went on to ask: "Is it not true that the British and American imperialists are blueprinting a Hitlerite future for the Jews? What is happening to the Jews of Palestine today, under British rule, does not differ essentially from what is happening to the Jews under Nazi rule."[20]

Predictably, the notion that there was nothing to choose between Nazi Germany and the democracies and that the war against Hitler was an imperialist war did not sit too well with many Jewish Communists. Several distinguished Yiddish writers, who had participated in Yiddish-speaking front groups, now drifted away. Leading members of the staff of *Freiheit,* the Yiddish Communist daily, resigned their posts. Former Yiddish-speaking Jewish party members and sympathizers formed an anticommunist organization, the League Against Fascism and Dictatorship. Serious losses also occurred in Local 22 of the International Ladies Garment Workers Union, which contained 20,000 Jewish dressmakers and had always been a radical stronghold. In December 1939, six leading Jewish Communists resigned their membership of the local's executive committee. As a result, the Communists lost control of Local 22, "a loss that reverberated throughout the Jewish labor movement."[21]

And yet, even among the Jewish Communists, the hard core remained loyal to the Party and many of them proved their dedication by vilifying those who had become apostates. Michael Gold wrote a series of articles for the *Daily Worker,* also published as a book under the title *The Hollow Men,* in which he castigated renegade intellectuals as weaklings and agents of the ruling class. Those intellectuals who supported the Allies, Gold wrote, had turned to the service of fascism since anyone "who is for America's entrance into the war must also demand an end to American democracy."

> These Mumfords, MacLeishes and Franks may go on spouting endless torrents of "spirituality," all the large, facile, greasy, abstract words that bookmen, like confidence men, are so perfect in producing. But basic tendencies remain. Where are they going after rejecting liberalism? Not to Communism surely, but toward the other pole, toward fascism.[22]

The Communist party's abandonment of the Popular Front and its new more militant line gave rise to a series of anticommunist measures which had wide support in the country. Browder and other Party leaders were indicted for violations of the passport law. During the year 1940, thirteen states arrested more than 350 Party members and charged them with offenses ranging from election fraud and disorderly conduct to criminal syndicalism and possession of explosives. Congress passed the Alien Registration Act, better known as the Smith Act, Title I of which made it a crime to teach and advocate the necessity or desirability of overthrowing the government of the United States.[23] Jerry Voorhis, one of the most liberal members of Congress, sponsored enactment of the Voorhis Anti-Propaganda Act, which required the registration of groups subject to foreign control and of those seeking the violent overthrow of the U.S. government.[24] In order to avoid registration, the Communist party dissolved its affiliation with the Comintern and modified its constitution.

The Voorhis Act had its origins in a proposal made by the noted civil libertarian Morris Ernst aimed at assuring openness and honesty in the marketplace of ideas. Propaganda, Ernst had argued, should be carried out under honest and adequate labels. So strong was anticommunist sentiment in the liberal camp after the Hitler-Stalin pact that even Freda Kirchwey, editor of the *Nation,* gave the Ernst scheme her qualified support. The proposal, she wrote, raised dangers, but "it would have the great merit of exposing to the light many unsavory relationships—financial and otherwise."[25]

The Imperialist War Becomes the People's War

On June 22, 1941, Hitler invaded the Soviet Union, and within hours the American Communist party once again changed its line. The members of the editorial board of the *New Masses,* who on that weekend had attended a meeting on foreign affairs at a camp in upstate New York, hurriedly returned to New York in order to change an article about to go to press in which they had called Roosevelt and Churchill warmongers. In the revised edition Hitler now became the warmonger and Roosevelt once again a peace-loving democrat.[26] The Western powers, who previously had been branded imperialist aggressors, now became allies in a common effort to defeat the Nazis. The Party called for developing the broadest united front against Hitler, the main enemy of mankind, and for a return to the Popular Front.

Old auxiliaries were discarded as no longer useful; new front organizations were created. The American Peace Mobilization, which as recently as June 21 had staged a "peace vigil" in front of the White House, on June 23 changed its name to American People's Mobilization and dedicated itself to achieving the military defeat of Germany. Its new slogan became "For Victory over Fascism." In the fall of 1941 the Communists formed the Russian War Relief to raise funds for food, clothing, and medical supplies to be shipped to the beleaguered Soviet Union. In the spring of 1942 the Party created the American Slav Congress, an organization for Americans of Slavic descent to seek to influence American policy toward resistance movements in Eastern Europe. In the fall of 1942 veteran fellow traveler Corliss Lamont helped organize the National Council of American-Soviet Friendship.[27]

Some of the Party's former allies were skeptical about these new fronts. The *New Republic* wrote on June 30, 1941, that "the Communists will no doubt make another attempt now to set up a United Front; we doubt whether they will succeed with anybody whose memory is good enough to go back a couple of years."[28] The *Nation,* too, expressed distrust of the Communists. Yet, in fact, memories proved weak and the desire for wartime unity, especially after Pearl Harbor and America's entry into the war, soon overrode all misgivings and hesitations. American Communists, who now could be American patriots and defenders of the Soviet Union at the same time, reached new heights of prestige. Government officials, senators, congressmen, generals, and captains of industry supported Communist fronts even when Communist dominance was only thinly disguised.

Between 1941 and 1944 party membership approximately doubled and reached 80,000 by mid-1944.[29] The Communists succeeded in strengthening their position in the Democratic party of California and Washington, a process of penetration begun during the late 1930s. They made major gains in New York, where they won control of the American Labor party. Individual party members, as a former activist later recalled, could become part of the political mainstream.

The rank and file were once again tasting the joy of being accepted by all groups. The party line made it possible during this period for ordinary members to be merely human beings and to act naturally, for their neighbors were now less frightened, and even listened to Communists explain that they were on the side of the American people.[30]

The first few months of the German invasion proved extremely difficult for the Soviet Union. Contrary to what the proponents of the German-Soviet pact of 1939 had assumed, Stalin had not used the intervening time to build up Soviet defenses. He had disregarded all warnings of a German attack, and Hitler's divisions at first, therefore, made rapid advances. Once the Germans had been halted in front of Moscow and Leningrad, however, the prestige of the Red Army soared and virtually all sectors of American life joined in celebrating the courage of the Russian people.

There now developed an unprecedented admiration for all things Russian. Dances, folk songs, and other music from Russia became highly popular. Publishers, always ready to capitalize on the latest fad, brought out numerous pro-Soviet books. A condensation of the best known book of this genre, Joseph E. Davies's *Mission to Moscow,* was published in *Reader's Digest,* previously and later no friend of the Soviets. In his book, which quickly became a best-seller, the former ambassador to the Soviet Union praised the achievements of Stalin. The "impractical" idea of communism, Davies argued, was being discarded in the Soviet Union and posed no threat to the United States. A Communist commentator, while disagreeing with Davis about the disappearance of communism, wrote that "we must be grateful for a book that confirms irrefutably the truth that many Americans had been fighting for during the Thirties."[31]

Many other Americans shared the view that Stalin's Russia was abandoning the earlier extremes of Bolshevik ideology and was now moving toward a more practical and less dictatorial society. Mrs. Tryphosa Duncan Bates-Batchellor, a leading member of the Daughters of the American Revolution, opined that "Stalin is a university graduate and a man of great studies. He is a man who, when he sees a great mistake, admits it and corrects it. Today in Russia, Communism is practically nonexistent."[32] The Soviet Union was admired as an efficient country in which things got done. The conservative businessman Edward V. Rickenbacker returned from a visit to the Soviet Union praising Russia's "iron discipline in industrial plants, severe punishment for chronic absenteeism, incentive pay, and compulsory overtime work."[33]

The Soviet Union, it was widely believed, was turning into a country with which the West could cooperate in the postwar world. The March 29, 1943, issue of *Life* magazine, devoted to the theme of "Soviet-American cooperation," acclaimed the Russians as "one hell of a people" who "look like Americans, dress like Americans and think like Americans." The NKVD, Stalin's dreaded secret police, was described as simply "a national police similar to the FBI" whose job it was to track traitors. *Mission to Moscow* was made into a film that presented the Soviet Union in an even more favorable light than the original book. *The North Star* and *Song of Russia* were other propaganda films glorifying America's "gallant democratic ally."[34]

Ministers and rabbis participated in the outbursts of enthusiasm for Russia that pervaded the country. Monsignor Fulton Sheen commended the conservative family legislation introduced in the Soviet Union in 1944 and exclaimed: "The family is higher in Russia than in the United States, and God, looking from heaven, may be more pleased with Russia than with us."[35] The Communists, in turn, praised the American churches for their contributions to Russian war relief. They discovered new meanings in religious holidays as when Abraham Chapman, a leading Jewish Communist, wrote in the *Daily Worker* in April 1944 that "the road to freedom this Passover is the road to collaboration with the Soviet Union."[36]

Any criticism of the Soviet Union was frowned upon. The book Trotsky was working on at the time of his assassination, *Stalin: An Appraisal of the Man and His Influence,* was turned down by publishers as "untimely" during the war years of good will. As late as 1945, Samuel Cross, the head of Harvard University's Slavic department, cautioned that the publication of the book would be detrimental to Soviet-American relations and sought to find ways not to release the manuscript of which Harvard had custody. It was finally published in 1946.[37]

In February 1943 the Soviet Union at last acknowledged that the well-known Polish-Jewish Socialists Victor Alter and Henryk Erlich, arrested in December 1941, had been executed for allegedly urging Red Army soldiers to "stop bloodshed and immediately . . . conclude peace with Germany." The idea that these lifelong anti-Nazis, who had taken part in the organization of the Moscow-based Jewish Anti-Fascist Committee, would have urged such a course of defeatism was preposterous on its face. The execution of these two world-renowned leaders of the Socialist Jewish Bund drew widespread condemnation. And yet there were those, including President Roosevelt and the labor leaders Sidney Hillman and Philip Murray, who maintained a discreet silence on the case. Others, while decrying the executions, warned that this monstrous crime should not be allowed to imperil Allied unity. The *New Republic,* for example, at first wrote that it was "time that we learned to know our ally . . . and not allow our admiration for his fighting abilities to blind us to the problems his participation in the war creates. The announcement of the deaths of Erlich and Alter should take the scales from our eyes." But a month later the editors cautioned that the Erlich-Alter case should not be allowed to interfere with American aid to Russia or cast a shadow over postwar cooperation between the allies. Citing the Sacco-Vanzetti executions, the *New Republic* declared: "All the chief United Nations have sins on their conscience like the Erlich-Alter case."[38]

On May 15, 1943, the Comintern announced its dissolution. A centralized leadership of the world Communist movement was said to be no longer necessary. Stalin himself, in an interview with a Western correspondent two weeks later, added the explanation that this action would expose the "calumny" that the Communist parties were agents of Moscow and would aid the unity of all progressive forces.

One of the few American intellectuals to warn against undue optimism over this move and against the widespread mindless glorification of Stalin's Russia was Max Eastman, long since cured of his earlier illusions about the Soviet Union. In an article published in the July 1943 issue of *Reader's Digest*, entitled "To Collaborate Successfully We Must Face the Facts About Russia," Eastman urged Americans, eager to cooperate with the Soviet Union against a common enemy, not to forget that communism was a totalitarian doctrine. In a six-page letter to the *New York Times*, printed on July 20, Eastman reminded his readers that this was not the first time the Communists had embarked on a turn to the right. Wartime imperatives, he warned, should not be allowed to create postwar illusions.

> For my part, I favor forthright cooperation with Stalin now and after the war. I favor giving all military and economic aid to Russia, all honor to her heroic soldiers and people. And I favor coming to their aid with as many western fronts as lie within our military power and judgment. But I think we should do this without kidding ourselves about Russia's total subjection to a totalitarian single party and its Boss, the close cooperation of that party with an exactly similar one here, and a not yet broken harmony in their plans and purposes.[39]

Eastman's words of caution found few supporters. In addition to the *Reader's Digest*, only the *New Leader* with its tiny circulation agreed with Eastman and did its own part in injecting a note of realism into reports about the Soviet Union. One of the few American liberals who refused to share the euphoria about "good old Joe" and the country he was ruling with an iron hand was John Dewey. In a letter to the *New York Times*, published on January 11, 1942, Dewey attacked *Mission to Moscow* as an apologia for Stalinist repression. To idealize the Communist police state, he argued, was to make a mockery of the ideals on behalf of which the country was fighting Hitler. When the film *Mission to Moscow* was released Dewey and Suzanne LaFollette pointed out its distortions. However, their efforts on behalf of the historical truth did not have much of an impact.[40]

American benevolence toward the Soviet Union did not necessarily mean a favorable attitude toward the American Communist party. Many liberals were wary of the Party's new Popular Front line and regarded the Communists as less than reliable allies. In 1943 the educators John Childs and George Counts published a book in which they argued that the American Communist party, as the experience of the past twenty-five years demonstrated, "adds not one ounce of strength to any liberal, democratic, or humane cause; on the contrary, it weakens, degrades or destroys every cause that it touches."[41] Another educator, Alexander Meiklejohn, expressed the view that the Communist party could not hope to become a "useful political party" until it abandoned "the procedures of the military mind, both in its internal discipline and its relations with other groups."[42] In 1944 Dwight MacDonald, formerly associated with *Partisan Review*, founded his own journal, *Politics*, which provided an outlet for anti-Stalinist intellectuals like Daniel Bell and Victor Serge.

From Class Struggle to Class Collaboration

In an exchange with Earl Browder at the end of April 1943, the editors of the *New York Times* suggested that the best service the Party could "render to America and to Russo-American relations is to follow the example set in Moscow and disappear."[43] A year later, the Communist party did exactly that. At its tenth convention, held from May 20–22, 1944, in New York City, the Party was dissolved and replaced by the Communist Political Association. William Foster, chairman of the national committee and Browder's long-standing rival, who earlier had opposed the dissolution of the Party, recommended approval and asked for the honor of nominating Browder as president of the new organization. Half an hour after convening, the meeting unanimously voted to constitute itself the founding convention of the Communist Political Association. The preamble to the constitution of the new group committed the association to "the principles of scientific socialism, Marxism," but otherwise stressed its democratic character:

> The Communist Political Association is a non-party organization of Americans, which, basing itself upon the working class, carries forward the traditions of Washington, Jefferson, Paine, Jackson and Lincoln. . . . It upholds the Declaration of Independence, the United States Constitution and its Bill of Rights, and the achievements of American Democracy against all

enemies of popular liberties. It is shaped by the needs of the nation at war . . . it looks to the family of free nations, led by the great coalition of democratic capitalist and socialist states, to inaugurate an era of world peace, expanding production and economic well being.[44]

The constitution of the association made any effort to subvert or over-throw America's democratic institutions an offense punishable with expulsion. Browder addressed the delegates as "Ladies and Gentlemen" instead of the customary "Comrades."

The dissolution of the Communist party had been foreshadowed by Browder's pronouncements and writings. For some time Browder had emphasized the need to subordinate the Party's long-range goals to war-time unity. After the Teheran meeting of Roosevelt, Churchill, and Stalin in late November 1943, Browder had called for class collaboration and national unity also in the postwar period. It is possible that what the Kremlin later called Browder's "liquidationist" policies went some-what further than Moscow had advised or desired. Browder perhaps had come to believe that the integration of American Communists into the political life of the country was a good in its own right. But on the whole, the dissolution of the Party at this point in time was in the in-terest of the Soviet Union and furthered Russia's goal of strengthening the wartime alliance.

The immediate results were promising. The association's spring 1944 recruiting drive brought in 24,000 new members. Total membership that year reached 70,000 with another 9,000 in the armed forces, about the same number as the Communists had been able to muster at the height of the Popular Front in 1938–39. Many of the new recruits belonged to the prized category of industrial workers, a success all the more remark-able in view of the fact that the Communists at this time were vigorous opponents of all strikes.

During the 1930s the Communists had made steady gains in the trade union movement. After some initial hesitation, the Party had played an important role in the new industrial unionism and by the start of World War II had gained a strong foothold in John L. Lewis's Congress of Industrial Organizations (CIO). Some liberals criticized the growing influence of the Communists in the CIO on the grounds that the Party subordinated the economic interests of the workers to the political goals of Russia's foreign policy, but this was a minority view. The Hitler-Stalin Pact and the Communists' agitation to keep America out of the Euro-pean war weakened the position of the Communists in some unions, but the Party was helped by the fact that John L. Lewis himself was a strong isolationist. In order to preserve their influence in the CIO, the Communists even voted for a resolution at the 1940 CIO convention, urged by their enemy Sidney Hillman, which rejected all foreign ideologies such as nazism, communism, and fascism.

During the years 1940–41 American defense industries experienced a string of protracted strikes which some contemporaries blamed on Communist machinations. "The epidemic of defense strikes," wrote the jouralist Eugene Lyons in 1941, "was no surprise to those who had been watching the communist penetration of American life. . . . It would be silly to deny that the series of defense tie-ups was communist in origin."[45] Later writers paint a somewhat more complex picture. They note that the Communists "were taking advantage of—not originating—a widespread labor insurgency" and that in "virtually all instances there were good and sufficient trade union reasons for striking."[46] At the same time it is clear that the Communists viewed the wave of strikes with satisfaction and that their main interest in them was political. On June 17, 1941, Communist leader William Z. Foster bitterly assailed Roosevelt's use of troops to halt a strike in California that had tied up 20 percent of American combat plane production as "a taste of the Hitlerite terrorism that Wall Street capitalists have in mind for the working class." Five days later the Soviet Union was invaded by Hitler, and from that date on the Communist party, no longer troubled by Roosevelt's "Hitlerite terrorism," insisted that all disputes in industry be resolved without interruption of production. Communist-led unions developed the best no-strike record and Browder proudly agreed to accept the label of "strikebreaker."[47]

Union leaders who disagreed with the Party's no-strike line were vilified as "agents of Hitler." Some of the harshest denunciations were directed at Trotskyist trade unionists because the Socialist Workers party, even after Hitler's invasion of Russia, continued to oppose the war as an imperialist conflict. After the government in 1941 had indicted twenty-nine Trotskyists under the Smith Act, most of them leaders of a Teamster local in Minneapolis, the Communists hailed the prosecution as a necessary action against a fifth column. Following their conviction, the *Daily Worker* declared: "The leaders of the Trotskyist organization which operates under the false name of 'Socialist Workers Party' deserve no more support from labor . . . than do the Nazis who camouflage their Party under the false name of 'National Socialist Workers Party.' "[48]

While the appeal of eighteen of the defendants wound its way through the courts, the Party submitted to the Department of Justice a collection of documents designed to help establish the guilt of the Socialist Workers party. One paper, entitled "The Fifth Column Role of the Trotskyites in the United States," argued that being a sabotage organization, concentrating upon the disruption of the war effort, the Trotskyites do not require a large organization. On the contrary, a smaller group is more easily controlled and efficient for their purposes. . . . The dangerous efficiency of this small group is shown by the fact that it succeeded in obtaining aid for the convicted Minneapolis traitors from the AFL and CIO unions representing 1,000,000 workers. . . . This core of saboteurs is small, but its underground influence is large. Remove the core and you wreck a strong fascist weapon in America.[49]

Well-known liberals like John Dewey and Edmund Wilson formed a committee to seek to overturn the conviction of the Trotskyists, and the American Civil Liberties Union supported the committee's appeal. But the Communists were unperturbed. In a memoir composed after his exit from the Party in 1958, the former Communist leader John Gates recalled that he and his comrades regarded the Trotskyists as counter-revolutionaries and their party as a conspiracy not entitled to a legal existence, the same position taken by the government in 1948 when it indicted the leaders of the Communist party under the Smith Act. "This failure returned to haunt us; it demonstrated that we were for civil liberties when it applied to our own rights but not in the case of our opponents."[50]

The Communists not only reversed their earlier militant line in the trade union movement, but they also moderated their policy with regard to the struggle for the rights of racial minorities. At a meeting of the Party's national committee in December 1941, Robert Minor insisted that blacks direct their efforts "in the first place against those measures of brutality, of the Jim Crow system, that prevent their participation in the war effort."[51] Liberals and black leaders argued that the best way to enlist the full energies of black Americans for the war effort was to do away with their second-class status entirely. Major black newspapers began a "Double V" campaign: Victory over Hitler abroad and Victory over Jim Crow at home. The Communists denounced this campaign as "disruptive."[52] Some Communist-controlled unions did stand up for racial equality; it would be going too far to conclude that the Party sought to suspend entirely the struggle for the rights of blacks. Yet it is clear that the Communists, intent upon wartime unity, insisted on forcing this struggle into narrow channels and thus antagonized many black activists.

The Communist record is worse with regard to the incarceration in detention camps of the country's Japanese Americans. The forced evacuation of 120,000 American citizens of Japanese ancestry at the time found few critics. The Communist press, which defended this shameful act as "a necessary war measure," therefore, was in the mainstream of American public opinion. Yet it was surely piling insult upon injury when Japanese American Communists, instructed or acting on their own, justified their incarceration as a contribution to the fight against fascism. In an article published in May 1942, Karl Yoneda, a longshoreman and veteran Communist organizer, praised conditions in his relocation camp where, according to his description, he and others busied themselves with drives to sell war bonds and conducted campaigns to save tin for the war effort. "The workings of democracy are clearly demonstrated before our eyes. . . . Those of us who are American citizens of Japanese ancestry are grateful to our government for the way this grave question of evacuation is being handled."[53]

The Fall of Browder

On May 20, 1945, the *Daily Worker* carried birthday greetings to Browder on his fifty-fourth birthday. Written on behalf of the staff by John Williamson, the organizational secretary of the Communist Political Association, the article praised Browder as one of the great leaders of the American people and as "the beloved leader of our movement. Your bold, matured Marxist leadership has enabled our movement to make a lasting contribution to our nation and to world democracy."[54] Two days later, on May 22, the New York *World-Telegram* reported that an article in the April issue of *Cahiers du Communisme*, the theoretical organ of the French Communist party, had denounced Browder as a "revisionist." The end had come for "the beloved leader."

The article that signaled Moscow's displeasure with Browder and his line of class cooperation was authored by Jacques Duclos, the French Party's second-in-command, and was entitled "On the Dissolution of the American Communist Party." Duclos charged that "the course applied under Browder ended in practice in liquidation of the independent party of the working class in the U.S." The concept of a "long-term class peace in the United States" represented "a notorious revision of Marxism on the part of Browder and his supporters." Finally, by "transforming the Teheran declaration of the Allied governments, which is a document of a diplomatic character, into a political platform of class peace in the United States in the postwar period, the American Communists are deforming in a radical way the meaning of the Teheran declaration" and were sowing dangerous opportunistic illusions. While severely criticizing Browder, the article included praise of William Foster's criticism of Browder.[55]

It is not clear whether the Duclos article was actually written in Moscow, but the American Communists understood correctly that this public rebuke could have come about only on direct orders of Stalin. It signaled Stalin's intention to push aggressively for maximum advantage in both Europe and Asia, and for this he needed pliant and obedient Communist parties all over the world. Stalin believed that the U.S. was heading for a severe economic crisis, the opposite of the notion of postwar prosperity Browder had welcomed in the Teheran declaration. This line was now outdated and Browder was left holding the bag.[56]

The response of the American Communists once again demonstrated their total dependence on their Russian masters. Those who previously had hailed Browder as the greatest leader of the American proletariat now repudiated him and his policies in an orgy of confession and self-abasement. The same individuals who earlier had voted unanimously to dissolve the Party now denounced the dangerous heresy of Browderism and, again unanimously, in July 1945 reestablished the Communist party. William Foster was elected chairman; in February 1946 an unrepentant Browder was expelled from the Party as a "social imperialist."

Reactions to the new Communist line and the reestablishment of the Party varied. The *Nation* welcomed the new militancy in domestic politics implicit in the repudiation of "Browderism":

> The attitude of the American Communists has been such a travesty on a working-class program that to maintain it after the fighting ended would have meant certain political suicide. It takes at least total war to sell co-operation with the Chamber of Commerce and the National Association of Manufacturers to American Workers.[57]

The *New Republic* saw the changes as another manifestation of the complete bankruptcy of the Communists. "The American Communists seem determined to make themselves as thoroughly and publicly ridiculous as possible." The reconstitution of the Party had taken place "to the accompaniment of public posturings so foolish that if any of the comrades are left who have the faintest sense of humor, they must be blushing all over." The Party was "a mess of hopeless incompetents" and the country was "still without what it badly needs: organized, sustained, drastic criticism by an intransigent, uncompromising and able Left."[58]

Whatever its domestic significance, the Duclos article indicated that Stalin, encouraged by the show of weakness displayed by Roosevelt and Churchill at the Yalta conference in February 1945, had adopted a new, hard line. The promise of postwar unity, celebrated in the Teheran Declaration of November 1943, was laid to rest. The Cold War had begun.

Liberal Anticommunism During the Cold War Era

The Impact of the Cold War

America entered the postwar period with the Popular Front mentality still widely prevalent. Criticism of the Soviet Union was limited; anti-communism invited distrust and raised cries of red-baiting. In the eyes of many intellectuals, the Communists were "extreme liberals," somewhat zealous, but essentially right on matters like world peace, racial equality, and other pressing social issues. George Seldes's pro-Soviet magazine *In Fact,* which had started in 1940 with a circulation of 6,000, by 1947 had a total of 176,000 subscribers and was the most widely read leftist publication in the country. Both the *New Republic* and the *Nation* were still enamored with the idea of common men everywhere forming a happy family, a favorite project of the future leader of the Progressive party, Secretary of Commerce Henry Wallace. If giving in to Russia was the price for realizing this scheme, they were willing to pay it. "Part of the style of American liberalism in the Roosevelt era," writes a historian of the period, "was a soft-heartedness (and soft-headedness) toward the Soviet Union and an abhorrence of Red baiting. This frame of mind could not change overnight."[1]

As late as November 1945, General Dwight D. Eisenhower sent a message of greeting to the National Council of American-Soviet Friendship, an organization of whose Communist front character few could have any doubts. Eisenhower praised American-Soviet friendship as one of the cornerstones on which to build the edifice of peace. "To achieve this friendship nothing is more important than mutual understanding on the part of each of the institutions, traditions, and customs of the other. As an American soldier and lover of peace I wish your council the utmost success in the worthy work it has undertaken."[2]

Anti-Stalinists like Norman Thomas and the editors of the *New Leader* expressed concern about the continuing sway of procommunist sentiments. In the fall of 1946, the *New Leader* published a special supplement by Norbert Muhlen entitled "Submission to Moscow: A Fellow-Travelog in the Empire of the Mind," which surveyed Communist and fellow-traveling activities in the United States. The Communist party, the author noted, still had 70,000 members, and its circle of sympathizers, concentrated especially in the universities and the media, was extensive. The Party controlled seventy national organizations and committees and scores of publications.[3] And yet, not only had the *New Leader* overstated the influence of the Communist party, but the magazine had paid insufficient attention to the rise of anticommunist thinking caused by an increasingly boisterous Soviet Union. America's honeymoon with Russia was coming to an end and so were the inroads of procommunist ideas.

Events in the world during the next few years more than the efforts of anticommunist intellectuals were soon to produce a radically new political climate in the United States. Western hopes for a harmonious relationship with the Soviet Union in the postwar world were collapsing in the face of Russian belligerence. In a speech delivered on February 9, 1946, Stalin described World War II as part of a long-term conflict which would eventually lead to the downfall of Western capitalism and the worldwide triumph of Communism. Heavy pressure was needed in 1946 to get the Russians to withdraw their troops from Iran and Manchuria. The Russians ignored promises of free elections and in 1947 established pro-Soviet regimes in all of Eastern Europe. In the eastern Mediterranean, Greece and Turkey were endangered. In February 1948, a coup overthrew the coalition government of Czechoslovakia and established an outright Communist regime. The Communist parties of France and Italy showed striking political gains. In June 1948, the Soviets instituted a blockade of Berlin.

America responded to these events by seeking to contain Soviet expansionism and halt the advancement of native Communist movements supported by Moscow. On March 12, 1947, President Truman announced that "it must be the policy of the United States to support free people who are resisting attempted subjugation by armed minorities or by outside pressures." After the Truman Doctrine came the Marshall Plan, which was aimed at preventing economic and social chaos in Europe. This blueprint for large-scale economic aid, announced by General Marshall in an address at Harvard University on June 5, sought to undermine the political influence of the European Communist parties that were benefiting from the continent's war-caused destruction and poverty. On April 4, 1949, eleven countries signed the North Atlantic Pact, which was followed by the creation of the North Atlantic Treaty Organization (NATO), designed to defend Europe against any Russian aggression. The war-born alliance between East and West was dead and the Cold War had gone into high gear.

The year 1949 brought new shocks. Early in the year, the inept Nationalist government of China, which had received extensive economic and military aid from the United States, was showing signs of collapse in the face of several successful military offenses staged by its well-organized Communist rival. In October 1949 the victorious Communists proclaimed the People's Republic of China and in December Mao Tse-tung and Chou En-lai traveled to Moscow to negotiate formal ties to the Soviet Union. The Communist bloc now governed almost a quarter of the earth's surface, signifying a dramatic change in the strategic situation and the world balance of power. In June 1950, Communist North Korea invaded South Korea, another case in a seemingly accelerating pattern of Communist expansionism.

Meanwhile a series of revelations about Soviet spy rings further undermined Western morale. In February 1946, the Canadian government announced the arrest of twenty-two persons for transmitting secret information to a foreign power. In May of that year, the British government convicted Alan Nunn May of leaking information about the atomic bomb to Russia. In 1948, Elizabeth Bentley and Whittaker Chambers began a series of public revelations about Communist espionage in the United States. At the end of 1948, Alger Hiss, a former highly placed official in the State Department, was indicted for perjury in denying that during the 1930s he had provided classified information to Chambers. In September 1949, the Soviets announced that they had exploded an atomic bomb; in February 1950, the former Manhattan Project physicist Klaus Fuchs confessed that he had been a Soviet spy since the early 1940s. And in July of the same year, Julius Rosenberg was arrested on a charge of conspiracy to commit espionage. Subsequent revelations brought out that the information provided by the Fuchs-Rosenberg network had saved the Russians many months of difficult and expensive research in developing their bomb.

An Age of Suspicion

All these developments could not but hurt the image of the American Communist party. The Communists had cheered on the Chinese Communists and they had provided unwavering support to Stalin's every foreign policy move. Between mid-1946 and April 1948, the percentage of Americans who thought that members of the Communist party were basically loyal to the Soviet Union rather than to the United States increased from 48 to 65 percent. By March 1947, 61 percent of Americans thought membership in the Communist party should be made illegal.[4]

Anxieties about the domestic Communist threat were fed by a series of headline-grabbing hearings held by the House Committee on Un-American Activities during the years 1947 and 1948. The Republican party in Congress, in particular, saw in the Communist issue a way of deriving political gains. President Truman, on the other hand, believed that the main threat faced by the United States was from the Soviet Union rather than from its agent within the country. He called the American Communist party "a contemptible minority in a land of freedom" and warned against overreactions. During the presidential campaign of 1948, he told an audience in Oklahoma City:

> The greatest danger to us does not come from Communism in the United States. The greatest danger has been that Communism might blot out the light of freedom in so much of the rest of the world that the strength of its onslaught against our liberties would be greatly multiplied.[5]

Truman sought to arouse public concern about the Soviet challenge to American interests abroad. Whether this stress on the danger from Communist expansionism also exacerbated national anxieties about domestic Communism and thus helped prepare the ground for McCarthyism is difficult to determine. We do not have adequate evidence to establish whether people actually listened to the President's speeches and understood their nuances. Rather than shaping public opinion, it is more likely, as one observer notes, that Truman conformed to it.[6]

Yet public opinion certainly was changing. The debacle of Henry Wallace's Progressive party in the election of 1948—he received only one million votes, half of them in New York—demonstrated that the American people had finally abandoned their wartime illusions about the benevolence of the Soviet Union. The dominant role of the Communists in the Wallace campaign, as we will see in more detail in a subsequent chapter, had further undermined the political fortunes of the Progressive party. Magazines like the *Nation* and the *New Republic,* previously associated with the Popular Front mentality, now lost subscribers. A clearly anticommunist liberalism, expressed in new magazines such as the *Reporter* and *Commentary,* was gaining ground. "Whereas the anti-Communist liberals were full of dynamism, élan and passion that so often accompany a newly discovered way of looking at things," Norman Podhoretz recalled years later, "the fellow travelers could marshal nothing but boring clichés and tired arguments."[7] This observation, at least in part, probably reflects Podhoretz's present political commitments, but it also captures an important trend in the political temper of the late 1940s.

Political pressures from the Right during these years undoubtedly played a role in causing President Truman to make several moves in the field of internal security. Attempting to head off more extreme demands made by several committees of Congress, in March 1947 Truman issued Executive Order 9835, "Prescribing Procedures for the Administration of an Employee Loyalty Program in the Executive Branch of the Government."[8] In the spring of 1947, the Justice Department began to expel alien Communists from the country. And in the face of demands from many Republicans within and outside of Congress to outlaw the Communist party, Attorney General Tom C. Clark in early 1948 approved steps leading to the indictment of the top leadership of the Party under the Smith Act.

Anticommunist fervor and a general sense of anxiety about the domestic Communist threat were reinforced by the Hiss case. If a person of such impeccable background and holding so important a government position could turn out to be a Communist spy, who could be trusted? The conviction of Hiss in January of 1950 gave credibility to other charges of widespread disloyalty among government employees and to the Republican accusation that the Democrats all along had been lax in handling loyalty and security cases. Both the conviction and the way many in the intellectual community reacted to the Hiss case undermined the reputation of American liberalism.

When the House Committee on Un-American Activities began its investigation of the Hiss case, President Truman dismissed it as a political red herring designed to distract public attention from the failure of the Republican-controlled Eightieth Congress to cope with inflation. Many liberals similarly rushed to the defense of Hiss and declared with assurance that he could not conceivably be guilty of the charges leveled against him by Chambers, a self-confessed liar. For many of those who during the 1930s had flirted with Communism and had been involved in various Popular Front activities, Hiss had to be innocent so as to vindicate the highmindedness of their own dedication to Popular Front liberalism. To believe that Hiss was guilty, wrote the ex-Communist James Wechsler with much insight, "required a confrontation of their own pasts. They had not been communists, but they had been foolish and credulous, and it was hard for them to face the disclosure that the movement they had once helped, however remotely, promoted such operations as espionage." The Hiss case compelled onetime Popular Fronters to examine their own delusions, never a pleasant task.[9]

For those like Wechsler who had been members of the Party, on the other hand, the accusations against Hiss rang true, because they could easily imagine the rationalizations which had led Hiss into espionage.

> In the decade that Chambers was testifying about, many men had become communists because they believed Russia was the great barrier to the fascist advance and, in particular, the only true ally of the Spanish Republic. To help the Russians was not in their view an act of treason to America, but an affirmative service to embattled democratic mankind; if one occupied a position in which government papers were available that might be helpful to what was then regarded as the citadel of anti-fascism, was it "inconceivable" . . . to pass the papers? In the Soviet mystique of the thirties, Stalin, unlike the diplomats of Downing Street and Pennsylvania Avenue, had no goal except to save the world from fascism. On this premise there could be no conflict between Russian national interest and the cause of peace and freedom; and—as the simple corollary—there could be no fatal hesitation about aiding the Russians through whatever means were available.[10]

A few weeks before his death in 1973, Earl Browder acknowledged the existence of this state of mind among Party members and sympathizers. Without reference to Alger Hiss or anyone else specifically, Browder confirmed what the Party has always denied and what numerous witnesses have repeatedly alleged, that is, that the Communist party was involved in espionage. "We had people," Browder told William M. Coombe of the United Press, "who would inform us from the enemy camp because they sympathized with our position. We didn't consider it espionage."[11]

There are others with a similar frame of mind. Hope Hale Davis, who worked in the Agricultural Adjustment Administration and joined the Communist underground in 1934, has explained why she and other like-minded individuals did not hesitate to obtain documents useful to the Party. They regarded it the fulfillment of "a Communist's 'internationalist' duties":

> We Communists, convinced that the cause we served was vital to the ultimate good of the world, could be sure that whatever we did to promote it was good. . . . I could quite honestly feel superior now to those "confused" liberals who were still making judgments by obsolete bourgeois codes of right and wrong, truth and dishonor. We could raise our heads and face the world proudly while actually living a lie.[12]

That Hiss himself was indeed part of a Soviet-run spy ring has since been established conclusively by Allen Weinstein's careful study, *Perjury: The Hiss-Chambers Case,* published in 1978. Today only Hiss himself and some circles in the radical Left still talk about his innocence.

Because the Communists and their friends during the 1930s advanced an image of the Soviet Union that was in basic harmony with that held by large segments of the noncommunist public, such people had no particular difficulty in obtaining positions in the government. There was nothing in New Deal liberalism that made it soft toward Communism. Yet, as Irving Howe and Lewis Coser note correctly, "it seems beyond dispute that *some* New Dealers, with their vaguely 'progressive' outlook, their floating sense of class identification, and their oppressive burden of class guilt, were prepared to be particularly friendly toward Popular Front rhetoric and to look upon Communists as somewhat impractical 'progressives in a hurry.' "[13] Liberals who insisted that Hiss had to be innocent and that the charges of Communist espionage in the 1930s were part of a new right-wing plot to smear the New Deal and its works unwittingly lent substance to these very accusations. Their protestations that liberals could not possibly have been involved in espionage were seen as an attempt to whitewash traitors and as proof that liberals and Communists were essentially of the same cloth.

It was this very charge that became a key argument in the demagogic rhetoric of the junior senator from Wisconsin, Joseph R. McCarthy, who made his public debut as the nation's chief red-hunter with a speech at Wheeling, West Virginia, on February 9, 1950. Charging that the State Department still employed 205 Communists, McCarthy began a series of sweeping accusations against alleged Communist spies that gained him widespread publicity. For McCarthy and his supporters the United States was threatened not so much by an expansionist Russian or Chinese Communism but by a far-flung conspiracy of American Communists and their protectors in high places. Liberals were considered crypto-Communists for having been members of Communist front organizations. All Communists were spies and traitors. There developed a climate of intolerance and suspicion in which accusation often amounted to guilt. In and out of government, people branded as unorthodox and politically unreliable were losing their jobs.

McCarthy used the forum of congressional investigations in order to browbeat witnesses and score points. He benefited from the indulgence of the Republican party, which tried to use McCarthy-style anticommunism in order to make up for the defeat of 1948 and regain power in 1952. Republicans had the assistance of conservative Democrats such as the chairman of the Senate Judiciary Committee, Pat McCarran, who considered President Truman a dangerous liberal. "From the viewpoint of intelligent liberals," recalls one such liberal, "the situation in the late forties and early fifties had a nightmarish quality about it. The Truman Administration found itself simultaneously denounced as the 'war party' because of its commitment to the lingering Korean War and as 'appeasers of Communism' because it had *not* saved China from the Communists or

Eastern Europe from the Soviets, which could certainly not have been accomplished without a major conflict."[14] The Democratic party's opposition to McCarthyite politics was undermined by Republicans denouncing the Democrats as the "Party of Treason."

Anticommunist hysteria led to a flood of anticommunist legislation. In 1950 Congress enacted the Internal Security Act, which called for the registration with the attorney general of Communist and Communist-front organizations. The act's sweeping provisions drew the veto of President Truman, but Congress overrode the veto and the legislation became law.[15] Anticommunist riders were attached to various kinds of social legislation. In 1954 the liberal Senator Hubert Humphrey was one of the co-sponsors of the Communist Control Act, which was billed as a law designed to outlaw the Communist party and went beyond anything Senator McCarthy had ever proposed.[16] Several states made it a crime to belong to the Party; many others barred Communists from the ballot and made them ineligible for public office or employment.[17] Much of that legislation was eventually invalidated by the courts, but in the meantime it contributed to the climate of insecurity and conformity.

The Debate over McCarthyism and National Security

The intellectual community was sharply divided in its reaction to McCarthy. For liberals like Freda Kirchwey of the *Nation*, anticommunism amounted to a witch hunt and attacks on the Communist party were regarded as red-baiting. The only threat to American liberties was McCarthyism. At the other end of the political spectrum were conservatives such as William F. Buckley, who acknowledged that McCarthy had been "guilty of a number of exaggerations, some of them reckless," but who defended McCarthyism "as a program of action against those in our land who help the enemy." The United States, Buckley argued in a book published in 1954, was at war against international Communism and in this situation the "McCarthyites are doing their resourceful best to make our society inhospitable to Communists, fellow-travellers, and security risks in the government." Buckley denied that liberals had anything to fear from McCarthyism. Their "jeremiads about the threat to free and independent thought and speech are self-refuting; they come from the tongues and pens of men who, in the very act of protesting against tyranny, i.e. in exercising their right to express opinions freely, expose their own hoax."[18]

Writing in the *New Leader*, Norbert Muhlen pressed the same points. There was no reign of terror and the real danger to America was not McCarthyism but the fight against it. If Communists "can make liberals think that McCarthyism is as much of a threat to freedom and justice as Communism, if they can divert the energies of liberals from the true and worldwide danger of Stalinism into a fight against a phantom ogre, then they will have achieved very much."[19]

Buckley and Muhlen were correct in maintaining that McCarthy had not succeeded in transforming the U.S. into a police state and that there existed no reign of terror in any meaningful sense of that term. At the same time, they paid insufficient attention to the spirit of conformity McCarthy had been able to impose on the country and which affected many of the less courageous souls. They also minimized McCarthy's depravity, his use of the big lie and the reckless smear, which deserved far more vigorous criticism than Buckley and the *New Leader* were willing to pronounce. Such a position of sharp condemnation of McCarthyism was taken by ex-Communist liberals James Wechsler and Granville Hicks.

In a book entitled *The Age of Suspicion* (1953) Wechsler warned against panic:

> Frightened men are forever telling us that the time for reflection is past. Senator McCarthy's followers assert that only the methods of primitives can save us, and that it no longer matters how many cruel injustices are committed and how many falsehoods spoken if a single enemy is finally caught somehow somewhere some day. A few ritualistic liberals tell us with equal intensity that any form of resistance to communism must finally make us all prisoners of McCarthy, as though it were impossible for rational men to use their minds in defending their liberties. These are rival absurdities of the age of suspicion.

The spread of know-nothingism, Wechsler argued, was at the moment "our gravest domestic threat," but this battle "will not be won by men who are so distracted by the McCarthy danger that they dismiss the external challenge of Soviet imperialism." That was the parallel of the McCarthy hoax. "For what he and like-minded men have done is to distort all reality by picturing the bedraggled American communists as far more menacing than the massive Soviet power, and by identifying with the communists all those who reject McCarthy's intolerant version of history."[20] Hicks made the same point in 1954 in suggesting that wrongheaded liberals like the editors of the *Nation* made effective resistance to both McCarthy and Communism more difficult for "they create confusion at a time when clear thinking is our great need." Such confused liberals, Hicks insisted, should be neither suppressed nor penalized in any way. They "should be free to say what they want to say. That is their right, just as it is our right to show what is wrong with what they say."[21]

The debate over McCarthyism inevitably became a debate over the entire problem of internal security and the position of antidemocratic extremists in a democratic society. By the early 1950s, under the impact of the Hiss and Rosenberg spy cases and the militantly pro-Soviet line taken by the American Communist party, most Americans and large segments of the intellectual community had come to agree with Norman Thomas and Sidney Hook that the Communists were outside the mainstream of American politics. Thomas, a veteran of many battles with the Communists, pointed out that the Communist party was not just an organization that advocated radical or revolutionary policies. Unlike earlier radicals, who had been honest in declaring their allegiance and proclaiming their purpose, the Party was a conspiratorial group:

> It is a rigidly disciplined body under control from Moscow which is actually engaged in secret conspiracy against not only the American government but the basic principles of democracy. The Communist party stridently demands rights which admittedly it would never grant to others should it come to power.[22]

Sidney Hook took the same position. The Communist party, he argued, was not a regular political party but a conspiratorial movement that claimed the rights and privileges of citizenship in order to do the work of a foreign power. "It does not offer its wares openly but by systematic infiltration into all organizations of cultural life, it seeks to capture strategic posts to carry out a policy alien to the purposes of the organization." Communist ideas, Hook maintained, are heresies which liberals have no reason to fear as long as they are openly expressed. "They should be studied and evaluated in the light of all the relevant evidence. No one should be punished because he holds them." The Communist movement, on the other hand, was something quite different from a heresy. Its threat to a free society could not be dismissed by a quotation from Jefferson.[23]

During those years, a majority of the U.S. Supreme Court agreed with this characterization of American Communism. In upholding the contempt conviction of a witness who had refused to answer questions regarding alleged membership in the Communist party before a subcommittee of the House Committee on Un-American Activities, Justice Harlan observed that "this Court in its constitutional adjudications has consistently refused to view the Communist Party as an ordinary political party, .and has upheld federal legislation aimed at the Communist problem which in a different context would certainly have raised constitutional issues of the gravest character. . . . To suggest that because the Communist Party may also sponsor peaceable political reforms the constitutional issues before us should now be judged as if that Party were just an ordinary political party from the standpoint of national security, is to ask this Court to blind itself to world affairs."[24] And Justice Frankfurter, in upholding the compulsory disclosure of Communist party members' names under the Internal Security Act, noted:

> Where the mask of anonymity which an organization's members wear serves the double purpose of protecting them from popular prejudice and of enabling them to cover over a foreign-directed conspiracy, infiltrate into other groups, and enlist the support of persons who would not, if the truth were revealed, lend their support . . . it would be a distortion of the First Amendment to hold that it prohibits Congress from removing that mask.[25]

And yet, agreement on the conspiratorial nature of the Communist party was only a first step in the process of deciding how to cope with the Communist problem. It did not necessarily signify agreement on concrete policies to be adopted. Some liberals, like Senator Hubert Humphrey, argued that since the Communists were part of an international conspiracy, "membership in that conspiracy should be punishable as a criminal offense, because members of such a conspiracy are, in fact, conspirators to overthrow the government of the United States by force and violence."[26] It was this reasoning which made Humphrey favor the adoption of legislation to outlaw the Communist party. Thinking along the same lines, the John Hopkins University professor Thomas I. Cook proposed outlawing the Party as "a Russian-sponsored anti-constitutional movement."[27] Others, like Adolf A. Berle, opposed outlawry as both "unnecessary and ineffective. . . . Communists are more dangerous when they are under cover than when they are exposed."[28]

Opinions were equally divided over the use of the Smith Act. The *Washington Post* hailed the conviction of the eleven Communist leaders under the act as "the most important reconciliation of liberty and security in our time."[29] Writing in the *New Republic,* the civil libertarian Morris Ernst similarly argued that the issue in the trial was not speech but secret conspiracy. The government could not be expected to wait until the danger is clear and present. The ACLU's Roger Baldwin, on the other hand, pointed out that the prosecution rested on public utterances and publications. "If the government knows of secret conspiratorial acts by the Communists, why did it not indict them for such acts?"[30]

Even those in the forefront of pressing the argument of the conspiratorial character of the Communist movement did not necessarily support the various anticommunist legislative measures enacted during the 1950s. Sidney Hook called the Internal Security Act "ill-advised" and "worse than useless because under its provisions we cannot even offer a haven of safety to former Communists whose information about our enemy's designs may be of incalculable value to us."[31] Norman Thomas agreed: "As a means to deal with sedition the law is on a par with an effort to stop burglars by requesting prospective burglars to register."[32] Hook also came out against "the plethora of needless loyalty oaths in education and other professional fields. The notorious fact is that no genuine Communist has ever been stopped from carrying on his activities by the requirement that he disavow his doctrines, intentions or actions. . . . The net result of the imposition of loyalty oaths has been the punishment of non-Communists."[33]

With regard to the Smith Act, Hook took the position that, in a democracy committed to peaceful change, there was no moral right to advocate the use of force and violence. At the same time, he felt that the Smith Act was "inept" because the prescription should have been placed not on speech to achieve revolutionary ends but on organizations controlled by a foreign power. Although he doubted the wisdom of enacting the law, he thought that the wisdom of repealing it was even more doubtful. Such repeal, Hook argued, "would give a new lease of life to an illusion whose widespread and pernicious character was to a not inconsiderable degree responsible for the original enactment of the law. This illusion is that the Communist Party is a political party like any other on the American scene, and therefore entitled to the same political rights and privileges as all other American political parties."[34]

The Loyalty Program

President Truman's loyalty program for government employees was another issue that divided the liberal community. Alan Barth, an editorial writer for the *Washington Post* and a frequent contributor to the *Nation*, charged that the program fell "far short of what has been established in this country as due process of law. The standards it employs for the measurement of guilt are wholly lacking in the definiteness usually required for official condemnation of American citizens." The administration had denounced Senator McCarthy for imputing guilt by association while "the loyalty boards, operating under a presidential order, had for two and a half years been condemning men on grounds of 'sympathetic association' with organizations arbitrarily called 'subversive' by the Attorney General."[35] Prominent liberals like Henry Steele Commager took the same position.

Sidney Hook criticized the loyalty program as too sweeping and called the practice of requiring security checks for all government employees, rather than merely for those occupying sensitive posts, "a needless, cumbersome and inefficient procedure." He suggested that the Attorney General's list of subversive organizations, used by the loyalty boards to evaluate the significance of membership in political groups, be based on more careful research and that it "should be published only after hearings have been conducted and the relevant evidence published, including the demurrers, if any, of the responsible officers of the organizations." At the same time, Hook argued that it was not unreasonable to infer intent from voluntary membership in an organization like the Communist party; a person's fitness for a position of trust had in part to be determined by his associations. "American tradition is opposed to the doctrine of *legal* guilt by association. But common sense has always recognized that there may be moral guilt by continuous association with disreputable persons, as when a city official is condemned because of the intimate cronies with whom he 'associates.' "[36]

Hook conceded that not every member of the Communist party would necessarily engage in espionage and that some would be more loyal to the United States than to the Soviet Union. This fact created a difficult dilemma, faced by the British Prime Minister, Clement Attlee. On March 15, 1948, he told Parliament about the establishment of new security measures for the civil service. Not all who adhere to the Communist party, Atlee acknowledged, would allow themselves to forget their primary loyalty to the state. "But there is no way of distinguishing such people from those who, if opportunity offered, would be prepared to endanger the security of the State in the interests of another Power. The Government has, therefore, reached the conclusion that the only prudent course to adopt is to ensure that no one who is known to be a member of the Communist party, or to be associated with it in such a way as to raise legitimate doubts about his or her reliability, is employed with work the nature of which is vital to the security of the State."[37] According to Hook, this was the rational and sensible way of dealing with potential security risks in sensitive posts.

The historian Arthur M. Schlesinger, Jr., too, saw the need for tough decisions. Liberals, he argued, "must reject the Communists as forthrightly as the British Labor Party has rejected them; it must not squander its energy and influence in covering up for them. This is the dictate of strategy as well as principle." There was overwhelming evidence that the Soviet Union was using the Communist party and its front organizations in order to recruit agents to penetrate sensitive branches of the government. "Discharge in advance of an overt act," Schlesinger admitted, "may seem a rough policy. Yet the failure to discharge suspicious persons may well imperil national security." The Truman loyalty program had serious defects. "Still, honest civil libertarians might better devote themselves, not to blanket abuse of any attempts to meet the problem but to the construction of alternatives which would better secure individual rights while still permitting the Government to deal effectively with the grim dangers of foreign espionage."[38]

The argument is often heard today that the loyalty programs established after World War II were a complete failure because they did not detect any acts of disloyalty punishable by law. "At a cost to federal agencies from 1947 to 1957 of about $350 million," writes one such critic, "the federal government was unable to uncover a single spy."[39] This objection misses the point, for these programs were designed not to catch the guilty but to exclude the potentially guilty. In view of the necessary shortcomings of a decent criminal law and of an imperfect counter-espionage system, a free society must attempt to protect the integrity of its government by assessing the probability of future misconduct, whether deliberate or through negligence or ignorance, on the part of those who occupy positions of trust and who could cause serious harm to the national interest. In recent years, most acts of espionage appear to have been motivated by financial greed rather than ideological sympathy for the Soviet Union or any other country. Yet human motives are complex and often composed of different elements; a weakened sense of patriotism may lead people to sell their country's secrets. Whatever the reasons for such treasonous conduct, it would be folly to ignore the possibility of serious damage which dishonest, alienated, and disloyal individuals will always be able to inflict upon the country's security. The need for vigilance, therefore, continues.[40]

The experience of the 1950s also demonstrates the need to pay attention to the costs of a loyalty-security program. There is general agreement that President Truman's loyalty program, too sweeping in its scope and administered by politically unsophisticated personnel, exacted a heavy price in its negative effects upon the morale and caliber of the civil service. A sober and experienced observer, the political science professor Robert K. Carr, noted in 1952:

> It is clear that the emphasis that has been placed upon loyalty and ortho-doxy among public employees has served to encourage mediocrity in the public service. Federal workers have learnt that it is wise to think no unusual thoughts, read no unusual books, join no unusual organizations, and have no unusual friends. What this has cost the government in terms of loss of indepedence, courage, initiative, and imagination on the part of its employees is impossible to say, but it is clear that the cost has been great.[41]

The Congressional Inquisition

In its response to the political investigations conducted by various congressional committees, the liberal community was again split betwen those who counseled complete noncooperation and others who, while critical of procedural and other shortcomings of these probes, accepted their basic legitimacy.

The need for Congress to have an investigatory power to aid it in its legislative function is fully established. The questions asked of a witness must be pertinent to the inquiry and the witness has a right to have that pertinency explained, but otherwise the courts have refrained from limiting the reach of such investigations. A legislative inquiry is basically justified by the need to gather information needed for the preparation of legislation, but it is doubtful that Congress has ever conducted an investigation that did not produce facts usable in legislation of clear constitutionality. Even in the area of speech and association, protected by the First Amendment, the courts have accepted the principle that the search for information must necessarily be allowed to have more scope than any actual legislation. Laws infringing on the rights of speech and association are subject to limiting criteria such as the "clear and present danger" test, but the right of Congress to investigate in this sensitive area is far greater. In 1948, in a decision left standing by the Supreme Court and never overruled, a Court of Appeals explained why the investigatory power necessarily had to be free from such limits:

> In our view it would be sheer folly as a matter of government policy for an existing government to refrain from inquiry into potential threats to its existence or security until danger was clear and present. And for the judicial branch of the government to hold the legislative branch to be without power to make such inquiry until the danger is clear and present, would be absurd. How, except upon inquiry, would the Congress know whether the danger is clear and present? There is a vast difference between the necessities for inquiry and the necessities for action. The latter many be only when danger is clear and present, but the former is when danger is reasonably represented as potential.[42]

As a corollary of this ruling, the courts have held that there is no absolute right under the First Amendment to remain silent about one's political activities or affiliations. And given the distinctive character of the Communist party, discussed earlier, disclosure of a witness's ties with the Party has been upheld as a valid object of questioning or at least an object beyond judicial scrutiny. There is no congressional power to expose for the sake of exposure, but the courts will not test the motives of congressmen. Similarly, despite the adverse effects which may follow the compelled disclosure of political relationships, not all such inquiries are barred. The right of Congress to legislate on matters of national security has been held to embrace the right of a properly constituted congressional committee to identify a witness as a member of the Communist party.[43]

Given this reality, since about 1950 most witnesses who did not want to answer questions about their membership in the Party have fallen back upon their right under the Fifth Amendment not to provide testimony that might incriminate them. In view of the many criminal statutes affecting membership in the Communist party, this use of the constitutional protection against compulsory self-incrimination was legally unassailable. Senator McCarthy and his supporters called such persons "Fifth Amendment Communists," but this was an improper inference. A person who had never joined the Party but who had been an innocent member of or contributor to many Communist front organizations could reasonably fear that such admissions could be used against him in an attempt to prove that he was a member of the Party after all. Thus such a person, too, was legally entitled to invoke the protection of the Fifth Amendment and any inference that he was a Communist was unwarranted.[44]

The House Committee on Un-American Activities (known as HUAC) conducted a probe into Communist influence in the motion picture industry in 1947. The many different issues raised by congressional investigations into Communism that for several years were to divide liberals received their first airing at this time. The Special Committee for the Investigation of Un-American Activities, under chairman Martin Dies (Democrat of Texas), had undertaken a similar investigation in 1940, but had received little notice. By 1947, there was more interest in the Communist problem. HUAC had become a permanent committee of the House, and its probe of Hollywood attracted considerable attention.

After holding preliminary closed hearings in Los Angeles, in October 1947 HUAC moved the investigation to Washington. The first testimony came from friendly witnesses who described Communist influence in the Screen Writers Guild and talked about the few pro-Soviet films Hollywood had produced, such as *Mission to Moscow*. Since these films had been made during the era of wartime collaboration with Russia, the damage done by Hollywood leftists did not seem to be too serious. There followed the appearance of ten unfriendly witnesses, eight of them screenwriters and all but one of them Communists.

The "Hollywood Ten," as they became known, at first had considerable support from the press and their Hollywood colleagues. A Committee for the First Amendment grew into a Committee of One Thousand, and even the heads of the studios warned against the danger of censorship. It was in large measure the raucous conduct of the Ten on the stand that soon lost them this initial show of sympathy. As Philip Dunne, one of the originators of the Committee for the First Amendment, and others recall, their friends had suggested that the Ten confine themselves to a simple and dignified statement explaining that they regarded any official inquiry into their political beliefs and associations as a violation of their rights under the First Amendment. They were then to call a press conference or buy time on national radio in order to declare their political affiliations. Such a principled refusal to answer the Committee's questions, coupled with full openness about their politics before the public, it was believed, would have gained them wide support. It also might have made it more difficult for Congress to cite them for contempt, for a jury to convict them, and for the Supreme Court to turn down their appeal.[45]

But events took a different course. The lawyers of the Ten argued against the defense strategy proposed by their liberal friends and the Ten agreed with their lawyers. They welcomed the hearings as a chance to express their hatred of the Committee and as a result became their own worst enemies. HUAC, in turn, played into their hands by not allowing John Howard Lawson, the first of the unfriendly witnesses, to read a prepared statement in which he accused the Committee of trying to introduce fascism into the United States and which contained other strident language. This, of course, was not the brief and dignified statement suggested by the Ten's liberal supporters. When Lawson persisted in his attempt to read this statement, he was gaveled into silence and there ensued a shouting match with the members of the Committee. The other nine witnesses were equally hostile. They refused to answer the Committee's questions without expressly invoking the First Amendment. This conduct strongly alienated most of their supporters. On November 24, 1947, the Motion Picture Producers announced the suspension of the Ten. The Hollywood blacklist had begun.

Dore Schary, a studio executive, in his autobiography concludes that this sorry spectacle had no heroes:

> My feelings then and now are that HUAC acted with malice and no evidence of the American values they were supposed to protect; that the Hollywood Ten were badly advised and provided an impetus for what happened following their appearance; that the producers behaved cowardly and cruelly.[46]

Even two writers who consider the Hollywood Ten "courageous activists" acknowledge that the conduct of the Ten on the stand and their failure clearly to base their refusal to testify on the First Amendment antagonized many would-be supporters. "They disarmed themselves of their clarion call to the American public in general and the Hollywood film community in particular."[47]

John Howard Lawson and Dalton Trumbo, the first two of the Hollywood Ten to go on trial for contempt of Congress, were found guilty on May 5, 1948. The Court of Appeals for the District of Columbia in June 1949 unanimously upheld the conviction on the grounds that it is "beyond dispute that the motion picture industry plays a critically prominent role in the molding of public opinion." In the context of the ongoing ideological struggle between democracy and Communism, the court concluded, "it is absurd to argue . . . that questions asked men, who, by their authorship of the scripts, vitally influence the ultimate production of motion pictures seen by millions, which questions require disclosure of whether or not they are or ever have been Communists, are not pertinent questions."[48] The other eight, whose trial had been postponed by agreement until the validity of the conviction of Lawson and Trumbo could be tested in the appellate court, now were also found guilty of contempt. In April 1950, the Supreme Court declined to review the convictions and in June the Hollywood Ten entered prison for a one-year term.

Until the late 1940s, the political influence in Hollywood of leftists of various degrees of radicalism certainly was substantial. In their study of Communism in Hollywood, Larry Ceplair and Steven Englund estimate that between 1936 and 1946 about 145 screenwriters, 50 to 60 actors, 15 to 20 directors and producers, and about 50 workers in front offices, animation departments, and so on were Communists. Many of these men were very well paid and provided the Communist party with substantial sums of money. Communist fractions in various Hollywood organizations, these two writers generally sympathetic to the Hollywood radicals note, "functioned exceedingly well, and it was through them that the policies, effectiveness and ideals (though not usually the dogma) of the Party were transmitted and magnified, well beyond actual Party strength in numbers, within a Union, a Popular Front organization, or a political campaign."[49] The Screen Writers Guild for a time was controlled by Communists. Even though constituting no more than 3 percent of the Guild's membership, recalls one of these men, Communists played "a vigorous and effective role. . . . Party membership was secret, but writers couldn't be prevented from speculating. Many of us in Guild leadership were simply assumed to be members."[50]

But were the Communist screenwriters, in particular, able to inject Communist propaganda into the scripts of the films they authored and thus, as the Court of Appeals had put it, in a position to "vitally influence" the motion pictures seen by millions of Americans? The answer, generally speaking, is no, but this was so not for lack of trying. The Communist writers saw themselves as radical artists with a duty to use their medium to change the way people thought about the world. Hollywood writers, Dalton Trumbo wrote in a letter to the editor of *Masses and Mainstream* in 1946, should "use art as a weapon for the future of mankind, rather than as an adornment for the variety of aesthetes and poseurs."[51] Edward Dmytryk, another of the Hollywood Ten, who broke with the Party while still in prison, recalls how he and another Communist writer were chastised and upbraided on several occasions for not accepting Party criticism of the way they had written certain movie scripts.[52] The Party also insisted that Communist writers not reveal their membership. In 1942, during the days of the wartime Popular Front, Lester Cole and Ring Lardner sought to follow the example of Dalton Trumbo, who in 1941 had come into the open, and asked for permission to shed the cloak of secrecy regarding Party affiliation. The Party ruled against this idea. "It was argued," Cole recalls, "that acknowledged membership would harm my effectiveness."[53] Presumably the Party expected something from its members' professional work that could be jeopardized if they were known to be Communists.

Yet, in practice, hardly any outright propaganda managed to get by the vigilant eyes of Hollywood's producers and executives—the front-office bosses, as they were known. These powerful men not only were worried about profitability but also saw themselves as guardians of public morality and patriotism. It was impossible, Cole writes, to sneak in revolutionary propaganda, though his political feelings were often represented in the attitudes of his characters.[54] The three pro-Russian films that Hollywood produced in 1942—*Mission to Moscow, Song of Russia,* and *North Star*—were done at a time when the Party line coincided with the generally prevailing euphoria about America's Russian ally, and even these films were not in-depth treatments of a Socialist society. The majority of the films made from the scripts of Hollywood Communists, conclude two students of the subject, "seem politically indistinguishable from the films made by non-radical screen writers." Despite the difficulties of getting their politics into films, the Communist writers stayed in Hollywood because of career considerations and because they did not want to miss a chance of using films for expressing their political views.[55] Such chances presented themselves only very rarely, though at times Hollywood Communists apparently were able to prevent the making of films they deemed strongly anticommunist. Arthur Koestler's book about the Moscow show trials, *Darkness at Noon,* is said to have been a casualty of such machinations.

The fact that the Hollywood Communists did not control production of films does not mean that the congressional probes into the industry were without legal justification. Under the wide latitude granted the congressional investigatory power by the courts, discussed above, there are very few subjects Congress cannot investigate. Needless to say, this observation about the legality of the Hollywood probes does not say anything about their political wisdom. Indeed, the hearings on Communist influence in Hollywood, which continued for several years, quickly turned into a hunt for anyone having the slightest connection to earlier Popular Front causes and became clearly punitive. "From 1951 on," writes the historian William O'Neill, who is not given to hyperbole, "HUAC turned up virtually nothing new but subjected witnesses to grueling and often humiliating ordeals. These were justified on the grounds that only the truly contrite were entitled to absolution. Confession was the proof of this, and was ruthlessly exacted."[56]

Those who refused to cooperate by taking the Fifth Amendment were blacklisted by the film studios, an industry that had never been willing to buck public opinion in matters of social mores and was even less prepared to resist the prevailing anticommunist hysteria. The Hollywood blacklist was supplemented by privately authored "graylists" like *Red Channels* that accused 151 named individuals in radio and television of subversive associations. Desperate people asked to be questioned by HUAC in order to clear their names.

On April 12, 1952, the movie director Elia Kazan, a day after appearing before the Committee, took out an ad in the *New York Times* in order to explain why he had freely testified about himself and others. The American people, Kazan maintained, needed to have the facts about Communist activities in order to protect themselves "from a dangerous and alien conspiracy and still keep the free, open, healthy way of life that gives us self-respect. . . . Whatever hysteria exists—and there is some, particularly in Hollywood—is inflamed by mystery, suspicion and secrecy. Hard and exact facts will cool it."

Kazan described how he had joined the Communist party in 1934 during the height of the Depression and under the impact of the ever growing power of Hitler. "The streets were full of unemployed and shaken men. I was taken in by the Hard Times version of what might be called the Communists' advertising or recruiting technique. They claimed to have a cure for depressions and a cure for Naziism and Fascism." He had left the Party a year and a half later because he had become disgusted with its system of discipline that suppressed personal opinions and tried to dictate personal conduct. He had held back from telling this story out of concern for the reputations and employment of people who, like himself, had left the Party many years ago. But there was another reason for his silence:

I was also held back by a piece of specious reasoning which has silenced many liberals. It goes like this: "You may hate the Communists, but you must not attack them or expose them, because if you do you are attacking the right to hold unpopular opinions and you are joining the people who attack civil liberties.

I have thought soberly about this. It is, simply, a lie. Secrecy serves the Communists. At the other pole, it serves those who are interested in silencing liberal voices. The employment of a lot of good liberals is threatened because they have allowed themselves to become associated with or silenced by the Communists. Liberals must speak out.[57]

The political and moral issues first raised by the Hollywood probe soon arose in many other contexts. While agreeing that silence before a congressional committee did not mean legal guilt, the intellectual community was divided over whether it was politically wise for persons questioned about their political views and associations to invoke the Fifth Amendment. Writing in the *Nation,* Laurentz Frantz and Norman Redlich argued that the refusal to testify was a necessary way of expressing disapproval of the "modern inquisition." The medieval inquisition, too, had put people under oath without specific charges in the hope of finding something damaging in the testimony. Liberals, they maintained, should not cooperate in such proceedings which could lead to criminal charges against them and undermined our free society.[58]

In an article published in *Commentary,* Alan F. Westin took the opposite position. Westin agreed that many congressional investigations into Communism had committed serious abuses. The procedures of these committees commonly did not give witnesses the procedural rights which appeared elementary to the American sense of fair play. Some hearings were designed to punish individuals by publicity, to achieve their discharge from jobs they held, to use accusations as charges, and to serve as substitutes for juries. Some Congressmen seemed more concerned with headlines than with the gathering of information for legislation. Cooperative witnesses usually were first questioned in executive session, which meant that the purpose of the public hearings was strictly ceremonial and designed to degrade. Still, Westin argued, liberty was not defended by silence. It created "in the minds of most well-intentioned people simply the image of one more Communist . . . cloaking his activities in the disguise of an appeal to civil liberties." Those who refused to testify helped the Communist party which wanted all witnesses to choose silence in order to camouflage the activities of the Party. Many persons had invoked the Fifth Amendment in order not to have to testify about former associates, but, Westin suggested, "a former Communist should think twice before reserving to himself the decision as to whether his former comrades are *presently* dangerous to American society." As a former Communist, he knew at first hand that Communists were capable of executing directives that could jeopardize civil liberties and the national security. "If the witness's associates have also left the party, they can say so; if they have not, then the former Communist must weigh a personal code of honor against the need for full disclosure in a free society under attack."[59]

Westin expressed some sympathy for the person who chose silence under the First rather than the Fifth Amendment. By affirming the right not to have to testify about one's political loyalties as a right of freedom of speech and association one risked a contempt citation, but there was the possibility that the courts would eventually accept this plea. Even if this were not to happen it was arguable that a prison term for the sake of the First Amendment could have a salutary impact on public opinion. In any event, the risk of punishment was not that much more serious. Those who invoked the Fifth Amendment also usually lost their jobs; this was a deprivation without any redeeming social value.

The cause of freedom, Westin maintained, was best served not by silence but by free speech. That had been the position of former Communists Granville Hicks, James Wechsler, and Robert Gorham Davis. Hicks had expressed the view that congressional investigations into Communist subversion were doing more harm than good, but felt that as an anticommunist he could not in principle oppose such probes. The only way to do justice to all of his convictions, therefore, was to testify and say what he thought both about Communism and congressional investigations. Davis, a professor of English, had made the same point in a letter to the *New York Times:*

> The investigations themselves offer a golden opportunity. There is much to object to in them, but in fighting for democracy and truth one cannot always choose one's battleground. The function of teachers is to teach, to clarify, to inform. The Congressional hearings offer teachers a captive audience of Senators and Congressmen more willing to learn than many people believe, and the widest possible publicity in the press.[60]

Irving Kristol, a former Trotskyist, also argued against silence. Such witnesses actually strengthened the hands of Senators McCarthy and McCarran, for whom the dissenter was per se a scheming subversive. The identification of free thought with underground conspiracy was the greatest imaginable spur to the despotism of public opinion. There was only one way, Kristol maintained, by which the despotism of public opinion could be resisted:

> That is for a person with unpopular views to express himself, loudly, brazenly, stubbornly, in disregard of the consequences. Such a person may have to suffer for his convictions, as others have suffered before him, and as

others will suffer after. But the responsibility for the mind's freedom in a democracy lies with the intransigent thinker, with his courage to shout the truth in the face of the mob, with his faith that truth will win out, and with his maddening commitment to the truth, win or lose.[61]

Many of those called before congressional committees, Kristol wrote, seemed more intent on preserving their well-paying jobs than on standing up for their convictions. They dodged and hedged and gave the appearance that being a radical was something to be ashamed of and to be concealed.

Some liberals took the view that because most of the congressional probers of Communism were so obviously motivated by the search for publicity and political advantage, the information they turned up could not possibly be true. This non sequitur led them to defend men like Alger Hiss. It also benefited those like the Soviet Asia specialist Owen Lattimore, who, while not Russia's top secret agent in the United States as charged by Senator McCarthy, in 1938 had defended the Moscow purge trials as a stroke for democracy and in 1950, when questioned by the Tydings Committee, still held the same view. To subscribe to such ideas was not a crime and it did not justify the harassment to which Lattimore was subjected both by congressional investigators and by the Justice Department. But Irving Kristol was largely correct in his criticism of liberals who in their zeal to oppose McCarthyism sought to whitewash Lattimore's fellow-traveling career:

> In his denunciation of Lattimore's pro-Communist record and in hurling unsubstantiated charges against him (chief of Soviet espionage, etc.), Senator McCarthy may well have been aiming a blow against independence of mind and nonconformity of spirit. For Messrs. Commager, Barth, and Chafee to defend Lattimore's pro-Communist record in order to defend such independence and nonconformity, is for them to play the Senator's game, on the losing side.

Lattimore, Kristol argued, belonged to a segment of American liberalism that had lent aid and comfort to Stalinist tyranny. This failing had to be acknowledged. Unless liberals distinguished between their achievements and their sins they disarmed themselves before Senator McCarthy, who was eager to have it appear that the achievements of liberalism *are* its sins.

> There is a false pride, by which liberals persuade themselves that no matter what associations a man has had with a Communist enterprise, he is absolutely guiltless of the crimes that Communism has committed so long as he was moved to this association by a generous idealism. There is a political

mythology, by which liberals locate Communism over on the "left," in a zone exempt from the unsparing verdict directed against the totalitarian "right."[62]

Professor Robert K. Carr, a professor of law and political science at Dartmouth College, in a careful study of HUAC published in 1952, undertook to review the Committee's accomplishments and shortcomings. If not necessarily valid for the free-wheeling fishing expeditions of Senator McCarthy, this assessment is largely applicable to most other congressional investigations of Communism. On the positive side, Carr pointed out, was the fact that HUAC had shed light upon the revolutionary aims of international Communism at a time when many Americans were inclined to believe that Communism and democracy could exist together peacefully in the same world. The Committee had revealed much useful information concerning the tactics of the American Communist movement—the establishment of cells in government agencies, the infiltration of labor unions, and the establishment of front organizations. HUAC had played a part in the exposure of the espionage activities of Communist agents like Alger Hiss.

Yet, on balance, Carr concluded, HUAC's failings and shortcomings outweighed whatever good it may have done. The record of the Committee made it clear that "one of its leading purposes has been to demonstrate the 'guilt' of certain persons for offenses not always defined in law and to see them punished in the sense of the destruction of their reputations and the loss of their means of livelihood." The Committee had usurped the functions of grand juries and courts and deprived individuals called before it of the presumption of innocence. It had been far more interested in exposing allegedly subversive *persons* than in exposing subversive *activity*.

Second, HUAC had to be held responsible "for having encouraged a widespread witch-hunting spirit both in government and in private life. This spirit has reached its peak in the shameful attacks made by Senator McCarthy upon federal employees and private persons. It may fairly be asserted that McCarthyism would never have been possible had not the Un-American Activities Committee, and its predecessor, the Dies Committee, paved the way from 1938 on." Third, the Committee had played a part in the demoralization of the federal civil service and through harassment had obstructed the recruitment of scientists into the public service. Fourth, by the antics of its members, its grossly unfair procedures, and its persistent overstatement of the extent of subversive activity in the United States, the Committee had diverted attention from a rational approach to the true problems of Communist conspiracy in a democratic society. Fifth, HUAC's numerous irresponsible acts had succeeded in discrediting the Congress of the United States in the eyes of many Americans. Last, the Committee had adversely affected the moral and intellectual atmosphere of the nation by making Americans distrustful of each other. All things considered, Carr suggested that the wisest course would be the abolition of the House Committee on Un-American Activities.[63]

This did not mean, Carr added, that Congress had to abandon entirely the study of the threat of Communist subversion. Other committees with a more clearly defined mandate than the vague charge to investigate "un-American activity" should undertake the necessary task of checking upon the adequacy of existing federal laws dealing with espionage, sedition, and sabotage and the enforcement of these laws by the executive branch of the government. It was not the mission of Congress to expose actual Communists and to demonstrate their guilt. The "informing function" should be minimized, "for the record clearly reveals that subversion is not a subject concerning which Congress is well equipped, in terms of either understanding or dispassion, to undertake to influence the minds of the American people."[64]

Other critics suggested that instead of relying upon congressional investigations the U.S. follow the British model, that is, make use of special bodies like the Tribunal of Inquiry or the Royal Commission. These were fact-finding institutions with no authority to impose sanctions of any kind. They heard witnesses in private and published as much or as little of the testimony as they saw fit. The publicity generated by congressional investigators, one critic pointed out, had the unfortunate result of keeping "in the party an unknown number of Communists, mostly young, who would get out if they were not afraid of being caught between reprisals by the party and ostracism by society."[65]

For many years, none of these suggestions of reform was acted upon. The House Committee on Un-American Activities continued until 1975, the Senate Judiciary Committee's Subcommittee on Internal Security until 1979. A Subcommittee on Security and Terrorism addressed similar concerns between 1981 and 1986, only to be abolished when the Republicans lost control of the Senate. What brought about an end to the congressional investigation of Communist subversion was a drastic and far-reaching change in the political climate produced, among other things, by a strong, negative reaction to the irresponsible and demagogic escapades of Senator McCarthy. We will discuss this change in the public mood in the next chapter.

Problems of Academic Freedom

Many of the persons summoned before congressional committees and questioned about their political affiliations were academics. Some of these professors testified freely; most of them invoked the Fifth Amendment. The question of how colleges and universities should react to such a refusal to cooperate and the larger question of whether they should retain known or suspected Communists gave rise to extended discussions.

By 1950 strong support had developed for the proposition that self-professed members of the Communist party were unfit to teach at any level of the educational system. At its eighty-seventh annual meeting held in July 1949, the National Education Association adopted a resolution on "Preservation of Democracy," which stressed the importance of teaching about Communism, but rejected advocacy of communism by Communist teachers.

> Members of the Communist Party shall not be employed in the American schools. Such membership involves adherence to doctrines and discipline completely inconsistent with the principles of freedom on which American education depends. Such membership and the accompanying surrender of intellectual integrity render an individual unfit to discharge the duties of teacher in this country.
>
> At the same time we condemn the careless, incorrect, and unjust use of such words as "Red" and "Communist" to attack teachers and other persons who in point of fact are not communists, but who merely have views different from those of their accusers. The whole spirit of free American education will be subverted unless teachers are free to think for themselves. It is because members of the Communist Party are required to surrender this right, as a consquence of becoming part of a movement characterized by conspiracy and calculated deceit, that they shall be excluded from employment as teachers and from membership in the National Education Association.[66]

The American Federation of Teachers, which in 1941 had expelled several Communist-dominated locals, took the same position, and so did most institutions of higher learning. The overseers of Harvard University declared in May 1953 that "membership in the Communist party is beyond the scope of academic freedom" and represents "grave misconduct justifying dismissal."[67] The same year, the New School for Social Research adopted a policy statement with the same conclusion: "The New School stoutly affirms that a member of any political party or group which asserts the right to dictate in matters of science or scientific opinion is not free to teach the truth and therefore is disqualified as a teacher."[68] In March 1953, the Association of American Universities (AAU) adopted a statement on "The Rights and Responsibilities of Universities and Their

Faculties," which declared that, since present membership in the Communist party required the acceptance of thought control and dictation of doctrines, "such membership extinguishes the right to a university position."[69]

The American Civil Liberties Union (ACLU), on the other hand, rejected the automatic dismissal of anyone solely because of his views or associations. In a statement published in April 1952, the ACLU declared that it did not oppose the ouster or rejection of a teacher found lacking in professional integrity. However, the organization opposed "any ban or regulation which would prohibit the educational employment of any person solely because of his personal views or associations (political, religious or otherwise). Even though a teacher may be linked with religious dogmatists or political authoritarians, the ACLU believes that he must nevertheless be appraised as an individual." The statement continued:

> If we accept the views of dominant forces current at any one time or place there will be no end to the tests imposed on the fitness of teachers. If Communists are the main target today, as anarchists, socialists and the I.W.W. were a generation ago there will be some other main targets tomorrow. . . . The harm done by a few teachers who might be undetected in misusing their teaching positions for political or religious ends, is far less than the harm that is done by making all teachers less responsible and less courageous. The political or religious screening of all teachers is far more dangerous than the presence of the occasional teacher who is misusing his profession. Intelligent, qualified persons are discouraged from going into the teaching profession by the knowledge that they may be dismissed for nonconformity.[70]

The American Association of University Professors (AAUP) similarly insisted that what counted was personal performance rather than political affiliation. "So long as the Communist Party is a legal political party, affiliation with that party in and of itself should not be regarded as a justifiable reason for exclusion from the academic profession." Dismissal was indicated, the 1947 AAUP statement continued, for professional unfitness such as use of the classroom for political indoctrination or lying and subterfuge with reference to political affiliation.[71]

The AAU statement of March 1953 had taken the position that professors owed complete candor both to the public and to their colleagues. If they invoked the protection of the Fifth Amendment they assumed the burden of proof to defend their continuing fitness to teach. Many colleges and universities adopted the same policy and dismissed only those professors who refused to testify before congressional committees and who also refused to be open to their colleagues.[72]

Sidney Hook agreed that an answer withheld from a congressional committee could legitimately be asked by peers. On the substantive issue of membership in the Communist party and the right to teach, Hook took a stand that differed from both the AAU and AAUP positions—he opposed automatic dismissals as well as complete reliance on individual performance. The test of competence, Hook argued, was not sufficient; a competent bookkeeper was not necessarily honest. One also had to ask whether a candidate for a position of trust would abide by the ethics of his calling. In the case of Communist teachers, Hook insisted, there was abundant evidence that such persons were not free agents and were under instructions to indoctrinate their students. Not every Communist teacher was necessarily intellectually dishonest, but since there existed no feasible way to detect indoctrination the only prudent course was to consider membership in the Party as a rebuttable presumption of unfitness. There might be a constitutional right to be a member of the Communist party but there was no constitutional right to be a teacher unless one was free to accept the duties of the search for truth inherent in the academic profession. The determination of individual fitness, Hook argued, should be made by the faculties themselves and not by administrators and trustees or legislative committees. Hook expressed his opposition to federal and state investigations of teachers, which, he said, usually were used by reactionary elements to hurl irresponsible charges against teachers whose views they disapproved.[73]

The crucial question of whether Communist teachers did in fact make it a practice to indoctrinate their students then as now has been a contested issue. Hook relied upon the Party's own instructions to its members. For example, in 1937 an article in the Party's theoretical journal, *The Communist,* had exhorted Communist teachers to "take advantage of their positions, without exposing themselves, to give their students to the best of their ability working class education." Teachers had to have a "thorough education in the teachings of Marxism-Leninism. Only when teachers have really mastered Marxism-Leninism, will they be able skillfully to inject it into their teaching at the least risk of exposure and at the same time to conduct struggles around the schools in a truly Bolshevik manner." In higher education, too, Communists were urged to set up party fractions in every department. Efforts had to be made to combat "omissions and distortions in the regular curriculum. Marxist-Leninist analysis must be injected into every class."[74]

In a recently published study, scholar Ellen Schrecker has minimized the significance of such instructions and has stated flatly that at least in the colleges and universities there was no indoctrination. Communist teachers, "both for professional and prudential reasons, did not try to proselytize in class." Communist professors, Schrecker writes, like their non-Marxist colleagues, were scholars devoted to the canons of "objectivity and fairness" and they therefore separated their politics from their teaching.[75]

Theodore Draper, who was a student of one of the professors held up by Schrecker as a model of detached scholarship, has pointed out that this idealization of Communist professors would have greatly surprised and offended these men. "If there was anything they did *not* believe in, it was classless 'objectivity and fairness.' . . . The Communists I knew in the universities would have been ashamed to admit that they thought the same way as everyone else, and that they did not know the class character of such bourgeois shibboleths as 'objectivity and fairness.' "[76] Schrecker herself acknowledges that she is "no believer in what is usually called 'objective' scholarship,"[77] yet she insists that Communist professors, though dedicated Marxists, were objective scholars.

Schrecker concedes that "even though Communist professors generally refrained from outright proselytizing in class, this does not mean that their political beliefs did not influence their academic work." In certain fields, she notes, Communist professors "sometimes taught their courses from what they considered to be a Marxist perspective. Some . . . even taught Marxism. Taught, not indoctrinated. The distinction is important, for whatever the intellectual quality of the Marxism these teachers purveyed, they all struggled to present it in an unbiased way. Many went out of their way to let students know that they were Marxists, if not Communists."[78]

Schrecker maintains that those Communist professors who taught their subjects from a "Marxist perspective" did so "in an unbiased way" and without hiding their philosophical and political orientation. Of course, it should be pointed out, bias does not cease to be bias when it is openly acknowledged. For the convinced Marxist, Marxism is *the* science of society and to teach from a Marxist perspective is simply to teach the truth. All teaching and scholarship involves acceptance of some theoretical point of departure, but for the non-Marxist his theoretical framework is not an ideological straightjacket. He can admit merit in rival theoretical constructs. The Marxist, on the other hand, insists that he alone has the truth. A contemporary Marxist political scientist, Bertell Ollman, who like Schrecker rejects the possibility of objective scholarship, has acknowledged the duty of countering bourgeois ideology with Marxism. "If non-Marxists see my concern with such questions as an admission that the purpose of my course is to convert students to socialism, I can only answer that in my view—a view that denies the fact-value distinction— a correct understanding of Marxism (or any body of scientific truth) leads automatically to its acceptance."[79] Ollman's frank admission that his purpose in the classroom is to make converts to Marxism would have been understood by the Communist professors Schrecker calls objective scholars, though like Ollman they would of course have insisted they were doing no more than teaching students the truth.

Not all Communists in higher education sought to indoctrinate their students. Professor Robert Gorham Davis, testifying in 1953 before the House Committee on Un-American Activities about the Communist unit at Harvard in the 1930s, remarked that such was not the Harvard way. "We had the lurking feeling that it wasn't quite good sportsmanship to try to influence young people—at least to make use of our position in the classroom to do this."[80] Davis added that this restraint was in part due to reasons of security—the risk of losing one's job was too high. The same point has been made by another member of the Harvard cell, Granville Hicks. We were anxious to make converts, he recalled, but we also knew there were limits. "Some of us felt that there were limits beyond which we should not go; all of us felt that there were limits beyond which we could not go."[81] Professor Harry Albaum, a professor of biology at Brooklyn College, in testimony before the Senate Internal Security Subcommittee in 1952, related that some of his Communist colleagues did misuse the classroom for purposes of indoctrination, while others did not. He noted that some took great pride in telling each other how they had managed to introduce principles of Marxism into their teaching.[82] In view of the well-known fact that not all Communists were good and docile Communists, this diversity of conduct is what one would expect to find. Since at the time it was difficult to find out who was doing what, it made sense for Hook and others to suggest a course of prudent caution in dealing with Communist professors, deciding each case on its merits.

Beyond the issue of what the Party wanted its members to do and what they actually did lies the question of how effective any indoctrination can be. Unfortunately we do not know with any precision to what extent teachers are able to influence the political thinking of their pupils. Most evidence suggests, writes a student of the subject, "that college experiences do not rework youths so that their initial characteristics are totally obliterated; what an individual is when he enters college amounts to most of what he is when he leaves."[83] A charismatic teacher probably will have a stronger impact than a mediocre one. In some cases students will be predisposed to accept the ideas of an indoctrinating professor. In all, the political influence of professors may well be somewhat less than radicals hope and conservatives fear. Needless to say, the success or failure of efforts at indoctrination has no bearing on the degree of culpability of such attempts.

Apart from the goings-on in the classroom, there were also the extra-curricular activities of Communist teachers to be considered. In the early thirties in particular, professors sometimes served as faculty advisers to leftist student clubs. This fact in itself is hardly a cause for reprobation except that both the professors and the clubs often operated under false cover. At the City College of New York, for example, the Liberal Club, and its day-session twin the Social Problems Club, formed the nucleus of the City College Communist party. "It spawned the Communist-run National Student League," reports Schrecker, "and supplied the Communist Party with a whole generation of dedicated cadres." In many instances the professors active as political mentors of students concealed or lied about their membership in the Party. They put out "shop papers" on local school matters as well as more general political issues without acknowledging their authorship.

Much of this subterfuge and secrecy may indeed, as Schrecker suggests, have been invoked for purposes of self-protection. However, one is inclined to think that such measures might not have been necessary in the first place if the Party had been a genuinely radical organization within the democratic framework rather than a conspiratorial group, loyal to a foreign power and committed to destroying the constitutional foundations of this country. Communists were under orders to keep their membership secret so that they could present themselves as liberals or independent radicals rather than as part of an organization laboring under the handicap of being perceived as an agent of the Soviet Union. Even Schrecker expresses some mild words of criticism of these deceptive tactics: "In retrospect, it would probably have been wiser for Communist professors to have been more open, especially during the Popular Front period."[84]

How did academic freedom fare during the 1950s? Schrecker speaks of a "witch-hunt" during which more than a hundred professors were dismissed or threatened with dismissal for political reasons.[85] Whatever one may think of the wisdom of and the procedures used for getting rid of Communist professors, the use of the term "witch-hunt" is surely inappropriate. There is no evidence for the existence of witches, but there could be no doubt about the presence of Communists in the educational system. It is also unfair to put the major blame for these dismissals upon the "moderate and respectable professors," for many of these professors opposed McCarthyism. The dismissals, whatever their justification, were implemented by administrators and trustees. Most faculty members, concludes another student of the subject—"those who were on institutional committees of inquiry and those who were merely powerless witnesses— behaved with decency, [while] the actions of most academic authorities were not honorable." Administrators generally were guided by a concern for public relations. Faculty members who came under attack "were judged by how much of an embarrassment they were thought to be."[86]

Contrary to the picture painted by Schrecker or contemporaries such as Robert M. MacIver and Robert M. Hutchins, the academy underwent no wholesale purge of non-conformists. Lionel S. Lewis found 126 cases at 58 institutions in which political issues surfaced as germane to the holding of an academic appointment during the 1950s, and not all of these cases ended in dismissals. At the time the country had 1,850 colleges and universities and 298,910 faculty members.[87] The French writer Raymond Aron, a frequent visitor to the U.S., observed in the early 1950s that "the European intellectual who travels in the United States, far from discovering an all-powerful McCarthyist reign of terror, meets almost everywhere he goes an anti-McCarthy conformism."[88] As the historian William O'Neill points out: "The professors who kept quiet were, by and large, those who never had been politically involved or engaged with controversial ideas."[89]

That having been said, it is also necessary to note that the demagogic antics of McCarthy and his supporters did create a climate of fear and insecurity in the country from which the academy could not escape. Institutions such as the University of California were seriously damaged by the cleansing of Communists and by the loyalty oath imposed upon its faculty. The widespread probes and dismissals could not but have had a chilling effect. As Sidney Hook writes in his autobiography, the excesses of McCarthy and other local worthies "who could not distinguish among liberals, New Dealers, democratic socialists and Communists, contributed to [the] impression of the United States culture being transformed into a menacing police state."[90]

There is thus no need to exaggerate. As a reviewer of Schrecker's study has pointed out, "American society and its institutions were severely tested by the Cold War. Since so few properly acquitted themselves, it is a pretty dismal story. . . . The case hardly needs to be dramatized or embellished."[91] Indeed, today, with the benefit of hindsight, one is inclined to agree with Nathan Glazer, who, in his review of Schrecker's book, has argued that "it would have been better if the few Communists and the larger number of ex-Communists on college and university faculties had been left to pursue their teaching and research—and agitation—undisturbed, except by the normal political debate that takes place in academic communities. Little harm would have followed from such a policy. But that is something that was not so clear in the later 1940s and early 1950s, with communism still advancing in Europe and a fierce war being waged in Korea."[92] Since Hook has often been painted as an extremist on these matters, it is worth recalling that he sounded a similar word of caution even in the midst of the red scare. "Although the exclusion of Communist party teachers from the academic community seems justified in principle," Hook wrote, "this by itself does not determine whether it is a wise or prudent action in all circumstances. Sometimes the consequences of removing an unmitigated evil may be such as to make its sufferance preferable."[93] Written in 1949, this judgment, too, has stood the test of time.

The American Committee for Cultural Freedom

Many of the divisions in the liberal camp that arose over the Communist issue and McCarthyism were mirrored in the disagreements within the American Committee for Cultural Freedom (ACCF). The Committee developed out of a counter-demonstration to a Communist-sponsored peace conference held at the Waldorf-Astoria Hotel in New York City in April 1949. Calling themselves American Intellectuals for Freedom, the group included men of varied political persuasions such as Sidney Hook, Arthur Schlesinger, Jr., A. J. Muste, Dwight MacDonald, Max Eastman, and Robert Lowell. They were united by the conviction that procommunist propaganda had to be answered. As Hook writes in his memoirs, although everyone recognized that "Communism as a world movement dominated and controlled by the Kremlin was a danger *to* America rather than *in* America, the agents and partisans of that movement, who had infiltrated strategic positions in government, trade unions, educational establishments, and centers for influencing public opinion, had to be exposed and opposed."[94]

The American Committee for Cultural Freedom was formally constituted in January 1951. The first chairman was Sidney Hook. The executive committee changed frequently on account of resignations and co-options. In addition to the original founders, it included at different times well-known liberals and socialists such as Hans Kohn, Daniel Bell, Diana Trilling, W. H. Auden, Ralph Ellison, George Counts, and Norman Thomas. The membership consisted of several hundred distinguished men and women in the cultural life of the country. The historian Christopher Lasch has sought to portray the Committee as a bunch of fanatics and "cold war intellectuals," held together by "their mutual obsession with the communist conspiracy."[95] At the time, however, the Committee enjoyed considerable esteem as is evidenced by an editorial in the *New York Times* in March 1955:

In the struggle against Communist efforts to woo the world's intellectuals, one of the key roles has been played in recent years by the American Committee for Cultural Freedom, whose membership includes many of the brightest stars in our own cultural and scientific life. The group's authority to speak for freedom against Communist slavery has been enhanced by its courageous fight against those threatening our own civil liberties from the Right. Backed by such famous figures as James Farrell, Thornton Wilder and Elia Kazan, to name but a few, the American Committee has carried freedom's story to key intellectuals abroad while defending freedom here.[96]

The Committee engaged in a variety of activities. It organized meetings and public forums, published pamphlets, and in a time of irrational fears of the Communist threat spoke up in defense of cultural freedom. It criticized the Post Office's ban on the distribution of *Pravda* and *Izvestia*. It deplored a raid by the Treasury Department on the office of the *Daily Worker:* "However much we abominate the *Daily Worker,* . . . we must protest even this much interference with the democratic right to publish freely." The Committee criticized the Agriculture Department's dismissal of the well-known advocate of land reform, Wolf Ladejinsky, and the Atomic Energy Commission's cancellation of the security clearance of J. Robert Oppenheimer, known as the "father of the atomic bomb." It fought the excesses of the McCarran Internal Security Act, which was used by bureaucrats in the Immigration Service to bar the admission to the United States of such eminent former Communists as Arthur Koestler and Czeslaw Milosz. The Committee combated the pressures of cultural vigilantism by protesting the harassment of Charlie Chaplin and by successfully resisting the efforts of the Catholic Church to ban the showing of the film *The Miracle.* Lasch, while listing many of the above actions, dismisses them as dealing with trivial issues. Yet at the time they were considered significant enough to call down upon the Committee the wrath of such rightist commentators as Walter Winchell.

From the beginning, the Committee was sharply divided over the attitude the organization should take toward Senator McCarthy. Some, including Arthur Schlesinger, Jr., and Diana Trilling, demanded a forthright condemnation. Others, such as Max Eastman and George S. Schuyler, a conservative black journalist, while critical of McCarthy's excesses, considered the Communist movement a greater threat to cultural freedom than McCarthyism. The split in the Committee was dramatized at a conference, "In Defense of Freedom," sponsored by the ACCF in March 1952. To the applause of some and hisses from others, Eastman here defended McCarthy and blamed his shortcomings on the failure of liberals to be sufficiently anticommunist.[97]

A month later the executive committee met to discuss a resolution on

McCarthy. After lengthy discussion a statement of condemnation was passed unanimously, but this vote merely papered over the sharp divisions that had emerged. By 1954, both Eastman and James Burnham, referring to themselves as anti-anti-McCarthyites, had resigned from the ACCF and, together with former radicals such as Dos Passos, gradually drifted toward the right wing of the Republican party. Motivated by the zeal of the convert, these men and many others who had gone through the same disillusioning experience turned into fanatics, never able to develop a calm and rational assessment of the true scope of the Communist threat. Many of these ex-Communists came to agree with the British editor of *The God That Failed* that "no one who has not wrestled with Communism as a philosophy and Communists as political opponents can really understand the value of Western democracy. The Devil once lived in Heaven, and those who have not met him are unlikely to recognize an angel when they see one."[98] This self-image helps to explain the sense of mission and self-righteousness exhibited by so many ex-Communists.

At the other end of the spectrum, the ACCF lost Schlesinger and David Riesman, who resigned on the ground that the organization had lost sight of cultural freedom and had become preoccupied with anti-communism long after the threat of domestic Communism had passed.[99] In an attempt to hold the organization together, the Committee sponsored a detailed inquiry into the truth of McCarthy's charges. Authored by James Rorty and Moshe Decter, *McCarthy and the Communists* was published in 1954. The book gave credit to McCarthy for having alerted the country to the danger of Communist infiltration in the federal government and to the lax and ineffective procedures with which several government agencies had handled this problem. At the same time, the authors sharply criticized McCarthy for his "cynical manipulation" of the Communist issue. The senator had seriously damaged the morale, recruitment, and day-to-day operations of the State Department, the Foreign Service, the Army, and other agencies. He had "wantonly injured the processes of constitutional government by stimulating and exploiting a network of private informers throughout the government." He had "spread disunity at home by attempting to undermine the nation's confidence in its highest civilian and military leaders, and by imputing disloyal motives to innocent citizens." McCarthy's "crusade," according to the authors, had encouraged a "spirit of anti-intellectualism, of vigilantism, of mutual distrust." McCarthy, they concluded, was "a power-seeking demagogue" who had used "deceit, innuendo, and falsehood." In addition to everything else, McCarthy had undermined and damaged an effective campaign against Communism.

McCarthy and the Communists also included a number of positive suggestions for the reform of security procedures and of congressional investigations into Communism. The book affirmed that faculties were the best judges of fitness to teach and warned against the activities of private organizations who "take it upon themselves to censor forum speakers, judge the political correctness of school textbooks, and evaluate the loyalty of persons suspected of being Communists." The authors expressed their regret over the fact that "genuine anti-Communists have allowed themselves to be set at odds—in attacking and in defending McCarthy. They have thus been diverted from the serious business of fighting Communist subversion at home and Communist aggression abroad—two aspects of a single struggle that cannot safely be disjoined."[100]

Rorty and Decter had produced a careful review of the activities of Senator McCarthy and of the consequences of his "crusade" against Communism. Yet the book failed to heal the divisions within the ACCF. Indeed, its very balance caused the disaffection of men like Eastman and Schlesinger, at opposite poles of the Committee's political spectrum. In the eyes of outsiders like the democratic socialists Irving Howe and Lewis Coser, too, the ACCF had not found the correct position. They argued that the Committee was dominated by hard-liners who failed to focus all energies against McCarthyism. Both of these men were active anticommunists, but they were never invited to become members of the Committee. According to Howe's autobiography, published many years later in 1982, he would have refused to join.[101]

Another divisive issue for the ACCF was its relationship with the Congress for Cultural Freedom (CCF). The Congress had come into being in 1950; its first meeting took place in West Berlin in June of that year. To put this event into its proper context, it should be remembered that this was when the independence of West Berlin had just recently been saved by the American airlift, purge trials were taking place in the East European countries, Zhdanov was mounting his attacks on "rootless cosmopolitan intellectuals" in the Soviet Union, and neutralism and anti-Americanism were spreading in European intellectual circles. It was in this atmosphere that more than a hundred intellectuals—including Jules Romains and André Philip from France, Alfred Weber and Carlo Schmidt from Germany, Ignazio Silone and Franco Lombardi from Italy, Julian Amery and Hugh Trevor-Roper from England, H. J. Muller, Arthur Schlesinger, Jr., and Sidney Hook from the United States—met to defend cultural and intellectual freedom against the forces of totalitarianism.

The American Committee, as we have seen, had come into being before the formation of the CCF. It became an independent affiliate of the Congress, but tensions emerged constantly because of what the Americans saw as the failure of the CCF to take a resolute position on important political issues. Sidney Hook, who served on the executive committees of both organizations, recalls that the Congress "was sensitive to any action of its affiliates that would give color to the charges of its enemies in Europe, namely that its main function was to further American political interests, and consequently leaned over backward to avoid taking positions that could be interpreted as more political than cultural."[102] Within the ACCF there were differences of opinion on how to handle this difficult relationship, until finally each group went its own separate way.

The most important achievement of the Congress was the sponsorship of magazines of high quality in several European countries, which reached a wide readership—in particular *Encounter* in England and *Der Monat* in West Germany. The CCF orchestrated international protests against oppression of intellectuals in the Soviet Union, Spain, Argentina, and Indonesia. It also organized a series of festivals of the arts, international conferences, and scholarly meetings that attracted some of the best minds of the day. "I can think of no group of people," George F. Kennan wrote Nicolas Nabokov, the Congress's general secretary in June 1959, "who have done more to hold our world together in these last years than you and your colleagues. In this country [the United States] in particular, few will ever understand the dimensions and the significance of your accomplishments."[103]

In 1966 it became known that the CCF had received financial support from the CIA. This revelation unleashed charges against both the Congress and its American affiliate, the ACCF, that these organizations had operated as intellectual fronts for the American government. They were conceived, wrote Carey McWilliams of the *Nation,* "as part of a CIA strategy to mute criticism of Cold War policies among intellectuals here and abroad."[104] Christopher Lasch spoke of "cold-war intellectuals" who had become "servants of bureaucratic power." The so-called campaign for cultural freedom, in his view, was a creation and tool of the state and the military-industrial complex.[105]

Sidney Hook has denied that the CIA subsidy had anything to do with the way the CCF functioned:

> There is not a single action that the congress took or failed to take that could be attributed to the fact that it was subsidized in part indirectly by United States funds. Not even its enemies can prove that its programs and activities would have been different had it been completely subsidized by the Ford or Rockefeller or any other private foundation. Its wisdom and foolishness, its successes and failures, were all its own.[106]

At the same time, Hook has conceded that while *morally* unassailable, in the perspective of hindsight, the decision to accept a CIA subsidy was *politically* unwise. "It was a foregone conclusion that sooner or later the source of the Congress's subsidy would come to light. When it did, it would discredit the Congress' work. . . . It would have been far better to have operated on a more modest scale with whatever private sources were available." Hook invokes the sense of crisis and the fear that the advances of Communism might lead to a new war in Europe as the reasons why he and others ignored the rumors about CIA funding of the Congress and overcame their uneasiness about it.

> If it was permissible to help keep free trade unions from being overwhelmed by the Communist trade unions with access to the unlimited resources of the Kremlin, if it was permissible to aid democratic political parties of Western Europe to carry on a political struggle in opposition to the Communist Parties funded by the Soviet Union, certainly a case could be made for the legitimacy of aid to those who were attempting to keep the alternative of a free culture open to the intellectuals and opinion makers of the same areas.[107]

And the fear that Communism might take over in Europe was not a paranoid obsession. Irving Howe, who is severely critical of the Congress's acceptance of CIA money, acknowledges that it was crucially necessary to strengthen European resistance to Stalinism. "That the communists in France and Italy never came close to taking power is by no means evidence that we overestimated the danger: I would say it is evidence of how necessary it had been to put barriers in their path."[108]

The same point has been made by Arthur Schlesinger, Jr., who considers the CIA's support as justified at the time when it began. "During the last days of Stalinism, before the Marshall plan had restored the economic energy and moral confidence of Western Europe, the non-Communist trade-union movement and the non-Communist intellectuals were under the most severe, unscrupulous, and unrelenting pressure. For the United States government to have stood self-righteously aside at this point would have seemed to me far more shameful than to do what, in fact, it did which was through intermediaries to provide some of these groups subsidies to help them do better what they were doing anyway." The mistake, Schlesinger argues, was to continue this covert program of support beyond the time of need.[109]

Still others, like the former *Encounter* editor Stephen Spender, have maintained that the concealment of the subsidy by the American editor, who knew about it, from his English colleagues misled the latter into making false statements about it. This deception introduced methods common in party politics "into the conduct of a magazine professing standards of intellectual integrity."[110] It was in part the desire to avoid self-defeating and morally demeaning situations of this kind that in 1983 led the United States, following the example of other Western democracies, to establish the National Endowment for Democracy, which uses public funds in a fully open program of support for democratic institutions abroad.

The American Committee for Cultural Freedom, too, for a time was a beneficiary of the Farfield Foundation, later to be revealed as a conduit for CIA funds. Unlike the Congress for Cultural Freedom, the ACCF, after hearing rumors of CIA involvement with the Farfield Foundation, decided to refuse further support from it. Soon thereafter, in 1957, the ACCF went out of existence, in good part on account of acute and persisting financial difficulties. Whatever one's judgment of the CCF, at least as far as the ACCF is concerned, it is therefore grossly unfair to vilify this organization as a willing tool of right-wing reaction. For much of its life on the brink of bankruptcy, the ACCF fought both Stalinism and McCarthyism and it was not just obsessed with anticommunism. It certainly did not, as one of its recent critics alleges, attempt "to curtail the individual's freedom of choice in thought, speech, and association" in order to impose conformity to its own form of anticommunism.[111]

7

The Revival of Anti-anticommunism

A Change in Political Mood

During the early 1950s, under attack from the federal government and harassment from many of the states, the American Communist party experienced severe losses in membership. In an attempt to strengthen an organization reeling from multiple blows, the Party announced in July 1951 that all members who had not re-registered would be dropped from membership, and this action resulted in the de facto expulsion of many inactive members. Others were expelled as unreliable or because they were suspected of being FBI informers. Several hundred of the best cadres were sent into hiding and stayed underground until 1955. Isolated from their comrades and thrown upon their own resources, many of these men and women developed strong doubts about the course of the Party. When Khrushchev revealed the crimes of Stalin at the Twentieth Congress of the Soviet Communist party in 1956 and revived the notions of coexistence of different social systems and a peaceful road to socialism, the cadres felt confused and shamed. These were the very ideas they had fought during the previous ten years. The impact of Khrushchev's speech on the American party therefore was devastating.[1]

George Charney, one of several leaders who left the Party during these traumatic years, recalls the overwhelming impact of Khrushchev's revelations. "They destroyed the image of Stalin but at the same time destroyed forever our blind faith in dogma, creed, ideology, vanguard, and all the gods. The party could never be the same."[2] There followed the brutal suppression of the Hungarian Revolution, which presented another serious challenge to the faithful. Within slightly more than two years after Khrushchev's speech the American Communist party lost 85 percent of its membership. An organization which at its peak had enrolled close to 100,000 members by the winter of 1957–58 was reduced to about 3,000, many of them FBI informants.[3] Upon abandoning the sinking ship, John Gates, editor of the *Daily Worker,* called the Party that remained "a living corpse."[4]

The decline of the Party coincided with the waning of McCarthyism. On December 2, 1954, sixty-seven senatorial colleagues of the junior senator from Wisconsin voted to censure McCarthy. In a series of decisions, the Supreme Court under Chief Justice Earl Warren invalidated, or at least limited, the reach of several pieces of antisubversive legislation enacted during the 1950s. With the end of the Korean War, the international situation looked more stable. The fear of Communism was receding. Writing in 1958, J. Edgar Hoover still argued that, despite its small size, the Communist party could under favorable conditions expand "overnight" into a mass organization of great potential power. "The present menace of the Communist Party in the United States," wrote the director of the FBI, "grows in direct ratio to the rising feeling that it is a small, dissident element and need not be feared."[5] Convinced that the Communists presented as great a threat as ever, the FBI in 1956 started a highly secret program known as COINTELPRO (Counterintelligence Program), a campaign to destroy the Communist party by having informants stir dissension, by circulating disruptive rumors about the Party and individual members, and by using other "dirty tricks."[6] Hoover's fears were shared by few.

One of the consequences of the declining fear of Communism was a revival of anti-anticommunism. The country's revulsion against the demagogic tactics of McCarthy was a key factor in both of these developments. The victims and opponents of as reactionary and vicious a politician as Senator McCarthy surely could not be all bad, it was felt by many, and deserved some sympathy and protection. McCarthy's brand of anticommunism helped discredit all anticommunism and provided a shot in the arm for a sentiment that had persisted in certain liberal circles ever since the Popular Front of the 1930s. Anti-anticommunists, albeit a small minority of the country's intellectual community, had continued to exist even during the red scare of the 1950s, as can be seen from a blast directed against them by Arthur Schlesinger, Jr., in 1952. Schlesinger gave this description of anti-anticommunism:

> This label applies to those who think it fine to be anti-fascist, anti-Republican, or anti-Democratic but who squirm and wince when someone in exactly the same sense is anti-Communist. All forms of baiting are okay for the "anti-anti-Communist" except red-baiting. Some of the "anti-anti-Commu-

nists" are not substantively pro-Stalinist. They just have a feeling that a Communist is a rather noble, dedicated fellow who deserves special consideration in a harsh and reactionary world.[7]

The Soviet "thaw" following the death of Stalin in 1953 also weakened anticommunism. The uproar in the American Communist party after the Khrushchev speech of 1956 denouncing the crimes of the Stalin era further strengthened the feeling among many intellectuals that the Communists were perhaps not beyond the pale after all. In 1957, the veteran anticommunist A. J. Muste organized the American Forum for Socialist Education, which brought together Communists and non-Communists in a series of conferences and debates held in various cities. To be sure, this drastic change in Muste's position did not go uncriticized. Norman Thomas argued that the Forum would help the Communist party, severely weakened after the suppression of the Hungarian revolt of 1956, to revive itself and confuse people politically. "The Forum gave some of those Communists the false impression that they could remain in the party and still be accepted in the community. The Communists don't belong in jail, but they also don't belong in any party with which I want to be connected."[8]

Part of the change in the attitude toward Communism was generational. The young people who came to political maturity during the late 1950s and early sixties had not experienced the manipulative behavior of the Party during the thirties or the Hitler-Stalin Pact. The only anticommunism they had known had been McCarthyism. Not surprisingly, for many of them this experience discredited the very idea of anticommunism and they quite deliberately embraced the doctrine of anti-anticommunism. This development can be seen most clearly in the case of Students for a Democratic Society (SDS), a new student organization created in January 1960, which we will discuss in detail in a subsequent chapter.

From about 1967 on, the growing opposition to the war in Vietnam and to the way the American military fought this war was the final element that gave a major boost to anti-anticommunism. In the eyes of many young people, in particular, anticommunists were those who sent American conscripts to their death in order to bail out a corrupt clique of generals in Saigon and who dropped napalm on civilians. Both unregenerate old leftists and what by then was known as the New Left blamed this misadventure on anticommunist liberals. The American intervention in Vietnam was held to be the logical consequence of anticommunist Cold War politics for which "Cold War liberals" were said to be responsible. Writing in the *New York Review of Books,* a citadel of radical chic and New Left revolutionism, Jason Epstein pressed this indictment in April 1967. "Was not Kristol's form of anti-Communism," he asked rhetorically, "likely to deaden the mind and feelings so that when the war in Vietnam fell into our laps some of us would have grown too rigid to feel the stupidity and arrogance from which it evolved and which continues to sustain it?"[9]

Support for this view came from the most unexpected quarters. In a book published in 1966, Senator James W. Fulbright argued that America had become involved in the fighting in Vietnam because we had come to regard "communism as a kind of absolute evil, as a totally pernicious doctrine which deprives the people subjected to it of freedom, dignity, happiness, and the hope of ever acquiring them. . . . This view of communism as an evil philosophy is a distorting prism through which we see projections of our own minds rather than what is actually there." Little more than ten years before the mass exodus of the boat people who were desperately seeking to escape their Communist liberators, Fulbright suggested that "some countries are probably better off under communist rule than they were under preceding regimes; . . . some people may even want to live under communism."[10]

Martin Luther King, Jr., was another important voice expressing opposition to anticommunism. At a meeting held in New York City on February 23, 1968, on the occasion of the centennial of the birth of W. E. B. Du Bois, King declared that it "is time to cease muting the fact that Dr. Du Bois was a genius and chose to be a Communist. Our irrational obsessive anti-communism has led us into many quagmires to be retained as if it were a mode of scientific thinking."[11]

Similar sentiments, as we will have occasion to see in more detail in a subsequent chapter, were spreading in the peace movement. In 1969 the American Friends Service Committee published a book-length study, *Anatomy of Anti-Communism,* in which anticommunism was described as a political strategy "that fights not only Communism, but neutralism and democratic revolution as well. It is based on antipathy to social change and a defense of the status quo." The legacy of anticommunism, the study argued, was the alienation of American youth and the subversion of the revolutionary aspirations of exploited, underdeveloped nations. "These consequences of a blind, emotional anti-Communism pose the most critical problem that American society presently confronts."[12] In a book published the same year, *The Anti-Communist Impulse,* the political scientist Michael Parenti explained that, until a few years ago, he had been an adherent of liberal anticommunism. "Vietnam was for me, as for many other Americans, a crucible for my anti-communist beliefs." He now viewed anticommunism with alarm because it had brought the country collective self-delusion and a gargantuan military establishment at home and nuclear terror and arms races abroad.[13]

A symposium in the September 1967 issue of *Commentary* took up the issue of anticommunism. Entitled "Liberal Anti-Communism Revisited," some forty prominent intellectuals of liberal or democratic socialist persuasion and known to have been anticommunists were asked to discuss the question whether, in their view, "the anti-Communism of the Left was in some measure responsible for, or helped to create a climate of opinion favorable to the war in Vietnam." They also were asked, "Would you call yourself an anti-Communist today?" and whether the recent revelations on CIA backing for magazines such as *Encounter* proved that liberal anticommunism "has been a dupe of, or a slave to, the darker impulses of American foreign policy."

The majority of the twenty-one persons who responded criticized the CIA subsidies for anticommunist activities during the 1950s as a political mistake but rejected the melodramatic phrase of "darker impulses of American foreign policy." Most also denied that liberal anticommunism should be blamed for the war in Vietnam, which they opposed. Arthur Schlesinger, Jr., called the developments leading up to the full-scale American involvement in the Vietnam conflict "a triumph of the politics of inadvertence." Lionel Trilling pointed out that the "position of liberal anti-Communism, as I understand it and adhere to it, has never been influential, quite the reverse." In the view of Daniel Bell the charge that liberal anticommunism had facilitated the American involvement in the Vietnam conflict made no sense "either as history or as sociology."[14]

Most of the respondents still regarded themselves as anticommunists. Irving Howe, the editor of the democratic socialist magazine *Dissent,* pointed out that for him and others who had experienced the debacle of socialism in the Soviet Union as the central fact of their intellectual development, "anti-Communism signified primarily *an effort to salvage the honor of the socialist idea.*" Those who had lived through the brutalities and deceits of Stalinism had to be anticommunists though they realized that anticommunism could also be "a protective mask for detestable politics." There was no such thing as a pure or unitary anticommunism, but that was no reason to refuse to take a principled stand against Communism. The anticommunism of the democratic socialist left, Howe maintained, had made "a contribution to intellectual health" for which he had no regrets.[15]

Arthur Schlesinger, Jr., too, presented himself "as an unrepentant anti-Communist—unrepentant because there seems to me no other conceivable position for a liberal to take." The real question therefore was not whether to be an anticommunist but what weight was "to be given to anti-Communism among all the factors shaping decisions of public policy." Sensible policy, Schlesinger argued, had to reject "obsessive anti-Communism" and incorporate a "rational anti-Communism—by which I mean anti-Communism graduated in mode and substance according to the character of the threat." There had been a time in the 1930s and 1940s, Schlesinger pointed out, when American Communists had penetrated labor unions, the liberal community, and even the government. Now, however, hardly any person could still claim with a straight face that Communism presented an internal revolutionary threat in the United States. During the Depression, Communism had "cast a powerful spell on young people in the democratic world adrift on a sea of economic insecurity. Today the glitter of modernity in the West casts an even more powerful spell on young people within the bleak and tacky Communist empire." This and other changes did not "diminish the obligation of the liberal to regard Communism with contempt or to reject its absolutisms. But it does gradually transform the character of the problem Communism poses for the democratic states."[16]

A minority of the participants in the *Commentary* symposium no longer wanted to be called anticommunists. The journalist Murray Kempton did agree that anticommunism had had an important share in bringing on the war in Vietnam and he had therefore stopped thinking of himself as an anticommunist. William Phillips, an editor of *Partisan Review*, stated that to be an anticommunist in 1967 one had "to be pathologically single-minded, allergic to change, and in love with existing institutions." Hence, though he had no more use for Mao than he had for Stalin, he was no longer an anticommunist. Philip Rahv, also an editor of *Partisan Review*, argued similarly that he had always been an anti-Stalinist rather than an anticommunist. "Insofar as cold-war anti-Communism implies implicit or explicit support of our society's present social and economic set-up—and, in my opinion, it implies no less than that—I cannot be counted among its partisans."[17]

The New History of American Communism

By the time the Vietnam War had ended, anti-anticommunism had become part of the conventional wisdom of wide strata of the American intellectual community. For some members of the New Left, anti-anticommunism became not only a prescription for the present but also a conceptual tool with which to rewrite the past. Since the 1970s there has emerged a body of scholarship in which one of the main villains in the recent history of the country is "Cold War liberalism," defined as an outlook that promotes the Cold War abroad and anticommunism at home. "Between the early 1930s and the end of the 1940s," writes Terry A. Cooney, "a majority of the New York intellectuals made the political trek from self-conscious radicalism to Cold War Liberalism."[18] According to two other writers belonging to the same school, from 1945 on, these liberals "not only blocked the formation of a liberal-radical alliance against a reactionary wave; they also . . . gave final legitimacy to the anti-Communist crusade." Liberal institutions and individuals "effectively widened the appeal and advanced the work of the [anti-Communist] crusade by praising it with faint damns."[19] Instead of creating a united front against the onslaughts of reaction, postwar liberals "excluded domestic Communists and popular-front leftists from the arena of permissible public debate and, as a result, lost sight of vital civil liberties and limited the free marketplace of ideas."[20] Liberals did not object to red-baiting; they were opposed only to "indiscriminate and irresponsible red-baiting." Liberals betrayed their earlier commitment to political tolerance. "In substance although not in degree, the rhetoric and tactics of ADA activists and other Cold War liberals did not differ from those of Martin Dies, J. Parnell Thomas, and Joseph McCarthy."[21]

For many of these writers any criticism of the Communist party amounts to red-baiting and all anticommunism is "mindless." Liberals, by refusing to make common cause with the Communists and accepting the need for such restrictions upon Communist inroads as the loyalty program in the federal civil service, violated the Communists' civil liberties. By considering the Party as no better than the fascists and developing a theory of "Red fascism," liberals are said to have destroyed "left-wing unity and effectiveness" and to have prepared the ground for McCarthyism.[22] Whatever else is wrong with this analysis, the blanket indictment of all liberals ignores the diversity of responses in the liberal community to McCarthyism described in the previous chapter. It represents, as William O'Neill concludes, "bad history."[23]

In this one-eyed picture of the country's recent history there is little room for Communist espionage. The U.S. never faced any kind of internal security threat—in the eyes of most of these authors, the Rosenbergs and Alger Hiss are seen as innocent victims of an FBI frame-up. The meticulous examination of these cases by Ronald Radosh and Allen Weinstein, who started out as critics and doubters of the government's case only to be overwhelmed by the massiveness of condemnatory evidence discovered by them, is dismissed an unconvincing. Books and film documentaries that argue for the innocence of Hiss and the Rosenbergs are praised no matter how flimsy their factual base.[24]

The revisionist reexamination of the past by New Left scholars has included in prominent place the nature and role of the Communist party. There has been an outpouring of dissertations and books on the history of the Party written, as one member of this group puts it, by "political activists of the 1960s who turned to scholarship in the 1970s in order to make sense of their own experience." Trading "the frustrations of politics for the pleasure of scholarship," there has emerged from this generation what Theodore Draper has called "a minor academic industry devoted to the history of the American Communist Party."[25] At a time when the New Left had lost much of its political effectiveness, the Communists seemed admirable because of the durability of their commitment. They were seen, as two former New Leftists observe with much insight, "as determined footsoldiers of progressivism who had fought the good fight, who had experienced defeat, disappointment, and even betrayal, but who had also learned how to survive and who thus might be good models for what was left of the Left."[26]

The new history of the Communist party "emphasizes the genuine achievements of the Communists in labor and political life during the 1930s and 1940s." While conceding that the Party was "obedient to the Comintern," the new historians argue that "American communism was also shaped by national experience."[27] The Party is criticized for having "enforced a type of disciplined and conspiratorial behavior," but such criticism is typically balanced by tributes to the Party for having been "a dynamic and often effective movement for social change."[28]

There prevails a tendency unduly to personalize the history of the Party. One such author, Paul Lyons, who characterizes himself as an advocate of democratic socialism and an adherent to a Marxist approach in the study of society, interviewed thirty-six "Old Leftists" in the Philadelphia area. He describes the members of the Party as "people committed to a vision of social justice and a strategy of social change that make them my political forebears. And like my biological parents, they merit a love that includes—in fact, requires—recognition of their faults and errors. Needless to say, such a love also rests on an honoring." Lyons disclaims any intention of glorifying the Old Left, but concludes that they were good and decent people. "Ultimately it was a party and a movement that energized hundreds of thousands of men and women to struggle for a more equitable social order."[29]

The new scholarship emphasizes social history and attention to the rank-and-file of the Party. Theodore Draper, who has reviewed the new history in a series of articles, argues that the effect "is to depoliticize the most political of all political movements. . . . The favoritism shown to the rank and file has the advantage of dealing with the people most removed from the making of Party policy and, therefore, seemingly most innocent of what was done in the name of the Party. . . . A social history of a Communist party divorced from its political organization and institutional structure is so far-fetched that it can only be explained by a 'hidden agenda' to draw attention away from the organization and the structure." The biography of individual Communists is interesting and occasionally important, but in the history of as hierarchically ordered an organization as the Communist party it cannot take center place at the expense of the leadership that determined the Party's political line. Sometimes, one should note, the political agenda of this kind of social history is not even hidden. According to Paul Lyons, the author of *Philadelphia Communists,* "scholars have only interpreted radical history in various ways, the point is to change its direction towards a socialist cultural hegemony."[30]

Draper has noted a number of other faults. Many of these historians stress that American Communists in the mid-1930s saw themselves "not only as faithful members of an international Communist movement but also as advocates of an authentic American radicalism." Draper points out that this idea of a blend between international Communism and national experience, which allegedly characterized the Party, slights the subservience owed to the dictates of Moscow. The general line was always set by the Comintern. "National and local factors 'complicated' the application of the 'dictates from Moscow'—but the dictates were still dictates, ultimately unchallengeable by those whose task it was to apply them." American Communists were not mere puppets, yet "whatever independent thoughts and actions American Party members had, their fealty to their Russian comrades ultimately prevailed."[31]

The years 1935–39 of the Popular Front are cited by the new historians as a time during which American Communists had an opportunity to root their radicalism in American soil. Draper points out that they also continued to root their radicalism in Soviet soil. Their "Americanization" took place at the behest of the Comintern and it was switched off again four years later when the Soviet Union needed a new and different line. "For these reasons, the Communist-style Popular Front did not and could not develop into an authentic American socialism or radicalism."[32]

In the past, Draper writes, radicals "have usually preferred to behold their promised land in the future; the post-New Leftists have been impelled to find it in the past. They have invented a radicalism of nostalgia." The rehabilitation of American Communism undertaken by them does not aim at a total rehabilitation of the Party; the "ostensible project is one of selective rehabilitation—Communists in the Popular Front, Communists in Harlem, Communists in the auto industry."[33] It is conceded that the Party made serious mistakes, but these are said to be balanced by the important contributions the Party allegedly made to such tasks as building the CIO or drawing attention to the problems of American blacks. The record is said to be mixed; Draper objects to this seemingly impartial verdict:

> Yet it might at best be considered "mixed" only if the alleged merits and demerits were commensurate. For example: the Party did not merely help to build the CIO. It also helped build itself in the CIO. It split the CIO. It sacrificed its own interests in the CIO as soon as conformity with the "dictates of Stalin's foreign policy" called for a break. But even this misses the main point. It is precisely the "mixture" of a central commitment to Stalin's Russia and an authoritarian structure with activity such as participation in the CIO that is the source of the deepest culpability: the exploitation of idealism in the betrayal of ideals. The disruption caused by the Communists, when they have to obey their central commitment and structure, is incommensurate with the "help" they give, the main motive for which is to provide themselves with a "mass base." A summing up that "the record is mixed" is a cop-out.[34]

While the new historians thus slide between praise and blame, Draper concludes, the one thing they cannot tolerate is anticommunism. They write "as if Communists were fallen angels and anti-communists were the devil's own disciples."[35]

The new attitude toward American Communism, exemplified by the revisionist history of the American Communist party, has also manifested itself in the world of culture. Films such as *The Front,* dealing with blacklisting in the television industry, and the documentary *Seeing Red: Stories of American Communists* present the Communists as persecuted defenders of American democracy. The abuses of McCarthyism are used to promote the innocence of the Communists. As Draper notes in his commentary on *Seeing Red,* "much of it is a historical travesty of the American Communist story . . . , making just enough glancing concessions to some minimum of reality to avoid being recognized as outright propaganda."[36] Another example of the same genre is Vivian Gornick's book *The Romance of American Communism,* which praises the Communists' intensity of commitment. "One would not know from seeing films such as *The Front* or reading books like *The Romance of American Communism,*" writes the historian William O'Neill, "that the heroes in them were apologists for Stalin's death machine."[37] The film *The Killing Fields,* dealing with Pol Pot's genocide in Kampuchea, studiously avoids any reference to the Communist ideology of the Khmer Rouge, which provided the impetus for the mass killings. The horrors portrayed have no discernible cause other than the American bombing.

The rewriting of history under the impetus of anti-anticommunism has included and benefited the Hollywood Ten and other hostile witnesses before the House Committe of Un-American Activities (HUAC). Thus the editor of an edition of letters of Dalton Trumbo calls him "a man to whom principle and honor are not just words but integral parts of his being and way of life." Trumbo's every word, action, and attitude is said to emanate "from his own basic honesty and sense of right."[38] One need not become a defender of the blacklist, which for political reasons denied employment to Trumbo and other Hollywood Communists, in order to wonder how a man of "principle and honor" could become a champion of Stalin's policies that caused the death of millions and the loss of liberty to many more.

In their history of radicalism in Hollywood, Larry Ceplair and Steven Englund have welcomed the rehabilitation of the former outcasts in public opinion as long overdue. Philip Dunne, on the other hand, has objected to the new mystique and "virtual deification" of the Hollywood Ten. At the time, Dunne had been among those of Trumbo's colleagues vainly to urge upon the Hollywood Ten reliance on the First Amendment and, after their appearance before the Committee, an open acknowledgment of their membership in the Communist party. Dunne now denied that these men had been warriors in defense of the Constitution. Communists, he pointed out in his autobiography, have never been "reliable champions of civil liberties" anywhere. When the American Communists took up unpopular causes like the Scottsboro Boys or Tom Mooney they did so not in order to advance the cause of freedom, a bourgeois value, but "only to serve their own political purposes."[39]

Among those to regain fame and fortune as a result of the new spirit of anti-anticommunism was the actress Lillian Hellman. Back in 1952, upon the advice of her counsel, Abe Fortas, Hellman had written to HUAC that she would be willing to testify about her own political views if the Committee would refrain from asking her to name other people. When this claim was denied she invoked the Fifth Amendment, yet in her later writings she presented herself as a great heroine who had defied HUAC. Hellman acknowledged that she had been mistaken about some aspects of Stalinism, but claimed that her pro-Communist activities and those of her fellow-traveling friends had done the country no harm. The anticommunist liberals, on the other hand, were accused by her of having prepared the ground for the Vietnam War and Watergate. Their refusal to come to her aid was attributed by Hellman to cowardice. "There was to her no chance," notes the historian O'Neill, "that anyone might be anti-Stalinist on principle. It had to be a pretext for doing the comfortable thing."[40]

In his book, *Naming Names*, published in 1980, Victor Navasky, editor of the *Nation*, also dealt with the question of how witnesses asked to testify about friends and colleagues should have conducted themselves. His conclusion, attained after laborious argument, was that the only moral course was to refuse to inform and to take the consequences. Some of those who chose to testify did so after considerable soul-searching. Elia Kazan, for example, has talked of the difficult moral dilemma he confronted and which he resolved in favor of agreeing to cooperate. The individuals named by him anyway were already known to the Committee as Party members or fellow travelers. Kazan felt that the one thing worse than testifying about others was to help the Communists maintain their deceptive tactics of secrecy. "I did what I did," Kazan has written in his recently published autobiography, "because it was the more tolerable of two alternatives that were, either way, painful, even disastrous, and either way wrong for me. . . . No one who did what I did, whatever his reasons, came out of it undamaged. I did not."[41] For Victor Navasky, on the other hand, to have called a Communist a Communist was red-baiting and unacceptable. Informing on the Communists was the cardinal sin. In the final analysis, it appears, Navasky remains opposed to any kind of anticommunism.

Another instance of rewriting the past has involved the nature and impact of McCarthyism. According to Richard H. Pells, McCarthyism began long before the junior senator from Wisconsin became prominent. It is said to have taken a variety of forms such as security checks, loyalty oaths, the attorney general's list, the trials of Alger Hiss and the Rosenbergs, and the expulsion of Communist-dominated unions from the labor movement.[42] Thus, since all action taken against Communists is considered McCarthyism, the clear implication is that the only legitimate response to the Communist issue is anti-anticommunism.

For the historian Robert Griffith, McCarthyism was not a passing aberration. "It was a natural expression of America's political culture and a logical though extreme product of its political machinery. What came to be called 'McCarthyism' was grounded in a set of attitudes, assumptions, and judgments with deep roots in American history. There has long been a popular fear of radicalism in this country." According to Griffith, "the mobilization and political articulation of these fears is the anti-Communist 'persuasion.' "[43] In other words, the fear of radicalism equals McCarthyism; anticommunism is just one form of antiradicalism. Presumably the only way to prevent McCarthyism is to abandon the fear of radicalism—to embrace anti-antiradicalism and therefore anti-anticommunism.

Most of these writers exaggerate the impact of McCarthyism and stress its link to "Cold War liberalism." The aim here is to show that McCarthyism created a reign of terror, and, in a revival of arguments already used during the 1950s, to blame anticommunist liberalism for failing to oppose this widespread repression. Obviously, the worse the consequences of McCarthyism for American society, the worse the moral and political failure of liberal anticommunism and the more important the need for the adoption of the posture of anti-anticommunism.

Useful ammunition for this thesis could be found in the book, *The Great Fear,* authored by the British writer David Caute. As suggested by the title, Caute speaks of "a desperate time" during which "the wealthiest, most secure nation in the world was sweat-drenched in fear." In schools, universities, and town halls "a pious mumbling of oaths was heard" promising not to have any independent thoughts. "Stalking their prey across the land, two-by-two, prowled the FBI, J. Edgar Hoover's G-men, hunters of radicalism whose dreary war of shadows was occasionally rewarded with real meat." The long shadow of security officers fell across factories, dockyards, ships and offices. "The great professional associations collapsed before the tidal wave, sacrificing their own black sheep to the wolves."[44]

The picture painted by Ellen Schrecker is only slightly less lurid. As a result of McCarthyism, college students are said to have become a silent generation. The "academic community's collaboration with McCarthyism . . . was, in many respects, just another step in the integration of American higher education into the Cold War political system. The academy did not fight McCarthyism. It contributed to it." Ultimately, the failure was that of liberals who "adhered to the ideology of Cold War anti-Communism, with its emphasis on the primacy of national security over individual rights."[45] A few short years after the end of McCarthyism, during the American involvement in Vietnam, it is relevant to note here, the country experienced an unparalleled outburst of political activism which demonstrated that, despite all anguished predictions and more recent misreadings of the meaning of McCarthyism to the contrary, American democracy had not suffered any lasting damage.

Several self-avowed anticommunists, too, who lived through this unhappy period of American history, have taken issue with the exaggerations propounded by writers like Caute and Schrecker. The McCarthy era, argues Irving Howe, was not a reign of terror. "In a reign of terror people turn silent, fear a knock on the door at four in the morning, flee in all directions; but they do not, because they cannot, talk endlessly in public about the outrage of terror."[46] Sidney Hook has similarly pointed out that even at the height of McCarthy's power "all the great organs of public opinion with the exception of one midwestern newspaper were hostile to McCarthy; all the Luce magazines with their fabulous circulation damned him for his demagogy; almost all church bodies denounced his methods; most radio and television commentators were caustic or savagely critical." McCarthy's tactics drew impassioned attacks on most of the nation's campuses. The impact on government employees, especially Foreign Service Officers, Hook writes, was damaging. McCarthy also had considerable grass-roots support. "All this is deplorable enough. But to exaggerate his influence, to speak of a reign of terror, or a climate of fear, is to do the sort of thing which has come to be associated with McCarthy's name."[47]

Anti-anticommunists blame liberal anticommunism for McCarthyism. Against this view one can argue that it was the failure of liberals to take realistic measures against Communist subversion that provided encouragement and support for the excesses of McCarthyism. Cord Meyer, a man who despite his high CIA position became a temporary casualty of the spirit of hysteria and political timidity that was indeed abroad in the land during those years, has correctly noted that McCarthy "would never have achieved his national prominence unless there had in fact been serious Communist penetration and evidence available to the public of the government's failure to cope with it."[48]

Much of the blame for the spread of McCarthyism must also be assigned to the Communists themselves. The intolerance for any dissent from political orthodoxy and the blurring of distinctions between liberals and Communists which afflicted the country during the 1950s was in part because the Communists, for the longest time, had cynically used liberalism as protective coloration. As put well by Peter Collier and David Horowitz: "It was they who hid their anti-democratic and anti-American agendas and commitments behind 'liberal' fronts and facades. If there was interest in ferreting Communists out of liberal institutions, it was . . . because Communists had infiltrated these institutions in the first place." If Communists had been above board and had openly acknowledged their membership in the Party it is unlikely that there would have been need to ask the most notorious question of that troubled era: "Are you now or have you ever been . . . ?"[49]

Signposts of a New Political Climate

In a speech given at Notre Dame University in May 1977, President Carter expressed his satisfaction that the United States had overcome its dread of Communism. "Being confident of our future, we are now free of that inordinate fear of communism which once led us to embrace any dictator who joined us in our fear."[50] Some three years later, as a result of the Soviet invasion of Afghanistan, Carter had reason to regret this remark. His reference in 1977 to the "inordinate fear of communism" probably was meant to apply primarily to fear of the Soviet Union. Many others, however, when speaking of the unreasonable fear of Communism do include in it the Marxist-Leninist philosophy and its domestic representative, the American Communist party.

One of the most ardent advocates of anti-anticommunism is the Washington-based Institute for Policy Studies (IPS). The Institute describes itself as "a source of radical scholarship," but, indicative of the new respectability of such ideas, IPS has been able to attract many liberals to its activities and functions. Its twentieth-anniversary reception in 1983, for example, was chaired by Paul Warnke, President Carter's head of the Arms Control and Disarmament Agency. The Anniversary Committee included Senators Christopher Dodd, Gary Hart, and Mark Hatfield and former Senators Birch Bayh, Frank Church, William Fulbright, Eugene McCarthy, and several well-known House liberals. IPS fellows have consistently opposed what they call "mindless anticommunism," though in the case of many of them it is difficult to imagine that any kind of anticommunism would pass muster.[51]

The anti-anticommunist mindset of IPS and those sharing its political outlook was well expressed in a letter to the *New York Times* written in November 1983 by then IPS fellow Michael Parenti. The occasion for this letter was the accusation made by Senator Jesse Helms that Martin Luther King, Jr., had had Communist associations. King's liberal defenders had labeled this accusation as "slanderous" and "obscene." But, Parenti asked, "what is obscene about associating with Communists?" The Communist party, he continued, had worked "long and devotedly" for civil rights, peace, and the rights of labor. Senator Helms's charge that King had associated with Communists, therefore, should be met simply with the retort "So what?"[52] True to his word, Parenti writes frequently for *Political Affairs,* the theoretical organ of the Communist party. In his articles he has praised Gus Hall and Yuri Andropov and he has condemned anticommunism.[53] Quite obviously, Parenti's position is not shared by anything like a majority of American intellectuals, but the fact that so benevolent a view of American Communism could be stated with such openness and confidence revealed the fundamental change in the intellectual climate that had occurred.

Perhaps following the French example, a few American intellectuals have recently begun to express anticommunist sentiments. Susan Sontag, earlier an admirer of Castro's Cuba and Communist North Vietnam, in a speech at New York's Town Hall in 1982 declared that "Communism *is* fascism." At the same time, these new converts to anticommunism go out of their way to distance themselves from the "coarse and vulgar" anticommunism which they claim to detect among the neo-conservatives in particular.[54] But even this concession has not spared Sontag and others having second thoughts about Communism the vigorous criticism of certain die-hards on the *Nation* and the *Village Voice*. Indeed, for some the appearance of anticommunism among the contemporary Left itself has been regarded as positively alarming.

One of the most heavily attended and hotly debated panels at the second Annual Socialist Scholars Conference held in April 1984 was on "The Revival of Left Anti-Communism." Most panel members, the *Guardian* reported, were highly critical of this development. Ilene Phillipson, associate editor of *Socialist Review,* argued that "the current wave of anti-communism is a facade for current political rifts using the political symbols of the 1950s." Victor Navasky of the *Nation* maintained that "the issue is not communism; the issue is poverty, hunger, and anticommunism and the evil they have brought throughout the world."[55]

The same sentiments surfaced at a conference on Socialism and Activism convened in December of the following year. One of the organizers was Sidney Lens, at one time an associate of A. J. Muste in the Trotskyist Workers party and most recently senior editor of the *Progressive.* In the August 1985 issue of his magazine, Lens once again had expressed his long-held view that opposition to Communism contributed to a Cold War mentality. But when in his talk at the December conference he made a reference to "the experiments in socialism in Europe which have brought forth forms of totalitarianism alien to most of us," the veteran anti-anticommunist found himself challenged. In the eyes of many participants this remark represented a form of anticommunism that was unacceptable. One respondent spoke against "denigrating existing socialism." He added that, while "there may be valid criticisms of the Soviet Union, it was wrong to begin to ally ourselves with the core of Reagan's philosophy of anticommunism and anti-Sovietism."[56]

Some forces on the left, an editorial in the *Guardian* of May 1, 1985, complained, made "significant concessions to anticommunism" and rarely defended Nicaragua. "While compromises are a part of politics and a full program of militant support for the Sandinistas would be suicidal in Congress, progressive groups undermine their own position in the long run by not finding ways to challenge the right-wing worldview. An effective anti-intervention movement, not to mention a strong left, can never be built on the basis of anticommunism."[57]

Just as Communists in earlier years insisted that any criticism of the Soviet Union irrevocably tainted a person, a new generation of radicals argues today that there is no greater evil than anticommunism. An article,

"The Victims of Anticommunism," in the new *Zeta Magazine* that appeared in January 1988 called anticommunism "the ideology of the dominant world system," an idea by means of which the Western powers lit "their way towards crunching internal opposition and justifying external ruthlessness." The author, Joel Kovel, a political scientist at the University of California, argued that anticommunism was the same kind of phenomenon as racism and "works hand-in-glove with racism, and, as a philosophy of killing, has generated corpses beyond imagination." Among recent "episodes of anticommunist slaughter" Kovel included two million dead in Vietnam and "100,000 in Nicaragua (adding the body counts attributable to Somoza and Reagan)." This was, of course, a typical instance of blaming the victim, for it completely ignored who started the hostilities in question. Presumably, those who died as a result of North Vietnamese aggression or those killed by the Sandinistas were not worth mentioning or counting. Kovel conceded that "socialism has not lived up to its shining promise," but he insisted that it was anticommunism and other dogmas that stood in the way of real emancipation and held back the human spirit.[58]

Kovel (by then Alger Hiss Professor of Social Studies at Bard College) was one of the speakers at a three-day conference on "Anticommunism and the U.S.: History and Consequences" held at Harvard University in November 1988. The conference, organized by the Institute for Media Analysis in New York, was attended by 1200 people and included 140 panelists. The main theme of the gathering was the need to overcome anticommunism, which was blamed for just about everything the participants considered bad in America. In his opening message, John Kenneth Galbraith called the convening of the conference "an important step back to reason." Communist leader Gus Hall characterized anticommunism as "the biggest hoax ever perpetrated against a whole people" and as a weapon used "in the struggle against democracy and peace." Anticommunism, he declared, "remains the main ideological justification for imperialist aggression and U.S. world domination. . . . The rich and the powerful will continue to benefit and the American people will suffer, until we rid society of the anti-Communist myth."[59] At the end of the conference, plans were announced to prepare curricula based on the proceedings. As one person noted, there are plenty of veterans of the 1960s teaching high school just waiting for this kind of material.[60]

It is tempting to write off pronouncements such as those made by Kovel in *Zeta Magazine* or at conferences of the kind just described as the insignificant utterings of far-out fringe groups. The organizations of the left to which most of these individuals belong indeed are numerically small, but what appears here in extreme language mirrors sentiments that in less strident form are widespread among larger intellectual circles. If during the years of McCarthyism all too many Americans suspected a Communist under every bed, the conviction now appears to be equally widespread that there are no Communists under any bed. A substantial segment of the American intellectual community today embraces a philosophy of anti-anticommunism no less reflexive than the obsessive anticommunism that did exist in some circles during the 1950s.

Not very long ago, most American liberals believed that anticommunism was a litmus test of political and moral integrity. Today, on the other hand, as the former radicals Peter Collier and David Horowitz have argued, anti-anticommunism has cast a spell on American political discourse. "Under this spell we censor ourselves and become incapable of speaking openly and honestly about a crucial aspect of our political culture. Under this spell we are led to believe that the only real enemy our country has is its own maligned self."[61] While nobody hesitates to raise the issue of membership in the John Birch Society or the Nazi party, in today's political climate it is considered bad form to refer to anyone as a Communist. "The prohibition on identifying Communists as such," writes the newspaper editor Eric Breindel, "is a fact of American life—it obtains in journalism, in politics, in the academy, indeed in virtually all mainstream political discourse. It's a rule widely acknowledged and obeyed, rather like a taboo." In the wake of the excesses of the McCarthy era, "many people tend to feel that by identifying someone as a Communist, they are doing something wrong—even when that identification is altogether accurate."[62] For example, Angela Davis, a highly placed Communist functionary and in 1980 and 1984 the Party's candidate for Vice President of the United States, most of the time is politely called by the media and other respectable voices a "black activist" rather than a Communist.

Communist leader Angela Davis has found praise as a person of significant achievements from the most unexpected quarters. In October 1988, Dartmouth College celebrated the anniversary of fifteen years of coeducation, and Angela Davis was the principal speaker. For reasons best known to the Dartmouth administration, the press was not permitted to record the speech, but one reporter took notes. The introduction was given by a Dartmouth dean who included among Davis's accomplishments the award of the Lenin Peace Prize in Moscow. The dean went on: "Angela Davis' life is an example of how one committed black woman activist has chosen to make a difference."[63] Not mentioned by the Dartmouth dean among the deeds that indeed have made a difference was an incident in 1970 that earned Angela Davis an indictment for kidnaping and murder. A gun owned by Davis was used in a violent attempt to free from jail the black militant George Jackson. The failed effort left five persons dead, and Angela Davis disappeared from sight. When she was caught the following year and tried, the prosecution was unable to prove that Davis had given the weapon to Jackson's brother, who was killed in the shoot-out, or that she had known what would be done with it, and she was acquitted. Those familiar with the case and her relationship with Jackson drew their own conclusions.[64] Today Angela Davis teaches philosophy, aesthetics, and women's studies at San Francisco State University. The dust jacket of a collection of her articles and speeches recently published by Random House, a book full of vituperation for America and including the usual apologetics for the Communist countries, mentioned her membership in the Communist party and in the same breath described her as "an internationally regarded writer, scholar, lecturer and fighter for human rights" and "one of the most incisive and forward-looking social critics and activists."[65] Even allowing for the flattery customarily practiced by publishers in speaking of their authors, this dose of hyperbole strikes one as rather extravagant.

Today Communists are found on the faculties of leading universities. In 1984 an alumnus of Harvard University inquired whether it was true that Professor John Womack, the chairman of the department of history, was a Communist. President Derek Bok replied that Professor Womack, who teaches Latin American history, was indeed a Communist but that Harvard saw no problem as long as the professor did not seek to indoctrinate his students. "Knowing Professor Womack," President Bok went on to say, "I would be very surprised if he were to abuse his authority by virtue of his political beliefs. He is a conscientious and principled person." This characterization left unexplained how a "conscientious and principled person" could be an adherent of Communism. William F. Buckley, Jr., who reported on this exchange in his syndicated column, asked whether one would call a member of the Nazi party "principled" if he defended the principle that racially inferior people deserved to be killed. President Bok had noted that Harvard professors were mostly Democrats and Republicans, but "we do have some faculty members who fall outside the spectrum being either libertarians or Communists or goodness knows what." Buckley asked whether we have reached the point where libertarians and Communists are regarded simply as complementary poles at the ends of the political spectrum.[66]

The refusal to name individuals and organizations by their right name today is widespread. In January 1988 it was revealed that for several years the FBI, operating under counter-terrorism guidelines, had conducted an investigation of the Committee for Solidarity with the People of El Salvador (CISPES). According to information made public by the State Department in 1981, CISPES was organized by Farid Handal, brother of the head of the Salvadoran Communist party, while on a tour of the United States in 1980. Handal had the assistance of Cuban intelligence officers operating out of the United Nations as well as from Sandy Pollack, a member of the central committee of the American Communist party.[67] Among those who have taken the trouble to familiarize themselves with the activities of CISPES there is general agreement that this organization operates as a support group for the FMLN, the coalition of Marxist-Leninist guerrillas fighting the elected government of El Salvador, providing the FMLN with money and a network of American supporters. Yet when the *New York Times* first reported the story of the FBI probe, it called CISPES "a liberal group that is opposed to President Reagan's foreign policy."[68] Scott McConnell, writing in a recent issue of the *National Interest,* correctly called this kind of reporting "a bizarre inversion of the worst of McCarthyism: rather than liberals being falsely identified as Communists, Communists are falsely labeled liberals."[69]

New York Times columnist Anthony Lewis, commenting on the CISPES probe about two weeks later, went even further. Lewis noted that the FBI had told the White House that CISPES "was established with the assistance of the Communist Party USA and the Communist Party of El Salvador." His comment on this information was: "It could have been said by Joe McCarthy. What makes the episode especially disturbing is that such Red-baiting and abuse of law-enforcement power seemed to be in our past. . . . The ideology of the Reagan years has brought them back."[70] Charges of McCarthyism and red-baiting here served as a convenient means for avoiding the confrontation of inconvenient facts, a tactic that until recently was used primarily by the Communists.

Ever since the 1930s, the American Communist party has attempted to shield itself behind the slogan of "red-baiting," claiming an immunity from criticism no other political organization is allowed to enjoy. The concept of red-baiting, as Paul Hollander has noted in his discussion of the adversary culture in America today, is intriguing, "implying at once that there is nothing wrong with being 'red' while at the same time signaling profound indignation over being called just that."[71] That a man of Anthony Lewis's standing should use this device in order to protect the deceitful activities of CISPES is symptomatic of the anti-anticommunist temper of our times. Subversion has become a forbidden subject and the government's attempt to cope with it is vilified as McCarthyism.

Not surprisingly, the Communist propaganda apparatus, both here and in the Soviet Union, has happily supported the anti-anticommunist conviction. Quoting from "The Road to Communism," the program of the Soviet Communist party, Georgi A. Arbatov, the director of the

Soviet Institute for Study of the USA and Canada, in 1970 called anti-communism "a reflection of the extreme decadence of bourgeois ideology." It consists mainly "in slandering the socialist system and distorting the policy and objectives of the Communist parties and Marxist-Leninist theory."[72] Y. Nalin, a Soviet propagandist, in 1978 described anticommunism as "the concentrated expression of the imperialist politics directed against all contingents of the revolutionary movement." The struggle against anticommunism, he went on to argue, "is an integral part of the general struggle for peace, democracy, national liberation, socialism and communism."[73] Henry Winston, national chairman of the American Communist party, in 1983 characterized anticommunism as "the main weapon the Reagan administration uses against the people."[74]

It is interesting to note that, while Communist propaganda argues against anticommunism, the Communist movement itself uses the term "Communism" less and less. An increasing number of Communist parties call themselves Workers party, People's Revolutionary party, and the like. As Joshua Muravchik has written in a perceptive article, "Communism . . . is the future that dares not speak its name." Muravchik has stressed the importance of restoring the terms "Communist" and "pro-Communist" as categories in our political discourse. "The ability to apply terms like communist or pro-communist," he argues, "is not something to be desired for the purpose of launching congressional investigations or police actions against these people. The purpose is to be able to discredit them, not as 'subversives,' but as people whose political perceptions or moral values are so deeply flawed that their counsels deserve no weight."[75]

While anti-anticommunism has made inroads among the intellectuals, the American people as a whole remain resolutely anticommunist. The discrepancy between the way the general population and more educated, elite groups view the Communist issue was first brought out in a survey undertaken by Samuel A. Stouffer in 1954. For example, while 51 percent of a national cross-section of the American people favored jailing admitted Communists, no more than 27 percent of community leaders supported this drastic move. Or again, while 68 percent of the national sample opposed the right of an admitted Communist to make a speech in their community, 47 percent of community leaders were in favor of this limitation.[76]

The Stouffer survey was undertaken at the height of the McCarthy era. A replication of this survey some twenty years later showed a considerable increase in tolerance toward nonconformists and Communists. For example, the percentage of the public who would allow an admitted Communist to speak in their community had risen from 27 to 53 percent. At the same time, community leaders continued to be more tolerant than the national sample.[77] Another study published in 1983 noted the continuing difference between the mass public and elite opinion, though the authors also remarked on the long history of opposition to the enjoyment of full civil liberties by admitted Communists. "Hostility towards left-wing ideologies, especially communism, and a desire to prohibit the dissemination of revolutionary opinions have been typical of the American public's response for as long as we have been able to measure that response through opinion polling."[78]

The surveys mentioned so far all measured the willingness of the American people to grant civil liberties to Communists, and there is little reason to rejoice at the results. A different type of study conducted in April and May 1987 revealed the strength of anticommunist sentiments as such. Fully 70 percent of a national sample interviewed identified themselves as strongly anticommunist, the most popular self-description listed, followed at a considerable distance by 49 percent who identified themselves as religious persons. The published results of this survey do not give us a breakdown between mass public and elite groups. A higher proportion of those over 50 years old are shown to support anticommunism as compared with those under 40, though even in the latter group 61 percent are strongly anticommunist. The authors of the survey comment: "As an identity anti-communism is virtually universal in America."[79]

Whether this strong anticommunist sentiment of the American people could at some point, especially at a time of new foreign policy reverses, lead to a revival of McCarthyism and new restrictions on civil liberties is a question on which we will not speculate here. It is clear, however, that the anti-anticommunism that has spread in the intellectual community is not shared by the general population. The great majority of the American people are not bashful about stating that they reject Communism. Since elections are decided by all those voting and not just by the minority of the population who are better educated and more vocal, this fact has obvious political consequences.

Following the defeat of Michael Dukakis in the 1988 presidential election, a liberal Democratic congressman, Barney Frank of Massachusetts, acknowledged that liberals had been hurt by failing to identify themselves with certain strongly held popular views, including anticommunism. Liberals, Frank argued, should come out and say that "in our era, certainly since the fall of Hitler, Communism has been by far the worst system of government in the world." Liberals thought that "to say you are anti-Communist . . . you will play into the hands of the far right and they will use it in bad ways." In fact, Frank noted, "what it does is that we make it plausible for Ronald Reagan to say that . . . we're not anti-Communist."[80]

The recent upsurge of anticommunist sentiments in the Communist world has led some American liberals to urge a reexamination of the country's political vocabulary. Senator Joseph McCarthy, columnist Meg Greenfield reminded her readers in the *Washington Post* in early May 1989, managed "to give anticommunism a bad name," and liberals became so preoccupied with fighting the excesses of this demagogue "that they seemed pretty much to forget what the main conflict was all about." It became suspect to be known as an anticommunist. Developments in the Communist world during the last few years, Greenfield pointed out, have demonstrated how perverse this logic was. "In the streets and assembly halls of Warsaw, Beijing, Moscow, Riga and Tbilisi . . . [y]ou don't hear the quite common (until lately) term of contempt, 'virulent anticommunist,' used any more." Liberals, Greenfield concluded, should remember that Communist systems "have been the greatest predators of liberal values."[81]

The wave of anticommunism sweeping the Communist bloc has not had much effect on some diehard anti-anticommunists in this country. In the fall of 1989, just a few weeks before the people of Eastern Europe toppled their Communist governments, the Church Council of Greater Seattle adopted a statement of "Affirmations and Confessions" which it recommended for use as litanies in worship. The people of the "free world" were said to be infected with racism and militarism as well as with the "cancerous disease of 'anti-communism.' " Americans were urged to liberate themselves "from the ever-growing disease of anti-communism."[82] Surely, one is tempted to remark, few ecclesiastical pronouncements have been issued in less appropriate circumstances.

Liberals such as Barney Frank and Meg Greenfield have acknowledged that anticommunism is not just a political obsession of the far Right. Indeed, given the historical record, it is hard to understand why anyone, East or West, concerned about democracy and liberty would be anything but hostile to communism. At a time when even the Soviet Union has begun to acknowledge the enormous human cost of Communism, Americans will be well advised not to be caught in outdated and politically self-defeating attitudes.

II

Organizational Responses: Cooperation with, Acceptance, or Exclusion of Communists

The American Civil Liberties Union Through Changing Times

Civil Liberties as an Instrument of Social Change

In 1915, after the outbreak of World War I in Europe, an organization was formed to prevent American involvement—the American Union Against Militarism. In the spring of 1917, Roger N. Baldwin joined its staff and established a Civil Liberties Bureau to handle the many complaints regarding freedom of speech and association, as well as cases of conscientious objectors, brought to the American Union. In October of that year, after some disagreement about tactics, the Civil Liberties Bureau became independent. In January 1920, the Bureau was reorganized and took on the name American Civil Liberties Union (ACLU).

The ACLU's founding officers and staff included the Reverend Harry F. Ward, chairman; Roger N. Baldwin, director; Lucille B. Milner, field secretary; and Louis F. Budenz, publicity director. Many of the members of the national executive committee, later renamed board of directors, were socialists and shared a strong animus against capitalism. Baldwin, in particular, wanted the ACLU to "serve the cause of freedom in the industrial struggle." The bureau had come into existence to handle wartime problems. "The cause we now serve is labor."[1]

The ACLU's first annual report stressed the view that capitalism thwarted the ideals of democracy:

Behind this machinery [of suppression] stand the property interests of the country, so completely in control of our political life as to establish what is in effect a class government—a government by and for business. Political democracy as conceived by many of America's greatest leaders, docs not exist, except in a few communities. This condition is not yet understood by the public at large. They are drugged by propaganda and blinded by a

press necessarily subservient to property interests. Dazed by the kaleido-
scopic changes of the last few years, the rank and file citizens accept the
dictatorship of property in the name of patriotism.

Civil liberty, the report continued, cannot be attained "as abstract principles or as constitutional guarantees." There was need for economic or
political power to assert and maintain rights. Freedom would be won
through "the union of organized labor, the farmers, radical and liberal
movements."[2]

One board member raised questions about the ACLU's anti-capitalist
agenda. In a letter to Baldwin, dated March 8, 1920, John Codman explained that his "interest in the American Civil Liberties Union is
entirely in the interest of maintaining civil rights guaranteed by the
Constitution. I am no more interested in these rights for the laboring
men than I am for anybody else and I do not like the idea of the American Civil Liberties Union becoming a partisan of labor, and I hope it
is not the intentions of the Union to do so."[3]

At the other end of the political spectrum was the young Communist
writer Joseph Freeman, who joined the ACLU in 1924 as a publicity man,
but who quit the organization after a while because of what he saw as
its failure to recognize that "the persecution of labor organizers was not
a violation but an *application* of capitalist law." The ACLU, he recalled
in his autobiography, was too legalistic; it "tended to obscure the political
factors involved and to encourage democratic illusions." Freeman praised
Baldwin's radical views. "It was, perhaps, his preoccupation with civil
liberties involving thousands of radical labor agitators, journalists, and
organizers that eventually propelled Baldwin ahead of the average liberal,
who wanted to redress social grievances in order to secure the continued
existence of bourgeois society." Still, the ACLU as a whole was not
sufficiently political for him. "Experience in the Civil Liberties Union
strengthened my conviction that under capitalism democracy was an
illusion."[4]

The 1920s and early 1930s were a time during which the rights of
labor were violated by the authorities in many parts of the country. In
1923, Upton Sinclair, a member of the ACLU, was arrested for reading
the Bill of Rights to a group of striking workers in Southern California.
In 1926, Norman Thomas, another founding member of the ACLU, was
arrested in Passaic, New Jersey, for attempting to speak against what the
local sheriff termed the "riot law," invoked to forbid assembly by striking
textile workers. A suit filed by Thomas eventually succeeded in enjoining
the sheriff from interfering with lawful meetings.[5] In view of the extensive repression that labor suffered in the 1920s it is therefore not sur-

prising that most of the cases handled by the ACLU during this period involved industrial conflict. The Union's intervention in the Scopes case, involving Tennessee's anti-evolution law of 1925, was not typical of ACLU activities. At the same time, it is necessary to point out that, until the early 1930s, for men like Baldwin and many of his colleagues, the ACLU's prolabor stance was dictated primarily by their politics and their concern for social justice. For Baldwin, the ACLU's struggle for civil liberties was a means and not an end. This is evident from Baldwin's published writings in this period.

Baldwin spent the year 1927 in Europe, studying political and economic conflict. For some two months of that time he was in the Soviet Union gathering material for a book that was published in America in 1928 under the title *Liberty under the Soviets*. The book was critical of the Russian prison system and the regime's practice of locking up many innocent people without trial or hearing. "I do not subscribe to the Communist idea," Baldwin wrote, "that a party machine, however self-critical it may be, can harness all the wisdom needed to work out [the regime's] great experiment with a minimum of blunders and waste." At the same time, Baldwin argued that far more significant than civil liberties as understood in the West was "the basic economic freedom of workers and peasants and the abolition of privileged classes based on wealth." The absence of political freedom and due process of law in the Soviet Union was necessary during the transition to a new society. "Repressions in Western democracies are violations of professed constitutional liberties, and I condemn them as such. Repressions in Soviet Russia are weapons of struggle in a transition period to socialism. . . . I see no chance for freedom from the repressions which mark the whole Western world of political democracy save through abolishing economic class struggle."[6]

Baldwin's indulgent view of repression in the Soviet Union drew criticism from Emma Goldman and others disillusioned with Communism. But Baldwin remained unperturbed. Indeed during the years of the Great Depression his political views, like those of many of his contemporaries, moved further to the left. In 1934 Baldwin published an article, "Freedom in the USA and the USSR," in *Soviet Russia Today*, the official organ of the Friends of the Soviet Union, one of the first front organizations established by the Communist party in 1921. In this article Baldwin explained why he fought for and supported free speech in capitalist countries and at the same time defended dictatorship in the Soviet Union. It was because he took "a class position . . . [which] is anti-capitalist and pro-revolutionary."

I champion civil liberty as the best of the nonviolent means of building the power on which worker's rule must be based. If I aid the reactionaries to get free speech now and then, if I go outside the class struggle to fight against censorship, it is only because those liberties help to create a more hospitable atmosphere for working-class liberties. *The class struggle* is the central conflict of the world; all others are incidental. *When that power of the working class is once achieved, as it has been only in the Soviet Union, I am for maintaining it by any means whatever.*

Baldwin went on to point out that, while he regretted that the means had to be dictatorship with its concomitant "personal distress" for many victims, he could not "get excited over the suppression of opposition when I stacked it up against what I saw of fresh, vigorous expressions of free living by workers and peasants all over the land. . . . No champion of a socialist society could fail to see that some suppression was necessary to achieve it."[7]

The following year, 1935, the editor of the Harvard College Class of 1905 Thirtieth Anniversary Yearbook sent a questionnaire to the members of the class asking them to describe their beliefs. Baldwin responded that he was active in defending the rights of workers to organize and strike, in the struggle against war and fascism, and in the fight for the conservation of birds, animals, and forests.

My chief aversion is the system of greed, private profit, privilege, and violence which makes up the control of the world today, and which has brought it to the tragic crisis of unprecedented hunger and unemployment. I am opposed to the New Deal because it strives to strengthen and prolong production for private profit. At bottom, I am for conserving the full powers of every person on earth by expanding them to their individual limits. Therefore I am for socialism, disarmament, and ultimately for abolishing the state itself as an instrument of violence and compulsion. I seek social ownership of property, the abolition of the propertied class, and sole control by those who produce wealth. Communism is the goal.[8]

As late as 1938, Baldwin appeared to subordinate civil liberties to the interests of labor. Early that year, the National Labor Relations Board (NLRB) had found the Ford Motor Company guilty of unfair labor practices. Ford not only was ordered to cease discriminatory discharges and other forms of intimidation of workers who sought to exercise their legal rights but also was told to stop circulating statements critical of unions. Ford had distributed such statements as part of its anti-union campaign. The issue for the ACLU was whether the NLRB prohibition violated the employer's constitutional right of free expression. The ACLU's labor committee of which Baldwin was a member came down on the side of the union and against Ford's right of freedom of speech. It concluded that since the dissemination of literature had consistently been accompanied by physical violence against workers, "speech [that] *is thus implemented by force* or by threats of discharge or violence . . . is not the free speech about which the ACLU is concerned."[9]

When the findings of the labor committee came before the ACLU board of directors, the well-known clergyman John Haynes Holmes, a member of the board since the founding of the Union, argued strongly against this position. "The very life, not to say the integrity" of the organization were at stake, he wrote Baldwin. "Under the impact of our real sympathy for labor's cause," Holmes told chairman Harry F. Ward, "we are allowing ourselves to become mere advocates of the rights of labor to the denial of those rights as exercised by those who are against labor." Our enemies, he continued, "have good reason for charging us with being partisan in the labor struggle, and using the civil liberties principle as a means of fighting labor's battles and the cause of radicalism generally."[10] Baldwin eventually worked out a compromise that allowed Ford to disseminate his anti-union views everywhere except on the bulletin boards of his factories, a position subsequently supported by the Supreme Court. The dispute demonstrated the tension between a principled defense of civil liberties and Baldwin's view that civil liberties were useful primarily as a means to advance the interests of labor.

Baldwin never joined the Communist party, though for many years he was the archetype fellow traveler active in numerous united front causes. J. B. Matthews, another man strongly attracted to the Party and, like Baldwin, eventually disillusioned as a result of his close dealings with the Communists, recalls that he and Baldwin participated together in so many Communist fronts that they came to be known as the "united front twins."[11] Baldwin's own recollections of this period help explain why so many liberals and socialists supported the united front with the Communists and how eventually they came to be disabused of their illusions about the Party. Since Baldwin was the dominant figure in the ACLU—his friend and colleague in the ACLU leadership Arthur Garfield Hays is supposed to have said "The American Civil Liberties Union *is* Roger Baldwin"—the significance of the veteran ACLU leader's views and activities extends, of course, well beyond the story of his personal life.

During the 1920s and 1930s, Baldwin's name appeared on the letterheads of some score of Communist fronts, and he was a board member of three of them: the League Against Imperialism, the American League Against War and Fascism, and the American Committee for Loyalist Spain. There was remarkably little criticism of these associations, Baldwin recalled years later. "Few seemed to sense the incongruity of civil libertarians cooperating with communist apologists for a dictatorship that suppressed all civil liberties." He was an innocent also, he admitted, "in relation to the inner workings of the party. I accepted communists in civil liberties work and in united fronts, but never inquired into their political reasons for joining such efforts."[12] The Communists were extremely energetic and determined. Hence they both inspired and ultimately dominated all the united front activities. And because they were so effective, the temptation to place them in key positions was well-nigh irresistible. Non-Communists like himself, Baldwin told his biographer Peggy Lamson, were deceived "into accepting the assurance that the officials we put into top spots were not party members. They simply lied about it, as some of them who quit the party told me later."[13]

It was also not until many years later, Baldwin related, that he discovered that the Communists used these fronts as recruiting grounds for the Party. If the treasurer happened to be a party member, funds would be siphoned off for party purposes. Eventually Baldwin recognized the futility of working with the Communists. "I recognized the lesson many others—but, unfortunately, not all liberals—learned: that no movement in which communists participate can successfully resist their manipulations for control. Whatever good they did was more than destroyed by the partisan ends they served when the common interest clashed with the party line, and by the confusions between communist and noncommunist liberals." A key event for Baldwin as for many other fellow travelers was the Hitler-Stalin Pact of 1939—he called it "the most traumatic political experience of my life. It was a union of opposites so shocking as to end for me any notion of choice between tyrannies. I became as outspoken an anticommunist as I had been an outspoken antifascist."[14]

Since Baldwin, as executive director of the ACLU, was regarded as the Union's chief spokesman, his many united front activities tended to get confused with the ACLU. In retrospect, he told his biographer in the 1970s, he and some of the other ACLU leaders "made a mistake in getting so deeply involved in United Fronts led by Communists. . . . I sometimes think now that we would have been more effective and it would have been better for the cause if I had stuck to our single purpose, or if the Union had been directed by a lawyer with no leftist or political connections."[15] After the Hitler-Stalin Pact, the same concern with the ACLU's effectiveness led to the exclusion of Communists from the organization's leadership.

The 1940 Resolution Against Totalitarians

Even before the Nazi-Soviet Pact strong opposition had developed among some ACLU leaders to the presence in the Union leadership of Communists and fellow travelers. Norman Thomas and John Haynes Holmes were the leaders of this faction, which also argued for the adoption of an explicit declaration of opposition to all types of totalitarian dictatorship. The board of directors rejected this request in a statement issued in April 1937 that declared it to be "the task of other organizations to engage in political controversy in defense of democracy."[16]

Though hardly surprised, Thomas was nevertheless incensed when ACLU board member Corliss Lamont, a veteran fellow traveler, was among the signers of a statement published in the *New York Times* of August 14, 1939, that accused anticommunists of sowing suspicions between the Soviet Union and other nations interested in maintaining peace. "With the aim of turning anti-fascist feeling against the Soviet Union they have encouraged the fantastic falsehood that the U.S.S.R. and the totalitarian states are basically alike." As it turned out, this letter was reproduced in the same issue of the *Nation* that announced the Hitler-Stalin Pact.

The new formal alliance between the Soviet Union and Nazi Germany strengthened the hand of the anticommunist faction in the ACLU. In October, Holmes warned that so "many of us are partisans of other causes, that again and again the cause of civil rights is so bent to the advantage of these other causes as to be warped and strained beyond recognition." In late November, following the Soviet invasion of Finland, John Dos Passos resigned from the ACLU national committee because the board included persons "still able to compromise with Communist-directed organizations."[17] After a special meeting the board issued a statement that affirmed the right of ACLU members to express their different political views without implicating the organization, but this compromise did not satisfy Norman Thomas.

In an open letter, Thomas attacked ACLU chairman Harry F. Ward, a well-known fellow traveler, charging that Ward's chairmanship of the Communist-dominated American League for Peace and Democracy (the new name of the American League against War and Fascism) disqualified him from further service to the ACLU. When Osmond K. Fraenkel accused Thomas of red-baiting, Thomas replied that the support of civil liberties for Communists and fascists was effective only when the ACLU excluded from leadership Communists and fascists who regarded the defense of civil liberties as a strictly temporary enterprise.[18]

Thomas spelled out his position in detail in an article published in the *Socialist Call* of December 16, 1939. The present ACLU board of directors, Thomas charged, included "six or seven Communists or fellow travelers of various degrees of closeness to the Communist party and the Communist line." These people damaged the work of the ACLU by taking positions that made them liable to be "indicted before the bar of public opinion as claiming in behalf of Communists in America those rights which openly or tacitly they support Stalin in denying where he has the power." It was not the business of the ACLU to defend civil liberties in Russia. And yet:

> It is equally clear that men and women of ordinary common sense should not entrust the defense of civil liberties in America to those who condone, or fail to denounce, Stalin's purges and his crimes against decency and humanity.
> Communists have the right to claim the protection of the American Bill of Rights. They cannot be accepted as honest advocates of them as long as they follow blindly all the changes of policy of the ruthless dictator, Stalin, who proved a thousand times over that he has as little or less conception of civil liberty than the fascist dictators.
> Communists belong on the Board of the Civil Liberties Union as much or as little as fascists who also want the protection of the Bill of Rights— until they seize power.

The ACLU, Thomas wrote, did not need a rigid creed, but there were boundaries beyond which it could not honestly go. To remove Communists from positions of leadership in the ACLU was no more a violation of political freedom than it was a violation of religious liberty to remove an atheist from a Christian pulpit.[19]

The debate within the ACLU about the presence of Communists and fellow travelers on the board coincided with attacks on the Union by the Dies Committee. In October 1939 ACLU general counsel Morris Ernst and Arthur Garfield Hays met with Congressmen Martin Dies and Jerry Voorhis. Shortly thereafter Dies unexpectedly absolved the ACLU of the charge of being a Communist organization.

The precise content of the conversation between the ACLU officials and the two congressmen is not known to this day. Ernst and Hays explained that they had met Dies and Voorhis with the sole purpose of obtaining for the ACLU a hearing to rebut the charges made against the Union. Corliss Lamont, pointing to the end of attacks on the ACLU by the Dies Committee and the drive to exclude Communists from the board that began soon after Dies's about-face, has charged that the October meeting sealed a deal—Dies would not investigate the ACLU if the Union would cleanse itself of Communists.[20]

Baldwin and others have denied that a deal was made, and there exists no way of resolving the dispute. The plausibility of Lamont's version of the event is weakened by the fact that the ACLU continued to be critical of the Dies Committee, an unlikely course of action if indeed there had been an explicit deal.[21] It is more likely that Dies abandoned his animus against the ACLU as a result of meeting with Ernst and Hays, two obviously sincere democrats and anticommunists. What is undisputed is that in early 1940 the Norman Thomas–John Haynes Holmes faction scored a major victory when the ACLU adopted a resolution barring supporters of totalitarian dictatorships from service in a leadership position.

The resolution, written by Baldwin, was first adopted by the nominating committee which met in the first days of February 1940 to propose new candidates for the board and national committee. The committee's action was unanimous; it was "intended to make ACLU's policy clear, both as to future elections and present membership, in the belief that it would create greater harmony on the basis of undivided loyalty to civil liberty." The resolution was then approved by the national committee by a vote of 30-10 and was given final approval at the annual meeting on February 5 by a vote of 43-14. The board of directors attended this meeting and the count included a mail vote of absentees. The resolution read:

> While the American Civil Liberties Union does not make any test of opinion on political or economic questions a condition of membership, and makes no distinction in defending the right to hold and utter any opinions, the personnel of its governing committees and staff is properly subject to the test of consistency in the defense of civil liberties in all aspects and all places.
>
> That consistency is inevitably compromised by persons who champion civil liberties in the United States and yet who justify or tolerate the denial of civil liberties by dictatorships abroad. Such a dual position in these days, when issues are far sharper and more profound, makes it desirable that the Civil Liberties Union makes its position unmistakably clear.
>
> The Board of Directors and the National Committee of the American Civil Liberties Union therefore hold it inappropriate for any person to serve on the governing committees of the Union or on its staff, who is a member of any political organization which supports totalitarian dictatorship in any country, or who by his public declarations indicates his support for such a principle.
>
> Within this category we include organizations in the United States supporting the totalitarian governments of the Soviet Union and of the Fascist and Nazi countries, (such as the Communist Party, the German-American Bund and others); as well as native organizations with obvious anti-democratic objectives or practices.[22]

In a statement to "members and friends," released to the press on February 5, the board of directors and the national committee of the ACLU sought to explain why they had adopted a resolution "that appears to set up a test of opinion." The Union, they pointed out, had always recognized that "membership in the Communist Party, as in certain other groups, involves a conception of civil liberties quite different from that of the Union. No member of the Communist Party was therefore ever elected or appointed to any position in the Union." The only member of the board presently a member of the Party was Elizabeth Gurley Flynn, one of the original incorporators of the ACLU, who did not join the Communist party until fifteen years later (in 1937, one year after her election to the board). "The occasion for raising this issue at this time is the increasing tension which has resulted everywhere from the direction of the Communist international movement since the Soviet-Nazi pact. The abandonment of the struggle against Fascism and the other changes in Communist policy have raised sharp issues which were reflected in the attitudes of members of our Board of Directors."[23]

Reaction to the resolution was mixed. At least thirty to forty members resigned in protest against what they regarded as the adoption of the principle of guilt by association. Among them was ACLU chairman Harry F. Ward. Others who had previously resigned or refrained from joining sent in contributions. The press and the general public responded favorably, and there were many strongly worded editorials approving the action. The *New Republic* expressed regret that the adoption of such a resolution had become necessary, but said that "the Union is right. Neither Fascists nor Communists share the democratic belief in individual freedom and there is an obvious absurdity in having such persons in a position of responsibility in this organization."[24]

At a regular meeting on March 4, the board of directors passed a resolution which, in line with the new policy, requested that Elizabeth Flynn resign her membership on the board. When Flynn refused to comply, board member Dorothy Dunbar Bromley, a newspaper columnist, read into the minutes the charge that Flynn "is not entitled to retain directorship on the Board on the ground that she is a member of the Communist Party." After Flynn had sharply criticized the board in two articles published in the *Sunday Worker* and the *New Masses,* two additional charges were filed against her to the effect that she was unfit to remain on the board because of the hostile and abusive comments made by her in these publications.

The "trial" of Elizabeth Flynn began in the evening of May 7 and ended in the early hours of the following day. After the three charges against her had been read by the secretary, Flynn demanded that the authors of the charges and chairman Holmes disqualify themselves so that her case could be decided by impartial judges. This procedural objection was rejected by the chairman and his ruling was sustained. Flynn next sought to defend herself against the first and most important charge involving her membership in the Communist party. The resolution under which this charge had been brought, she argued, was contrary to the principles and purposes of the ACLU and violated traditional policies. She had joined the Communist party in 1937 and had not changed her position on issues of civil liberties since then. Offering as evidence the constitution of the USSR, which showed the country to be a socialist state of workers and peasants, Flynn denied that the Soviet Union was a totalitarian state. Referring to the constitution and by-laws of the American Communist party, she argued that membership in this party was not incompatible with defense of the Bill of Rights. The attempt to oust her from the board was an instance of red-baiting.[25]

Flynn's doctrinaire defense of the Soviet dictatorship doomed any chance that her defenders might have had to prevent her ouster. The February resolution clearly was a departure from previous policies. Several members of the board were prepared not to apply it retroactively or to keep those Communists who were sincerely committed to civil liberties. Flynn's obvious and simple-minded enthusiasm for the Soviet regime probably lost her crucially needed supporters. When Arthur Garfield Hays asked Flynn whether "members of the Communist Party believe in civil liberties and democracy as a way of life, or merely that they are useful methods to be used in a democracy towards bringing about a Communistic system and a dictatorship of the proletariat," she refused to answer the question on the grounds that it was hypothetical.[26] The fact that Baldwin himself at one time had held this same instrumental view of civil liberties did not help Flynn in the changed political climate of 1940. Neither was it necessary to prove that her activities had violated ACLU principles or been inconsistent with civil liberties. Flynn's proud acknowledgment of her belief in communism and her defense of Stalin's dictatorship put her squarely among those defenders of totalitarianism whose service on the governing organs of the ACLU was forbidden by the resolution of February 5.

The vote on the first charge, demanding her ouster on the grounds that she was a member of the Communist party, resulted in a tie which was broken by chairman Holmes. The first and most important charge thus stood approved by a vote of 10-9. The charges of misconduct were sustained by votes of 12-8. The final motion to expel Flynn carried 11-8. Arthur Garfield Hayes, who had voted against the first charge, and John F. Finerty, who had abstained, now voted in favor of the expulsion of Flynn. The meeting which had started at 8 p.m. on May 7 adjourned at 2:20 a.m. the following day. Three months later the Union's national committee ratified the board's action by a vote of 27-12, with 12 abstentions.[27]

For prodigious fellow travelers like Corliss Lamont, the 1940 resolution against totalitarians and the expulsion of Elizabeth Flynn marked a crucial point in the history of the ACLU. These actions, Lamont wrote in 1956, "made anti-Communist militancy and purity the main qualifications for the nomination and election of individuals to the Board of Directors and National Committee. It is hardly surprising that the quality of Directors and national committeemen steadily declined. For experience has demonstrated that passionate animosity towards Soviet Russia and communism is no assurance of a man's devotion to civil liberties in America."[28] Recent revisionist writers have seen the events of 1940 as the beginning of liberal Cold War anticommunism which, as we have seen in a previous chapter, are blamed for the eventual emergence of McCarthyism.[29]

The notion that the adoption of the 1940 resolution weakened the ACLU's commitment to the Bill of Rights has been rejected by Osmond K. Fraenkel, a general counsel of the Union, who voted against both the resolution and the expulsion of Flynn:

> In the decades following, the Union remained steadfast to its only purpose of defending the Bill of Rights for all, including Communists and other advocates of political unorthodoxy, even while asserting its separation from those doctrines. This occurred in cases defending the right of Communists to teach and to hold government jobs; and in resisting numerous Smith Act prosecutions, the federal loyalty program, and the outrageous depredations of the McCarthy and House Un-American Activities Committees.[30]

Alan Reitman, an associate director of the ACLU in the 1970s, has defended the 1940 resolution as a necessary measure in view of the "mood of national revulsion against the German-Russian Pact as an abdication of principle, and the havoc created by Soviet supporters' takeover of organizations through anti-democratic methods." Failure to take this stand might have meant the destruction of the organization. The action taken, Reitman argued, "was based not on the desire to court majoritarian approval or right-wing support but on the need to prevent impairment of the Union's function, and consequent loss for civil liberties, a serious reduction of credibility before courts and legislatures when the ACLU defended the civil liberties of all persons and groups, even those inimically regarded because of their noxious political views."[31]

Roger Baldwin, who had a key role in passing the 1940 resolution, until the end of his life stood by his conviction that Communists have no place in the leadership of an organization defending civil liberties. The ACLU, he told his biographer in the early 1970s, is like a church. "You don't take nonbelievers into the church. We are a church; we have a creed and only true believers should lead us." Communists, Baldwin argued, are nonbelievers. They "accept dictatorship and that is a denial of civil liberties."[32]

Divisions in the Ranks

The ACLU continued to adhere to this view of the role of Communists in the Union until the convulsive political changes of the 1960s, though disagreements regarding the Communist issue began to surface well before that time. In 1945 the board of directors authorized an inquiry into charges that the Chicago affiliate had become infiltrated by Communists. When the local committee did not satisfactorily cooperate with the inquiry, the board unanimously adopted a resolution which called upon the affiliate to show cause why it should not be disaffiliated. The dispute ended with the Chicago affiliate breaking its ties to the national organization.[33]

In 1977 documents obtained under the Freedom of Information Act revealed that for many years, but especially in the 1950s, ACLU officials had maintained close relations with the FBI. The main purpose of these contacts was to seek the assistance of the FBI in determining whether or not Communists had obtained positions of influence with state affiliates. Herbert Monte Levy, who was ACLU staff counsel from 1949–55 and who was one of the officials in regular contact with the FBI, has argued that this relationship has to be understood in the context of the times. During those years, the Union frequently was under attack as a Communist front. Hoover's record in the area of civil liberties, on the other hand, at that time was considered good. Predictably, Corliss Lamont has charged that "the collaboration between the ACLU leadership and the FBI was a scandalous betrayal of American civil liberties. It stemmed directly from the fanatical anti-Communism of the times."[34] The ACLU's own official inquiry into the matter concluded that no overt improprieties had taken place.[35]

The climate of insecurity during the 1950s led to a number of actions designed to make clear the Union's opposition to Communism. In 1951 the ACLU constitution was revised, and the 1940 resolution against totalitarians was incorporated into it. Two affiliates, Iowa and Northern California, cast dissenting votes, but the response of the others was "overwhelmingly favorable." In 1953, the board decided to put the following statement on all membership application forms and promotional material: "The ACLU needs and welcomes the support of all those—and only those—whose devotion to civil liberties is not qualified by adherence to Communist, Fascist, KKK, or other totalitarian doctrine."[36]

In late 1952, several members of the board, including Norman Thomas and Morris Ernst, began to press for the adoption of a statement on the Communist party and related issues such as academic freedom and the Fifth Amendment. Their concern was not only to demonstrate the Union's anticommunism but to differentiate their position from that of Senator McCarthy and his followers, then at the height of their power. Other influential figures on the board, such as Osmond K. Fraenkel, Arthur Garfield Hays, and Walter Gellhorn, voiced their concern that the ACLU not weaken its stand for civil liberties. After considerable debate, in the spring of 1953 the board appointed a special committee which drafted a lengthy resolution consisting of three statements largely reflecting the thinking of Thomas and Ernst. After prolonged discussion, this resolution was approved by the board in late April.[37]

Fraenkel and others opposed to the resolution thereupon initiated a referendum to the corporate membership of the ACLU provided by the by-laws. The corporate membership consisted of the board of directors, the national committee, and the boards of the Union's twenty-three local affiliates. Enclosed with the resolution were affirmative and negative arguments written by James L. Fly, former head of the Federal Communications Commission, and Osmond K. Fraenkel respectively. These materials were sent out in September 1953.

In his argument in support of the first statement, dealing with the nature of the Communist party and the significance to be attached to membership in it, Fly stressed the importance of having a "recognized landmark" from which specific decisions in civil liberties cases could be derived. The statement held the Party to be antidemocratic and subservient to a foreign power and recognized that in certain situations membership in such an organization, radically different from traditional American political parties, could be relevant to a particular judgment. The statement affirmed the ACLU's duty to defend the constitutional rights of Communists and, as Fly reminded his readers, did not embrace the principle of guilt by association. No automatic guilt was attached to the fact of membership. "The character, extent and currency of the association are to be weighed. And every qualifying or countervailing factor is to be thrown into the scales of reasoned judgment."

The second statement dealt with academic freedom and employment practices of the United Nations. The first part reaffirmed the ACLU's position on "Academic Freedom and Academic Responsibility" approved in April 1952. Teachers should follow their own "free and unbiased pursuit of truth and understanding" and those lacking in professional integrity could be dismissed. However, teachers should not be penalized solely because of their "personal views or associations (political, religious, or otherwise)," and even members of authoritarian organizations were to be judged as individuals. The second part stressed the importance of U.N. employees serving the United Nations and not the interests of any particular government. Fly considered both parts axiomatic and not in need of special supportive argument.

The third statement spelled out some general principles to be applied in regard to congressional investigations. It denied that reliance on the Fifth Amendment's protection against self-incrimination justified an inference of criminal guilt, but recognized that in certain situations "a person's exercise of the privilege may be inconsistent with his duty of full disclosure toward an employer, whether public or private." Fly pointed out that the statement did "not endorse the idea that a refusal to answer in an investigative forum is in itself grounds for discharge by an employer. It only provides that certain specified employers may inquire into all the facts (including, but not limited to, this refusal to answer) relevant to the competency of the employee."[38]

Fraenkel argued that a statement on the character of the Communist party was unnecessary and exceeded the function of the ACLU. "If Communists attack civil liberties, we should condemn them; if their rights are violated, we should come to their aid. There is no need for any statement of policy to reassure the public of our position in these matters, nor do we think it necessary to reaffirm our own political rectitude." For the same reason, Fraenkel opposed the second statement. "In order to avoid any misinterpretation with regard to the meaning of this referendum," Fraenkel wrote, "we suggest that those who [cast a negative vote] indicate that they are doing so because they believe the proposals unnecessary." Fraenkel urged defeat of the third statement dealing with the Fifth Amendment because he considered it badly formulated and liable to be "misunderstood and misinterpreted."[39]

When the votes in the referendum were counted in October 1953, it turned out that the policy statement had been rejected by a vote of 21,271 to 18,995. Most of the negative votes came from the affiliates. The board, however, refused to accept the outcome of the referendum as final and by a vote of 14-4 (with 5 abstentions) held that the substance of the rejected statement expressed "in essence the policy of the Union." This action was possible as a result of a by-law adopted in 1951 which allowed the board to disregard a referendum for "vitally important reasons" to be explained to the corporation. The executive director of the Union was now directed to reformulate the form, but not the substance, of the policy statement in order to take into account the changes proposed by various board members and affiliates.[40]

The ACLU corporation met in February 1954 and this time the affiliates prevailed. It was agreed that a special committee representing the affiliates, the board, and national committee would rewrite the statement. This revised version spoke of the dual character of the Communist party: "It is both a political agitational movement and a part of the Soviet conspiracy. Insofar as it is the first, its members have all the rights of members of other parties; to the extent that it is the second, its members may in some particulars be restricted by law." The statement also reaffirmed "the policy of the American Civil Liberties Union not to have as an officer, Board Member, committee member or staff member, national or local, any person who does not believe in civil liberties or who accepts the discipline of any political party or organization which does not believe in civil liberties or which is under the control or direction of any totalitarian government, whether Communist or Fascist."[41] Changes in the other two statements were minor. The tripartite committee then unanimously approved the entire policy statement; the vote in the board on August 2, 1954, too, was unanimous. Basically, the Union had reaffirmed its anticommunist posture.

Some liberals and leftists, critical of what they regarded as the ACLU's concessions to the political climate of the Cold War, in 1951 formed the Emergency Civil Liberties Committee (ECLC). Corliss Lamont, who in 1953 had lost his seat on the ACLU board, became a member of the ECLC's executive committee and in 1955 became vice chairman of the organization. Many members of the group's national council had similarly long records as fellow travelers. But the leadership of the ECLC also included men such as Clark Foreman, its director, and Professor I. Emerson of Yale University, who had resigned from the Progressive party in 1950 when the procommunist leadership of that party had blamed South Korea for starting the Korean War.

The ECLC's Statement of Principles, adopted on May 15, 1954, declared that the organization did not seek "to supplant other groups fighting for the Bill of Rights." At the same time, the statement quite deliberately sought to differentiate the ECLC from the ACLU. The organization would not "be drawn into controversies dealing with American foreign policy and international affairs" and it would "not take a position on economic and social systems." In a paraphrase of the ACLU's statement on membership, the Committee declared that it sought "the support of all those—and only those—who believe with us in the all-inclusive application of the Bill of Rights." It invited the support of all such persons, irrespective of their "varying political, economic and social viewpoints"—conservatives, liberals, and radicals.[42]

In the charged political climate of the 1950s, such a stance and the presence within the ranks of the ECLC of so many avowed leftists led to some harsh attacks. The American Committee for Cultural Freedom called the ECLC a Communist front, a charge which it was later forced to retract and apologize for.[43] When in the spring of 1954 the Committee held a conference at Princeton to celebrate Albert Einstein's seventy-fifth birthday, Norman Thomas declined to attend and tried to get Einstein to withdraw as well. "Prominent and dominant personalities in the Emergency Civil Liberties Committee," he wrote Einstein on March 9, 1954, "have shown through the years anything but a consistent love of liberty. . . . I am thoroughly persuaded, as I think you are, that the test of freedom in America and indeed among thoughtful men everywhere is a capacity to oppose both Communism and the thing that in America we call McCarthyism."[44] Einstein rejected the suggestion and defended the ECLC as an organization that upheld civil liberties "with a decisiveness and in a sense which is close to my convictions."[45] All these attacks, however, did put the Committee on the defensive and, in a rare departure from its general practice, at the end of March 1954 it released a statement which rejected a "double standard" of political conduct: "We will not judge our country by one standard, and other coutries by a less rigorous democratic standard. . . . We condemn without reservation, anti-democracy, anti-Semitism, and political persecution wherever they occur. We condemn these practices in the Soviet Union."[46]

The Repeal of the Exclusionary Policy

Within the ACLU, too, the Communist issue would not go away. By the late 1950s and early 1960s, several of the most outspokenly anticommunist leaders had retired and a new generation that did not share the earlier anticommunist consensus had begun to assume the helm. For many of these younger people the excesses of McCarthyism had discredited the very idea of anticommunism, and they quite deliberately embraced the doctrine of anti-anticommunism. There was also the impact of the civil rights movement in the South, which encouraged a more critical attitude toward American institutions. At the same time, the Soviet "thaw" which followed the death of Stalin in 1953 had generally weakened anticommunism and undermined what came to be called deprecatingly the "Cold War mentality."

The affiliates of the Union had always been less supportive of a strong anticommunist stand than the board of directors, dominated by old-timers. In 1964 ACLU members from affiliates in Iowa, Southern California, and Northern California began to contact like-minded individuals in other affiliates in order to press for a revision of the 1940 resolution in particular. At the plenary board meeting in April 1965, George Slaff, president of the ACLU of Southern California, announced that his affiliate had adopted and circulated to the other affiliates a proposed "Criterion for ACLU Membership and Eligibility for Office," and he urged a full review of the issue. The criterion which the ACLU of Southern California wanted to be adopted read:

> Support of civil liberties as guaranteed in the Constitution of the United States and particularly in the Bill of Rights is the one and fundamental qualification for membership or office in the American Civil Liberties Union.

In support of this proposed change the ACLU of Southern California argued that the 1940 resolution failed to evaluate each individual as an individual, embraced guilt by association, probed into belief and opinion, and pronounced a bill of attainder. By banning persons under the control and direction of governments hostile to civil liberties, the Union was said to be "proscribing every employee of a state such as Alabama or Mississippi."[47]

The board agreed that this matter would be taken up at its next plenary meeting, and the national office circulated to the affiliates relevant materials and position papers. In a memo dated June 7, 1965, Baldwin opposed any change in the 1940 resolution. The ACLU, he argued, had always excluded from its governing boards those whose views or associations were inconsistent with its purpose. Qualifications for a public post should be open to all regardless of political or religious views, but a private association with a single declared purpose could promote this purpose only with the help of those who shared it without conflicting interests. The concept of "guilt by association," Baldwin insisted, was valid when applied to qualifications for a private organization.[48]

Norman Thomas also favored retention of the 1940 resolution. The resolution, he pointed out, simply says "that those who favor Chinese or even Russian standards of state control which make any measure of civil liberty a gift of a totalitarian government, not a right, do not belong on our governing boards." Algernon Black of the Society for Ethical Culture argued that the ACLU had been able to do an effective job largely because its energy had not been diverted from its purpose and because its officers and staff were fundamentally committed to that purpose. Arguing on the other side was the attorney William Kunstler, who favored the adoption of the Southern California proposal in order to make ACLU policy consistent with what the Union supported for others.

A count conducted in January 1966 indicated that seventeen affiliates favored retention of the 1940 resolution, fourteen favored a change though not necessarily adoption of the Southern California proposal, and eight had not yet reached a decision. On January 30, 1966, after some discussion, the plenary board approved an amended version of a proposal made by the Michigan affiliate which called for the establishment of a tripartite committee, composed of representatives of the affiliates, the board, and the national committee. Instead of focusing simply on the 1940 resolution, the committee was to "consider the total problem of maintaining the integrity, effectiveness and viability of the ACLU and to prepare appropriate recommendations for By-law and Constitutional changes which may be necessary to effectively achieve this goal consistent with our principles and democratic purposes."[49] The committee was asked to submit a report to the first plenary board meeting in 1967. Subsequently, board chairman Ernest Angell appointed a special joint committee consisting of the constitution committee and a special committee on the 1940 constitution made up of six members from the board and affiliates.

Discussion in the special joint committee involved most of the old substantive arguments but also attention to the impact of a repeal of the 1940 resolution. Co-chairman George Soll stressed that he did not want either ACLU members or the media to think that the Union now invited Communists to serve on its governing organs. It was wrong to worry only about public images, but it was perfectly appropriate for an organization to pay some attention to public relations. "Communist philosophy," Soll argued, "is alien to ACLU principles and I think it is worthwhile saying so on the merits and for public relations considerations."[50]

At its March 1967 meeting, the board considered the report of the special joint committee and two minority recommendations. A lengthy debate over section 7(D) of the Union's constitution, dealing with qualifications for service on the board and staff, ended with the adoption of the following new language:

The ACLU's leadership and staff should be comprised of those—and only those—whose devotion to civil liberties is not qualified by advocacy of those communist, fascist, racist or other doctrines which reject the concept of democratic government and of civil liberties for all people in the United States and its possessions.

The final vote on this new section was 36–10. By a voice vote the board also agreed to drop from the Union's membership application forms the sentence: "The ACLU needs and welcomes the support of all those—and only those—whose devotion to civil liberties is not qualified by adherence to Communist, Fascist, KKK, or other totalitarian doctrine."[51]

The board's action represented a compromise. It continued the exclusion of Communists from the Union's governing organs and staff, but dropped the disavowal of Communists as members. When the change in the constitution was presented to the ACLU corporation for ratification, it was approved by 56 percent of the electorate. However, this was less than the two-thirds required for a constitutional amendment and the status of the 1940 resolution was thus left unchanged.

During the course of the year 1967, new efforts to repeal the 1940 resolution were made by several affiliates and members of the national committee. Most of these proposals aimed at doing away with the distinction between members and governing organs and therefore sought to eliminate entirely section 7(D) with its reference to the 1940 resolution. The board discussed the matter once again at its December 1967 meeting and after considerable debate adopted yet another compromise solution to this thorny problem. Section 7(D) was changed to say that all persons serving on the Union's governing bodies and staffs "shall be unequivocally committed to the objectives of the Union" and "to the concept of democratic government and civil liberties for all people." In addition, the board adopted a resolution which stated that this requirement "be understood to preclude support of those principles which reject or qualify individual liberties and minority rights for all people equally, regardless of race, sex, religion or opinion; or which reject or qualify the freedoms associated with the forms and processes of political democracy."[52]

The vote in the board on this new compromise was unanimous. The ACLU corporation ratified it by 95,683 to 10,221, well in excess of the required two-thirds' margin. For a time, all parties to the controversy appeared happy with the new language. Roger Baldwin, who had played a prominent role in devising the compromise, felt that the new policy did not constitute a change of principle but merely expressed the old requirement in new language. Corliss Lamont, on the outside, thought that the ACLU still maintained a requirement of "political purity." The ACLU, he declared in 1968, would never "win the unqualified support of principled civil libertarians until it rescinds its new 'loyalty' resolutions and repudiates the action of the 1940 Board of Directors in expelling Miss Flynn."[53]

In the early 1970s Lamont's wishes were to be fulfilled. Lamont's way of thinking about Communists and civil liberties by that time had become widely shared by the New Left. With anti-anticommunism gaining ground in the intellectual community, the ACLU now took several additional steps to get rid of its earlier anticommunist stands. In the 1971 edition of the ACLU Policy Guide, the statement "ACLU and Communism" was renamed "ACLU and Totalitarianism." The old statement, adopted in 1954, had noted the dual character of the Communist party— "both a political agitational movement and a part of the Soviet conspiracy." The new statement merely spoke of the Union's opposition "to any governmental or economic system which denies fundamental civil liberties and human rights."[54] In the new political climate of the 1970s, any specific reference by name to Communism was no longer acceptable.

In January 1974, George Slaff, president of the Southern California affiliate, asked that the board put on its agenda the 1940 expulsion of Elizabeth Gurley Flynn. "The Catholic Church," Slaff argued, "reversed the trial of Joan of Arc and canonized her."[55] Elizabeth Flynn, too, had been unjustly treated and this mistake should be acknowledged.

Osmond Fraenkel was one of several board members to announce his opposition to this move. At the time, he had voted against both the 1940 resolution and Flynn's expulsion, but he now saw "no useful purpose being served by our beating our breasts about this in public." Such an action, he wrote his fellow board members in late January 1974, might rekindle old charges and be taken as a rewriting of history. "We are not here concerned with the rehabilitation of a person unjustly convicted of a crime she did not commit. Miss Flynn was concededly a member of the Communist Party, and, therefore, came within the literal term of the 1940 Resolution." He had opposed the expulsion because he did not believe that the resolution should have retroactive effects, but recision was a needless exercise "without any real gain for the Union and considerable possible harm."[56]

Seventeen members of the national advisory council, including Roger Baldwin, also communicated to the board their opposition to the Slaff proposal. Elizabeth Flynn, they argued, was dead and "neither she nor her heirs, also deceased, can benefit." Rescinding the expulsion would inevitably be interpreted to mean that members of the Communist party or others in conflict with our principles are now eligible for service on the ACLU board of directors.[57]

The Slaff motion to amend the agenda with regard to the 1940 expulsion of Elizabeth Gurley Flynn was taken up by the board at its February 9, 1974, meeting, and, after a short debate, lost by a vote of 27–22. Slaff thereupon gave notice that he would move the adoption of a resolution on the subject of guilt-by-organization at the next board meeting. This resolution, he stated, had become necessary because the statement signed by the members of the national advisory council included a possible misinterpretation of the 1967 actions.[58]

At its April 1974 meeting, the board, after adding a few words, unanimously approved the Slaff resolution. It read:

> It is the understanding of the Board of Directors that the policy of the ACLU is that no member of any political party or any other association in the United States is ineligible for membership on the Board of Directors of the Union or of any affiliate or on the staffs thereof merely by reason of being a member of such party or association.

The resolution went on to affirm that "this understanding supplements and is not in denigration of the Resolution adopted by the Board in December, 1967" and then quoted the 1967 resolution in full.[59] Presumably, under this new policy guidance, it was still possible to bar a person who, while a member of the Communist party, was not devoted to the principles of civil liberties and not committed to "the forms and processes of political democracy." Implicit in the ACLU's new position was the assumption that a person could be a member of the American Communist party, one of the most Stalinist Communist parties in the world, and at the same time be devoted to civil liberties and democracy.

In November 1975, George Slaff once again asked that the board consider rescinding the Flynn expulsion. The ACLU, he wrote his colleagues on the board, had explicitly reversed the 1940 resolution pursuant to which Flynn had been expelled. "But we still permit to remain on our books the fact that we expelled a person from our Board because of what she thought, because of what she said, because of her associations." This "day of infamy" in the history of the Union should be remedied. "We owe it to the ACLU, I think, but we also owe it to the memory of Elizabeth Gurley Flynn."[60]

The executive committee agreed to place the Slaff proposal on the agenda of the next board meeting, but this action drew some sharp criticism. Board member Frank Haiman argued that to rewrite ACLU history would be "a symbolic act of self-flagellation for which I see no rhyme or reason. . . . Obviously, there are several axes each of us could grind if a majority of the Board permits any of us to indulge in this process. I hope we will say "NO" to everyone, and to George *for the second time*. Maybe he will finally get the message."[61] Attorney Paul Meyer, a board member from Oregon, expressed his concern that Slaff had been able to place the Flynn matter on the agenda of the board despite the fact that the board as recently as December 1975 had instructed its executive committee to confine the agenda to matters of pressing current business. In a lengthy memo which he asked be distributed to the board, Meyer pointed out that many on the board today were too young to have experienced the trials and tribulations of the united front period. "It would be a display

of arrogance for an ACLU board in 1976—three and a half decades later—
to second-guess those who fought the good fight in the 30s and 40s: to
presume to judge how they should have acted." The ACLU, Meyer stated,
unlike most other liberal organizations, had survived that turbulent period. "Whether this would have been true had the Communists been
allowed to apply their 'rule or ruin' policy to ACLU, as they did to virtually all liberal organizations during those years, is something we can
never know."[62]

Similar arguments were made when the board took up the Slaff proposal at its April 1976 meeting. The minutes record an unnamed member
pointing out that "in the 1940's any Communist in the ACLU would
have voted against civil liberties for a Nazi. The Board's 1940 resolution
represented a considered judgment that membership in the Communist
Party was inconsistent with a commitment to civil liberties. Today we
operate in a different climate, where an individual can be a Communist
and a civil libertarian." Taking the opposite position, another member
argued that the 1940 expulsion of Flynn should be repealed "not only
because of what it did to the individual, but because it signalled one of
the worst periods of the ACLU in which for twenty years we engaged in
redbaiting and would not put out a brief without a disclaimer. . . . The
repeal of this action will signal that the ACLU judges the individual and
is not a redbaiting group."

After lengthy debate, the board agreed to rescind the 1940 expulsion of
Elizabeth Flynn. The Slaff resolution, adopted by a vote of 32–18, praised
Flynn for the great service rendered by her to American labor and for her
long service to the cause of civil liberty. Flynn had been expelled in the
absence of any evidence that she had ever committed an act in violation
of the ACLU's basic principles. The resolution noted that Flynn had not
been permitted to vote on the motion to expel her, while three members
of the board who had brought formal charges against her had been
allowed to vote. During the 1974 discussion Osmond Fraenkel had pointed
out that this procedure conformed to Robert's Rules of Order and the
Union's by-laws, but this time around a majority of the board brushed
this point aside. The resolution concluded with the finding that "the
expulsion of Ms. Flynn was not consonant with the basic principles on
which the ACLU was founded and has acted for fifty-four years." The
board also agreed that a statement should be drafted to indicate that the
members were pleased that the 1940 resolution was removed from the
ACLU constitution in 1967.[63]

By the early 1970s, the ACLU not only had repealed the exclusion of
Communists from its governing organs and changed its stated position on
the nature of the Communist party, but it had come to accept the service

of individuals such as the radical lawyer William Kunstler, an avowed defender of violence. For example, in a 1970 interview with *Playboy* magazine, Kunstler argued that if the government did not "respond to the urgent needs of the people," the movement should "move from resistance to revolution." Resistance to a college that did not end its ROTC program could take the form of "the burning down of a particular college building at a safe time . . . when no danger to human life is involved." Kunstler criticized the violence of the Weathermen, at that time engaged in a wave of bombings, as "not tactically sound," but he added, "I am not against violence on a philosophical level nor on an emotional or a moral basis. . . . I don't condemn those who have engaged in burning and bombing."[64] Until shortly before he made these statements, hardly an example of commitment to the concept of democratic government, Kunstler was a member of the Union's board of directors. In 1970 Kunstler was named a member of the national advisory committee, a position he held until the 1980s. In 1982 the board named to the same national advisory committee the playwright Lillian Hellman, whose pro-Stalinist record has few rivals.

When in 1970 I raised questions about the service of Kunstler in the government of the ACLU, executive director Aryeh Neier wrote me that even if "everything you say about William Kunstler is correct," and since "the same comments could not be made about more than 1 or 2 of the 150 or so other members of the Board and National Advisory Council of the ACLU, is it more destructive to civil liberties to have Mr. Kunstler in his place or to engage in a trial of his views and possible eventual purge?" This reply, of course, failed to address the question why a person of Kunstler's views had been named to these posts in the first place.

In the light of the events outlined in the preceding pages, it is hard to resist the conclusion that the ACLU today has come to share the notion of anti-anticommunism so widely prevalent among the liberal community. The 1940 resolution was repealed with the help of the argument that to exclude Communists from the government of the Union represented redbaiting. The ACLU today criticizes anyone who has the temerity to raise the issue of the Communists' role in the nuclear freeze or other peace groups. As two dissenting members of the Union pointed out in a recent perceptive article, "questioning the propriety of conscious associations with pro-Communist groups is itself improper."[65]

There are those who regard these developments as a manifestation of the ACLU's increasing politicization. During the last twenty years or so, these critics argue, the Union has gone well beyond its traditional concern with civil liberties and has returned to the left-leaning political agenda which dominated ACLU activities during the twenties and early thirties.[66] Examples of such political forays with little or no discernible connection to the Bill of Rights abound. In February 1969, as the Vietnam War became increasingly unpopular, the Union gave "top priority" to a campaign to end the draft. In June 1970, it decided to oppose the war itself, declaring that "the present military involvement of the United States itself is unconstitutional." At the time, Professor Joseph W. Bishop, Jr., of Yale University Law School, argued that "only by a process of self-hypnosis can a lawyer take seriously the idea that the draft will be held unconstitutional" and that it was nearly as unlikely that the Supreme Court would consider the war in Vietnam unconstitutional.[67] Subsequent court decisions fully validated Bishop's judgment that these kinds of activities were clearly political in nature and were a waste of ACLU money, better spent on real issues of civil liberties.

Since then the ACLU has continued to pursue various liberal political causes, many of them with no clear relationship to civil liberties. Citing "basic concerns of fairness, dignity and privacy" the ACLU today opposes work requirements as a condition for eligibility for welfare benefits. The Union supports "the concept of comparable worth as the essential next step in achieving full equality for women and minorities."[68] In 1982, it voted to work toward halting military aid to El Salvador on the grounds that this support helped the death squads and violated the human rights of the people of El Salvador.[69] In 1989 the ACLU urged enactment of legislation to prohibit covert operations to influence the election in Nicaragua scheduled for February 1990.[70] All of these positions are arguably wise or unwise, but most of them have little to do with the Bill of Rights.

During the 1988 presidential campaign, the ACLU's left-liberal outlook drew the criticism of Vice President George Bush. Some of this criticism was unduly harsh and slighted the Union's courageous defense of unpopular groups like the segregationist National States Rights party or the American Nazi party. At the same time, the basic substance of these attacks was on target. The ACLU today, in many ways, is back to where it began: in at least some of its activities, the defense of civil liberties functions as a means of promoting a political agenda.

When in October 1973 the ACLU took out a full-page ad in the *New York Times* calling for the impeachment of President Nixon, Roger Baldwin opposed this action as not clearly related to the Union's commitment to civil liberties.[71] Today, with Baldwin and others of his generation passed away, those who might seek to return the ACLU to its traditional role as a champion of the Bill of Rights are few in number and definitely no longer the controlling force in the government of the Union.

9

The Peace Movement: The Difficulty of Learning from Experience

The Comintern's Way of Struggling for Peace

For much of its history, the Soviet Union has encouraged peace activities aimed at protecting its own territory and weakening the armed strength of the capitalist world. In some instances this has led to tactical alliances with pacifists and other peace groups. At the same time, the leaders of the Soviet Union and of the world Communist movement have often voiced their disdain for pacifism, which they consider a bourgeois ideology that fails to recognize the class character of war. During World War I, even before the victory of the Russian Revolution, Lenin criticized pacifists for their failure to distinguish between just and unjust wars: "We are not pacifists. We are opposed to imperialist wars for the division of spoils among the capitalists, but we have always declared it to be absurd for the revolutionary proletariat to renounce revolutionary wars that may prove necessary in the interests of socialism."[1]

In the years since the Bolshevik revolution of 1917, the Soviet Union has continued to encourage pacifist thinking in the West while at the same time Soviet leaders have warned against the spread of pacifist ideas among their own people. Lenin stressed the importance of exploiting pacifists for the goals of Soviet foreign policy at the time of the Conference of Genoa which met during the spring of 1922 in order to discuss the economic reconstruction of Europe. In his letters to the Commissar for Foreign Affairs, G. V. Chicherin, Lenin reminded his representative at the conference that, even though pacifism was incompatible with the program and interests of the revolutionary party, it was important to strengthen and support the pacifists in the bourgeois camp in order "to demoralize the enemy."[2]

During the twenties and thirties, the German Communist and Comintern functionary Willi Münzenberg developed the exploitation of noncommunist intellectuals for Soviet purposes into a fine art. Implementing Lenin's advice to reach out beyond the Communist party, Münzenberg became an expert at setting up front organizations that attracted artists, writers, and professors. It was he who coined the term "Innocents' Clubs" for these groups.[3] Arthur Koestler, who worked with Münzenberg, called him a genius of organization and an inspired propagandist: "Willi produced Committees as a conjurer produces rabbits out of his hat; his genius consisted in a unique combination of the conjurer's wiles with the crusader's dedication."[4]

One of Münzenberg's early successes was the establishment of the League Against Imperialism, founded at a congress held in Brussels in February 1927. For the first time, this organization united European socialists and liberals with movements for colonial independence. The Communists had strict instructions to keep in the background, yet they managed to dominate the League from the start. Roger Baldwin, who was one of five delegates from the United States, served for a year on what struck him as a multiparty executive committee. Yet the key post of secretary was occupied by Münzenberg, and the Communists were able to control the committee's deliberations and decisions without too much trouble.

Upon his return to the U.S., Baldwin became chairman of the League's American section, but he was purged two years later when he proved insufficiently obeisant to the real masters of the organization. To his great surprise, Baldwin recalled years later, "at a routine meeting of the executive committee . . . at which I presided, I found the room packed with members who had never attended before . . . mostly communists and fellow travelers. It became apparent at once what was up. The secretary, a party member, read a long indictment of me for deviations. Had I not supported Gandhi by a telegram or letter endorsing his nonviolent resistance? Was I not an accomplice of bourgeois elements and a victim of bourgeois illusions? It took them less than fifteen minutes to present and adopt by overwhelming vote a resolution of censure, expelling me as a member and chairman."[5]

The League Against Imperialism did not survive these heavy-handed tactics and went under in 1931. A year later, Münzenberg was able to put together a new enterprise that was to use more sophisticated tactics and prove more long-lived. In the spring of 1932 Japan had conquered Manchuria and in Germany the Nazi vote was rising. These events increased the Comintern's long-standing fear of a capitalist encirclement of the Soviet Union and made them renew their efforts to prevent an attack upon the USSR. This, then, was the background for the calling of the World Congress Against Imperialist War, which met in Amsterdam in late August 1932.

Münzenberg's preparations for this event were meticulous. Except for Maxim Gorki, the head of the convening committee, not a single Russian name appeared in the advance publicity. Of the 2,196 delegates from 35 countries, only 830 were Communists, but of the 1,041 delegates without a specific party affiliation a large number belonged to various party auxiliaries or fronts. About one-third of the delegates were members of national branches of the Friends of the Soviet Union and could be counted on to support the party line. There were 32 delegates from the United States, among them the writers Theodore Dreiser and Sherwood Anderson. Practically all of these delegates had been selected by various Communist-controlled organizations such as the John Reed Clubs, the International Workers' Order, and the Friends of the Soviet Union.[6]

Münzenberg's careful design even extended to the name of the gathering. In Communist publications it was referred to as the World Congress Against Imperialist War while for non-Communists it was called simply the World Congress Against War. The latter name suggested that the congress was opposed to all wars though in point of fact the real focus was on protecting the Soviet Union.[7] The call to the congress, issued by two popular French intellectuals, Romain Rolland and Henri Barbusse, declared that the purpose of the meeting was "to arouse the peoples of the world against the bloody catastrophe threatening them as a result of imperialist rivalry, and specifically the danger of an attack on the Soviet Union."

While the organizers of the congress went out of their way to play up the role of liberals and pacifists, the Communist position was never challenged. A manifesto, unanimously adopted by the congress, defended the peace policy of the USSR. Only the destruction of the capitalist system would finally do away with war. Another decision was to set up a World Committee Against War. In order to promote the goals of the Amsterdam congress in the United States, the American delegates formed the American Committee for Struggle Against War.[8] Within a short time, this group, renamed American League Against War and Fascism, was to become one of the most successful Communist auxiliaries in the United States, claiming millions of members and enjoying the backing of many well-known American intellectuals.

The American League Against War and Fascism

The American Committee for Struggle Against War had the backing of many prominent Americans. Theodore Dreiser was elected honorary chairman. Among the sponsors were John Dos Passos, Upton Sinclair, Sidney Hook, and Thornton Wilder. Despite the shabby treatment he had recently received from the Communists in the League Against Imperialism, Roger Baldwin agreed to serve on the board of the new organization. The board was headed by J. B. Matthews, a Methodist clergyman known for his leftist views, secretary of the pacifist Fellowship of Reconciliation, and known as an ardent fellow traveler. It was Matthews who was charged with planning the First United States Congress Against War.

The arrangements committee for the congress included only three known members of the Communist party—Earl Browder, Robert Minor, and Donald Henderson. Yet together with delegates from various party auxiliaries, the Communists controlled the twenty-five-member committee. The Socialists at first agreed to participate in the planning for the congress, but withdrew when the Communists continued to attack the Socialist leaders as men who "pretend to fight fascism" while actually paving its way. The withdrawal of the Socialist left the remaining non-Communists without effective direction and cohesion and enabled the Communists to dominate the congress with relative ease.[9]

The First United States Congress Against War convened in New York City on September 29, 1933. There were 2,616 delegates, many of them non-Communists, but the Party was in firm control. When the French Communist Henri Barbusse entered the hall to give the keynote address, the orchestra struck up "The International" and hundreds of delegates greeted Barbusse with the red salute—raised right arm and a clenched fist. The Communists' determination to have their way was also demonstrated when the congress rejected the nomination of Jay Lovestone to the presiding committee. The Party was eager to have the participation of prominent non-Communists, but a Communist "renegade," ousted from the Party in 1929 upon orders from Moscow, was clearly unacceptable. When the proposal to nominate Lovestone came before the delegates, it was "drowned out in a thunderous roar of disapproval," as the *Daily Worker* reported. When Baldwin a bit later tried to raise the issue a second time, arguing that the congress should be a symbol of true antifascist unity, a disturbance ensued and the services of Browder had to be enlisted to restore order. Baldwin's motion was then overwhelmingly defeated.[10]

This blatant display of power angered Baldwin and other non-Communists on the presiding committee, who threatened to walk out unless a

Lovestoneite was added to their ranks. Eventually a compromise was reached and Charles Zimmerman, an ally of Lovestone, was put on the presiding committee as a representative of Local 22 of the International Ladies' Garment Workers' Union. When Zimmerman appeared on the platform of the congress to speak he was received with boos and hisses. Browder again had to intervene to get his followers to calm down.[11]

Otherwise the congress proceeded as planned. Several well-known non-Communists including Reinhold Niebuhr and A. J. Muste were allowed to speak, but the manifesto adopted by the delegates clearly reflected the Communist party line of the day. It denounced American imperialism, demanded an end to the manufacture of munitions and other war materials, opposed the "growing fascization of our so-called 'democratic' government," and praised the peace policies of the Soviet Union as "the clearest and most effective opposition to war throughout the world."[12] The congress also voted to change the name of the organization to the American League Against War and Fascism, and it elected a national committee divided between Communists and fellow travelers.

Browder was satisfied with the job done. He told the thirteenth plenum of the executive committee of the Comintern in December 1933: "The Congress from the beginning was led by our Party quite openly but without in any way infringing upon its broad non-Party character."[13] When the manifesto adopted by the congress was published in the *Communist,* the theoretical organ of the Party, an excerpt from a resolution adopted at the Sixth World Congress of the Comintern was added which clarified the tactical intentions of the Party. "In the struggle against pacifism" Communists had to draw a distinction between the masses who "become a prey to pacifist swindlers, and the swindlers themselves, the pacifists of various shades. The masses must be patiently enlightened as to their error and urged to join the revolutionary united front in the struggle against war. But the pacifist swindlers must be relentlessly exposed and combatted."[14]

Most American pacifists had no illusions about the real intentions of the Communists, but in view of the rising danger of war many of them were willing to give the League the benefit of the doubt. Devere Allen, a leader of the Fellowship of Reconciliation (FOR), wrote after attending the League's first congress: "The pacifists and other non-Communists who entered into this Congress did so with their eyes open, knowing well enough that the major interest of [the] Comintern was the prevention of a war against Soviet Russia, and knowing that in accord with Communist tactics, the Communists could be expected to conceive of a united front only as united primarily behind their own particular doctrines."[15] An editorial in the *Christian Century,* entitled "Imperialist War or All War," voiced agreement with the Marxist view that the destruction of the capitalist order was a prerequisite to a lasting peace. But, it insisted, "this sentiment can be aroused and organized only as this peace movement sets itself against *all* war."[16] Kirby Page, vice chairman of the FOR, on the other hand, argued against the very idea of cooperation with the Communists. The united front, he charged, was a Communist game aimed at destroying movements "that stand in the way of their winning the workers to violent revolution and civil war."[17]

The correctness of Page's assessment of Communist tactics during those years was demonstrated by an event that took place in New York City on February 16, 1934. On that day the Communists violently disrupted a mass meeting called by the Socialist party in Madison Square Garden in order to protest the suppression of the Austrian workers by the Dollfuss government. As a result of this riot, the American League Against War and Fascism suffered a severe setback. The events of February 16, an editorial in FOR's unofficial organ, *The World Tomorrow,* pointed out, confirmed the impossibility of any united front with the Communists. Cooperation "depends upon fair play and ordinary honesty in dealing with fellow-workers. The Communists regard these virtues as bourgeois prejudices."[18] On February 20, Devere Allen resigned from the League. The Communist party, he declared, "considers the League as an opportunity, primarily, to disrupt and attack the various other participating organizations."[19] Soon thereafter, A. J. Muste's American Workers party dropped its membership. "The League," the party's organ *Labor Action* declared, "is not a broad genuine united front against war and Fascism . . . but in fact represents only one substantial organized labor group, the Communist Party and its affiliates."[20]

Other affiliated groups such as the League for Industrial Democracy and the National Association for the Advancement of Colored People also withdrew from the League because of the Madison Square Garden riot. Also damaging was the resignation of Matthews as the League's chairman. Roger Baldwin, on the other hand, was prevailed upon by Browder to retain his active role. Browder told him that it had all been a mistake and that Baldwin could help restore the united front by persuading ACLU chairman Harry F. Ward, a Methodist minister and professor at Union Theological Seminary in New York, to assume the chairmanship of the League and replace Matthews. "I was doubtful," Baldwin recalled in a memoir of the thirties, "but agreed to ask him. Dr. Ward, to my surprise, accepted the proposal; he had no disinclination to working with communists. . . . My surprise at his acceptance of the league chairmanship was due to my ignorance of the intensity of his attachment to the Soviet brand of salvation. We had never discussed it."[21]

For the Communists the accession of Ward to the chairmanship of the League was a coup. Born in London in 1873, Ward had come to the United States in 1891. During the twenties he had emerged as one of the most articulate champions of radicalism in the churches, with a strong hatred of capitalism. In 1931 he spent close to a year in Russia and he returned fired with ecstasy over what he had seen. The Soviet system, he now argued, was a fulfillment of the ethics of Jesus. Communism was crushing the profit motive and replacing it with incentives for service and sacrifice. The United States should follow the example of the Soviets.[22] Given these opinions and in view of Ward's great capacity for hard work, it is not surprising that Browder had nothing but high praise for Ward's contribution to the work of the League. "Such selfless and consistent service to a progressive cause," Browder wrote, "will always receive the unstinted recognition and support of the Communist Party."[23]

Under the energetic direction of Ward, the League grew again and gained the support of many liberals. Still, there was concern about the prominent role of the Communists in the organization. Referring to these concerns, Baldwin wrote to Browder in July 1934 and urged that at the forthcoming second congress of the League to be held in Chicago in September there be "less Communist party representation in proportion to the whole. Special efforts should be made in Chicago to get out a large non-Communist representation, particularly of foreign language groups, trade unionists and the middle-class church and antiwar crowd." With the consent of the executive committee, Baldwin wrote to Norman Thomas and offered to let him speak either as an individual or for the Socialist party, but Thomas refused.[24]

The second congress of the American League Against War and Fascism met in Chicago on September 28–30, 1934, with no dissidence to spoil the spirit of harmony. Well over 70 percent of the 3,332 delegates were members of the Communist party or its auxiliaries. A request to make public the names of the affiliated organizations, many of them paper organizations set up to provide cover for Communist activists and to enable them to claim delegate status, was turned down. In his address to the congress, Ward went out of his way to quell the fears of those who fretted about Communist domination. "It is quite illegitimate," he stressed, "for any political group to seek to dominate this organization for parties or purposes." At the same time, Ward defended the leading role of those most dedicated, which, of course, referred to the Communists. "Legitimately, the group which can offer to this movement the most valuable suggestions concerning program and tactics, which can offer the most dynamic active force for carrying it out, will gain political activity in this League and are entitled to do so."[25]

Ward also presided over the third congress of the League, held in Cleveland on January 3–5, 1936. As before, the leadership refused to reveal the list of the affiliated groups. The complete dependence of the League's program on the latest shift in the party line also continued. Prior to the second congress the League had denounced the League of Nations as a mouthpiece of the imperialist powers. These attacks ceased after the Soviet Union joined the League of Nations. Between the second and third congresses the Comintern had switched to the Popular Front line and the League again quickly fell into step. Franklin Roosevelt and Leon Blum now won endorsements for their support of the policy of collective security. The change in line reached its final ratification at the fourth congress, held in Pittsburgh on November 26–28, 1937, when the organization's name was changed from American League Against War and Fascism to American League for Peace and Democracy.

In conformity to the new conciliatory political line, the League adopted a rule that no political party could be affiliated, and the Communist party now withdrew from the League. The Communist party, Browder announced in November 1937, as the only party affiliated with the League, had become "the subject of all the attacks of our enemies who try thereby to label the American League as a Communist organization."[26] Needless to say, this action did not mean that the Party was no longer in control of the League. It maintained fractions in most branches and continued to hold key executive positions.

By 1937, the League claimed an affiliated membership of over four million. Actual dues-paying members, however, probably were less than 10,000. Still, the League had succeeded in broadening its base. It had gained many adherents on account of its defense of the Spanish Republic, its protest against Mussolini's invasion of Ethiopia, and other good causes. During the days of the Popular Front, as John Roche notes in his memoirs, the League "drew a considerable body of supporters who were totally unconcerned about the *nature* of the group but gave their endorsement to its *program*."[27]

The *New Republic* was among those liberal publications that gave the League much favorable coverage. "During the first two years of its life," an article published in January 1936 pointed out, "the League was handicapped in its growth because of the suspicion held by some that it was merely an instrument of the Communist Party. But it now seems reasonable to say that these suspicions have proved groundless. . . . It is clear by now that the CP's interest in the League is only seeing that it becomes the largest and broadest front possible against the common menace of war and fascism." The *New Republic* failed to inform its readers that the author of this article, William Mangold, was national treasurer of the League and thus hardly a disinterested observer.[28]

By the late thirties, on the other hand, the League had lost practically all its pacifists, whose judgment of the Communists' devotion to the cause of peace proved more adroit than that of many liberals. "Communists have nothing but contempt for religion and for pacifism," Kirby Page, vice chairman of FOR, wrote in 1935. "They use the united front as a means of boring from within."[29] Consequently FOR decided against affiliating with the League.

The Women's International League for Peace and Freedom (WILPF) authorized its executive secretary, Dorothy Detzer, to participate, but Detzer soon developed serious concerns about the Communists' mode of operation within the organization. In her memoirs she recalls that it was disconcerting to discover that "Communists imagined that if five of them yelled louder than twenty other members of a subcommittee, the noise they made constituted an affirmative vote on a given question. Or that it was perfectly ethical to postpone a vote on a motion until most of the non-communist members present had to leave to catch trains." Finally, in 1937, the WILPF withdrew from the League. Experience had shown, Detzer concluded, "that there is no basis for co-operative ventures where there is no basis of moral integrity. The clash of ideas, the conflict of thought can be healthy adjuncts to human effort, but only, I am now convinced, when they are secured by the veracity of the pledged word. Trust and good faith are the necessary underpinnings of co-operation."[30]

Another reason why American pacifists lost interest in the League was, of course, the League's endorsement of collective security. During those years pacifists sought to keep the United States out of the threatening European conflagration. They supported the Emergency Peace Campaign, which opposed increased military appropriations and promoted a nation-wide propaganda campaign against the idea of collective security. A new world war, it was argued, would mean the end of American democracy. It was the League's strong antifascist stand, on the other hand, that gained it many recruits and sympathizers and replaced the isolationists.

At its fifth congress, held in Washington in January 1939, the League claimed that the membership of affiliated organizations had gone above seven million and that the dues-paying membership was almost 20,000. Secretary of the Interior Harold Ickes sent a letter of welcome which stated: "The name of your organization must mean that you are committed to the policy of peace and the policy of democracy." Greetings were delivered by Representative Walter Judd, Judith Epstein, the national president of Hadassah, and J. Finley Wilson, Grand Exalted Ruler of the Improved Benevolent and Protective Order of the Elks. The League had become one of the most successful instruments by which the Communist party was able to reach and ingratiate itself with congressmen, labor leaders, and many other important public figures. Because of its respectability, the League also made it possible for the Party to reach other, less fully dominated organizations.[31]

This imposing edifice collapsed practically overnight as a result of the Hitler-Stalin Pact of August 1939. The controlling role of the Communists in the League was again demonstrated when a special congress convened in October passed resolutions in support of the Soviet Union's "peace policy" and refused to condemn the Nazi-Soviet agreement. The executive committee, meeting in closed session, turned down a resolution offered by LeRoy E. Bowman, a member of the staff of the U.S. Office of Education, which condemned both Germany and Russia for attacking Poland. The vote was 14–1. Another resolution offered by Bowman, which called for the dissolution of the League since it was no longer a genuine united front, lost by the same margin. Bowman thereupon quit the organization, followed by Roger Baldwin and many other non-Communists. When the fellow travelers who until then had provided the Communists with a safe majority balked at the invasion of Finland and showed a dangerous spirit of independence, the League was dissolved. On February 1, 1940, a meeting of League officers adopted a resolution saying that the outbreak of the war "has created a situation in which a different program and a different type of organization are needed to preserve democratic rights in war time and to help keep the United States out of war."[32] Thus ended an organization which, as Baldwin has correctly pointed out, functioned "as the most powerful of the united fronts . . . and as an agency which compromised more patriotic Americans than any other."[33]

By October 1939, the League had come under sharp attack by the Dies Committee on Un-American Activities, and the discussion of the question of Communist control of the League continued after its dissolution in early 1940. In his testimony before the Dies Committee, Harry Ward had denied that the League was dominated by the Communists and he repeated this denial in a book published in 1940. The Communists, he argued, had done no more than work for "the adoption of the party's view of what the united effort should be." They had done so democratically and, after the organization had become the American League for Peace and Democracy, without the use of fractions—"our Communist members acted as individuals in our National Congress and did not caucus."[34]

The picture painted by Ward was too simple. It is true that for many years the Communist party line and the views of certain liberals and fellow travelers in the League leadership had been identical. "If the League followed the line of Moscow," one of these liberals, Robert Morss Lovett, has written, "it was not because the policy emanated from Moscow but because it was our own line, especially in the matter of collective security and the punishment of aggressors." The Communists, therefore, were able to have their way "democratically." At the same time, as Baldwin has noted, the Communist role in the League was so indispensable that they had, in effect, a built-in veto. The Communists were the driving force of the organization "and everyone—except a few innocents or persons who did not care who ran a good cause—knew it. The liberal support and the prominent letterhead names disguised the essential backing." This meant, Baldwin went on to point out, that we were "prevented from taking any position in opposition to Communist policy, for they would have withdrawn and thus wrecked the united front." This is what happened after the Hitler-Stalin Pact and the Russian invasion of Finland. "The League," Lovett recalled, "could not approve these acts, and the Communists could not agree to denounce them. To that extent it may be said that the Communists controlled its existence."[35]

And there was more. We now know of at least one officer of the League who claimed to be a non-Communist but actually was a secret member of the Party and functioned at its call. "Months after the league dissolved," Baldwin has written in a memoir, "our former secretary, chosen as a man independent of politics and specifically noncommunist, called on me to confess that all along he had been a secret party member, taking orders not from his board but from party headquarters. The Nazi-Soviet Pact had uprooted him. I am confident that Dr. Ward did not know of the deception."[36]

Students Against War

The same manipulation of peace sentiments in the interests of Soviet foreign policy which wrecked the American League for Peace and Democracy also brought to grief the student antiwar movement of the thirties. In late 1931, the Communists formed the National Student League (NSL), which claimed to be "affiliated to no political party and [be] controlled by the membership itself."[37] Among the manifold activities of the League, issues of war and peace ranked high from the very beginning. A delegate of the NSL attended the Amsterdam World Congress Against War in August 1932. At the urging of Henri Barbusse, one of the organizers of the Amsterdam meeting, the NSL convened a national student antiwar conference in Chicago in December of the same year. There were close to

700 delegates, including members of the Young People's Socialist League (YPSL), the Student League for Industrial Democracy (SLID), and representatives of pacifist groups. Communists and non-Communists agreed on the need to struggle against imperialist war. When Jane Addams, founder of the Women's International League for Peace and Freedom and recipient of the 1931 Nobel Peace Prize, pleaded that it was necessary to oppose all violence, she was answered by J. B. Matthews, who pointed out the importance of distinguishing between imperialist and non-imperialist wars. This bit of Marxist wisdom drew enthusiastic applause.[38]

In the following year, the NSL addressed an open letter to the Student League for Industrial Democracy proposing a merger of the two groups. This offer was rejected by SLID leader Joseph Lash on the grounds that the NSL was the student wing of the Communist party, with which the Socialists had major disagreements. The young Communists, Lash wrote in an article published soon after the merger proposal, "envision amalgamation as a god-given opportunity to smash the influence of the Socialist movement and socialist ideas in the student field."[39] The two groups, nevertheless, did agree to cooperate in certain antiwar activities. Pacifist ideas had been spreading on the campuses, the reflection of a spirit of uncertainty and alienation from a society engulfed in the misery of the Great Depression. Consequently, on April 13, 1934, the NSL and SLID, aided by the American League Against War and Fascism, organized the first student antiwar strike. Some 25,000 students participated in a one-hour stoppage of classes at which a pledge not to support the government in any future war (borrowed from the pledge of the Oxford Union in England that it would "not fight for King and country in any war") was administered. The following year, the event attracted 150,000 students and received the endorsement of prominent intellectuals. James Wechsler, then a leader of the young Communists in New York City, recalled years later: "I led 3,500 students in a solemn recitation of the Oxford pledge and numerous faculty dignitaries participated."[40]

Many of the young Socialists were more militant than their elders and there was strong support for left-wing unity. When in the summer of 1935 the Comintern formally endorsed the concept of the Popular Front an important barrier to an organic union of leftist students was removed. At a convention held during the Christmas break of 1935 at Columbus, Ohio, the NLS and SLID merged into the American Student Union (ASU). Lash had abandoned his strong opposition to an amalgamation of the two groups, but within a year, confirming his earlier fears, the new organization was to pass into the effective control of the Communists.

There was tension from the very beginning. About half of the 500 delegates who attended the unity convention were neither Socialists nor

Communists; many of them adhered to pacifist sentiments. The young
Communists caucused each night and laid plans for getting the ASU to
endorse the concept of collective security. This idea troubled the pacifists
and Socialists who sought a strong antiwar stand.[41] The focus of the
debate was the Oxford pledge, considered by the Communists an outdated antiwar slogan. In the interest of adhering to the Party's united
front policy, the young Communists showed themselves conciliatory and
agreed not to push for an immediate repudiation of the pledge. Nevertheless, the resolution which was finally approved named only Germany,
Japan, and Italy as threats to world peace, a clear concession to the strong
antifascist stand sought by the Communists.[42]

The American Student Union never gathered more than 20,000 members, yet it became an important force on the American campus. In 1936,
about half a million students joined in the annual antiwar strike. These
accomplishments, however, were accompanied by growing internal dissension. At the ASU convention of 1936, a YPSL-sponsored resolution
opposing collective security lost by a narrow margin. In a spirit of compromise it was then agreed not to take any position on the contested idea.
But a year later, the Communists finally asserted themselves. They were
helped by the defection of Lash, who, by 1937, as he put it later, had
become "a non-Party Communist." The ASU convention, meeting at
Vassar College in December 1937, now formally abandoned its commitment to the Oxford pledge and by a vote of 282–108 endorsed the principle of collective security. This step brought the ASU into full alignment
with the party line. On October 5, President Roosevelt had given his
Quarantine Speech. The United States, the President had urged, in order
to avoid war should join with the "peace-loving" nations of the world to
"quarantine" aggressors. The Communists had given their full support to
Roosevelt and the ASU now had followed suit.[43]

The ASU thus had abandoned its antiwar stand and had become
respectable. President Roosevelt sent the 1937 convention his greetings, a
gesture he repeated in 1938, at which time the ASU endorsed the New
Deal. Most of the young Socialists by then had left the organization. The
ASU, they charged, founded as the agency of American students to combat
war, war preparations, and militarism had become an agency to support
war, justify war preparations, and condone militarism.[44]

The Hitler-Stalin Pact for a time returned the ASU to an antiwar
position. With the young Communists now in undisputed control, the
ASU once again switched gears and accepted the latest twist in the party
line. At its December 1939 convention the erstwhile antifascist organization denounced the war against Hitler as "imperialist." A motion to condemn the Soviet attack upon Finland lost by a vote of 322–49. Joseph

Lash, who had wanted to stick to the collective security line, was expelled. ASU propaganda echoed the slogan "The Yanks Are Not Coming."[45]

The final chapter of the ASU was written after the Nazi invasion of the Soviet Union, which required yet another about-face. The Communist party itself realized that, as a result of all these many twists and turns, organizations like the ASU had become completely discredited. The student group, like other relics of the thirties, was finally allowed to die. Once again, a cause supported by idealistic, if occasionally naïve, aspirations had become a casualty of the manipulative embrace of the American Communist movement, subservient as ever to the interests of its foreign master.

The American Peace Mobilization

After the American League for Peace and Democracy had been unceremoniously dissolved in early 1940, the Party turned to the formation of new peace groups. There was the Hollywood Peace Forum, the Peace Committee of the Medical Professions, the Mother's Day Peace Council, and even a Milwaukee Indians' Peace Group. On the East Coast alone there were said to exist 300 Emergency Committees for Peace. Borrowing ideas and slogans from both pacifism and isolationism, the Party organized numerous "peace rallies," all with the central objective of keeping America out of the "imperialist war."[46]

By the end of the summer of 1940, the groundwork for a new national organization had been laid. During the Labor Day weekend, an Emergency Peace Mobilization convened in Chicago. Among those signing the call to this gathering were many clergymen as well as the governor of the Virgin Islands, the veteran fellow traveler Robert Morss Lovett. Most of the 5,653 delegates came from Communist-controlled unions, fraternal groups, and youth organizations. When a delegation of non-Communist auto workers from Flint, Michigan, had the audacity to offer a resolution that condemned aggression of all kinds, specifically naming both Germany and Russia, the Communist managers of the gathering ruled it out of order on the grounds that resolutions from individual groups could not be considered; there was to be only one general declaration of policy. That statement, when finally adopted, made no mention of aggression, but did attack the "war policies" of President Roosevelt.[47]

The new organization was named American Peace Mobilization (APM). Its leaders included Carl Sandburg, Franz Boas, Theodore Dreiser, and other innocents. For the post of executive secretary the Party tapped the millionaire Frederick Vanderbilt Field. In his recently published autobiography, Field described how he was approached by Browder "some time before the APM was formally organized" and asked whether he would accept the post of executive secretary. Field agreed and his "election" took place without a hitch. There were no rival candidates for the position and Field was elected unanimously and without discussion. Most of the delegates, Field recalls, did not know him by sight, let alone by any qualifications he might have had for the post, yet "they evidently had been told that I was to have the job."[48]

The APM never became large, but it carried on an energetic campaign against Roosevelt's attempts to provide aid to beleaguered Britain. In January 1941 Roosevelt submitted the Lend Lease Bill to Congress, a plan for turning the United States into the "great arsenal of democracy." The Communists swiftly joined the opposition. At the annual Lenin memorial meeting held in New York's Madison Square Garden, Browder accused the President of resorting to the "Hitlerian tactic of concentrating upon a single step at a time" in leading the nation into war. Another party leader, Israel Amter, declared that the "Soviet Union has a policy of peace while President Roosevelt pursues a policy of war."[49] The APM also reportedly made overtures to the isolationist America First Committee, but this attempted cooperation was eventually dropped.[50]

One of the news-making activities of the APM in 1941 was a "perpetual peace vigil" in front of the White House. The strength of the line varied from a handful of demonstrators late at night to several hundred during weekends. After Congress had passed the Lend-Lease Act in March and President Roosevelt had announced plans to protect merchant ships carrying supplies to Britain, the picket line started to carry "No Convoys!" signs. On June 21, Field climbed on the White House fence and told a group of several hundred picketers that the vigil had surpassed 1000 hours and was to be terminated for now. A new antiwar campaign was to be started in Washington at the end of July. On the following day, June 22, 1941, Hitler invaded Russia. Now plans had to be changed. Instead of an antiwar position the Communist auxiliaries now were called upon to defend a vigorous prowar line.[51]

On July 23, the American Peace Mobilization announced that it had changed its name to American People's Mobilization. This choice allowed the new organization to use the same acronym—APM. The official slogan now was "For Victory over Fascism." Nothing more was heard about British imperialism and American warmongering. Soon thereafter the APM was dissolved. It had outlived its usefulness. New times demanded new fronts.[52]

The way in which the Communist party after June 1941 worked for the total mobilization of the home front and the kinds of new auxiliaries it utilized for this purpose have been described in Chapter 5. American pacifists, who spoke up for a negotiated peace, were attacked as disloyal. "Any honest win-the-war liberal who continues to blink at the menacing, disruptive nature of these so-called 'pacifist' groups in this country," the *Daily Worker* warned, "is doing a disservice to real liberalism and contributing to sabotage of the war effort."[53] Former allies had become enemies.

A New Peace Campaign

The end of the wartime alliance and the outbreak of the Cold War brought with it a new Communist peace offensive. The Soviet Union had swallowed Eastern Europe, but it was lagging behind the United States in the development of nuclear weapons. The West had committed itself to a policy of containment and had created the North Atlantic Treaty Organization (NATO) in order to protect Western Europe. The Wallace campaign of 1948 had sought to discredit these defensive moves, but the results had been disappointing. The Cultural and Scientific Conference for World Peace held in March 1949 at the Waldorf-Astoria Hotel in New York City marked the beginning of the new peace campaign in the U.S.

The Waldorf conference was organized by the National Council of the Arts, Sciences and Professions, a descendant of the Independent Citizens' Committee of the Arts, Sciences and Professions which had supported the Roosevelt candidacy in 1944 and Henry Wallace in 1948. By that time it was generally regarded as a Communist front. Many prominent American intellectuals allowed themselves to be listed as sponsors. Leonard Bernstein, Aaron Copland, Norman Mailer, Budd Schulberg, Arthur Miller, and Thomas Mann were among those who responded to the call to come together "to discuss and seek a basis for common action on the central question of peace." Also among the sponsors were a large number of persons known as Communists or staunch fellow travelers such as Howard Fast, Lillian Hellman, William Gropper, Donald Ogden Stewart, and Harlow Shapley. Many members of this latter group had attended a Soviet-sponsored World Congress of Intellectuals in Wroclaw, Poland, in August 1948, which had vilified the United States as a bastion of imperialists and monopolists bent on world domination. The Waldorf conference, it turned out, was largely the work of the continuations committee of the Wroclaw congress, one of several "peace" conferences scheduled to follow the Wroclaw meeting.[54]

The veteran pacifist A. J. Muste asked for a place on the program, but his request was turned down. Sidney Hook requested permission to present a paper entitled "Science, Culture and Peace," and, not surprisingly, the organizers of the conference, despite the alleged focus of the gathering on science, culture, and peace, could find no place for him either. Hook thereupon organized an ad hoc group, Americans for Intellectual Freedom, which sought to counter what Hook regarded as a grandiose fraud on the American public. Except for Norman Cousins, not a single person openly critical of Soviet foreign policy or of the Communist party line in any of the fields of the arts and sciences had been invited. The Communists, Hook recalls in his memoirs, "were posing as champions of peace at a time when the Soviet Union was threatening the peace of Europe with their blockade of Berlin, and as advocates of a free culture at the height of the Zhdanov purges and the imposition of Lysenkoism on Soviet scientists."[55]

The ad hoc group stressed that it had no objection to the holding of the meeting. It criticized the State Department for refusing to issue visas to some of the Communist delegates from Western Europe—the State Department had granted visas to delegates from the Soviet Union and Eastern Europe—and it also condemned the noisy picketing of the conference by the American Legion and other right-wing groups. The group's main aim was to draw attention to the false pretenses of the conference and to prevail upon the non-Communist sponsors to withdraw their support.

The conduct of the conference confirmed the apprehensions of the critics. Questions asked by members of the ad hoc group who attended the meeting were either turned aside or evaded. No real discussion was allowed. When Norman Cousins told the gathering that the Communists did not speak for America and that they were regarded by Americans as discredited spokesmen for a foreign power, he was roundly booed. The chief Russian delegate, A. A. Fadayev, secretary of the Union of Russian Writers, gave a speech that praised the peace policy of the Soviet Union. Dwight McDonald noted that this speech drew "thunderous applause." The great majority of those present at the gathering, he concluded, were obviously on the side of the Russians. The conference "was strictly a Stalinoid affair."[56]

Yet the efforts of the ad hoc group were not entirely in vain. A counter-meeting at Freedom House drew a capacity crowd of 450 and several thousand more listened to the proceedings through loudspeakers set up in Bryant Park. This meeting was addressed by Sidney Hook, A. J. Muste, Arthur Schlesinger, Jr., Max Eastman, the Nobel laureate H. J. Muller, and other well-known public figures. The counter-demonstration received wide coverage in the press and demonstrated the absurdity of the claim of the Waldorf conference to represent American culture. It also was able to show that the Waldorf gathering had been convened not to further the cause of peace but to propagandize for Soviet foreign policy.

The next major move in the Communist peace offensive came in Paris a month later, in April 1949, with the formation of the World Committee of the Partisans of Peace. In November 1950, this group changed its name to World Peace Council (WPC). Until 1951 the WPC was based in Paris. Expelled from France for "fifth column activities," the WPC moved to Prague and then to Vienna where it remained until banned in 1957 for "activities directed against the Austrian state." However, the WPC continued to operate in Vienna as the International Institute for Peace until it moved to its present location in Helsinki, Finland, in 1968. Today the WPC claims 140 national affiliates. It describes itself as "the largest international, non-governmental organization dedicated to the achievement of peace, disarmament and detente." The general secretary of the WPC since 1966 and its president since 1977 has been Romesh Chandra, a member of the central committee of the pro-Soviet Communist party of India. Among students of Communist affairs there exists a consensus of opinion that the WPC functions as an unfailing supporter of Soviet foreign policy and represents the archetypical international front organization.[57] Indicative of the contemporary unwillingness to call Communist fronts by their right name or perhaps the result of just plain ignorance, a recent article in the *Washington Post* that made reference to the WPC noted that "conservative groups call [the Council] a communist front,"[58] thus raising subtle doubts about a characterization that no knowledgeable person outside of the Communist camp has ever challenged.

A meeting of the Partisans of Peace held in Stockholm in March of 1950 issued the so-called Stockholm Peace Appeal. Addressed to "all men and women of good will throughout the world," the appeal demanded the "outlawing of atomic weapons as instruments of intimidation and mass murder of people." It called for "strict international control to enforce this measure" and declared that "any government which first uses atomic weapons against any country whatsoever will be committing a crime against humanity and should be dealt with as a war criminal." The appeal appeared at a time of clear Soviet nuclear inferiority (the first Soviet test of a nuclear weapon had taken place just six months earlier), although the Soviet Union possessed overwhelming superiority in conventional weapons. After the Soviet Union had caught up with the West and in 1953 had exploded a thermonuclear device, the Stockholm Peace Appeal was suspended.[59]

The Stockholm Peace Appeal appeared to be well-timed. Three months after it had been issued, on June 25, 1950, Communist North Korea attacked South Korea. It is assumed today that the Soviet Union, at the very least, had given this attack its implicit approval. Whatever its role, the Soviets backed the contention of its ally that the South had fired the first shot, and they condemned American assistance to South Korea as "aggression." Meanwhile Communist parties all over the world and their auxiliaries began to circulate the Stockholm Peace Appeal. No responsible statesman in the United States at that time thought of using the atomic bomb in Korea, but the appeal nevertheless served to call into question the West's policy of nuclear deterrence.

In the United States a Sponsoring Committee for the World Peace Appeal (the official name of the Stockholm declaration) was formed. Hundreds of peace groups sprung up which went from door to door soliciting signatures to the appeal. There was the Harlem Women's Committee on Peace, Veterans for Peace, the U.S. Youth Sponsoring Committee for the World Peace Appeal, and many more. Many people, unaware of the appeal's Communist origins, signed what appeared to be a message of peace. The number of signers in the U.S. is said to have been more than two million; there were allegedly more than 273 million around the world. Typical of the many sincere people who signed the appeal was the comment of a retired Episcopal minister in Boston who said that he believed "in favoring every proposal or action that tends to promote peace rather than against peace."[60]

The Stockholm appeal was promoted by a host of new fronts that made wide inroads among the churches in particular. One of the religious figures to take a leading role in pushing the appeal was the Methodist lay theologian Willard Uphaus. A man of genuine idealism, Uphaus had drifted into the Communist orbit in the late 1940s. In 1950 he went to Warsaw to attend the Second World Peace Congress which created the World Peace Council, the most important propaganda instrument of the worldwide Soviet peace campaign. In his address to the congress, Uphaus upbraided the United States for its "overweening arrogance." A ten-day visit to the Soviet Union, on the other hand, left him convinced that Soviet society, "despite all its wrongs and mistakes," had as its purpose "cooperative living and social justice, with economic plenty, education, health, and cultural fulfillment."[61]

In June 1951 Uphaus, together with Thomas Richardson, a black union leader, became a director of the American Peace Crusade, which quickly became the principal front group behind the Stockholm appeal. He had, he said, no objection to working with Communists for peace. The crusade organized prayer vigils and sought to end the American role in Korea. According to Uphaus, the United States there was allied "with the British and French imperialists, expending blood and treasure, in a futile effort to stop the onward march of the colored people to freedom and independence."[62] The crusade was asked by the Justice Department to register under the Internal Security Act as a Communist front, but instead decided to dissolve.

The war in Korea and the growing fear of a nuclear conflict that could end human civilization on earth made many well-meaning Americans susceptible to the Communist peace slogans. At the same time, the intolerant political climate of the McCarthy years and the often crude ways in which the Communists and their fronts exploited the peace issue also lost that drive many potential supporters. Probably the most important reason why all groups working for peace, Communist-run or not, were weakened during the fifties was the heating up of the Cold War. The outbreak of open hostilities in Korea, the crisis over the islands of Quemoy and Matsu off the coast of China in 1954, the danger of an American involvement in the French war in Indochina the same year, and other international trouble spots all appeared to prove that the prospect of a peaceful resolution of international differences was at best utopian and at worst treasonable.

The death of Stalin and the accession of a somewhat less bellicose leadership in the Soviet Union helped the peace movement in the late 1950s. The fear of fallout from nuclear testing led to the creation of the Committee for a Sane Nuclear Policy (SANE), which gained backing from many people outside the traditional peace constituency. The spread of "nuclear pacifism" strengthened the demand for disarmament. This new situation provided fertile ground for a revival of the Communist peace offensive and led to new attempts to infiltrate the peace movement. Arnold Johnson, national legislative director of the American Communist party, in 1958 called on Communists to support, encourage, and help the developing movement for peace. The Party, he stressed, had to be prepared to take advantage of the new opportunities:

> We need to be flexible in how we present proposals. For instance, it is perfectly reasonable in working with pacifists and conscientious objectors to find formulations so that they can function with enthusiasm. And in working with others, it often means finding a new formulation in a speech which is more expressive of the common objective. . . . Peace is the central issue of our era. Peace must therefore be the central issue of our politics and our organization.[63]

In his keynote speech to the seventeenth national convention of the American Communist party in December 1959, Gus Hall made the same point. The sentiment for peace, he noted, was widespread, and the Party had to align itself with "the existing mass organizations of the people" in order to help build and guide the peace movement. It had to address the specific interests of different groups. "With some, unrestricted trade with the socialist countries will be the starting point, with others it will be the dangers of fallout. For still others, disarmament will be the point of greatest interest."[64]

SANE, as we will see in more detail in a later chapter, at that time was not taken in by these maneuvers, and it adopted rules to protect itself against Communist infiltration. The pacifist groups, too, were skeptical of Communist pretensions of peace made at the very same time that the Soviet Union was actively promoting violence in many parts of the world. The refusal to work with the Communists was a continuation of policies followed since the 1930s. The Fellowship of Reconciliation (FOR), for example, in 1951 reaffirmed its unwillingness to participate in Soviet-sponsored peace activities. A statement issued in May of that year suggested that "the best way to test any 'peace' project or joint effort which is proposed" is to discover whether its promoters clearly stated "that it is opposed to militarism and war preparations *both* in Russia and in the United States, that it is critical of the foreign policy of both countries, and opposed to all forms of totalitarianism, including the Communist." The Soviet Union, declared FOR leader John M. Swomley in 1953, was not really interested in world peace. "The Communist 'Peace Offensive' operates in the interests of one group of power states."[65]

Other pacifist leaders such as A. J. Muste similarly opposed collaboration with the Communists. Members of the Party, Muste argued in 1949, "use deceit and violence at the behest of the Party; they do conceal and lie about membership in the Party; they do penetrate organizations for all kinds of ulterior purposes and without hesitating to resort to the most egregious chicanery." Communists, Muste declared in 1956, are human beings whom Christians had to love like other children of God. But, he went on, "I do not take this to mean that we have to work with them politically or be sentimental and naive about certain aspects of their behavior and strategy."[66] When Muste a year later organized the American Forum for Socialist Education, which brought together Communists and non-Communists in a series of conferences and debates, he was criticized by Norman Thomas. The forum, Thomas argued, would help the Party, badly weakened after the suppression of the Hungarian revolt of 1956, to revive itself and would confuse people politically.[67]

Alfred Hassler, executive secretary of FOR, took the same position in 1963. There was a tendency among many Americans revolted by the excesses of McCarthy, Hassler pointed out, to reject automatically anything that sounded as though the State Department might agree with it. "Confronted by an official America that argues that nothing the Communists say can be believed, the peacemaker is tempted to act as though nothing the Communists say may be disbelieved. . . . Official America seeks to exclude Communists from everything; therefore, a 'sincere' peace movement may exclude them from nothing." This reaction, Hassler stated, was understandable but not defensible. One could not build peace by allowing oneself "to be used to advance one side of the cold war against the other."[68]

Peaceful Coexistence and the New United Front

Not surprisingly, the Communists vigorously criticized those in the peace movement who refused to make common cause with them and to praise those who accepted the idea of a new united front. Writing in 1963 in the Party's theoretical journal, *Political Affairs*, Arnold Johnson called Women Strike for Peace "the most vital mass force in the peace movement" because they were an "all-inclusive" organization. Johnson related with approval how Dagmar Wilson, the founder of the group, had refused to assure the House Committee on Un-American Activities that she would exclude Communists. The Women's International League for Peace and Freedom (WILPF), too, drew Johnson's commendation because it had "a healthy attitude to other organizations," including the role of Communists. On the other hand, there were those such as Homer Jack, the executive director of SANE, who were preoccupied with keeping Communists out of the peace movement. Johnson stressed the importance of countering such people and fighting "the poison of anti-Communist slanders."[69]

The year 1962 marked the beginning of a systematic Communist campaign against anticommunists who were accused of deliberately perpetuating the Cold War. Anticommunism was held to be one of the greatest barriers to peace and international understanding. The danger of a new world war was said to come from those who did not trust the good intentions of the Communists. This campaign against anticommunism benefited from the accession to positions of leadership in the American peace movement of a generation who had not experienced the struggle against the Communists during the 1930s. For these younger people the only acquaintance with anticommunism was McCarthyism. Most of them, therefore, embraced the New Left's anti-anticommunism and refused to exclude anyone who claimed to share their concern for peace. This policy of nonexclusion became one of the trademarks of the movement against the war in Vietnam, a subject we will take up in detail in a later chapter.

By the time the war in Vietnam had come to an end in 1975, American peace groups had behind them ten years of cooperation with the Communists and various Marxist-Leninist fringe groups in the antiwar movement. Men like FOR leader Alfred Hassler, who had opposed the new united front, had been eased out of positions of responsibility. Peace organizations like the Women's International League for Peace and Freedom now regularly attended meetings of the World Peace Council and other Communist front organizations.[70] The war in Vietnam had radicalized large segments of the peace movement, had alienated them from American society, and had therefore made them susceptible to the new Communist overtures. Both the Communists and the peace movement now expressed their support for so-called national liberation movements and anti-American Third World dictators like Fidel Castro.

In 1977, the U.S. Peace Council (USPC), an affiliate of the World Peace Council, came into being. As of 1984, it had chapters in 75 American cities. The group's executive director since its founding has been Michael Myerson, a member of the central committee of the Communist party. Another key member until her death in January 1985 in the crash of a Cuban Airline flight from Havana to Nicaragua was Sandy Pollack, a member of the Party's national council. A memorial service held at Riverside Church in New York City was attended by a thousand people and there were eulogies from many non-Communists. The Reverend William Sloane Coffin noted that "Sandy may not have believed in God but God sure believed in Sandy."[71]

The USPC flaunts its pro-Soviet stands, and it has therefore occasionally experienced difficulties in winning acceptance by other American peace organizations. In 1981, the Coalition for a New Foreign and Military Policy, which included the National Council of Churches, the Union of American Hebrew Congregations, the War Resisters League, and other groups, by a vote of 18–4, with 4 abstentions, rejected the USPC's application for affiliation. According to the minutes of the meeting, the majority felt that it had to make clear that "the positions the Coalition takes that are critical of the U.S. government and its policies come from our own independent analysis and conclusions and are not influenced by organizations that may have associations of some sort with a foreign power."[72] Despite considerable contentiousness over this issue, the coalition held to this position until its demise in the summer of 1988.

On the other hand, both the USPC and the American Communist party have been accepted by Mobilization for Survival (MfS), an umbrella organization which had come into being in 1977 as a result of efforts by Sidney Lens and Sidney Peck. Lens was a former Trotskyist, Peck a onetime Communist party organizer. Both men had played a prominent role in the movement against the war in Vietnam and had long been involved in various united front activities. MfS today has some 200 affiliates, among them pacifist groups such as the Fellowship of Reconciliation and the War Resisters League, and a variety of environmental groups. Among its proclaimed goals are disarmament and the abolition of nuclear weapons. MfS is also for "nonintervention"; that is, it opposes the use of military power by the United States.

A self-portrait published in 1982 in the *Mobilizer,* the organization's journal, noted: "There is in this country a need for a political organization that has a clear and comprehensive left-of-center perspective . . . without being sectarian or a party, that is militantly antiwar without being exclusively pacifist, and that has a spiritual core without being rooted in organized religion."[73] The Mobilization is quite deliberately all-inclusive and has successfully resisted the efforts of some of its affiliates to limit the role of the Communists and other hard-left groups. Cofounder Sidney Peck, looking back on the first ten years of MfS, in 1987 expressed the hope that the American people eventually would reach an appreciation of the need for radical change in this country: "We know from history and experience that the private interests of the ruling groups in our country directly contravene the social, economic and political interests of the American people as a whole. And that when the American people are conscious of these differences, they will respond to programs of mass action."[74] In other words, Peck expected that the American people sooner or later would shed what Marxists call "false consciousness" and assume a truly revolutionary role. Quite clearly, for activists like Peck, MfS has a political agenda that transcends the search for peace.

During the 1970s and early 1980s, despite the fact that the Soviet Union strongly outspent the United States in arms expenditures, most segments of the peace movement spoke of the "myth of the Soviet threat." Not surprisingly, Communist propaganda made major efforts to support and strengthen this benevolent view of the Soviet Union. At the same time, the Communists stressed that they were not pacifists and that it was necessary to distinguish between just and unjust wars. The Soviet Union was said to be committed to peaceful coexistence with the capitalist West, but peaceful coexistence, it was argued until most recently, did not overrule the "immutable laws of historical development" which inevitably move the world toward the victory of Communism. "Peaceful coexistence," wrote a Soviet official in 1972, "applies only to relations among states and does not include the ideological struggle between the two systems, the class struggle in the capitalist states, or the national liberation movements of the oppressed peoples."[75] Soviet foreign policy was characterized as based on a Leninist policy of peace. However, "peace cannot be lasting until a just political and economic order has been secured for all the world's peoples."[76] Hence, "the CPSU and other Marxist-Leninist parties resolutely support the national liberation wars of oppressed peoples lending them assistance by all means possible under the given circumstances."[77]

In order to advance these objectives, the American Communist party continues to emphasize the importance of working with and within the non-Communist peace movement. In addition to the USPC, the Party uses for this purpose the National Council of American Soviet Friendship (NCASF), a front organization established in 1943.[78] The success which the Party has had in hiding its hand is illustrated by the following episode in which this author played a minor role. In October 1984, Alan C. Thomson, the executive director of the NCASF, was the featured speaker at a meeting in Northampton, Massachusetts, where I lived at the time. His visit was sponsored by an Ad Hoc Committee for Dialogue, Peace and Friendship with the USSR, which had the support of many well-meaning local residents. Publicity for the meeting described the NCASF as an organization with no governmental or political affiliation. A letter to the editor of the local newspaper, in which I pointed out the Communist connections of the NCASF, drew charges of slander. On February 7, 1989, Thomson was arrested by the FBI on charges of violating U.S. currency laws. He had just returned from the Soviet Union with $17,000 which he had received from the USSR Society for Friendship and Cultural Relations with Foreign Countries. Upon entering the U.S., he had failed to declare this sum of money and then proceeded to deposit it in two separate bank accounts in order to prevent the money from being reported by the banks. The arrest was reported in the *Washington Times* and *Washington Post* of February 8, but this kind of news is unlikely to reach the American hinterland where organizations like the NCASF ply their mischievous and deceptive trade.

Today, once again, the Communists look upon pacifists as allies. During the late 1930s, when the Soviet Union favored collective security, wrote a Communist publicist, pacifism had to be rejected because it sabotaged conditions for the defeat of Hitler. Now, however, when the socialist world and its allies in the Third World seek to prevent global war and contain U.S. imperialism and aggression, "pacifism becomes an ally, particularly within the aggressor country."[79] "The place of every Communist," urged James E. Jackson, a member of the Party's Politburo, in 1982, "is in this army of fighters for peace." Communists had to provide leadership and push the ideological struggle against the violators of unity. "We will not accept the legitimacy of anti-Communism. Anti-Communism is U.S. and world imperialism's preferred stock-in-trade device for dissolving the unity and power of the peoples for peace and progress." Communists, Jackson argued, had to drive home the point that "responsibility for the arms race and the peril to peace belongs exclusively to the powers of U.S. and world imperialism, which have the defeat of the Soviet Union and the national liberation movements as their designated objective." The Soviet Union was said to be *"the* great power for world peace." The fight for peace required solidarity with the "liberation struggles of oppressed peoples" and resistance to "all acts of U.S. intervention and all acts of aggression by imperialist powers."[80] In other words, aid to Communist-led guerrilla movements as in El Salvador is an act of solidarity and "socialist internationalism." American assistance to governments under attack represents "imperialist intervention."

In keeping with the Communist party's well-established policy of using other mass organizations as hunting grounds for converts, Jackson urged Party activists "to recruit from our contacts peace cadre into the Communist Party,"[81] yet even this frank acknowledgment of ulterior motives has not been allowed to stand in the way of cooperation. Demonstrations against American policy in Central America and South Africa or in opposition to U.S. arms control positions for many years now have been fully nonexclusive. The Communists refuse to accept any criticism of Soviet policies, and non-Communist peace activists have gone along with this demand in the interest of unity. Slogans at such demonstrations are based on the lowest common denominator, or what is called "minimum consensus." Concretely this means that the United States is routinely portrayed as the source of all the world's ills and problems. None of the marches and mobilizations against "interventionism" held in Washington in recent years has included demands for a Soviet withdrawal from Afghanistan or for a Cuban pull-out from Angola. One of the effects of this one-eyed view of the world is to undercut support for less-than-perfect allies of the United States in the Third World. Why, for example, should the American public in the long run continue to support countries like South Korea against its enemy in the North if all it hears is a steady barrage of criticism directed against human rights violations in South Korea but nothing against the infinitely worse human rights abuses in Communist North Korea?

During the early 1980s, non-Communist peace organizations like the American Friends Service Committee defended these coalitions as necessary to create a broad-based movement of protest against the Reagan administration's policies. The peace movement was said to have liberated itself from the repressive, red-baiting outlook of the 1950s. The relatively young leaders of these groups are blissfully ignorant of the fact that the peace movement's earlier opposition to such alliances with the Communists was formulated in the 1930s and 1940s—that is, well before the anti-communist hysteria of the 1950s—because of experience with the dire consequences of working with the Communists and not because the peace movement had succumbed to a Cold War mentality or compulsive anti-communism.

The Communists have expressed their satisfaction with this development. After the large demonstration held in New York City in June 1982 in conjunction with the special United Nations session on disarmament, an article in the Party's magazine *Political Affairs* noted that the peace movement now more and more rejected anticommunism. Contingents of the Party at the June demonstration had been well received. "During the entire campaign not once were they publicly red-baited."[82] In his report to the twenty-fourth convention of the Communist party in August 1987, General Secretary Gus Hall noted the decline of anti-Sovietism and anti-communism and stated that "the possibilities for a broad Left unity have increased greatly."[83] Following the approval of the INF treaty, Michael Myerson, head of the USPC, claimed that this milestone in disarmament had been made possible by "our active, principled opposition to anti-communism. . . . It helped us overcome division and mistrust within our own movement."[84]

E. P. Thompson, a leader of the British Campaign for Nuclear Disarmament, has repeatedly pointed out the danger of working with the Communists, and he has warned against collusion with the far-flung operations of the World Peace Council. His assertion that such cooperation would make the Western peace movement in effect a movement opposing NATO militarism only—a sure recipe for its political isolation—has found little support in the American peace movement. In an exchange with Thompson, the director of FOR's disarmament program, Norman Solomon, argued that the peace movement had to be careful that it did not "unwittingly reinforce chronic American-Soviet antipathies. . . . We cannot reduce our society's cold war fervor by adding to it."[85] Thompson, on the other hand, maintained that it was not honest to remain silent about the suppression of Solidarity, the Polish free trade union, or the persecution of the Group for the Establishment of Trust Between the USSR and USA, an independent peace organization in the Soviet Union established in June 1982. The problems of Western society, Thompson wrote, did not justify "fellow traveling sentimentalism" about the Soviet Union. The Soviet peace offensive was strictly for export. The Soviet Union made sure "that the infection of the peace movement is halted at its borders." Its peace offensive, Thompson pointed out in 1983, was directed toward the West, while at the same time the East was being placed under quarantine. With the independent peace movement effectively repressed, public opinion in the Soviet Union could scarcely influence the rulers of the country.[86]

Thompson has played a prominent role in European Nuclear Disarmament (END), an umbrella organization comprising several West European independent and non-Communist antinuclear groups. An American counterpart to END is the Campaign for Peace and Democracy/East and West, established in 1982, which stresses "the importance of breaking out of the Cold War straitjacket, of rejecting a choice between East and West."[87] The Campaign has protested the persecution of independent peace activists in Czechoslovakia, East Germany, and the Soviet Union. It was critical of the Soviet occupation of Afghanistan. Since the spring of 1984, the Campaign has published a magazine, *Peace & Democracy News*. The size of the group is not known, though it appears to be relatively small and not a major voice in the U.S. peace movement.

The activities of the Campaign for Peace and Democracy point up the ambiguous role Western peace groups play in the promotion of world peace even if they try to be evenhanded. In the early 1980s the Campaign opposed the deployment of Pershing II and cruise missiles in Europe. It also expressed opposition to the Russian SS-20 rockets targeted on Western Europe which the American deployment program aimed to counter. Yet, predictably, this agitation had an impact only in the West; the Soviet Union could easily ignore the pronouncements of those few Western peace activists who were sincerely interested in nuclear disarmament by both sides. Had the agitation against the deployment of the American missiles, pushed by the nuclear freeze and other peace organizations, succeeded, the Russians would have had no incentive to dismantle their missiles and to agree to the INF Treaty of 1987, which eventually banned all medium-range missiles.

The same dilemma arose in 1985 when the Campaign came out against American aid to the Contras, the armed resistance to the Sandinista regime in Nicaragua. A statement entitled "Independent Voices, East and West, Speak Out Against Reagan's Nicaragua Policy" and published as a large advertisement in major U.S. newspapers protested what was called "the Reagan administration's escalating war on Nicaragua." The nature of the Sandinista regime was said to be not the issue.

> We defend the democratic right of every nation to self-determination in complete freedom from superpower control, whether that domination is justified by the Brezhnev doctrine in Eastern Europe and Afghanistan, or by Reagan's claims of U.S. special interests in Central America and the Caribbean. The application of force against weaker nations blocks democratic social and political change, tightens the superpowers' grip on their respective blocs and spheres of influence, and fuels the arms race with catastrophic consequences for all of us. . . . We challenge the U.S. to set an example of non-interventionism, and we ask the Soviet Union to do the same in Eastern Europe and Afghanistan.[88]

In addition to officers of the Campaign for Peace and Democracy, the statement was signed by many former activists in the movement against the war in Vietnam such as Richard Barnet of the Institute for Policy Studies, Noam Chomsky, David McReynolds of the War Resisters League, Daniel Ellsberg, and Richard Falk. Also among the signatories were several members of the independent East European peace movement such as Sergei Batovrin, the founding member of the Trust Group in Moscow, who now lives in the U.S., and Gyorgy Konrad in Hungary. The statement was also signed by E. P. Thompson in Britain.

The statement on Nicaragua, typical of the thinking of those who take a position of moral equivalence toward America and the Soviet Union, ignored several important matters. It accepted without questioning the legitimacy of the Sandinista regime, while in point of fact the Sandinistas derived their power from appropriating the genuine democratic revolution that overthrew the Somoza dictatorship in order to build their own system of dictatorial rule. The statement equated the Brezhnev doctrine, which justified the continued domination of Eastern Europe by the Soviet Union, with the granting of aid to a native resistance movement that seeks to restore democracy. Most important, and raising the same issues discussed above with regard to the stationing of medium-range missiles in Europe, the opposition to aid to the Contras, despite a show of evenhandedness by also opposing Soviet hegemonic designs, necessarily had to have one-sided results. Until the advent of Mikhail Gorbachev's "new thinking," the Soviets ignored the call to abandon their grip on Eastern Europe and Afghanistan while the pressure on the U.S. to abandon the Nicaraguan resistance—playing on Western fears of war—could and indeed did prove highly effective. Good intentions and appeals for peace alone generally have little effect on the hard realities of world politics.

The Impact of Mikhail Gorbachev's "New Thinking"

Two recent developments in Soviet thinking about war and peace may introduce new dynamics into the relationship between the peace movement and the Communists. First, until very recently, the Soviet Union and its ideological instruments maintained a barrage of criticism against what they called the theory of "equal responsibility" held by segments of the Western peace movement like European Nuclear Disarmament (END). The *Peace Courier,* the monthly magazine of the World Peace Council (WPC), in October 1984 called it "pernicious" to claim "that the US and the Soviet Union share equal responsibility for the threat of nuclear war."[89] To blame both superpowers for the ongoing arms race was held to mask the real source of the danger of war. "Those who adhere to the position of dual responsibility," a Soviet magazine declared in early 1986, "are for all intents and purposes contributing to weakening the struggle for peace, since they cannot concentrate on the genuine enemy—imperialism."[90] "Imperialism" was the Soviet codeword for the United States; as the Soviets saw it, the struggle for peace had to be waged solely against the United States and its allies. This view led to friction between the WPC and END. There are indications that the Soviets' clumsy attempts to bend the Western peace movement to Soviet interests and steer it in an anti-American direction have recently given way to more conciliatory attitudes.

The meeting of the WPC held in Sofia in 1986 took up the tensions that had developed between the WPC and some segments of the Western peace movement. President Romesh Chandra was criticized for the bureaucratic manner in which he had run the organization, and this criticism was renewed with more vigor in 1988. Several articles and letters published in the *Peace Courier* charged that the WPC was too sectarian and had yet to accept the spirit of "new thinking" to which the Soviet Union under the leadership of Mikhail Gorbachev had committed itself. Changes were said to be needed in the structure and activities of the WPC. At the end of the year, the newsletter of the USPC announced that Chandra would not run for reelection. "So the discussion of changes in the WPC contains the recognition that the changes must include a change in leadership."[91]

The demand for "new thinking" in the WPC has not gone unchallenged. In November 1988, Johannes Pakashlahti, a Finn who had been general secretary of the WPC since 1986 and who was known as an advocate of "bloc-free" thinking and a greater role for the national affiliates, was stripped of his responsibilities by the WPC bureau. But the momentous events of the year 1989 quickly changed the political line-up once again. Following the downfall of Communist governments in Eastern Europe, national affiliates of the WPC in several of these countries dissolved themselves; the organization is said to be suffering a massive financial crisis. At a meeting in Moscow in December 1989, a representative of the newly formed Polish Peace Coalition called the WPC a "Stalinist organization," and there is now open talk of the possibility that the WPC may break up.[92]

The second new element involves the principle of "peaceful coexistence," which, as we have noted above, until recently was always considered by the Soviets as a specific form of the class struggle. Foreign Minister E. A. Shevardnadze, in a speech given at a conference of the Soviet Foreign Ministry on July 25, 1988, declared that this view was "erroneous" and indeed "anti-Leninist." The realities of the nuclear age and the crucial importance of economic strength to national security, Shevardnadze argued, required a new way of thinking about peaceful coexistence.

> Quite validly we refuse to see in it a specific form of class struggle. Co-existence which is based on such fundamental principles for all as non-aggression, respect for sovereignty, national independence, noninterference in internal affairs, and so forth, cannot be identified with the class struggle. This, of course, does not eliminate the patterns of class struggle and the thesis that a state's policy is determined by the interests of the classes ruling it. But these class interests can and should have common human interests as their common denominator.

The survival of mankind, Shevardnadze continued, depended on genuine coexistence, and "the clash between capitalism and socialism can occur solely and exclusively in the forms of peaceful competition and peaceful rivalry." There was need for the peaceful resolution of regional conflicts, confidence-building measures, and a reduction in the levels of military confrontation by relying on nonoffensive defense and "reasonable sufficiency" in weapons. The continuation of the arms race could bleed the enemy dry, "but truly at the price of undermining one's own economic and social base" and leading to economic exhaustion.[93] Earlier Soviet leaders, conceded Stanislav Kondrashov, a political columnist for *Izvestia,* had "exceeded all possible limits in building up military might in Europe and other regions of the world." This military burden had resulted "from exaggerated if not false notions about the West's aggressiveness. . . . Stalin exaggerated the hostility of the capitalist world in order to back up his thesis about the 'intensification of class struggle' and justify mass terror." There was need now "to 'de-ideologise' relations between states and accept the supremacy of human values over class interests. . . . Contrary to previous views, peaceful coexistence of socialism and capitalism is not a transitional period or form of class struggle, but the only natural means of survival in this pluralist world."[94]

Time will tell to what extent these new ideas will be followed by deeds. The signals so far are mixed. In a speech delivered during his visit to Cuba in April 1989, Gorbachev made repeated references to the glories of Castro's revolution and its role in helping "the tide of national liberation to reach unheard-of heights."[95] The year 1989 saw a surge of Soviet arms shipments to Afghanistan, Ethiopia, and Cambodia. As Secretary of State James A. Baker III noted with concern prior to the Malta Summit in 1989, Soviet-bloc weapons continued to end up in Nicaragua.[96] On the other hand, the Soviet Union has begun to cut back its large military forces, and its negotiators have made important concessions on methods of arms control, including previously rejected measures of verification.

Soviet officials have begun to downplay their role as the patron of black revolution in South Africa and to express their preference for a political settlement. "We do not want to emphasize the need to enlarge the armed struggle," declared Yuri Yukalov, head of the Foreign Ministry's Department of African Countries at a roundtable discussion in Moscow on March 15, 1989. "South Africa should not be destroyed. . . . There should be a dialogue."[97]

The change in line has been noticed and criticized by Western advocates of Third World revolution. "The new foreign policy stance toward Southern Africa," wrote an American supporter of the African National Congress, "is based on the same derelict reordering of priorities that caused China to abandon its theory of 'people's war' all over the globe. . . . Such a shift involves subverting and repressing one's revolutionary principles and spirit of proletarian internationalism to accommodate a new sense of urgency in dealing with domestic concerns."[98] In a press interview given prior to a clandestine congress of the South African Communist party held in 1989 and in an article published in the *World Marxist Review,* Joe Slovo, one of the top leaders of that party, sharply criticized the Soviet's Union's "new thinking" in international affairs as coming "dangerously close to prescribing the abandonment or the toning down of conflict in internal class struggles" in the interests of international equilibrium.[99]

Of course, this would not be the first time that the Soviet Union sacrificed its support of revolutionary movements to more pressing policy considerations. To mind come sudden switches like the adoption of the Popular Front line in 1935 or the abandonment of the antifascist struggle after the Hitler-Stalin Pact of 1939. Whatever the long-range results of the changes now under way in the Soviet Union, the American peace movement would probably be well advised not to ignore the historical record. Its credibility depends on being seen as a movement that defends the interests of the United States and of world peace rather than the ever-changing requirements of Soviet foreign policy.

10

The Travail
of Progressivism

Several American liberal organizations have had encounters with the Communist party, encounters that sometimes proved crucial to their very survival. The outcome of these contests has depended on many different factors. The adoption of formal constitutional provisions regulating the acceptability of Communists has been helpful though not necessarily decisive. The resolve of leaders to protect their organizations against Communist infiltration has been important. Last but not least, the location of these clashes, the kind of electoral system in existence, and the importance attributed by the Communists to the prize were often crucial in determining whether Communist takeovers would succeed.

The American Labor Party

During the presidential election of 1936, several union leaders in New York, who wished to support President Roosevelt but were unwilling to be identified with the corrupt Democratic machine of New York City, formed the American Labor party (ALP). New York electoral law made it possible for a candidate to be the nominee of more than one party. The new organization drew the support of Jews and Italians, resentful of the dominant role played by the Irish in Tammany Hall, the Democratic organization of Manhattan. Others to make common cause with the ALP were municipal reformers eager to improve New York City governance and the members of the Social Democratic Federation (SDF), the right-wing "Old Guard" who had recently broken away from the Socialist party.

Taking a leading role in the formation of the ALP were David Dubinsky of the International Ladies Garment Workers Union, Sidney Hillman of the Amalgamated Clothing Workers of America, and Alex Rose of the Milliners Union. The needle trade unions of New York were traditionally anticommunist, and so were the "Old Guard" Socialists. The new party therefore adopted provisions barring Communists or Communist-run unions from membership, but this rule was to prove less than effective. During the election of 1936 the Communists failed to poll the minimum number of votes necessary in order to continue to qualify as a political party. For this and other reasons they therefore decided to enter the ALP en masse. "The building of the American Labor Party," declared Party leader Israel Amter in December 1936, "is a central task" for the Communists.[1]

New York City had the largest concentration of Communists in the country—some 30,000 by 1938. Together with their sympathizers, they constituted a powerful voting bloc. The Party mobilized its forces and the results were soon apparent. Applying their great energy, the Communists helped organize district clubs and brought in new members. Given the traditional low turnout in primaries, the Communists found it easy to influence the outcome and thus the choice of party leaders. By 1938, they controlled the Manhattan organization of the ALP. The needle trade union leaders refrained from challenging the Communists because the Party worked loyally for ALP policies, such as support of the New Deal. The Communists also were weak in upstate New York and therefore did not appear to be a threat on the state committee of the party, the governing body of the ALP. That committee consisted of five members from each of the 150 assembly districts in the state. At the time, only 62 of these districts lay within New York City, and Communist strength in the city was therefore easily balanced by non-Communist members.[2]

The *New Leader* and other Socialists raised their voices against the growing power of the Communists. In May 1939, the labor lawyer Louis Waldman told the New York City convention of the Social Democratic Federation: "In Manhattan the Communists captured most of the clubs. In Brooklyn some clubs are fully dominated by the Communists. In others, though they were defeated, it was only by narrow margins. Considering the progress that they have made, it is only a matter of time before the Communists dominate the vast majority of ALP clubs in New York."[3] The convention thereupon called upon the ALP to enforce the constitutional provision against Communists, but this demand went unheeded.

The first showdown between non-Communists and Communists in the ALP came in the fall of 1939, following the Hitler-Stalin Pact. The ALP state committee passed a resolution denouncing the pact. It also expelled Mike Quill, the president of the Transport Workers Union, for echoing the Communist party's defense of the Nazi-Soviet agreement. Known in New York as "Red Mike," Quill never openly admitted his membership in the Communist party, but until his falling-out with the Party in 1948 he worked closely with the Communists and later admitted attending Party caucuses.[4] Quill's ouster was criticized by the *New Republic*. An editorial published in November 1939 agreed that the ALP "should free itself from Communist influence, and as a voluntary association has a perfect right to do so. This is not an infringement of civil liberties, so long as the Communists are allowed to have their own party and are not expelled from unions on account of party membership." On the other hand, it was wrong to apply "dogmatic tests of eligibility, carried out on the basis of suspicion and inquisitorial rituals."[5] Reacting to the editorial in a letter, Norman Thomas defended Quill's expulsion and accused the *New Republic* of "crypto-Stalinism."[6]

The struggle for control of the American Labor party continued. At the 1940 convention, the ALP leadership succeeded by a narrow margin in endorsing Roosevelt for a third term. The Communists by then had decided he was an imperialist and warmonger. ALP meetings during this period, writes a historian of New York State politics, "became so acrimonious that managers of hotels and convention halls shied away from renting space to the ALP for meetings, and police riot calls were frequent."[7] The Communists eventually succeeded in taking over the Brooklyn organization and they made gains in Queens. Getting control of the Bronx proved more difficult, for the garment-center workers living there were conscientious in attending club meetings and frustrated the tactics of the Communists by coming early and staying late.

By the fall of 1941, the Communists had captured the ALP organization in four of New York City's five boroughs. SDF leader Louis Waldman by then had resigned from the ALP, charging that it provided the Communist party with a respectable front behind which it could carry on its tactics of disruption. During the next three years ALP leaders Dubinsky and Rose increasingly lost ground. Dubinsky and Hillman had long had strained personal relations, exacerbated now by jurisdictional disputes between their two unions. In the spring of 1944, Hillman teamed up with the Communists in order to wrest control of the ALP from Dubinsky. In the primaries of that year the Hillman-Communist coalition swept all five New York City boroughs and also gained strength upstate. As a result, Hillman had the support of a majority of the ALP state committee, and he was elected chairman. At that point, Dubinsky and Rose led their followers out of the ALP and organized the anticommunist

Liberal party. The ILGWU's newspaper *Justice* noted: "The primary results leave no doubt that Mr. Earl Browder has captured the American Labor Party."[8]

The Liberal party was at first small, but it made steady gains and continues to this day as a significant political force that seeks to keep the New York Democratic party honest. The ALP, on the other hand, started a period of gradual decline. In 1948 it became an important organizing force behind the candidacy of Henry Wallace, at which point the Amalgamated Clothing Workers withdrew from it. In April 1948, Mike Quill resigned and denounced "the screwballs and crackpots who will continue to carry on as if the Communist Party and the American Labor Party were the same house with two doors."[9] In August 1950, Lee Pressman, formerly general counsel of the Congress of Industrial Organizations (CIO) and until then a secret member of the Communist party, announced his resignation. The policies and activities of the ALP, Pressman charged, "do not represent the democratic or progressive interests or aspirations of the American people but rather the Communist party."[10] The ALP lost its status as a legal entity in New York State in 1954 when it failed to muster the 50,000 votes necessary to stay on the ballot. The party was formally dissolved in October 1956. The Communists by then had lost all interest in the ALP. An organization without innocents to create a façade of respectability was of no use to them.

Henry Wallace and the Progressive Party

Henry Wallace was never a fellow traveler of the Communist party, but like many American liberals during the days of the Popular Front of the 1930s and 1940s he held a highly simplistic view of the Soviet Union. Russia, he declared in an address at Ohio Wesleyan University in March 1943, did not want to conquer the world. Communism was rooted in poverty, not the machinations of the Soviets. It would succeed only if the West failed to solve the problems of poverty and unemployment.[11] On a trip to Siberia in 1944 Wallace had no eyes for Stalin's slave labor camps there and instead waxed enthusiastically about the grandeur that comes when men work wisely with nature. Dwight MacDonald characterized Wallace's mindset harshly but probably not inaccurately when he wrote: "Wallace land is the mental habitat of Henry Wallace plus a few hundred thousand regular readers of *The New Republic, The Nation* and *PM*. It is a region of perpetual fogs, caused by the warm winds of the liberal Gulf Stream coming in contact with the Soviet glacier."[12]

Wallace believed the Soviet Union had achieved economic democracy while avoiding some of the abuses of political democracy. The United States, on the other hand, needed somewhat less political democracy and more social justice. Both Russia and America, he was fond of saying, favored the common man. The American and Russian peoples should insist on pushing the "people's revolution," which would guarantee the peace of the world and the "century of the common man." In a speech at Madison Square Garden in New York City on September 12, 1946, Wallace stressed the importance of a soft policy toward the Soviet Union. "The tougher we get, the tougher the Russians will get." When the pro-Soviet audience booed some references perceived as anti-Soviet, Wallace omitted other critical allusions to the Soviet Union in order to quiet the crowd.[13] The *New Republic* praised the speech: "We lead the world as progressives or not at all. In voicing our progressive spirit, Wallace stands as a world leader."[14]

Wallace had been secretary of agriculture and later a Vice President in the Roosevelt administration. At the time of the Madison Square Garden speech he served as President Truman's secretary of commerce. Even though Truman held a rather different view of the world and American-Soviet relations, he had approved the text of the speech. But there were many unfavorable reactions to Wallace's address, and, under pressure from his secretary of state, James F. Byrnes, Truman forced Wallace's resignation. The *New Republic,* seeking to support the dismissed secretary's fight for peace, offered him the editorship of the liberal magazine. Wallace accepted. He wrote a weekly column, but otherwise did not play a very active role. "The *New Republic,*" writes a historian of the period, "presented Wallace a stage on which to play the role of liberal public figure."[15]

Wallace and the *New Republic* were not the only voices critical of President Truman. To many liberals it appeared that Truman would undo many of the achievements of the Roosevelt era. Labor leaders like David Dubinsky were unhappy with the President's policies on inflation and housing, and so was Dubinsky's rival, Sidney Hillman. In 1944 Hillman had created the National Citizens Political Action Committee (NCPAC) which brought together Communists and well-known liberals such as Freda Kirchwey and Max Lerner, as well as businessmen, labor leaders, and bankers—a replay of the Popular Front. Like John Lewis in the thirties, Hillman sought to tap the organizational energy of the Communists. The group's executive secretary was C. B. ("Beanie") Baldwin, a secret Communist. In December 1946, the NCPAC, leaderless since the death of Hillman earlier that year, united with a genuine Communist auxiliary, the Independent Citizens Committee of the Arts, Sciences and Professions, to form the Progressive Citizens of America (PCA). The new organization stated its willingness to accept "all progressive men and women in our nation, regardless of race, creed, color, national origin or political affiliation." The door to Communists, it was thus made clear, was open. Avowed anticommunists did not attend the gathering.[16]

The PCA chose the progressive label in order to present itself as an authentic American radical movement and in an attempt to capture the prestige, and perhaps some of the adherents, of Robert LaFollette's Progressive movement of 1924. As Arthur Schlesinger, Jr., pointed out at the time, this was a rather unscrupulous maneuver because LaFollette had vigorously opposed any cooperation with the Communists. "To pretend that the Communists can work with the Progressives who believe in democracy," LaFollette had written, "is deliberately to deceive the public." The Communists, he had argued, are enemies of democracy. "I believe, therefore, that all Progressives should refuse to participate in any movement which makes common cause with any Communist organization." There was little excuse, Schlesinger charged, for Henry Wallace to appropriate "the name of LaFollette's party while abandoning LaFollette's unconditional opposition to totalitarianism."[17]

Wallace was the featured speaker at the founding conference of the Progressives, and he cheered the gathering by expressing sharp criticism of the Democratic party, to which he was still nominally committed. "We have less use for a conservative, high-tariff Democratic Party," he declared, "than we have for a reactionary, high-tariff Republican Party. If need be we shall first fight one and then the other." The preamble of the group's program also raised the issue of a third party: "We cannot . . . rule out the possibility of a new political party. . . . We, the people, will not wait forever—we will not wait long for the Democratic Party to make its choice."[18]

During the spring of 1947 Wallace went on an extensive national speaking tour. By now he was spreading hints that he might head a third-party ticket. In May he told newsmen in Olympia, Washington, that he would lead a third-party effort if he thought doing so would help prevent war. In September Wallace declared that he would continue fighting within the Democratic party to "prevent it from committing suicide," but that, if the Democrats continued in their present direction, "the people must have a new party of liberty and peace."[19] Pressure on Wallace to commit himself to an independent course was building from several left-run CIO unions and the PCA.

Speaking to large and enthusiastic audiences in various parts of the United States and during a highly publicized tour of England and the Continent, Wallace sharply attacked the Truman Doctrine and continued to plead for peace and understanding with Russia. His opposition to the

Marshall Plan was more ambivalent, but the combined effect of these pronouncements was, nevertheless, to highlight his closeness to the pro-communist left in the PCA, and this convergence of views began to hurt him politically. Yet for the PCA there was no turning back. In mid-December 1947, its executive committee voted to request Wallace to seek the presidency on an independent ticket. On December 20, Wallace announced his candidacy; the second convention of the PCA, meeting in January 1948, endorsed Wallace and laid the groundwork for the formation of a third party.[20]

The Communists, as we will see, played a key role in the Progressive movement and the Wallace campaign. This campaign began, as Wallace put it, like "Gideon's Army," but turned out to be, as Wallace later acknowledged, "a division of Stalin's foreign legion."[21] This raises the question of what part the Communists had in the formation of the Progressive party and the Wallace candidacy. When did the Communists decide to go all-out in support of a third party?

There was talk about the possible creation of a "broad people's party" as early as February 1946, after the ouster of Earl Browder, but no commitment appears to have been made until the fall of 1947. At that point, two important considerations were involved in the decision finally to press ahead with the formation of a third party. On October 5, representatives of nine Communist parties had met in Poland to form the Communist Information Bureau (Cominform). In a speech at that meeting, Soviet leader Andrei Zhdanov stressed the menace of American imperialism and the need to prevent war and fascism. The American Communists apparently decided that their contribution to this struggle would be to press ahead with the formation of a broad-based antiwar party, a coalition in which the working class, led by the Communist party, would play the leading role. The second impetus was provided by rumors that the Truman administration was about to arrest the leading Communist leaders. This information came from O. John Rogge, a former assistant attorney general, who claimed to have heard about these repressive steps from Attorney General Tom C. Clark. In the eyes of the Communists this threat confirmed their fears of an imminent American fascism and led to preparations to go underground. In these circumstances, it was believed, the existence of a Communist-dominated Progressive party would provide cover and protection for Communist cadres.[22]

After breaking with the Communists, Michael Quill revealed that in late October of 1947 he had attended a meeting between several left-wing labor leaders and high Communist officials, in which the possibility of a third party was discussed. The final decision to form a third-party ticket headed by Wallace apparently was conveyed by the Communists to friendly union leaders at another meeting held on December 15. Shortly thereafter the PCA announced that they had asked Wallace to run.[23]

The prominent role which the Communists had played in the creation of the Wallace candidacy shocked some PCA members. Frank Kingdon, a co-chairman of the organization, concluded that he had underestimated Communist control of the PCA and that he could no longer work with the Communists. Wallace, he wrote in the *New York Post* on December 31, was the hand-picked candidate of the Communists. "I am no red-baiter. I believe it possible for American liberals to cooperate with Communists for social ends immediately desirable. The saddest lesson I learned in 1947 was that this is impossible. . . . All citizens, including Communists, have a right to put forward a candidate. All I am saying is that their candidate is theirs. They are his sponsors. He is named by them to serve their ends."[24]

The Communists probably never expected to win the election of 1948. Their main aim, at this point in time, was to create an independent "people's party." They hoped to defeat Truman, the architect of a strong anticommunist foreign policy, expecting that the isolationist elements in the Republican party would force a Republican President to conduct a much less assertive foreign policy. For Wallace, too, next to getting even with Truman for removing him from his cabinet post, peace was the most important issue. He hoped that a large vote for him would have a moderating impact on whoever won the presidency. As it turned out, the Wallace vote was to be far smaller than expected.

The large progressive people's movement expected by Wallace and his supporters never developed. The Progressives drew some support from students and left-leaning liberals, but the numbers were disappointing. Even procommunist labor leaders were less than enthusiastic in backing the third-party ticket, fearing that such endorsements would split their unions and create problems with the CIO leadership. That leadership vigorously opposed the Wallace candidacy and put much effort into convincing the CIO affiliates to work for the Democratic ticket.

World events and Wallace's reactions to them further damaged the Progressives. In October 1947, the national board of the PCA had condemned both the Truman Doctrine and the Marshall Plan for "all but destroying the unity which existed among the nations that fought the Axis in World War II."[25] In January 1948, Wallace put forth his own alternative to the Marshall Plan, a reconstruction fund to be administered by the United Nations which would provide aid to any needy nation. This proposal happened to be largely identical with a plank of the PCA. Under such a plan American funds would have gone to Communist countries; this idea proved highly unpopular.[26]

On February 25, 1948, the Communists seized power in Czechoslovakia. The Beneš government had shared power with the Communists, but when the Communists overthrew this last outpost of democracy in Eastern Europe it proved to many the futility of such cooperation. Wallace deplored the death of Czech democracy, but argued that it was the result of American provocations and the Cold War, which he was going to end. A bit later, Wallace criticized the American airlift, organized in the wake of the Russian blockade of West Berlin. The blatant manner in which Wallace followed the Communist line frightened away potential supporters. Wallace seemed determined to confirm the charges of his opponents that the Progressive movement identified with the interests of a foreign power. A Wallace presidency, it was widely feared, would mean surrendering to Soviet aggression.

For liberal journalists such as Max Lerner, Wallace's apology for the Czech coup was the last straw. Liberals, he wrote, had to defend the rights of Communists, but they could not work with them. This was the lesson of Czechoslovakia, which "demonstrated for all except the willfully blind that the Communists use a Popular Front only as long as it is useful to them and smash it at their first chance to capture power."[27]

The Wallace candidacy was hurt even more by the prominent and overbearing role of the Communists in the Progressive movement. The Party instructed its members to seek positions of leadership at all levels of the organization; the aggressive manner in which the Communists carried out this call and quickly attained control of numerous local organizations antagonized many non-Communist progressives. Wallace himself showed no interest in organizational and administrative matters and ignored Communist influence in his campaign. To make things worse, in April the Communist party announced the beginning of a drive for 15,000 new members, to be recruited from the ranks of labor, youth, and the Progressive Citizens of America. "The Grass Roots Movement which is rallying millions of Americans to the new People's Party," the Communist leaders proclaimed with their usual hyperbole, "reaches into thousands of towns and communities never before stirred to political action. In these towns and communities hundreds of men and women are awakening to the basic issues of our time. Some of them are ready not only for the New Party's answers but for the more basic answers only our Communist party can give."[28] By thus using the Wallace campaign as a hunting ground for new converts, the Communists further alienated many of the moderates among the Progressives.

The defensive manner in which Wallace handled the touchy issue of Communist support for his candidacy proved equally damaging. Such explanations ranged from professions of ignorance about the political nature of communism to assertions that it would be undemocratic to discriminate against people just because they hold communist beliefs. Most basically, Wallace was a sincere believer in the ideals of the Popular Front. The Communists he had met, he was fond of saying, were good Americans and to denounce them was red-baiting. When asked in May 1947 whether he would accept the support of known Communists, Wallace replied: "Anyone who will work for peace is okay with me. . . . Folks have found out they don't have to be scared of the word 'communism,' this word 'red' seems to lose its terror."[29] To affirm the principles of openness, Wallace felt, was particularly important at a time of growing anticommunist feeling. "I am not afraid of Communism," he declared during his national speaking tour in the spring of 1947. "If I fail to cry out that I am anti-Communist, it is not because I am friendly to Communism but because at this time of growing intolerance I refuse to join even the outer circle of men who stir up the steaming cauldron of hatred and fear."[30]

As his campaign for the presidency got under way and the Communists assumed an increasingly visible role in it, Wallace began to fear the stigma of his association with the Communists. He continued to defend the right of the Communists to be an active political force, but he also began to acknowledge the political cost of Communist support. In an interview with Edward R. Murrow in Albuquerque, New Mexico, in June of 1948, Wallace stated: "According to the newspapers, I'm getting a lot of support from the Communists, and the Communist leaders seem to think they have to endorse me every day or so. There's . . . no question that this sort of thing is a political liability." He then affirmed once again his position of nonexclusion. "I will not repudiate any support which comes to me on the basis of interest in peace. . . . If you accept the idea that Communists have no right to express their opinions then you don't believe in democracy. And if you accept the notion that it is impossible to live in a world with sharply differing opinions, then you accept the inevitability of war. I don't believe in the inevitability of war. I do believe in democracy. If, during the war, we had accepted the idea that you don't work with Communists, we might not have succeeded in our joint efforts to stop Hitler."[31]

A few days later, in Burlington, Vermont, Wallace went even further in expressing his unhappiness at the role of the Communists in his campaign, a role he felt unable to repudiate on grounds of both principle and practical necessity: "If the Communists would have a ticket of their own, the New Party would lose 100,000 votes but gain four million."

Wallace repeated this statement on June 28 at a lawn party in Center Sandwich, New Hampshire: "I'm never going to say anything in the nature of Red-baiting. But I must say this: if the Communists would run a ticket of their own this year, we might lose 100,000 votes but we would gain three million. I know if the Communists really wanted to help us, they would run their own ticket this year and let us get those extra votes."[32] The Communists, of course, had their own plans and were not about to accommodate Wallace. The hapless Wallace ended up with paying the price adherents of the Popular Front usually have to pay for their alliance with the Communists.

Liberal Anticommunism Reaffirmed: Americans for Democratic Action

The Progressive party was formally launched at a convention held in Philadelphia during the last week of July. The control of the Communists and their reliable friends over the machinery of the organization was by then assured, but a liberal, anticommunist organization, Americans for Democratic Action (ADA), decided to use the opportunity to engage their opponent at close quarters. For this purpose it dispatched to Philadelphia its executive secretary, James Loeb, who was to present the ADA position before the platform committee of the Progressive party.

ADA had its origins in a small group of socialist and liberal intellectuals of the prewar period, Union for Democratic Action (UDA), organized in 1941, and having the well-known theologian Reinhold Niebuhr as its first chairman. Niebuhr had been a member of the Socialist party and he was a former pacifist. Most of the other members were likewise Socialists opposed to the isolationism of party leader Norman Thomas. The organization was unique in excluding Communists from membership, thus putting it ahead even of the ACLU, which barred Communists from being officers but not from membership.[33]

The executive director of UDA was James Loeb, Jr., who in the spring of 1946 began to explore the idea of broadening the small group. In a letter published in the *New Republic* in May of that year, Loeb called on American progressives and liberals to face up to the complexities of the world situation and to commit themselves to the defense of human freedom. It was not enough, he argued, to blame all problems on the United States and to consider economic security the sole object of the progressive movement. Democratic progressives, Loeb maintained furthermore, could not strive for the goals of economic betterment and individual liberty within the same organization as the Communists.

No united-front organization will long remain united; it will become only a "front." This is sometimes, but not always, due to the fact that the Communists are more active, more consecrated, more zealous than their liberal associates. More pertinent is the fact that independent liberals, whether we like it or not, simply will not group themselves into a disciplined, semiconspiratorial caucus whose aim is to retain or obtain control of the organization. Thus they are handicapped in their competition with even a small number of disciplined Communists who automatically follow their own leadership and make use of any legitimate differences of opinion to further their own strategic advantage.[34]

On January 3, 1947, UDA convened a conference in Washington, D.C., which brought together over four hundred liberals, ready to establish a progressive anticommunist organization. This was the beginning of Americans for Democratic Action (ADA). The new group included many of the big names in American liberalism. There were labor leaders David Dubinsky and Walter Reuther; former New Dealers such as Eleanor Roosevelt, Leon Henderson, and Paul A. Porter; and well-known intellectuals such as Elmer Davis, Stewart Alsop, Morris Ernst, John Kenneth Galbraith, Arthur Schlesinger, Jr., and Reinhold Niebuhr. The gathering approved a declaration of principles which rejected "any association with Communists or sympathizers with Communism as completely as we reject any association with Fascists or their sympathizers. Both are hostile to the principles of freedom and democracy on which this Republic has grown great." Article II, section 2 of the constitution adopted by ADA barred from membership any person "who is a member or follower of a totalitarian organization or who subscribes to totalitarian political beliefs or who does not in good faith accept the basic principles of Americans for Democratic Action."[35]

Max Lerner criticized ADA for excluding Communists and for equating them with fascists. Freda Kirchwey of the *Nation* argued similarly that it was wrong to lump together Communists and fascists and she deplored the disagreement between ADA and the Progressive Citizens of America (PCA), established a month earlier, over the Communist issue. There was no need for two liberal organizations.[36] James Loeb, secretary-treasurer of ADA, responded to these arguments in a lengthy "Letter of the Week" in the *New Republic*. The question whether liberals could or should cooperate with the Communists, Loeb argued, was not trivial. Rejection of any alliance with Communists and their apologists was "an essential prerequisite to the aggressive fight for democracy that we propose to wage. No movement that maintains a double standard on the issue of human liberty can lay claim to the American liberal tradition." Ties with the Communists bestowed a political kiss of death. The ADA's unequivocal rejection of such links expressed "the painfully acquired conviction of American progressives that there can be no organizational compatibility between Communists and liberals, regardless of any coincidental agreement on specific issues."[37]

The battle lines between two kinds of liberalism and progressivism were thus drawn. In the eyes of the PCA one could not be a liberal and an anticommunist; the exclusion of Communists amounted to red-baiting. ADA, on the other hand, regarded the Communists as a menace to the vitality and independence of American liberalism and therefore opposed any cooperation with them. Members of ADA were resolved not to forget the calamities that had resulted from previous attempts at a united front, and they rejected the accusation, thrown at them then and later, that they were leading an anticommunist witch hunt. As the Hollywood liberal Philip Dunne has put it in his memoirs: "To differ publicly with Communists, which we did, is hardly the same thing as persecuting them, which we did not."[38]

The first annual convention of ADA was held in Philadelphia in late February 1948 and condemned the third-party candidacy of Henry Wallace: "It is an established fact that it owes its origin and principal organizational support to the Communist Party of America." The only result could be to elect a reactionary and isolationist Congress.[39] At the same time ADA continued its effort to defend the exclusion of Communists in the court of liberal opinion. Writing in *Commentary*, the journalist Robert Bendiner insisted that to call a Communist a Communist was not red-baiting but simply an adherence to correct labeling. There was no right to anonymity which facilitated the infiltration of liberal organizations by Communists. The Communists were numerically weak, but they also were "a source of untold mischief." To keep them out of ADA was therefore a necessary measure in order to cope with their secret and conspiratorial tactics of deceit. Moreover, Bendiner argued, the Communists' "entire philosophy, not to mention their current political line, is utterly at variance" with that of ADA.[40]

In July Loeb stated ADA's political position before the platform committee of the Progressive party. ADA had fought for a strong and unequivocal declaration on civil rights in the United States at the Democratic convention. Accordingly, Loeb declared, "we propose to concentrate here on making sure that solicitude for freedom and minority rights does not wither away beyond the three-mile limit. We challenge the new party to renounce its double standard of political morality; to make clear that it opposes the police state and totalitarian dictatorship everywhere in the world—whether in Mississippi or in the Soviet Union." The third party, Loeb pointed out, "has an unprecedented opportunity—possibly its last— to show its independence of communism and totalitarianism." It could do so by supporting the Marshall Plan and by withdrawing third-party candidates from congressional and local races. These candidates had no chance of being elected and would only help reactionary and isolationist Republicans defeat valuable liberals such as Paul Douglas in Illinois and Hubert Humphrey in Minnesota.

Loeb expressed his doubt that the Progressive party, an instrument of Soviet policy, would follow this advice. The presence of Wallace at the head of the ticket did not obscure the fact that "the Communists and their collaborators guide the major policies and word the major pronouncements of this party."

> We know that we speak for the great non-Communist liberal and labor majority when we state our conviction that your movement is a dangerous adventure undertaken by cynical men in whose hands Henry A. Wallace has placed his political fortunes. It is our conviction that, were the Communists to withdraw from your party today, your organization would soon join that long list of discarded groups which testify eloquently to the inevitable failure of the so-called "united front"—which always becomes decreasingly united and increasingly "front."[41]

Loeb's testimony was headline news all over the country. Until then, charges that the Progressive party had come under Communist domination had been made for the most part by right-wing papers such as the *Chicago Tribune*. Many liberal readers had reacted to these allegations with skepticism. ADA, however, had unquestionable liberal credentials, and its challenge to the Progressive party therefore had a far stronger impact.

The End of Progressivism

The publicity resulting from Loeb's appearance benefited ADA, but it was unable to stop Communist control of the Progressive party convention. Every committee was staffed by Communists and their reliable allies. The chairman of the platform committe was Rexford Tugwell, one of the few genuine liberals in the upper reaches of the party machinery, but he was flanked by men such as Lee Pressman, former general counsel of the CIO and a secret Communist, and veteran fellow travelers such as Professor Frederick Schumann of Williams College and singer Paul Robeson. The platform of the new party therefore faithfully reflected the Communist line. It condemned the Marshall Plan and the American proposals for control of atomic energy. The domestic plank called for the nationalization of the largest banks, the railroads, the merchant marine, the electric power and gas industry, and other industries primarily dependent upon government purchases.[42] There were some comic moments as well. When Congressman Vito Marcantonio, for many years a close ally of the Communists, rose to speak, he began with a robust "Com—" only to correct himself quickly and, in embarrassment, shift to "Fellow Delegates."[43]

Communist and procommunist control of the proceedings manifested itself during the discussion of the platform. As the convention was about to adopt the foreign policy section, James Hayford, a delegate from Vermont, proposed an amendment stating, "It is not our intention to give blanket endorsement to the foreign policy of any nation." This timid appeal for a less one-sided view of the world was buried in a flood of rhetoric protesting such a concession to reaction. "In rapid succession," recalled James Wechsler, "American Communist dignitaries and others who were trying to imitate the accents of earnest, idealistic liberals rose to announce that they were shocked by these words. . . . Thus while it was deemed the height of political propriety to accuse the American Government of every form of sin from fratricide to genocide, it was intolerable to state in explicit form the possibility that Moscow might deserve criticism."[44] Rex Tugwell and Lee Pressman helped defeat the amendment by arguing that the point was already in the platform. To demonstrate this, Pressman referred to a statement in the platform that stated that avoiding war was the joint responsibility of Russia and the United States.[45]

Another embarrassing incident involved a plank supporting independence for Macedonia from Greece, a longstanding demand of the Communists. However, since the draft of the platform had been printed the Macedonians had turned for help to Marshal Tito of Yugoslavia, which was now in revolt against Moscow. The provision dealing with Macedonian independence was therefore hastily stricken from copies of the platform distributed to the delegates. When a delegate from Minnesota questioned the discrepancy he was silenced by an "explanation" that nobody could understand. Bill Lawrence, who was covering the convention for the *New York Times,* Wechsler recalls, leaned over to him and murmured: "What in God's name are these people trying to do—hang themselves?"[46]

Otherwise everything proceeded according to script. Wallace was duly nominated. His acceptance speech explained once again why the Communists were so pleased with him. Speaking of the Berlin airlift, Wallace declared: "We gave up Berlin politically and we can't lose anything by giving it up militarily in a search for peace."[47] It is probable that this and other speeches delivered by Wallace were written by his principal ghostwriter, Lewis Frank, Jr., a man of pronounced procommunist views. Wallace's extemporaneous campaign speeches are said to have been quite different in both tone and content from his prepared speeches for large gatherings, composed for him by Frank and other speechwriters.[48]

On August 24, Wallace finally made a statement on the Communist issue that, had it been issued months earlier, might have helped his campaign. In an interview in Louisville, Kentucky, Wallace stated, "I solemnly pledge that when I am elected President neither the Communists nor the Fascists nor any other group will control my policies."[49] But by August 1948, such a declaration could no longer turn things around. Even the *Nation* was sufficiently disgusted by the Communist capers at the convention to come out against Wallace. Nobody was going to be fooled by the party's name into thinking that this new Progressive party in any way resembled those of Theodore Roosevelt or Robert LaFollette, Freda Kirchwey declared in an editorial. "The new party's platform and the speeches of Mr. Wallace and Senator Taylor echoed the party line closely enough to dispel any idea that a break with the Communists is likely." The failure of the platform to couple its critique of American foreign policy with a corresponding criticism of the Soviet Union, Kirchwey argued, would repel independent voters. The repudiation of the Marshall Plan also was a bad mistake. "Only a handful will accept the thesis that it [the European Recovery Program] is nothing more than a 'capitalist conspiracy' to enslave the world and force it to buy American goods."[50]

When the votes were counted in November, Wallace's showing turned out to be the disaster many had predicted. The Progressive ticket received a mere 1,157,140 votes, 2.37 percent of the total and less than that cast for the Dixicrat candidate, Strom Thurmond. Truman won reelection despite a three-way split in the Democratic camp and in the face of forecasts of sure defeat made by the pollsters.

Wallace himself emerged from defeat bitter and increasingly detached from public affairs. He now spent most of his time on his farm, devoting himself to an earlier love, agriculture. It was said that he remained a member of the Progressive party out of a sense of loyalty to the surviving non-Communist progressives. Wallace briefly attended the second convention of the Progressive party held in Chicago in February of 1950 and in a major address belatedly tried to draw a line between the Progressive party and the Communists. It had been a mistake, he conceded, to turn down the Vermont resolution which had sought to make it clear that the Progressive party did not want to provide a blanket endorsement of the foreign policy of any nation. "We must not allow anyone the slightest, legitimate reason for believing that any working member of our

Party puts Rome, Moscow or London ahead of the United States." It also was necessary, Wallace declared, to give the American people the facts about the attitude of the Progressive party toward the Communists.

The way in which Wallace carried out this attempt at clarifying the Communist issue demonstrated that his political thinking had changed but little. It was inevitable, Wallace began, "that all peace-loving people in times like these should be attacked as Communist dupes." In fact, he insisted, "the policies of the Progressive party are its own. . . . Our policies are not determined and controlled by anyone who owes his supreme allegiance to any other party and we do not—and will not—permit any organized factions or groups within our party." The principles of the Progressive party, Wallace continued, were different from those of the Communist party. "Our program is based upon progressive capitalism, not socialism. . . . It is the only program that can save capitalism from itself."

The Progressive party, Wallace reasserted, sought the support of "all those who believe wholeheartedly in it no matter what party they belong to. We will not attempt the purge of any individual because of past or present labels." At the same time, the Progressive party had to convince the American people that it fought for peace because the world needed peace and not because any foreign power wanted it. "We must make it clear that there are no concealed strings manipulating us." The Progressive party also had to show that civil liberties are indivisible. "We believe in civil liberties in Eastern Europe but we recognize that except for Czechoslovakia there has been no democratic tradition on which to build." Wallace concluded with another affirmation of the distinctiveness of the two parties: "The Communists have their party. We have ours. We agree with the Communists that peace with Russia is possible—but that doesn't make us Communists."[51]

The Communists had no problem with this speech and its recommendations. The convention this time did approve a resolution stating that both the United States and the Soviet Union had made mistakes in foreign policy. Otherwise, all remained as before, in fact more so. Wallace's tame words of independence notwithstanding, nobody could have any illusions about the continuing key role of the Communists in the Progressive party. I. F. Stone was one of the few well-known non-Communists still defending the idea of a Popular Front with the Communists and expressing his admiration for Wallace, whom he called "the heir to Roosevelt, a giant in the pygmy world of the Left, a man with international prestige."[52]

A few months later, in August 1950, Wallace resigned from the Progressive party when the Progressives, following their mentors, condemned the U.S.–U.N. defense of South Korea. The Communists now attacked him savagely, listing Wallace among the "enemies of mankind."[53] Many of the remaining non-Communist leaders resigned with him. The Progressive party still lingered on for several years, but without a non-Communist following it eventually expired. In an interview with Edwin A. Lahey, in the *Chicago Daily News* of March 31, 1951, Wallace finally conceded what had been obvious to others for a long time: "You know, I didn't actually realize how strong the Communists were in the Progressive Party. I think now that they were out to knife me."[54]

The collapse of the Progressive party gave rise to discussions and recriminations that have continued to the present day. For a time, the dismal failure of the Wallace movement seemed to prove the bankruptcy of Popular Front and pro-Soviet thinking. "The crushing setback suffered by the Progressive Party," wrote James Wechsler in 1953, "marked the turning point in American communist fortunes in the decade of the forties. They never recovered from the blow."[55] More recently, some authors in line with the currently fashionable anti-anticommunism, have resurrected the heroic image of Wallace and the ideas for which he stood. "With his prophetic fight against the Cold War crusade at home and abroad," writes Richard J. Walton, "he established himself as one of America's authentic heroes." Wallace led a "courageous but futile struggle against the Cold War policies of Harry Truman" which eventually led the country into the Indochinese civil war. According to Walton, the Communists supported Wallace, but they did not dominate the Progressive party. "Communists were an important and influential part of the Progressive party. That was so, and there was no moral or ethical reason why it should not have been so. Communists should have the same rights of political participation as other Americans." Wallace, argues Walton, "almost uniquely among important political figures, saw Communists as humans, not devils."[56]

The notion that the kind of conciliatory policy toward the Soviets favored by Wallace would have prevented the Cold War or Communist expansionism is highly questionable. Equally dubious is the idea that the exclusion of Communists from a political movement represents a denial of civil rights. Wallace, like many other liberals, could have repudiated both anticommunist hysteria and Communist support for his movement. The Communists were not devils, but they had richly earned their reputation of moral depravity and political deviousness. For years they had faithfully and obtusely defended the crimes of Stalin, acknowledged by today's Soviet rulers. They had built a long track record of wrecking organizations and causes with which they allied themselves. There thus were ample reasons to consider the Communists as unacceptable partners.

The Progressive party was not a typical Communist front, but, as even friendly historians like Norman D. Markowitz admit, the Communists were the indispensable core of the Progressive movement. The Communist party created the Progressive party; its cadres ran the presidential campaign and wrote Wallace's key speeches. Communist control of the Wallace campaign was helped by Wallace's muddled political thinking and by the gradual withdrawal of non-Communist elements from the Progressive party. Rexford Tugwell and others have suggested that a more active role played by moderates could have prevented Communist domination,[57] but that assumption is questionable. It was extremely difficult for liberals to rival the organizational efficiency of the Communists, especially in a situation where Wallace, the nominal leader of the movement, was weak and manipulable. At the same time, it is no doubt true that Communist influence grew in direct proportion to the flight of non-Communists from the movement until eventually they were left in full control. Paradoxically, this success also guaranteed failure. A Progressive party dominated by the Communists could neither win an electoral victory nor become the kind of popular mass movement the Communists had set out to create.

The Expulsion of the Communists from the CIO

Another unintended consequence of Wallace's third-party movement was to bring to a head the Communist issue in the Congress of Industrial Organizations (CIO). The decision of a majority of the CIO board in early 1948 to oppose a third party and the insistence of several Communist-dominated unions to support the Progressive party ticket were key factors in the expulsion of these unions from the CIO in 1949.

Tensions within the CIO had begun to build at the end of World War II. The Communists at that time controlled international unions with a membership of about one million, or about 15 percent of the CIO's total, and they used this influence to push their harsh criticism of President Truman's foreign policy. This agitation, in turn, strengthened the anticommunist elements in the CIO. The first major defeat of the Communists occurred when in 1946 Walter Reuther won the presidency of the United Auto Workers. A year later his group took control of the union's executive board. Irving Howe and Lewis Coser note that the rise of Reuther signaled "a change in the whole relationship of forces within the CIO by providing it with a gifted anticommunist leader who could criticize the party from a sophisticated radical perspective and who had a grasp of political ideas quite exceptional in the trade-union movement."[58]

Philip Murray, president of the CIO, resisted the anti-Communist pressure. He was a devout Catholic and an unequivocal anticommunist, but he feared that a split would significantly weaken the organization and encourage raiding from its rival, the American Federation of Labor (AFL). He therefore continued the important role played by left wingers such as Lee Pressman and Len DeCaux, who had made themselves indispensable despite the fact that one was known as a not-quite-secret member of the Party and the other as a faithful fellow traveler. In order to defend himself against growing criticism, Murray pushed through a resolution at the CIO convention held in November 1946 which declared that the delegates "resent and reject efforts of the Communist Party or other political parties and their adherents to interfere in the affairs of the CIO. This convention serves notice that we will not tolerate such interference."[59]

Several state CIO organizations went much further. The Massachusetts CIO, for example, banned Communists from its offices. But Murray continued his ambivalent course. By early 1947 American liberalism had split between the Progressive Citizens of America (PCA) and Americans for Democratic Action (ADA). Murray sought to remain on good terms with both groups. He did not protest when the founding convention of the PCA in December 1946 elected him vice president. Two months later, he sent two high-ranking officers of the CIO as his personal representatives to attend the organizing meeting of ADA. When the conflict within the executive board over the PCA/ADA rivalry heated up, Murray resigned as PCA vice president and got the board to adopt a resolution recommending that all CIO officers pull out of both organizations.[60]

Of the two organizations, ADA was much more effected by this move. Mrs. Roosevelt, a prominent supporter of ADA, wrote Murray asking him to rescind the directive. His neutrality, she argued, "actually operated in favor of the Communists since most influential CIO members have shunned the PCA and given their backing to ADA."[61] All through the year 1947, meanwhile, left-wing union leaders ignored the directive and continued to furnish financial and organizational backing to the PCA. By early 1948, Murray and many of his associates had concluded that the Progressives were under the domination of the Communists, and that the only purpose of the Wallace candidacy was to defeat Truman and the Marshall Plan. In late January, over the opposition of the representatives of ten Communist-controlled unions, the executive board of the CIO adopted a resolution which denounced the formation of a third party in 1948 as "politically unwise." In February, Murray declared the earlier resolution of neutrality as no longer binding, thus paving the way for a full alliance between the CIO and ADA.[62]

In late summer of 1948, the CIO endorsed Truman. The split within the CIO was exacerbated by the sharp attacks on Murray by the Communists. Murray himself, a generally warm and friendly person, now began to respond in kind and sharply denounced the Communists and their backers in the CIO. Those members of the board who opposed the Truman administration's policy of containment and supported Wallace, he maintained, were demonstrating thereby their sympathy with the Communists. "They follow the Line, and they live to follow the Line."[63] The dismissal of Pressman as CIO general counsel because Pressman was running for public office on the Progressive party ticket was a sign of things to come. And the poor showing of Wallace in November in labor strongholds provided a further impetus for the ouster of the dissident unions which had defied the CIO leadership.

In the spring of 1949, the executive board of the CIO voted to withdraw from the World Federation of Trade Unions because the Federation, increasingly under the influence of the government-run unions of the Eastern bloc, had refused to support the Marshall Plan. The CIO board also endorsed the North Atlantic Treaty Organization (NATO). The sharp split within the board was heading for a showdown. The division, as all agreed, was political in nature. "You can't beat around the bush about that," Murray declared. "It is one of Communism and anti-Communism."[64] In May 1949, the executive board adopted a resolution which required all members to enforce the CIO constitution and to carry out the directives of the board. Those board members unwilling to do so were called upon to resign.

By the time of the CIO's annual convention, October 31, 1949, in Cleveland, Murray and his supporters had more or less decided to get rid of the Communist-dominated unions. The last straw for Murray may have been the vicious attacks upon his leadership by the Communist press. "Leaders of unions who wish to be judged as responsible men," Murray told the delegates in his opening report, "have accused your President of subservience to corporate interests; of selling out the interests of American workers; of race baiting; of company unionism; of repudiation of the democratic principles to which your President, through all the years of his life, has remained steadfastly loyal."[65] When the United Electrical Workers refused to take their seats at the convention, charging that the "main business of the CIO Convention would be a red-baiting spree for the gratification of the anti-labor commercial press and the politicians to whom the CIO now subordinates itself," Murray was finally pushed into action on expulsion.

By a large vote the convention voted several amendments to the CIO constitution. The first barred members of "the Communist Party, any fascist organization, or other totalitarian movement, or [those] who consistently pursue policies and activities directed toward the achievement of the program" of such totalitarian organizations from membership on the CIO executive board. The second amendment gave the executive board the right to expel, by a two-thirds' vote, any union whose policies and activities were "consistently directed towards the achievement of the program or the purposes of the Communist Party, any fascist organization, or other totalitarian movement, rather than the objectives and policies set forward in the constitution of the CIO."[66]

The convention itself expelled the United Electrical Workers (UE) and the Farm Equipment Workers. "We can no longer tolerate within the family of CIO," the resolution on the UE declared, "the Communist Party masquerading as a labor union. . . . There is no place in the CIO for any organization whose leaders pervert its certificate of affiliation into an instrument that would betray the American workers into totalitarian bondage." Contrary to the overwhelming sentiment of the rank and file membership, the resolution charged, this leadership had betrayed the economic, political, and social welfare of the CIO. At the signal of the Cominform, the UE leadership had "assumed its true role as a fifth column. Its agents in the labor unions followed the Communist Party line" and sacrificed the needs of the workers to the interests of the Soviet Union.[67]

In accordance with the new constitutional provisions, William Steinberg, a member of the executive board, now filed charges against ten Communist-dominated unions, asking that their charters be revoked. At hearings that began in December 1949, the CIO did not attempt to prove that the left-wing union leaders were Communists, a difficult and perhaps impossible task. Instead the committees conducting the hearings sought to establish that the unions in question, through their publications and political activities, had consistently followed the Communist line rather than the "objectives and policies set forth in the Constitution of the CIO," a relatively easy matter.[68] The Mine, Mill and Smelter Workers were said to have opposed the Marshall Plan, to have converted their newspaper "into a Progressive Party organ," and to have subordinated trade union news to "Progressive Party propaganda." The United Office and Professional Workers of America, it was charged, had consistently followed the program of the Communist party. By following "the twists and turns, the zigs and zags of the Communist party line," the union had lost membership and by November 1949 had dropped to the "pitiable" figure of about 12,000.[69]

On February 15, 1950, the committees made their recommendations to the executive board. Within a few weeks the board expelled nine of the ten unions accused of being Communist-dominated. CIO President Philip

Murray stated that he was delighted at these actions. "We have cleaned our house; we have rid ourselves of these Communist influences within the family of our trade unions and we have rendered a distinct service not only to American workers but also to our country."[70] The CIO now granted charters to new unions and allowed its affiliates to raid the expelled unions. By the time the CIO and AFL merged in 1955, the influence of the Communists in the labor movement had come to an end. As a result of their expulsion from the CIO and government-imposed requirements that union leaders sign non-Communist affidavits, the Communist-run unions had severe losses in membership. "The decisiveness of the CIO victory over the CP," noted Max Kampelman in 1957, "is in a measure illustrated by the fact that Communist-led unions in 1949 claimed a membership of more than two million and are today estimated to represent no more than two hundred thousand workers."[71] This figure amounted to less than 1 percent of total American trade-union strength.

Critics of the Communist purge from the CIO have argued that the left-run unions were expelled primarily because they had become a political liability. "It was only after the escalation of the Cold War and after the bitter debates over American foreign policy," writes Mary Sperling McAuliffe, "that Murray concluded that the presence of Communists in the CIO was a danger."[72] Irving Howe and Lewis Coser note that the proceedings to oust the ten unions raised "grave and knotty issues of union autonomy and democracy" and they question whether it was right to impose political uniformity. "Granted the desirability of eliminating Communist influence from the trade-union movement, one might still have argued that the mass expulsions not only were a poor way for achieving this end but constituted a threat to democratic values and procedures."[73]

There can be little doubt that the expulsion of the Communist-led unions from the CIO was strongly influenced by the charged political climate of the late 1940s, a tension to which both Communists and anti-Communists had contributed. At the same time, it is clear that the issues that led to the ouster were legitimate issues that perhaps should have been addressed much earlier. Experience had shown that the Communists used trade unions as they used all other mass organizations—to recruit members for the Party and to obtain backing for their political objectives, especially to win support for the foreign policy of the Soviet Union. This meant that sheer bread-and-butter trade union issues were always subordinated to larger political concerns, and as a consequence the interests of workers often suffered. The Communists were active and energetic members of the trade-union movement not in order to end the exploitation of the working class but to gain adherents and support for their party.

The Communists regularly made decisions on strikes in terms of purely political considerations. James Wechsler related how in 1941, when he was a labor editor for the newspaper *PM*, he was asked to report on the background of the New York City bus strike then in the making by the pro-Communist Mike Quill.

> One of my first steps was an interview with the attorney for the Transport Workers Union. I tried to get some evidence from him that the bus employees had a compelling economic case, based on comparisons with other cities and even with equivalent employment. In a moment of remarkable candor the attorney said that it would be hard to assemble such data. The case, he admitted, was a close one. And then he added: "I think a strike would be a good thing anyway because we're in a period of imperialist war and the workers have to be toughened up for the big fights ahead." He said this jauntily, as if even a poor fool ex-communist ought to understand him.

Wechsler noted that "the bus enterprise was a failure because it was based on an essential dishonesty or naiveté—the notion that the communist-led Transport Workers Union was uninfluenced by the vaster politics of international communism and that its economic crusades could be divorced from its political designs."[74] Many labor leaders had long since shed this illusion, and they had therefore come to regard the Communists as, at best, unreliable allies. The anticommunist political climate of the Cold War years gave them the incentive and opportunity to act on this insight.

The Revival of Progressivism

In 1947 ADA had come into being in order to create a voice for anticommunist liberals. Uniquely for its time, the organization excluded Communists from both leadership and membership. During the election campaign of 1948 and in the years that followed, ADA played a key role in exposing the fraudulent character of the Progressive party. ADA, noted James Wechsler with pride in 1960, probably "did more than any other single agency to expose the frauds and the fallacies, the double-think and double standards through which the Communists tried to entrap American liberals in the late 1940s as they had in the mid-1930s."[75] Paradoxically today, some forty years later, ADA is part of the anti-anticommunist Left, and the ban on working with Communists, never formally repealed, has become a dead letter.

The key factor that fundamentally changed the political character of ADA was the Vietnam War. The following decisions are the milestones in a process of radical transformation that took but a few years. In March 1967, the annual convention of ADA, by a vote of almost 2–1, strongly criticized President Johnson's policies at home and abroad. In February 1968, the national board of ADA, by a vote of 65–47, endorsed Senator Eugene McCarthy for President, a decision that led to the resignation of several veteran ADA leaders such as John P. Roche and Paul Seabury. In June 1970, the ADA convention, overturning a recommendation of its foreign policy commission, came out for unilateral withdrawal from Vietnam. In April 1971, the national executive committee endorsed the End-the-War demonstrations planned for April 24 in Washington by the National Peace Action Coalition, an organization created and dominated by the Trotskyist Socialist Workers party. In early May 1971, an ADA contingent participated in the large Washington demonstration that had the avowed purpose of bringing the operations of the government to a momentary halt. ADA chairman Joseph Duffey was one of the speakers at that demonstration which resulted in mass arrests. In May 1972, ADA supported yet another demonstration in Washington organized by the National Peace Action Coalition, one of the last big demonstrations of the Vietnam War era.[76]

The embittering and polarizing experience of the American involvement in Vietnam left ADA with a new political outlook characterized by a profound distrust of the exercise of American power. Today ADA is positioned uneasily between the left wing of the Democratic party and the so-called "peace and justice" network. This group of organizations, the offspring of the New Left and the radical antiwar movement, is strongly anti-anticommunist and considers the United States the cause of most of the world's problems. Working in coalition with these organizations, ADA during the last fifteen years has taken a stand against practically every new weapons system adopted by the United States. It has opposed the Trident I and II nuclear submarines, the B-1 bomber, the neutron bomb, and the MX missile. In 1982, ADA came out for nuclear disarmament, arguing that the production and possession of nuclear weapons was morally wrong.[77]

ADA has fought recent American policies in Central America. In late 1980, the Carter administration, after receiving information that Nicaragua was materially supporting the Marxist-Leninist guerrillas of El Salvador, threatened to cut off aid to the new Sandinista regime. ADA opposed this step and expressed the hope "that the myopic anti-communist forces in Congress can be defeated in their efforts to halt the aid package."[78] Some years later, when Bruce Cameron, the author of this statement, abandoned his positive assessment of the Sandinista revolution and came out in favor of aid to the Nicaraguan resistance, the Contras, Cameron was summarily drummed out of ADA. In 1983, Robert F. Drinan, the president of ADA, argued that the United States, by sending military aid and advisers, was supporting "a cruel and unrepresentative government in El Salvador." U.S. policy toward both El Salvador and Sandinistra-ruled Nicaragua, Drinan maintained, was motivated by a "pathological fear of Communism."[79]

The anti-Communist provisions in ADA's constitution are by now a clear anachronism. In 1973, the ADA convention elected to its board Bella Abzug and Gene LaRocque, two persons whose anticommunist credentials it would be hard to substantiate. ADA has given top rating to several congressmen whose political record is outright procommunist. The ADA voting record for 1983 listed Congressman George Crockett with a score of 100 percent and Congressman Ronald V. Dellums with a score of 95 percent. Crockett is a former vice president of the National Lawyers Guild and until well into the 1970s was a regular at major Communist social events. In 1983, when ADA praised his voting record, he was one of only two members of Congress (John Conyers, who also received a 100 percent rating by ADA, was the other) who pointedly abstained on a House resolution, which passed 416–0, condemning the Soviets' shooting down of Korean Air Lines flight 007.[80] Representative Dellums is a vigorous proponent of CISPES, a support group for the Marxist-Leninist FMLN of El Salvador. His special assistant, Carlottia A. Scott, in an April 1982 letter to Maurice Bishop, the head of the Communist New Jewel government of Grenada, described Dellums as an ardent admirer of Bishop and Castro.[81] The political record of Dellums fully bears out this appraisal. By 1987, Dellums had made the list of "ADA All Stars" with a 100 percent rating of approval.

The striking political transformation of ADA is part and parcel of the anti-anticommunist climate of opinion that has taken hold among certain segments of the American intellectual community. That a political organization with such views can still call itself "liberal" indicates the leftward drift of the American political spectrum. Progressivism, declared dead after the demise of the Progressive party in the 1950s, has staged a dramatic come-back.

11

The Committee for a Sane Nuclear Policy: From Center to Left

The idea of forming a national organization that would work for a moratorium on the testing of H-bombs came from Lawrence Scott, peace education secretary of the American Friends Service Committee (AFSC) in Chicago. On April 22, 1957, Scott convened a meeting in Philadelphia that was attended by veteran peace activist A. J. Muste, civil rights leader Bayard Rustin, Robert Gilmore, executive secretary of AFSC in New York City, and other peace and church leaders. The group decided to work for the establishment of a broad-based organization that would enlist the support of both pacifists and nonpacifists. Scott then contacted Norman Cousins, the editor of *Saturday Review* and a leader of the United World Federalists, as well as Clarence Pickett, secretary emeritus of the AFSC. Both men agreed to call a meeting of people of national stature for June 21. Attended by twenty-seven churchmen, scientists, businessmen, authors, and others, this gathering formed the Provisional Committee to Stop Nuclear Tests. In September the name of the group was changed to National Committee for a Sane Nuclear Policy.[1]

Norman Cousins and Clarence Pickett became co-chairmen of the new organization, generally known as SANE. An executive committee composed of peace activists and prominent public figures was formed, and a statement of goals and purposes was drafted. This statement proposed the immediate cessation of nuclear weapons tests by all countries, enforced through an agreement monitored by the United Nations. SANE was to serve as a clearing house for information. It would prepare and distribute materials, issue public statements, and encourage the formation of local committees. Looking beyond the short-term objective of an end to nuclear testing, SANE set itself the goal of working toward disarmament and leading mankind away from the danger of nuclear war.

On November 15, 1957, SANE ran its first full-page advertisement in the *New York Times*. Headlined "We Are Facing a Danger Unlike Any Danger That Has Ever Existed," this statement stressed the importance of going beyond the "national interest" to "the sovereignty of the human community" where man could breathe unpoisoned air and work on uncontaminated soil. It called on Americans to press their government for an immediate suspension of nuclear testing. The statement declared that, while "the abolition of testing will not by itself solve the problem of peace or the problem of armaments, it enables the world to eliminate immediately at least one real and specific danger."[2]

Concern about the danger of radioactive fallout from bomb tests had been growing for some time. Fallout was said to be especially threatening to children whose bodies mistook radioactive strontium-90 in milk for calcium. The November advertisement therefore struck a ready chord, and what had started out as an educational campaign quickly turned into a grass-roots movement with considerable momentum. The statement was reprinted in thirty-two local newspapers and there were 25,000 requests for reprints. People from all over the country inquired how they could help; by the summer of 1958 SANE had 130 chapters with about 25,000 members. As one of its leaders recalled later, "SANE gave anxious citizens from varied background a single meaningful issue on which to act—the cessation of nuclear weapons testing."[3]

In March 1958, the Soviet Union announced a moratorium on the testing of nuclear weapons. In August the United States followed suit and both nations agreed to meet in Geneva to begin negotiations for a treaty that would ban the atmospheric testing of nuclear bombs. With the issue of nuclear testing thus in negotiation, SANE broadened its goals. A national conference held in New York City on September 29 decided that SANE would seek international control over delivery systems and the stockpiling and production of nuclear weapons. In addition, the national committee was authorized "to take positions at its discretion on those areas of United States foreign policy impinging upon possible nuclear war."[4] The conference also decided that use of the committee's name should be restricted to local committees that accepted the policy guidance of the national committee. Local committees were required to clear all policy statements made in the name of the organization with the national committee.

Meeting the Threat of Communist Infiltration

SANE leaders had been apprehensive about the Communist issue from the very beginning. In a memo dated April 30, 1957, Lawrence Scott had warned that an organization of the kind he and others had in mind would be vulnerable to vilification as a Communist front on one hand and vulnerable to Communist infiltration on the other. Scott urged that the proposed organization follow a middle ground. "We will be neither naive concerning this problem nor hysterically expend our energy refuting false charges."[5]

During the tense political climate of the 1950s, these were not idle fears. Advocates of nuclear testing were indeed charging that those who called for a suspension were helping the Communist cause. In April 1958, *Time* magazine pointed out that Linus Pauling and others who had signed the SANE ad of November 1957 had been active in various Communist front organizations. The caption under a picture of the signers read: "Defenders of the unborn . . . or dupes of the enemies of liberty?"[6]

The threat of Communist infiltration also was real. In a letter to Trevor Thomas, SANE's first executive secretary, written on June 13, 1958, Norman Cousins urged: "We must develop a razor-sharp vigilance against the danger of Communist infiltration or control as the issue of nuclear testing, perhaps more than any other issue in recent years, provides an attractive sphere of action for Communists." The situation in the local chapters in New York, Oregon, and Missouri, he pointed out, "could be potentially harmful," and this situation "serves as a stern warning that we must have both the policy and the means to deal effectively with the problem when it arises."[7]

By the summer of 1958, Cousins had become so concerned that he contacted the FBI and requested that the Bureau furnish SANE with the names of any individuals known to them as attempting to infiltrate any of the local committees in New York City or in other places. The aims of SANE, Cousins wrote, were highly important and he "did not wish to see it hampered by being used by an individual who did not have the best interests of the United States at heart." The FBI responded to Cousins that it "could not legally give him any assistance."[8] FBI files, later obtained by SANE under the Freedom of Information Act, indicate that by December 1959 the FBI had obtained evidence of Communist infiltration into the Greater New York Committee for a Sane Nuclear Policy. In January 1960, FBI Director Hoover authorized an investigation.[9]

By this time, the issue of Communist infiltration of local committees had become a matter of serious concern to other leading figures of SANE. In early 1960, Norman Thomas warned the executive committee "that unless it faced up to the Communist issue, this organization placed itself in dual jeopardy: on the one hand, there was the danger that increasing Communist activity on the local level would compromise or undermine the organization; on the other hand, there was the danger that our inability or unwillingness to recognize the problem would increase the likelihood of official attack, with our defense crippled in advance." Thomas expressed special anxiety about Henry Abrams in New York City, a leader of the Greater New York Committee for a Sane Nuclear Policy.[10]

After a discussion of this problem in SANE's administrative committee, Homer A. Jack, a Unitarian minister and one of the founders of the organization, prepared a statement which he sent to Cousins and several other key figures. The problem of Communist infiltration, Jack noted, was "obviously a divisive issue which could wreck SANE if we did nothing and could equally wreck SANE if we did the wrong thing." Jack proposed that the board of directors adopt a statement to the effect that SANE sought the support only of persons free to criticize the actions of all governments and free from totalitarian ties. Local chapters were to be advised to follow this principle when electing their own officers.[11]

During the following three months, the administrative committee spent several long meetings discussing a draft of such a statement. By late April, they had come close to an agreed formula, but then time ran out. On May 13, 1960, Henry Abrams was subpoenaed by the Senate's Internal Security Subcommittee, chaired at the time by Senator Thomas J. Dodd. Abrams was a former leader of the American Labor party and he had been active in the Wallace campaign. At the time of the subpoena, Abrams was the main organizer of a large SANE rally at New York's Madison Square Garden, scheduled for May 19. The Committee sought to question Abrams about his alleged membership in the Communist party, but Abrams invoked the Fifth Amendment. He was then called in by Cousins, who asked Abrams to be frank with him and the other board members so that SANE could defend Abrams against the Dodd committee. Abrams agreed to answer questions related to his work for SANE, but declined to discuss allegations of Communist party membership. He did state that "he was not under the orders or instruction of any outside agent or organization, and that his sole concern was to make SANE a success." Cousins considered this response unsatisfactory and he asked Abrams to offer his resignation. When Abrams refused, Cousins suspended him.[12]

Cousins next hurried to Washington and asked Senator Dodd to hold off the publicity about his committee's investigation until after the May 19 rally. Dodd was a neighbor of Cousins in Connecticut and a friend; he agreed to comply with this request. Cousins assured Dodd that SANE was not hiding anything and that the Abrams case should not be used to cast an unfavorable light upon the entire organization. The New York rally consequently was able to proceed without a hitch. Some 20,000 persons heard speeches by a roster of prominent public figures including Mrs. Eleanor Roosevelt, Governor G. Mennen Williams of Michigan, and labor leaders Walter Reuther and A. Philip Randolph.[13]

A few days later the floodgates of publicity opened up. On May 25, Senator Dodd gave a major speech before the Senate in which he accused SANE of having moved too slowly on the issue of Communist infiltration.

> I believe that the heads of the Committee for a Sane Nuclear Policy have a serious contribution to make to the great debate on national policy. But they can only make this contribution effectively if they purge their ranks ruthlessly of Communist infiltration and if they clearly demarcate their own position from that of the Communists, first, by stressing the need for adequate inspection; second, by reiterating at every opportunity their opposition to the tyranny of communism.

SANE, Dodd charged, had had every reason to expect a concerted effort at infiltration—some of its leaders had warned against this danger—and yet the organization had not taken "the necessary measures to create a climate that is inhospitable to Communist infiltration." Perhaps, Dodd suggested, this was a situation "in which private citizens must have the assistance of Government to cope effectively with a movement that operates by stealth and by secrecy."[14]

There followed articles in the press which alleged that it had been Cousins who had urged Dodd to undertake an investigation of SANE and that Cousins had accused Abrams of plotting to have Communists take over the Madison Square Garden rally. Cousins denied all of these allegations. This, then, was the situation when SANE's board of directors met on May 26 to discuss the growing public controversy. Clarence Pickett, Robert Gilmore, and Stewart Meacham—all of the American Friends Service Committee—proposed a statement which declared that SANE had not and would not let itself be controlled by the Communist party or any other outside organization. The statement also affirmed that "SANE has not and will not trim its sails to suit opponents of a sane nuclear policy whether they be members of congressional committees, private citizens, or anonymous accusers." This language was turned down by a majority of the board which instead adopted a more explicit ban on the participation of Communists in the leadership of the organization.[15]

Entitled "Standards for Sane Leadership," the policy statement declared that SANE's program necessarily involved the organization "in searching criticism of those positions of the U.S., USSR, or any other country which block the attainment of adequate disarmament agreements."

> Therefore members of the Communist Party or individuals who are not free because of party discipline or political allegiance to apply to the actions of the Soviet or Chinese government the same standard by which they challenge others are barred from any voice in deciding the Committee's policies or programs. This statement was originally approved in principle by the Committee soon after its organization, long before there was any action by the Senate Subcommittee on Internal Security. It is now reaffirmed herewith.

The statement went on to deplore "the intrusion of a congressional committee into the affairs of an organization which during its entire life has acted only in accordance with its declared principles." SANE, the statement concluded, was "entirely capable of carrying out its principles and guaranteeing that it will not permit their betrayal or subversion under any pressure from, on the one hand, investigations directed to its hurt or, on the other, by the actions of its own local chapters or their leaders."[16]

Donald Keys, SANE's executive director, communicated the board statement to the local committees. His letter explained that, in order to provide against "the cooperation of unwanted people on the one hand and attack from those who basically disagreed with its policy on the other," the Committee had "created a deliberately autocratic organization in which the ultimate power of decision and policy making resides in the members of the corporation, a small number of the national leadership." Local groups had to be chartered, and those deviating from the declared policy of the organization were subject to disaffiliation. The national office, Keys affirmed, was not using "a screening process based upon innuendos or questions regarding previous affiliations." Instead the emphasis was on performance. If the performance of a group or its leaders varied from duly established policies a warning would be issued and disaffiliation would be voted by the national board only after "due and careful consideration." The Committee, Keys stressed, would not be stampeded into the establishment of a "divisive screening machinery which will violate the basic principles of democratic process in which a man is judged on the basis of his current allegiances and actions rather than those of the past, or on the beliefs that he may be alleged to hold. The machinery for the removal of undesirable elements exists. It will not be abused, but will be used to the degree that seems prudent and just."[17]

The board's action drew criticism. On June 27, Robert Gilmore resigned from the board. SANE, he argued, "could have responded to Senator Dodd's attack with a ringing challenge to the cold war stratagem of discredit and divide, with a clear affirmation of the right of everyone to debate and dissent. . . . The fact that SANE turned down this opportunity is, to my mind, a great tragedy."[18] Objections were received also from several local committees. The executive committee of the Long Island Committee for a Sane Nuclear Policy informed the board that it disapproved of the fourth paragraph of the May 26 statement. "This paragraph presupposes, and apparently approves of, a continuation of the cold war and thus works against what may be one of the necessary conditions for achieving one of Sane's leading objectives—ending the threat of nuclear war." The statement assumed, the Long Island committee argued, that members of the Communist party were unable to meet the test of independent judgment. "This denies the right of Communist party members to be treated as individuals. . . . Also its implementation may lead to humiliating investigations and unfortunate personal conflicts within the Sane organization." A similar objection was voiced by the Skokie (Illinois) Committee for a Sane Nuclear Policy. SANE, it was maintained, "is not a political organization [and] we should not be forced to single out any one group such as the Communists for special attention."[19]

In a letter addressed to all local committee chairmen, national co-chairmen Cousins and Pickett noted that they were "on the whole pleased with the responses" to the May 26 statement. "Looking over the country we find general acceptance of the policy." In a few instances, groups and individuals had "reacted rather violently against the policy statement, assuming or alleging that its acceptance would mean the initiation of a 'witch hunt' and/or a capitulation to government pressure that would be the end of an effective SANE." These allegations, the two leaders assured the local committees, were baseless and probably arose from the fact that the statement had been distributed without a detailed plan of implementation. After consulting with attorneys versed in civil liberties, such a plan was prepared by the staff and the national committee. There was no intent to require a loyalty oath and the procedure was not aimed at persons who might have made a mistake in the past. It was designed to enable SANE to say to the public and to its supporters, "Our house is in order." Local committees were asked to review the plan carefully and to inform the national office when they had done so.

The plan of implementation involved several steps. In the first instance, individual leaders were to exercise "self-judgment and self-discipline" in deciding whether they accepted the principles of the May 26 statement excluding Communists from positions "deciding policy implementation and program." If individual leaders or staff members had their good-faith adherence to the statement questioned, the national committee would decide whether the case merited investigation. It would ask for a full and forthright response from the individual concerned, and if such frankness was not forthcoming it could ask for the person's resignation. The refusal of an individual to testify before a congressional committee was not itself a reason for action by the national committee. "However, representatives of the National Committee will expect to have full and frank private conversations with those individuals in order that they defend them to the fullest." If such a candid response was not forthcoming or if attitudes or background were revealed that placed the individual in the proscribed category, that is, membership in the Communist party, a resignation could be requested. All local committees wanting to use the name of the Committee for a Sane Nuclear Policy were asked to take out a charter before September 1, 1960.[20]

The requirement that all local committees obtain a charter from the national office was designed for situations like New York City, where more than fifty committees had been chartered by the Greater New York Committee for a Sane Nuclear Policy and thus were effectively beyond the supervision of the national organization. Greater New York SANE was the committee about which several national SANE leaders had been concerned for some time and which had become the target of Senator Dodd's probe. During the months of August, September, and October of 1960, the Senate Internal Security Subcommittee subpoenaed twenty-seven persons associated with Greater New York SANE. In a memo sent to all local committee chairmen on September 29, Cousins and Pickett noted that SANE had not given any names or lists to the Dodd committee and that it had retained counsel to represent without charge any member called by the Senate committee. Those asked to testify had been advised not to invoke the Fifth Amendment. The committee's current procedure was to respect the wish of witnesses who answered questions about themselves not to testify about others. But even if a witness disregarded the advice of SANE counsel and took the Fifth, Cousins and Pickett affirmed, this would not be automatic cause for dismissal from SANE. The Dodd committee had given assurances that all testimony would be in executive session, that the names of the persons called to testify would not be made public, and that the SANE board would be informed about the committee's findings before any public statement was made. "The decision as to what action is to be taken will be entirely at the discretion of SANE Board of Directors."[21]

A national conference of SANE was held in Chicago from October 14 to 16 and revealed continued unrest within the organization over the Communist issue. Cousins told the national board on October 24 that "there were substantial reservations and [that] the local organizations are not entirely behind the National Board." Nevertheless, with only Stewart Meacham of the American Friends Service Committee dissenting, the board voted to reaffirm the May 26 policy statement and the subsequent plan of implementation. It also voted that the policy of SANE is that "members of the Communist party, fascists, or individuals who are not free because of party discipline or political allegiance to apply to the actions of the Soviet Union or the Chinese government the same standards by which they challenge others are not welcome on any level of this organization." By this action the board added a declaration to the effect of "We do not welcome Communists even as members" to the formal ban on Communists in policy-making roles adopted on May 26. The administrative committee was to make the determination where this statement should be publicized.[22] It carried out this mandate by requiring the following statement on all brochures describing SANE: "The national committee needs and welcomes all persons whose support is not qualified by adherence to Communist or other totalitarian doctrine."

The board also discussed the status of the Greater New York SANE. SANE's counsel William Butler argued that there existed a basic incompatibility between national and New York SANE and that the problem of revoking its charter should be frankly discussed. Others warned against so drastic an action. Cousins suggested that those opposed to the current SANE policy team up with Linus Pauling. This well-known scientist, a national sponsor of SANE, was in favor of a peace movement open to all. He had therefore declined an invitation, extended to him after Pauling's run-in with the Senate Internal Security Subcommittee, to join SANE's board of directors. Following the board meeting, Hugh C. Wolfe, head of the administrative committee, notified Walter Lear, chairman of the executive committee of Greater New York SANE, that on November 7 the board would act on whether the committee's charter should be terminated. Greater New York SANE, Wolfe charged, had failed to reorganize its executive committee in order to bring it into line with the May 26 policy statement barring Communists.[23]

The final showdown had arrived. On November 7, the national board of SANE asked the Greater New York Committee to dissolve and reconstitute itself as a coordinating council of local committees who would have to be chartered directly by the national organization. Unless this reorganization was implemented by November 15, the resolution declared, "the charter of the Greater New York Committee shall be automatically terminated on November 15, 1960."[24] Two days later, Greater New York SANE surrendered its charter. The vote was 9–7, with 21 abstentions. In its place, a new Greater New York Council for a Sane Nuclear Policy was formed. About half of the local committees in the Greater New York metropolitan area, some twenty-five out of perhaps fifty, refused to take out charters and were expelled from SANE.

There exists uncertainty as to how many members and leaders of Greater New York SANE actually were Communists. Most of those who appeared before the Senate Internal Security Subcommittee, some of them chairmen of local committees, took the Fifth Amendment and refused to testify. It would appear that the number of actual party members was relatively small, while a far larger number were ex-Communists who, while no longer under party discipline, nevertheless had not really changed their political outlook. Together with many who had never joined the Party, these individuals were temperamentally and intellectually committed to a fellow-traveling interpretation of the world. They had a special loyalty to the Soviet Union, the first socialist society, while the capitalist United States was regarded as definitely inferior. The presence of large numbers of such people in many New York SANE committees, noted the sociologist Nathan Glazer in a perceptive article that was published soon after these events, "meant that a tone was established which could only repel sophisticated anti-Communists who might have wished to work for disarmament. It also repelled the broad mass of Americans and made the peace movement suspect in influential political quarters."[25]

Glazer thought that the exclusion of what he called the "Communist-minded" from SANE reflected "political wisdom." These people could not criticize the totalitarian countries with the same standards by which they judged the Western democracies and thus did not fulfil the requirement for membership which SANE had adopted. Glazer expressed the hope that this action would enable SANE to reach out to a far larger constituency. Others felt that the purge of the Communists and their allies represented a capitulation to McCarthyism. A. J. Muste agreed that "an effective United States peace movement cannot be built by liberals or other people who are emotionally pro-Soviet or pro-Communist," but he took exception to the means adopted by SANE for getting rid of such individuals.[26]

As a result of the anticommunist provisions adopted by SANE in 1960, the organization lost some supporters from among radical pacifists and students who objected to what they regarded as a witch-hunt and a demand for ideological conformity. On the whole, however, SANE weathered the crisis quite well, and, after a brief setback, its membership continued to expand. As executive director Homer A. Jack was able to report in the spring of 1961, out of the total of eighty-five persons who made up the national board of directors and national sponsors, only three had resigned—Robert Gilmore, Stewart Meacham, and Linus Pauling. In the past six months, Jack noted, "SANE has sponsored more programs and other activity than ever before in its three-year history."[27] The view expressed by some younger historians that, as a consequence of this episode, SANE suffered serious damage appears to be less a correct description of actual developments than a view dictated by the nonexclusionary principles adhered to by these authors. For graduates of the student left of the 1960s, anticommunism is a symbol of Cold War politics and a result of a craving for respectability for which they have little sympathy.[28]

For the next few years, SANE continued to criticize both legislative probes of the peace movement and political double standards. On March 19, 1961, the Senate Internal Security Subcommittee released Part II of the hearings held in 1960, entitled "Communist Infiltration in the Nuclear Test Ban Movement." This transcript included the names of those persons, many of them formerly active in the dissolved Greater New York Committee for a Sane Nuclear Policy, who had refused to cooperate with the Senate committee. In a statement adopted on April 17, the national board of SANE deplored "the subpoenaing, questioning, and release of testimony of any citizen for other than a legislative purpose." SANE, the statement stated, "does not believe that any congressional investigations of private organizations have a valid legislative purpose." SANE, therefore, "strongly reiterates its resentment of the intrusion of the Senate Internal Security Subcommittee into its affairs."[29]

A year later, after the House Committee on Un-American Activities (HUAC) had subpoenaed members of Women Strike for Peace, SANE issued another statement critical of such probes. "A Congressional investigation of any organization concerned with preserving the peace," the national board declared on December 7, 1962, "represents an act of intimidation against the right of citizens to express their opinions on matters of human survival, and also threatens the exercise of the right of all nongovernmental organizations to maintain an independent political position. . . . No valid legislative purpose can be served by the present action of the House Committee on Un-American Activities."[30] At the same time, SANE made it clear that, unlike some segments of the worldwide peace movement, it was opposed to totalitarianism and stood for peace *with* freedom. An article published in same issue of the organization's newsletter which criticized HUAC stressed SANE's independence and evenhandedness: "We want no part of the double standard which judges American foreign policy with principles different from those used in judging the policies of other nations. Herein we differ from those peace organizations in some parts of the world which tend to speak for government, not to government. We praise our government when we can, yet we do not hesitate to criticize our government or any other government when we must."[31] On another occasion, SANE's newsletter criticized apologists for the Soviet Union who were "passionately eager to picket the White House during the Cuba crisis [of 1962], but who refused to picket the Soviet Embassy, although the crisis was triggered by the introduction of Soviet missiles into Cuba."[32]

The Exclusionary Policy under Attack

SANE was an early critic of the American involvement in the Vietnam conflict, though the organization went out of its way to stress that it sought a negotiated peace and had no intention of supporting a military victory by the North Vietnamese or anyone else in the war. When SANE organized a march against the war in Washington on November 27, 1965, the organization insisted that the demonstrators carry only authorized slogans. Signs for an immediate withdrawal of the United States were not allowed. Norman Thomas told the audience that he did not want to burn the American flag but cleanse it of the defilement of the war in Indochina.[33] It was this very posture of moderation and balance which for the second time in a decade brought about a major crisis for SANE.

The movement against the war in Vietnam, as we will have occasion to see in more detail in a later chapter, began as a coalition between liberal groups such as SANE concerned about the political and human cost of the conflict, pacifists opposed to any war, the budding New Left which blamed the military-industrial complex of capitalist America for leading the country into a colonialist adventure, and Old Left groups such as the Trotskyist Socialist Workers party, who were avowed partisans of the Vietnamese Communists. As the American involvement deepened, disagreements developed between these different elements. The leadership of the antiwar movement increasingly fell into the hands of radical activists who became dissatisfied with the emphasis of the moderates on electoral politics and who insisted on taking their protest into the streets. Many of these radicals, though not themselves Communists, were convinced that the National Liberation Front deserved to win and they demanded the unconditional withdrawal of American troops from Vietnam rather than the negotiated settlement of the war sought by liberal critics such as SANE. In the eyes of the New Left, it was liberalism and its support of the Cold War that had brought about an imperialistic war against Vietnamese peasants. "It is already clear to everyone except SANE and its allies," wrote Robert Paul Wolfe in the early summer of 1966, "that

one cannot protest the war in Vietnam in the name of a more sophisticated version of anti-Communism without lending credence to the very
myth which has produced the war."[34]

By the spring of 1967, serious tensions over these issues had begun to
surface within SANE itself. The beginning of the year saw the formation
of the Spring Mobilization to End the War in Vietnam. The goal of this
effort, stated coordinator A. J. Muste, was the development of a "radical
anti-war coalition" that would be based on the principle of nonexclusion—it would welcome the participation of all groups irrespective of
their political goals or ideological commitments. Muste died unexpectedly on February 11, but the broad-based movement he had helped initi-
ate went forward with Dr. Benjamin Spock, co-chairman of SANE, and
the Reverend Martin Luther King, Jr., becoming co-chairmen.

Dr. Spock, the well-known pediatrician, had become an active member
of SANE in 1962. By 1965, he had embraced a sharply critical view of
the United States, a fact which endeared him to the more radical elements
in SANE. In a speech delivered at a SANE rally held in New York's
Madison Square Garden on June 8, 1965, Spock accused the U.S. of a
"ruthless disregard of the rights of other nations." America "violates international agreements, jeopardizes the very existence of the United Nations, alienates its allies, antagonizes the neutral countries, is ready to
attack or intervene in any small country by which it feels threatened."
Why, Spock asked rhetorically, had the country developed such an unreasonable fear of Communism? "Why are so many of us ready to launch
a holy war against any Communists in the world, and to detect them
everywhere in our own country?"[35] At the time Spock delivered this
speech, these ideas had relatively few adherents in SANE; such words
were soon to become standard vocabulary in the antiwar movement.

Spock's assumption of a leading role in the Spring Mobilization of
1967, taken on without the approval of SANE's board of directors, drew
objections from several leading board members. As Cousins commented
later: "We didn't like the style of the thing. Some of the leaders had black
racist tendencies streaked with violence. Some were Vietcong supporters.
Some were opposed to negotiations. We couldn't control what those people would say or do, and we didn't want SANE to be taxed with ideas
that most of us didn't share." Norman Thomas also favored nonpartici-
pation on the grounds that "there should be some earnest organization
of people who still try constructively to influence the government's actions rather than simply demonstrate against one side—our side—in terms
of objections to mass murder which of itself would not be stopped simply
by our withdrawal." Spock, on the other hand, argued that only by participating in such protests could SANE exert any influence over them. A

policy of excluding some elements in the peace movement would encourage dissension. "I believe in going with other groups as long as their aims are roughly those of SANE. I believe in solidarity."[36]

Meeting on February 12, a decisive majority of the board agreed with Cousins and Thomas. By a vote of 22–4 it adopted a resolution which stressed that SANE had to concentrate on its own program and therefore did not endorse the marches planned by the Mobilization in New York and San Francisco for April 15. The resolution reaffirmed guidelines on participation in peace demonstrations adopted in 1963 which had ruled out cooperation with organizations whose policies were at variance with those of SANE. Specifically, SANE was not to "identify itself with unilateral and pacifist . . . or with Soviet apologist positions."[37] This decision drew strong objections from several local committees who sided with Spock and voted to support the April 15 mobilization. Others agreed with the board's action and expressed the hope that Spock would rethink his position.[38]

Relations between Spock and SANE's executive director Donald F. Keys, a centrist, had become tense as a result of this disagreement. In a letter addressed to Spock on February 20, Keys explained why he had thought it necessary to bring the issue to the attention of the board:

> To this point in SANE's history, the Board has been consistent in deeming it unwise, undesirable and self-defeating to have SANE identify with or become involved in what might be termed popular front or united front actions with groups representing the radical left of this country. Few Board members knew about the Spring Mobilization, or understood that if SANE were involved it would in effect be assisting the establishment of a new radical anti-war movement. Surely I had a responsibility to make clear the use to which SANE would be put.[39]

One of the local committees to endorse the Spring Mobilization was the Washington, D.C., chapter of SANE. On April 7, the *Washington Post* published an article entitled "SANE Is Split on Militancy of Dr. Spock." With the dispute in the organization thus in the open, SANE on April 14 issued a public statement regarding the Spring Mobilization. The statement explained why SANE had not officially endorsed the demonstration, but stated that the organization had not attacked or obstructed it either. The board "respects the position of Dr. Spock in wishing to freely endorse as an individual action of groups other than SANE," while at the same time it "also respects the position of executive director Donald Keys in implementing the majority view of the board."[40]

The demonstrations on the following day attracted a large turnout. In New York the marchers included housewives pushing baby carriages and other middle-class "straights" but also members of the Communist party with their own banner and other radical groups carrying Viet Cong flags. "Many of the younger marchers," report two historians of the antiwar movement, "chanted 'Hell, No, We Won't Go!' and 'Hey, Hey, LBJ, How Many Kids Did You Kill Today?' "[41] These were the kinds of features of a demonstration against the war in Vietnam which Cousins and Thomas had anticipated and with which they had sought to avoid entanglement.

The meeting of the national board on April 27 was characterized by sharp exchanges. Dr. Spock and his supporters berated executive director Keys for his opposition to cooperation with organizations like the Spring Mobilization and demanded his resignation. After a bruising discussion, the board finally adopted two resolutions. The first, approved unanimously, declared that "SANE shall maintain cordial relations with all groups and individuals seeking world peace." SANE would try to participate with other organizations in the formulation and execution of peace policies and joint projects. "Where SANE's established policies, programs and priorities do not allow actual participation, SANE shall maintain an attitude of goodwill and respect for the intentions of others, recognizing that division of labor leaves ample room for multiple efforts toward our common goal." National officers and staff were not to "take action contravening SANE's policies nor publicly endorsing new movements and programs without prior consultation with SANE's Board or the policy committee." Efforts should be made "towards harmony and efficiency within the staff and as between the staff and the officers."

The second resolution provided for an enlargement of the national board to sixty members. It also required "that at least 50% of its members be elected from the Chapters and the members at large" and that "provision be made for representative voting from the members." A special committee was to work out the necessary details.[42] These actions of the board mirrored a definite shift in political outlook. The first resolution put some restraints on the freewheeling activities of Spock which the latter, however, felt free to disregard; the second, by adding members of local committees who were known to be more radical than the existing board, clearly strengthened the Spock faction.

A month later the members of the SANE Corporation, the original founders of the organization bearing legal and historical responsibility for it, admonished the board to adhere to the original goals and methods of SANE. These methods emphasized "policy change," based on changing American public opinion, and differed from the "social protest" approach used by other organizations that often opposed democratic values. SANE, the statement declared, affirms that its goals "can be attained using present U.S. political institutions. . . . Sane applies a single standard of judgment to the actions of the U.S. and other nations." Those who insisted on the social protest viewpoint, the statement concluded, "must stand aside so that work can continue."[43]

Homer Jack, director of the Unitarian Universalist Association and one of the members of the SANE Corporation, expressed his apprehension about the threatened leftward drift of SANE in even more forthright language. In a talk given at Cornell University, Jack criticized the failure of the New Left to learn from the past. The New Left's willingness to work with all persons and groups irrespective of ideology was basically admirable, but their intolerance of those who opposed Communism was annoying. "There were communists in some organizations and they were using these organizations for their own party ends. To dismiss this history as latterday McCarthyism is sheer political innocence. Beyond innocence there is a romantic anti-intellectualism."[44] On June 22, Jack warned Richard J. Neuhaus, a Lutheran pastor and a new member of the board, that "increasingly I see a conspiracy to take over National SANE (for which no doubt I will be called paranoid if not senile) not by communists, but by pro-communist types."[45]

Concern about the inroads of the New Left was also building up in some of the local committees. In late February 1967, a group of present and former officers of the Chicago Area SANE warned the membership that Chicago SANE was experiencing "a rather brazen bid for power on the part of a small minority that is unrepresentative of SANE, either nationally or locally." Those reaching for power, the dissenters charged, assumed "that the principal source of trouble in the world is American military power; that 'united front' activities are not only acceptable but preferable; that SANE's best hope for the future lies with the New Left, the alienated and rejectionist student groups . . . and that SANE's principal mission should be to consolidate all the forces on the Left who oppose the war in Vietnam, for whatever reason."[46] In June of 1967 occurred a portent of things to come on the national level. Chicago SANE voted to eliminate from its by-laws the until then standard SANE provision that "those who are not free, because of party discipline or political allegiance, to criticize the actions of totalitarian nations with the same standard by which they challenge other nations are barred from membership in the Committee and thus from any voice in deciding the Committee's policies and programs." Proponents of this change argued that SANE's anticommunist statement was "a manifestation of the McCarthy period" and likely to perpetuate "a climate of suspicion, name calling and rigidity of outlook in foreign policy."[47]

On August 2, Keys sent a memo marked "Confidential" to the officers of national SANE in which he informed them "that Ben [Spock] is violating the spirit and letter of the Board resolution of April 27." He cited three "important recent instances" in which Spock, without prior consultation with the board, had participated in activities contravening SANE policies: (1) Spock had led a peace march in Los Angeles sponsored by the Peace Action Council, "a catch-all group dominated by far left dissidents." (2) At a recent SANE press conference, called to state that SANE was not prepared to support third-party activity, Spock had declared his willingness to be a third-party candidate. (3) Spock had appeared at a press conference of the National Conference for New Politics and thus had publicly assumed a leadership position in a group known for the view that American institutions were no longer workable. Keys noted that he had refrained from making public comments on peace movements issues, but that he did not see how he could "be expected to continue to do so as long as the Co-Chairman enunciates policies not accepted by SANE."[48]

Unperturbed by this complaint lodged against him by SANE's executive secretary, Spock continued to disregard the April resolution. He served as co-chairman of the National Conference for New Politics held at the Palmer House in Chicago during the Labor Day weekend of 1967. Ten local SANE committees were also formally represented. The gathering, marked by an orgy of self-abnegation on the part of the white majority, finally decided not to support a third-party movement, but its shrill, radical rhetoric very clearly had little in common with the moderate politics national SANE was then supporting. Nevertheless, when this matter was brought up at the September meeting of the SANE board, the Spock forces succeeded in tabling a motion that reaffirmed SANE's position on various issues discussed in Chicago and thus would have highlighted the differences between the two organizations. This led to a threat from Cousins to resign from the board. Next, Irving Howe, editor of the democratic socialist magazine *Dissent* and a critic of the New Left, offered a resolution affirming the incompatibility of SANE and National Conference on New Politics policies. The resolution declared that officers of SANE therefore should not serve as officers of the National Conference. This motion was ruled out of order.[49] Despite this backing from the SANE board, Spock at the end of September submitted his resignation as co-chairman of SANE, stating that he "did not think he could do justice to both jobs, especially in view of all the controversy involving the National Conference for New Politics."[50] He did remain a member of the board and continued to play a key role in SANE.

The highhanded tactics of the national board, dominated by Spock supporters, by then had driven some old-time leaders of SANE to the conclusion that the organization was beyond repair. On September 20, the officers of the SANE San Francisco regional committee asked the members of the SANE corporation to constitute a new national board and to submit this action to the judgment of the SANE membership. If the corporation failed to act by October 20, they would resign. In lengthy memos addressed to the corporation and the board, the California leaders expressed the view that "the present National Board has fundamentally altered the goals, the political direction, the assumptions about American and International politics" of SANE. It had failed to repudiate the leadership of Spock despite the fact that the co-chairman had given his name to "the National [Conference] for New Politics (now committed to supporting all 'wars of liberation'), and a dozen other events and groups whose peace position amounts to a justification of one side of a war."

In the past, the California group pointed out, SANE had fought "the rigid anticommunism of the Cold War" while at the same time it had opposed the "hesitation by liberal forces to criticize the policies or goals of Communist nations or political organizations." Now, on the other hand, the board had come under the domination of individuals who supported the radical segment of the antiwar movement, a coalition of forces united by "opposition to present U.S. power and influence in world politics and an agreement . . . to silence all criticism of communist activity whether undertaken from Havana, Peking or Moscow." These individuals and groups, while purporting to speak for peace, saw America as the single villain in Vietnam, charged that America was engaged in the deliberate and systemic extermination of colored people in a racist war, and found American actions indistinguishable from Nazi genocide. "SANE," the California leaders stated, "can more effectively and honestly review the terribly mistaken judgments of past U.S. policy in Vietnam and the horror of our present military action there, when SANE distinguishes itself from such views." SANE should affirm its commitment to democratic values and not gloss over "its differences from groups committed to the expansion of the power of totalitarian structures or to racist ideologies."[51]

The California leaders were not alone in reaching these conclusions. On October 10, fourteen leading officers, sponsors, and board members of SANE submitted a letter of resignation and announced the formation of a new organization that would carry on and expand the work done by SANE in the past. The group included founding members Norman Cousins, Donald Harrington, Lawrence Meyer, and Orly Pell, as well as Irving Howe, Victor Reuther, and other well-known public figures. The signers solicited support for this step from other SANE leaders, but stated that *"the resignation will not be tendered or made public* until it is clear that the conditions which have brought us to this decision cannot be remedied."

The "Letter of Resignation" declared that the signers had concluded with regret that "further association is no longer an effective way of serving the cause of peace. . . . [W]e no longer have faith in the capability of the Board of Directors to function effectively in advancing SANE's goals—an end to the war in Vietnam, safeguarded disarmament and a strengthened United Nations." For almost a year, the letter declared, SANE had been immobilized by sharp differences over goals and tactics which reflected divisions in the peace movement generally.

> There is a basic division in the "peace movement" between those groups and people who support the use of democratic means to bring about change in policy and those who believe the society must be overturned before peace is possible. The former, of which SANE has been one, seek to communicate with and to convince both the public and policy makers to adopt needed changes democratically through education, political activity and public pressure. The latter accept the view—or are prepared politically and intellectually to subordinate themselves to those who accept the view—that American society cannot be significantly reformed, that foreign policy cannot be changed through action within the democratic process, that a negative and sometimes nihilistic attitude of "alienation" is desirable, and that it is necessary to emphasize forms of protest which in our judgment can only be self-isolating and self-defeating. While both groups want an end to the Vietnam war, their basic policies and expectations of America are vastly different and irreconcilable.
>
> Recent action of the Board of SANE has effectively turned control of the organization over to those elements within SANE which hold the views of the negatively oriented and anti-democratic groups or support close cooperation with them.

It was understandable, the letter declared, "that the frustration over the Vietnam war would lead some to seek common cause with groups whose interpretation of America are radically different from those of SANE, but it is also inevitable that by doing so SANE would lose its integrity of purpose and power to convince."[52]

Meeting on October 19, the SANE board adopted an amendment to the organization's by-laws, proposed by Chairman H. Stuart Hughes, which reaffirmed its fidelity to the democratic process and the principle of non-violence. As a concession to the Spock forces, the amendment also stated that SANE opposed intervention or interference in the affairs of other nations. While SANE believed that a single standard of judgment had to be applied to all nations, as American citizens they had a special responsibility to influence the policies and actions of their own government.[53]

This compromise formulation of SANE's political position was adopted unanimously, but the action did not allay the apprehensions of the members who had submitted their conditional resignation.

On October 20, the *New York Times* reported the crisis among SANE's leadership in a front-page story which left the impression that the resignation of the fourteen had already taken place. In a new communication, issued four days later, the original signers of the letter of resignation expressed regret about the leak. They also announced that nineteen other sponsors of SANE, including Roger Baldwin, Nathan Glazer, and Leonard Bernstein, had meanwhile added their names. Eventually, a total of forty-nine SANE leaders stood ready to resign unless reforms were instituted. Most of them eventually withdrew their threatened resignation as a result of concerted efforts by conciliators within the organization who succeeded in adding to the board members-at-large agreed upon by both factions. But these changes merely papered over a deep and fundamental split which effectively left the Spock forces in control of SANE.

On October 21, the National Mobilization Committee to End the War in Vietnam (the new name of what earlier had been called the Spring Mobilization) staged its march on the Pentagon. Advance publicity had called for resistance, not protest, and for "putting bodies into the gears of the war machine" by blocking Pentagon entrances. The SANE board had taken no stand on this demonstration though it authorized local committees to take part. However, the Spock forces on the board had managed to pass a resolution which condemned the SANE San Francisco chapter for publicly criticizing the planned march and threatened to withdraw its charter.[54] This action provided the last straw for the leadership of the Northern California SANE committee, who now submitted their resignation. In a letter sent out on the day of the Washington demonstration, chairman Clarence Heller and vice chairman Robert Pickus explained that they had taken this step because of their belief that "the present national board is leading SANE into cooperation with a coalition that has agreed to oppose only Washington's policies and to silence any criticism of the military policies of various elements of the Communist world." Their reason for resigning, they explained, was "not that this coalition is dominated by leadership from various communist, New Politics and Black Power groups. We would welcome these elements in a genuine peace movement, but when we see SANE refusing to differentiate itself from a coalition which is more anti-Washington than anti-war, in which these elements play crucial leadership roles, we must resign from SANE."[55]

Others to resign included SANE founder Norman Cousins and executive director Donald Keys. In a letter addressed to the members of the board, Keys explained that his resignation was a result of the failure of the board to adopt the reforms and clear political policy demanded by the forty-seven board members and sponsors who had submitted a pending letter of resignation. "The Board of SANE has failed to state that it will not take part on the basis of differences in principle and belief in joint activities with organizations and groups which reject the democratic process, encourage violence and offer only protest and opposition without constructive alternative foreign policy proposals." The board had instituted a method of electing board members "the effect of which grants control of the organization to those elements within SANE which either hold the views of the negatively-oriented and anti-democratic 'peace groups,' sympathize with them, or actively support cooperation with them." The two major trends in the peace movement, Keys maintained, were by their nature "incompatible and mutually divergent. It is tragic that SANE is unwilling to make this divergence clear either within its organization or to the public it is attempting to reach and serve."[56]

In the view of Keys, the crisis of SANE was of importance not only to SANE but to the entire peace movement. He therefore accepted the invitation of the magazine *War/Peace Report* to discuss the meaning of the events that had taken place for a larger public. In an article entitled, "SANE's Wayward Drift to the Left," Keys argued that under the heat of the Vietnam War the Old and New Left had coalesced, "the latter providing the dynamism and numbers, the former attempting to channel the newly available energies to its own ends and to the service of its own analysis of our society." This new movement was supported by Dr. Benjamin Spock and his supporters in SANE who favored a policy of "non-exclusion" and sought the unity of all peace forces irrespective of their political outlook. "Neither Spock nor his followers seem to understand that alliances with the left preclude effectiveness in reaching the broader American public that alone can force policy change."

The radical peace movement, which the forces newly in control of SANE were supporting, Keys argued, pursued goals at variance with those favored by SANE until now. "For the peace movement far left, there can be no peace in the world until American society is dismantled and rebuilt—to their prescription. It is this conclusion regarding the United States that has led to peace movement links with the Maoist factions of the Communist party, to identification with 'all wars of liberation,' and in particular to active support of Hanoi and the National Liberation Front, in contrast with efforts of other segments of the peace movement to bring the conflict to an early conclusion through a negotiated settlement." The split within SANE over these issues, Keys concluded, had been "papered over by accommodation and expressions of good will, but whether the glue will hold through the next good rain is difficult to predict."[57]

SANE Becomes Part of the Social Protest Forces

Donald Keys's pessimistic prognosis for SANE was soon born out by events. Under the embittering experience of the Vietnam conflict, the organization moved steadily leftward and its rhetoric became increasingly shrill. Today it is part of the "peace and justice" network that considers the United States the major cause of the world's problems and fights American "interventionism." The original stress on evenhandedness has been lost and so has the policy of excluding from SANE those unable to apply to other nations the same standards of criticism that are used in judging the United States. SANE today works in coalition with any and all political groups opposed to the foreign policy of the Reagan and Bush administrations, including Communist fronts like the U.S. Peace Council and the Committee in Solidarity with the People of El Salvador (CISPES). There have been individuals and groups, it should be noted before we look at this record, who have taken *some* of the same positions on these issues as SANE. But no group other than those belonging to the anti-American Left have taken *all* of these stands, the cumulative effect of which, if adopted, would have been to make the United States a second-rate power unable to defend its vital interests.

The following are some of the milestones in this process of far-reaching change: At a press conference in September 1969, Spock announced SANE's new policy of "immediate, total and unilateral withdrawal" of U.S. forces from Vietnam, and from that time on the organization joined most of the direct action protests of the radical antiwar movement. In early 1971, SANE adopted as a new program priority the demilitarizing of American society and called for opposing "the power of an oppressive military machine." SANE, the five-year strategy statement declared, had to question the Cold War assumption that the United States "must defend the 'free world' against aggressive communism." In fighting the military-industrial complex and the "tendency to intervene in underdeveloped countries" such as Indochina, SANE should seek out new allies—even from among those organizations "whose social philosophy may disagree with ours in certain areas." The goals to be pursued included a sharp reduction in military spending, multinational efforts to achieve disarmament, and a shifting of resources to build a humane society.[58]

An advertisement run in the *New York Times* on June 20, 1971, headlined "America Has a Tapeworm," described the U.S. as "armed to the teeth and rotting to the core." In line with this view, during the last twenty years SANE has opposed the development of practically every new weapons system proposed for the United States—the B-1 bomber, the Trident nuclear submarine, the neutron bomb, the MX missile. SANE was a strong supporter of the nuclear freeze movement and sought to block the deployment of Pershing II and cruise missiles in Europe. In 1985, it went on record as opposing the Strategic Defense Initiative (SDI), commonly referred to as Star Wars.[59]

In 1976, SANE came out against American intervention in Angola and for a withdrawal of U.S. forces from South Korea. Marcus Raskin, a founder of the Institute for Policy Studies—often referred to as the "Think Tank of the Left"—and later a co-chairman of SANE, in 1981 stated that SANE "is committed to a system of international organization that opposes unilateral interventions and covert operations, and neither skirts international law nor beats up on developing nations impoverished by generations of imperialism." Together with CISPES, SANE has opposed U.S. military aid to El Salvador. An article in *SANE World* in 1981 accused the Reagan administration of having "launched a Cold War crusade against alleged Soviet and Cuban intervention in El Salvador." Sending military aid and advisers, it was said, would repeat the mistakes of Vietnam and Iran and could only "prolong El Salvador's strife."[60]

From early on, SANE has defended the Sandinista regime of Nicaragua and it has been in the forefront of those opposing military aid to the Nicaraguan resistance. In 1982, SANE participated in a delegation of twelve American peace organizations that visited Nicaragua at the invitation of the Nicaraguan Peace Committee. Reporting on this visit, the SANE delegate noted that Nicaragua had problems, but that "people are being organized to participate in the political and economic decisions that affect their daily lives." SANE executive director David Cortwright, who was in Nicaragua during the elections of 1984, related upon his return that he had found the elections to be "fair and open. . . . I came away with great respect for the Nicaraguans and a renewed determination to prevent American intervention." SANE has argued that there is no proof of the export of arms from Nicaragua to the guerrillas in El Salvador. The Sandinista regime, an article in *SANE World* in early 1986 declared, could be "legitimately criticized on some grounds" but was not totalitarian. "Even under continued economic and military siege by the U.S., policies of the new government have brought education, land, health care, and better nutrition to the lives of most Nicaraguans." Later that year, Cortright called the American air raid on Libya "part of an orchestrated campaign to whip up military frenzy in this country so that the

President can stampede Congress into supporting his request for aid to the Nicaraguan terrorists."[61]

Since the 1970s, SANE has abandoned its prohibition on the acceptance of Communists and procommunists into the organization. In 1960, it will be recalled, SANE had decided to discourage the affiliation of Communists and other totalitarians by inserting in all of its promotional pamphlets the sentence: "The national committee needs and welcomes all persons whose support is not qualified by adherence to Communist or other totalitarian doctrine." In 1966, this language was changed to:

> SANE welcomes as members all persons who put humanity above ideology, race or nation, who work for human survival and for realization of a world community of nations with freedom and justice under law, who are in general agreement with SANE's policies and programs and who are free to apply the same standards of criticism to the actions of all nations.

The national board, in adopting this new language, went on record as stating that "the changes in wording did not constitute a change in the position of the Board on the matter of affiliation."[62] But by the early seventies the leadership of SANE had changed and from that time on even the milder language adopted in 1966 has no longer appeared on SANE publicity.

During the last ten years, SANE not only has ceased to adhere to the original exclusionary policy, but some of its leaders have political credentials that very clearly would not have passed muster during the organization's first twenty years. In 1977, SANE appointed as its new executive director David Cortright. The thirty-year-old Cortright had been active in the movement against the war in Vietnam and in 1975 had published *Soldiers in Revolt*. This study of "the struggle within the American military against repression and the Indochina intervention" had been prepared during almost three years of study under Marcus Raskin at the Institute for Policy Studies (IPS). In his introduction to the book, Raskin praised Cortright for teaching us that the "struggle was not only against the war, but also against an authoritarian military machine oiled for world imperialism."[63] Raskin himself in 1985 became a co-chairman of SANE. The other co-chairman, since 1979, has been William Winpisinger, president of the International Association of Machinists. In January 1978, Winpisinger was a member of a national committee that sponsored a "Dialogue on Disarmament and Detente" held in Washington with a delegation from the World Peace Council.[64] His political views are in line with that of Raskin and other New Left figures.

The composition of SANE's board of directors has also undergone a decisive change. The place of moderates such as Homer Jack and Irving

Howe has been taken by members of the left such as Jesse Jackson, Michael Klare of IPS, antiwar activist Cora Weiss, and Representative Ronald Dellums, a promoter of CISPES and other hard-left causes. Serving with Raskin and Winpisinger on the board's executive committee is Jack O'Dell, active in the World Peace Council and, in the words of the *New Republic,* a man "with a long record of public identification with Stalinism, American style," whose "politics will not bear scrutiny."[65] In view of O'Dell's frequently enunciated procommunist views, the question of whether O'Dell is technically still a member of the Party is essentially irrelevant.[66]

It is not surprising that in recent years SANE's public activities have been fully nonexclusive. In 1983, SANE joined the Campaign for Peace with Justice in Central America which, in addition to pacifist groups like the American Friends Service Committe and the Women's International League for Peace and Freedom, included CISPES and the U.S. Peace Council.[67] In 1985, SANE was a sponsor of the April Actions for Peace, Jobs and Justice held in Washington, which was endorsed by a similar roster of organizations. In early 1988, SANE joined the "Disarmament and Common Security by the Year 2000" network composed of the usual "peace and justice" groups, including the U.S. Peace Council.[68] In March 1989, SANE participated in nationwide demonstrations against American aid to El Salvador, organized by a new coalition, Stop the U.S. War in El Salvador, which includes CISPES, the Pledge of Resistance, and other groups of what is often referred to as the "Solidarity Left." Clearly SANE has come a long way since the days when it ruled out joint activities with pacifist and pro-Soviet organizations.

Even the American Communist party itself is considered by SANE to be pro-peace. When in October 1980 *SANE World* reviewed the qualifications of the presidential candidates, it concluded that Carter had capitulated to the right wing because during his presidency "the military budget has grown by leaps and bounds," and it dismissed Ronald Reagan as having a "zealous and obsessive cold war mentality." In view of this dismal choice, the SANE publication therefore recommended attention to "independent political parties" such as the Communist party which "is on the ballot in more than 20 states and has traditionally emphasized the issues of peace, disarmament and detente."[69]

By the time of the election victory of Ronald Reagan, SANE's membership was down to little more than 8,000. The Reagan administration's arms buildup and newly assertive foreign policy helped revive the fortunes of the peace movement, including SANE. By 1987, SANE had over 150,000 members and was considered the largest and most effective peace organization in the country. In January of that year the SANE board of directors approved the merger of SANE with the Nuclear Weapons Freeze Campaign. The new organization became known as SANE/FREEZE; the Reverend William Sloane Coffin, Jr., agreed to be its first president. In 1988, SANE/FREEZE claimed 180,000 members and over 250 chapters. Soon thereafter, with peace breaking out all over, the organization experienced a new crisis. Like other movements that had thrived on the Cold War and the fear of nuclear Armageddon, SANE/FREEZE now was hit by a serious fall-off in contributions and was forced to lay off a quarter of its national staff. Morale is said to be low.[70]

In a history of SANE, published in 1986, the author welcomed the then pending merger as a historic step that would further strengthen the American peace movement. SANE, Milton R. Katz wrote, had started out as a "product of Cold War liberalism" and for a long time had been an organization that had spent "too much time and energy grappling with the issue of working with Communists and more radical peace activists and protecting the process of consensus-formation as the way to influence American foreign policy." By the late 1980s, however, Katz concluded with approval, SANE had evolved "into the nation's largest peace membership organization that has left its elitist and exclusionist policies far behind."[71] Katz is correct in his assessment of SANE's place on the contemporary political spectrum, for SANE today indeed considers itself a part of America's Left. Commenting on SANE's 1986 national peaceworks conference, the organization's director of communications described SANE as "the realization of the New Left dream: a multicultural, multi-issue coalition—now grounded in political pragmatism."[72]

The degree of pragmatism that is said to characterize SANE can be open to debate, but that SANE today represents the fulfillment of some of the New Left's aspirations is undoubtedly true. Whether this development is to be welcomed or regretted is also a matter on which opinions will differ. Some of the founders of SANE are less than happy with the changes that have taken place. Homer Jack, who stayed with SANE's directorship until he was eased off the board of directors in 1984, has noted that the present leadership of America's peace organizations "is reinforcing or creating a peace and justice ghetto" that does not reach middle America.[73] The abandonment of SANE's anticommunist posture may well be one of the important reasons for this failure to escape the ghetto of the radical Left.

12

The Nonexclusionary Policy Triumphant: SDS and the Movement Against the Vietnam War

The late 1950s and early 1960s saw a limited revival of campus radicalism. The country was recovering from the climate of conformity created by McCarthyism; the civil rights movement was beginning to stir; and the fear of nuclear war created a sense of urgency about safeguarding world peace. C. Wright Mill's book *The Power Elite,* published in 1956, challenged the notion that American democracy represented the best of all possible worlds. The book found a sympathetic response among young people searching for a vision of radical social change. Mills, recalls former SDS leader Tom Hayden in his memoirs, combined "the rebel life-style of James Dean and the moral passion of Albert Camus with the comprehensive portrayal of the American condition we were looking for."[1]

New organizations were born, such as Students for a Sane Nuclear Policy and the Student Peace Union. Older groups such as the Young People's Socialist League (YPSL), the youth arm of the Socialist party, and the Student League for Industrial Democracy (SLID), the descendant of Upton Sinclair's Intercollegiate Socialist Society, experienced a modest growth in membership. In January 1960, SLID changed its name to Students for a Democratic Society (SDS). By 1962, SDS had become the most important radical student group; soon thereafter it became virtually synonymous with what came to be called the "New Left."[2] What attracted young people to the New Left, recall Peter Collier and David Horowitz, leading figures of this new social movement, "was the opportunity to be Leftists in a new way: not as servile agents of a foreign power but as the shapers of an indigenous radicalism."[3]

Students for a Democratic Society Reject Anticommunism

From its beginnings, SDS included among its leading figures a considerable number of "red diaper babies," the offspring of Communist parents. "As one read about the student radical leaders in the press," Norman Podhoretz recalled in his autobiography, "one kept coming upon scions of what could be called the First Families of American Stalinism."[4] Equally significant, in a generational revolt designed to differentiate itself from its parent body, the League for Industrial Democracy (LID), SDS from early on adopted a self-conscious anti-anticommunism. Ironically, it was the commitment of SDS to a policy of nonexclusion, openness, and participatory democracy that some years later enabled a Maoist faction of Marxist-Leninists to infiltrate and ultimately destroy SDS.

In June 1962, SDS held its founding convention at Port Huron, Michigan, and adopted a political program that became known as the Port Huron Statement. Some of the most heated debates developed over the Communist issue. It began with the question of whether a member of the Communist-sponsored Progressive Youth Organizing Committee could be seated as an observer, and continued in regard to several other parts of the new program. The YPSL faction present, some of them veterans of many battles with the American Communist party, argued for a tough anticommunist stand. The majority that prevailed, however, insisted on a new start and quite deliberately attacked some of the dogmas of the anticommunist Old Left. The Port Huron call for a "new left," drafted by a 1961 graduate of the University of Michigan, Tom Hayden, and approved by the convention with only minor amendments, therefore came out against "Cold War anti-communist" politics. Anticommunism, the statement maintained, presented itself as a defense of individual freedom. "But actually 'anti-communism' becomes an umbrella by which to protest liberalism, internationalism, welfareism, the active civil rights and labor movements."

> An unreasoning anti-communism has become a major social problem for those who want to construct a more democratic America. McCarthyism and other forms of exaggerated and conservative anti-communism seriously weaken democratic institutions and spawn movements contrary to the interests of basic freedoms and peace. . . . Even many liberals and socialists [read: LID members] share static and repetitious participation in the anti-communist crusade and often discourage tentative, inquiring discussion about "the Russian question" within their ranks.[5]

In line with this thinking, the convention also modified the exclusion clause in the constitution of SDS, which was seen as too negative and "redbaiting." In place of language that barred from membership "advocates of dictatorship and totalitarianism," the new provision read: "SDS is an organization of democrats. It is civil libertarian in its treatment of those with whom it disagrees, but clear in its opposition to any totalitarian principle as a basis for government or social organization. Advocates or apologists for such a principle are not eligible for membership."[6]

At the time SDS adopted the Port Huron Statement, the organization's anti-anticommunism did not imply any sympathy for the Soviet Union or the political doctrine of communism. On the contrary, the program approved by the 1962 convention included several references meant to make clear that SDS was "in basic opposition to the communist system" and did not regard the United States as solely responsible for the Cold War. Still, to the thirty-four-year-old Michael Harrington, who attended the convention as a representative of the LID, the young radicals were engaged on a dangerous course that smacked of heresy. "The world's oldest young socialist," as he described himself, therefore vigorously and passionately argued for a more strongly anticommunist platform. The fact that the convention had voted down an amendment to the constitution forbidding cooperation with procommunist or profascist groups was far more significant to him than the avowals of opposition to Communist doctrine.

As Harrington later related in an autobiographical work published in 1973, his anticommunism, shaped by years of sectarian strife and traumatic events like the Soviet suppression of the Hungarian Revolution of 1956, "was not simply a theory, but an emotion as well." For Tom Hayden and his fellow SDS activists, on the other hand, the American Communist party was a discredited remnant, and for these young people the recent Bay of Pigs invasion of Cuba was much more alive than memories of Hungary. Hence, Harrington wrote, "my notion of a progressive, Leftist anti-Communist made as much existential sense to them as a purple cow. For them, anti-Communism was *simply* the excuse American reactionaries used whenever they wanted to masquerade their own viciousness in some noble rhetoric." In the eyes of Harrington, "a resolute struggle against reactionary anti-Communism, including a principled defense of the rights of Communists, required, in the name of democratic and socialist values, an equal struggle against Communist totalitarianism. My logic," Harrington concluded in this retrospective, "was compelling. But the students at Port Huron had not shared the experiences that made this logic so vivid to me."[7]

The Port Huron convention was followed by what can justly be described as a comedy of errors, even though for the participants at the time it was undoubtedly a highly serious affair. After his return to New York, Harrington was informed by one of the YPSL observers at the convention that the changes in the program agreed upon after much discussion had been left out of the final version ratified by the gathering. This led to a "hearing" before the LID executive board at which SDS leaders Tom Hayden and Al Haber received a dressing-down for being soft on Communism and running their organization on principles opposed to those upheld by the LID. The elder statesmen decided to cut off SDS funds and to change the locks on the SDS office. Eventually, the complete text of the Port Huron Statement became available, and it was discovered that it did not contain anything completely unacceptable after all. After mediation by Norman Thomas, tempers cooled and SDS was restored to its former position. Still, as former SDS leader Todd Gitlin has correctly noted, "The patchwork could not last. Errors and accidents aside, two generations glowered at each other across a deep historical divide of experience as well as belief."[8]

The divide between the two groups and generations involved substantive issues as well as perceptions of the world. For the LID anticommunism was at the core of political identity. The battles they had fought with the Communists sometimes had been not just ideological contests. At a meeting with the young people, one LID leader is said to have taken off his shirt in order to show Al Haber the scars Communists had inflicted on him at the Madison Square Garden riot of 1934. For SDS, on the other hand, anticommunism was essentially synonymous with McCarthyism and anti-anticommunism was therefore a political as well as moral imperative. They had hopes that Third World revolutions such as that of Castro's Cuba would redeem the socialist ideal betrayed by the Soviet Union. They saw these revolutions achieve the kind of closely knit community which they hoped to build in America.

The commitment to a strong sense of community also meant that personal persuasion was seen as the preferred way to deal with dissenters. Many of these young people had never seen a live Communist. They knew little about the history of radicalism in America, yet they believed that Communists, however perverted by Stalinism, at least stood for radical change. This view of the Communists had been taught to them by the children of the Old Left in their midst, for whom they had much admiration. "The majority of SDSers, from liberal or social-democratic backgrounds," writes Gitlin, "had been drawn (like me) to red-diaper babies as living, breathing carriers of the radical tradition, conscientious objectors to the American Celebration."[9] In reaction to Harrington and the LID, who brandished history as a weapon of ideological combat, SDS members embraced a deliberate agnosticism about what they saw as the sterile debates of earlier days. "A disregard of the past—a calculated innocence," remarks another former SDS leader, "became a perverse badge of their own political independence."[10] Eventually, SDS was to pay a heavy price for this ignorance of history.

The infatuation with revolutionary movements in the Third World led SDS into identification with Vietnam's National Liberation Front and into early opposition to American intervention in Southeast Asia. On May 2, 1964, SDS participated in a demonstration in New York City against American involvement in Vietnam. This protest had been organized by the May Second Committee, a student group formed at Yale University and dominated by the Progressive Labor party, a Maoist breakaway from the Communist party. In 1966, the May Second movement dissolved itself and its members entered SDS. Already in 1964, however, the ideas and vocabulary of the group left their imprint on SDS's political thinking and exerted a radicalizing effect. The SDS president's report published in October 1964 declared: "We must disconnect the concerned peace activist or scholar from his belief that American foreign policy is benign and motivated by a concern for the 'protection' of democracy, and make him face the reality of American imperialism and the forces that sustain it."[11]

On August 7, 1964, Congress passed the Gulf of Tonkin resolution, which authorized President Johnson to "take all necessary measures" to prevent Communist aggression in Southeast Asia. In February 1965, against the background of a deteriorating situation in the fighting in South Vietnam, the administration started a series of bombing raids against North Vietnam. On March 8, the first American ground combat units went ashore on the beaches north of Danang. Soon thereafter, SDS issued a call for a march on Washington on April 17 to protest the growing American involvement. The call made it clear that the demonstration was to be nonexclusionary. "We urge the participation of all those who agree with us that the war in Vietnam injures both Vietnamese and Americans and should be stopped."[12] As Thomas Powers, a supporter of the principle of nonexclusion, put it in his history of the war at home some years later, "To have excluded the Communists from its [the movement's] ranks would have fatally weakened their argument that fear of Communism was not a proper justification for the devastation of Vietnam."[13]

Some other critics of American policy in Vietnam did not see it this way. On the eve of the march, several prominent American peace activists—including A. J. Muste, Bayard Rustin, Norman Thomas, and H. Stuart Hughes—issued a statement which, while it supported the demonstration, sought to discourage the participation of Communist organizations: "We welcome the cooperation of all those groups and individuals who, like ourselves, believe in the need for an independent peace movement, not committed to any form of totalitarianism or drawing inspiration from the foreign policy of any government."[14] For Michael Harrington, the issue was primarily one of prudence: "I felt that any movement that appeared to be a fifth column for Communists doing battle with Americans would have no chance of winning the people of the country to the idea of withdrawal from Indochina."[15] This was also the thinking of several peace organizations such as the Committee for a Sane Nuclear Policy (SANE) and Turn Toward Peace, a coalition of some sixty national organizations organized in 1961 in order to build momentum for disarmament without surrendering democratic values. These groups consequently declined to endorse the march which appeared to them more opposed to the American side in the conflict than to the war itself.

The policy of nonexclusion—the refusal, on principle, to rule out joint activities with Marxist-Leninist groups—was reaffirmed at the annual convention of SDS held in June at a camp near Kewadin, a small town in upper Michigan. The gathering, attended by some five hundred people, also eliminated from the SDS constitution the exclusionary clause barring advocates of totalitarians. It now read: "SDS is an organization of democrats. It is civil libertarian in its treatment of those with whom it disagrees, but clear in its opposition to any anti-democratic principle as a basis for government or social organization." In vain did Tom Kahn, the LID emissary, warn that this change would lead to a break with the parent organization. In fact, Kahn's threat may well have provided additional impetus for passage, though the adoption of the new membership clause did indeed bring about the final parting of ways between SDS and the LID, which took place in October. "The capacity of a disciplined cadre to take over or paralyze a mass organization had been amply demonstrated in the Left of the Thirties and Forties," writes former SDS leader Todd Gitlin, "but that thread of history was either lost—like most other knowledge of what had happened in ancient times, i.e., before 1960—or glibly discounted as a useless relic, or worse, a recrudescence of bankrupt 'anti-Communism' (the very term now becoming a curse word). The amendments passed overwhelmingly."[16]

There was an irony to this development that Gitlin has noted with the benefit of hindsight and a newly acquired political maturity. "SDS stripped itself of its strongest line of defense at just the moment PL [the Maoist Progressive Labor party] was moving in. . . . Eight months after Kewadin, PL dissolved the relatively unruly M2M [May Second Movement], and its cadres promptly flocked into the happy hunting grounds of SDS." But at this point in time, SDS was a cocky, fast-growing movement that believed, as its new president, Carl Oglesby, put it, "democracy is nothing if it is not dangerous."[17]

Al Haber, the first president of SDS, provided a lengthy defense of the policy of nonexclusion in a pamphlet issued by the organization in 1965. "Nonexclusionism," Haber affirmed, "is both a moral and a pragmatic necessity." It was related "to a rejection of anti-communism as the primary principle of democratic radicalism." Haber acknowledged that the "new left" 's anti-anticommunism had complex psychological roots.

> These undoubtedly involve elements of pugnacious defiance, generational rebellion, limited historical experience, repugnance of loyalty oaths and their association with McCarthyism and profound estrangement from mainstream America. Basically the "new left" represents a desperate search for new ways in the face of failure of the old. They are repelled by the history of left sectarianism (though without knowing the history). They seek a style of politics which is direct, which speaks to the immediate issues and which deals with people as individuals, assuming their good intentions or basic morality. They believe that ideology evolves from action, and that any imposition of predetermined standards or categories of analysis narrows the creative potential of the movement.

Yet beyond these "gut feelings," Haber insisted, there were important other reasons for choosing anti-anticommunism—it was necessary as "a political response to the nature of anti-communism in America."

> Anti-communism has become the chief ideological weapon of defenders of the status quo, by which they not only justify political imperialism abroad, but also by which they outlaw the expression of radical vision and dialogue at home. . . . Communism, however defined, is the central category dividing good and evil. . . . Left anti-communism may have a different motivation, formulation and intent—it certainly derives from a clearer understanding of the realities and complexities of the "communist world." But as it *functions* and is heard by the American public, these subtleties are lost; its absolutism is translated into just one more prop supporting all-American consensus anti-communism.

The "new left," Haber argued, had to challenge anticommunism as the public's political frame of reference. Communists symbolized in America the threat to the country's basic institutions of free enterprise, private property, and the market. Inasmuch as SDS, too, was opposed to these cherished elements of the American way of life, it had to defeat the rhetoric of anticommunism and fight the exclusion of the Communists. "We must defend their right to participate, to express with us their views and to be heard on the merits of their views. For we demand nothing less than that for ourselves. . . . This does not mean that we embrace 'communism' or espouse its values, but we should be under no misapprehension that this may not put us in 'working alliance' with people whose values we oppose—just as we work with people to our 'right.' "

Nonexclusionism, Haber admitted, posed "certain inherent organizational problems and it requires a tremendous commitment to discussion and internal democracy." Yet he felt sure that contact with nondemocrats will not "convert or corrupt us" and that in a "free debate we have confidence in our conviction and our power to persuade." There also was no danger "that alien elements will 'take over' control of our organization," for it lacked "centralized levers of organizational power" as well as "hard-minded, cynical, doctrinaire manipulators so much feared." In sum, the "new left" had to risk the misuse of the principle of nonexclusionism. "The only way to determine who your friends are is to work with them and gain an understanding of their ideas and ultimate goals through continual discussion on the specifics of social progress that follow from those ideas."[18]

Haber's sense of sureness that SDS could not be taken over was based in part on SDS's decentralized and highly informal mode of organization which spurned all structure as a manifestation of "elitism." "They can't take us over because they can't find us" was the standard joke. When SDS president Oglesby addressed the annual dinner of the *National Guardian* on November 20, 1965, he argued similarly that SDS had no need of loyalty pledges or detectives in order to keep out undesirables. It is hard to see, Oglesby declared, "how a group could be 'taken over' unless it has handles of power that can be seized, some 'central apparatus' that can enforce orders. SDS has no such apparatus—only a beleaguered hot-spot in Chicago—and it is a main hard point with us that it never shall."[19]

Central apparatus or not, the struggle for SDS got under way just a few short months after these words of bravado had been uttered. In February 1966, the Progressive Labor party dissolved the May Second Movement and directed its members to enter SDS. Thus began what later SDSers were to call the invasion of the body-snatchers.[20] At about the same time, the Communist party urged members of the Du Bois Clubs of America, an organization controlled by the Party, to join SDS in order to recruit suitable cadres or at least "save" SDS from the Maoists.[21] Yet when the issue of "Communists in SDS" was discussed at the SDS 1966 convention, held in late August at Clear Lake, Iowa, a motion that anyone belonging to a disciplined party declare so before running for office in SDS was defeated by a resounding vote of 41–3. The idea that Communists could take over SDS was still regarded as a joke.[22]

The influx of various kinds of Marxist-Leninists coincided with the radicalization of SDS caused by the emergence of new leaders. In 1964, many of the original SDSers had gone into the slums in order to organize the poor. They were replaced, writes Hayden, "by a younger leadership, who knew only the bitterness of the mid-sixties, not the intellectual excitement and political hope of the decade's beginning. The early spirit of pragmatism and experimentation was steadily replaced by the adoption of more radical, abstract and ultimately paralyzing ideology. Instead of Camus, there were Sartre, Fanon, and then Herbert Marcuse." Marxism tended to appear in debate. "The language and style of the Old Left were beginning to seep into the New as the politics of Port Huron were rejected as 'liberal' and 'reformist.' "[23]

By early 1967, the influence of Progressive Labor (PL) within SDS had begun to make itself felt. In a sympathetic account of "the new radicals" published in 1966, Paul Jacobs and Saul Landau had described the "kids" as "open and searching. Even those emotionally *simpatico* with the Chinese or Cuban revolutions are not moral monsters. They are not comparable to the hard, ruthless party aparatchiks of the 1930's."[24] Yet in fact the PL cadres turned out to be every bit as hard and ruthless as the Communists loyal to Moscow, and the emotionally defined leftism of SDS proved incapable of withstanding the dogmatic Marxism-Leninism pushed by the shrewd and disciplined PL forces. Those members of SDS who had groped their way to radicalism through opposition to the war in Vietnam, writes Kirkpatrick Sale in his account of SDS, "found an undeniable appeal in PL's ready-made formulas. . . . And those who were simply young and easily swayed could be impressed by the PLers' open espousal of revolution, thoroughgoing anti-Americanism, unselfish devotion to the workers' cause, forthright declarations of communism—and, not least, their readiness to take on the hard jobs involved in running a chapter, a devotional task willed upon them by the party and applauded by all their fellows."[25]

Open warfare between the rival factions of SDS broke out at the group's 1968 convention held in June at Michigan State University. The well-organized caucus of the PL forces, the Worker-Student Alliance (WSA), included only about one-quarter of the delegates, but they could sway many of the uncommitted. They were opposed by the so-called National Office (NO) faction which, in a mood of desperation, finally discarded the sentiments of love and trust and openly attacked PL as an "external cadre" that was using SDS for its own selfish ends. In a speech to the delegates, NO delegate Robert Pardun declared:

We must demand that external cadre operate in a principled fashion. It's simply not principled to move into SDS in order to recruit members for another party. Your function should be to bring in ideas. It's not principled either to pack meetings in order to manipulate acceptance of a line or to tie up valuable time discussing issues that the collective does not wish to discuss.[26]

This admonition to respect participatory democracy predictably failed to impress the PL cadres, though all of the delegates realized that the principle of nonexclusion had finally reached a crucial test. Another denunciation of PL was delivered by Tom Bell, a longtime SDSer and one of the founders of the Cornell chapter. Bell angrily charged that the PL people had obstructed constructive discussion by injecting their line at every meeting. Because of the organized opposition of PL it had been impossible to adopt a program. Unless SDS did something about this now, Bell argued, the organization would surely collapse. Sale's description of the reaction to this call for action against PL deserves to be quoted in full:

At that one PLer from the floor began shouting at the platform; Bell paused. Redbaiting, the PLer called, all you guys from the NO faction are simply redbaiting us because we're communists. Bell was stunned, his color livid, his voice quivering. "Redbaiting! *Red*baiting!? *I'm* the communist here, not you guys from PL who are holding this organization back from being *really* communist, from *really* getting on with the revolution. "PL out," he shouted into the microphone, "PL OUT." The cry was taken up immediately on the floor—possibly spontaneously, but more likely by pre-arrangement among the NO people hoping to stampede PL off the floor and out of the organization: "PL OUT! PL OUT! PL OUT!" Feet stamping in rhythm, hands clapping, chairs banging. . . . The din went on for two full minutes, then three, and four, turning the hall into a maelstrom of bitterness. . . . Soon the tumult faded: no more than two hundred of the delegates could be enticed into the outburst, and most of the rest just sat, . . . shocked at the flouting of SDS's antiexclusionism.[27]

Bell's claim that he was the true Communist was in keeping with SDS rhetoric in this turbulent year of 1968. The exanding war in Vietnam with its rising casualties and the sense of frustration resulting from the failure to end the conflict had radicalized SDS as it had other segments of the antiwar movement. Almost overnight everyone had become a Marxist revolutionary. Moreover, the contest with the PL forces had had the effect of making Marxism, and then Marxism-Leninism, the unofficial language of SDS. "Marxism," recalls the former SDSer James Miller, "became a tool seized on by both sides, not only as a theory for interpreting the world, but as a weapon in an internal power struggle."[28] There was much dramatic posturing. Bernardine Dohrn, soon to attain notoriety as a leader of the Weatherman faction of SDS, picked up a following at the 1968 convention when she declared she was a "revolutionary communist" with a small c, which meant a supporter of the NLF, of Castro's Cuba, and Third World revolution in general.[29] Ultimately, the competition over who could be the most ardent revolutionary was to contribute to the descent of an important faction of SDS into terrorism.

PL saw the failure of the attempt to expel it from SDS as a victory over anticommunism. The charge that PL represented an "external cadre," wrote Jeff Gordon, one of the leaders of the PL faction, in October 1968, was "an appeal to narrow organizational chauvinism and to anti-communism. 'External cadre' is no different than the term 'outside agitator,' which is used by the ruling class to attack those it can't defeat by other means." The appeal to anticommunism, Gordon noted, had been set back at the convention, but "the struggle promises to go on; anti-communism must be met more sharply and decisively each time it raises its ugly head. The future of SDS as a positive factor in the American revolution is at stake."[30]

PL's opponents in SDS, meanwhile, sought to blunt the all-out invasion of SDS by the Progressive Labor party by seeking ties with other revolutionary groups such as the supporters of Cuba and the left wing of the Communist party. The superior expertise of the Communists in ideological debate, it was hoped, could be used to halt the PL offensive and perhaps drive them from the organization. Another way of stealing the thunder from PL's association with Marxism was to outdo the Maoists in violence. During the Democratic convention in Chicago in November, the SDS contingent threw itself into cat-and-mouse games with the "pigs," the shotgun-toting Chicago cops who were easily provoked. "Youth Will Make the Revolution," recalls Gitlin, was one improvised poster in the SDS movement center near Lincoln Park. Barricades were built, rocks were thrown, and streetfighting was seen as a prelude to revolution. Those who felt qualms about particular tactics muffled their voices "for fear of derailing the onrushing movement."[31]

American casualties in Vietnam during 1968 were at an all-time high. The assassinations of Robert Kennedy and Martin Luther King, Jr., contributed to the atmosphere of crisis and violence. ROTC establishments and Selective Service offices were attacked with explosives and firebombs. In January 1969, several high-power transmission towers in and around Denver, Colorado, were dynamited. Following the tumultuous events of Chicago, SDS was at the peak of its strength. "We won," claimed a SDS statement. "We have a base in the millions of young people who have no place and want no place in plastic poverty pig America. . . .

Call us revolutionary Communists—you better. But you better call us the people because that's who we are."[32] SDS now had chapters on 350 to 400 campuses and perhaps as many as 100,000 members. Many more sympathized with the organization's militancy even if they did not themselves participate in disruptive demonstrations and confrontations. The National Office faction of SDS saw its strategy of "resistance" vindicated and considered itself the vanguard of the developing revolutionary forces. The PL bloc regarded Chicago a mistake because it had alienated the working class, on which they relied to "make the revolution." Everyone, however, now quoted Lenin, Stalin, and Mao in order to bolster his case and support his ongoing strategy. The reformist spirit of the civil rights movement, so important in the early history of SDS, had been superseded by a doctrinaire Marxism-Leninism and a commitment to revolutionary violence.

Outwardly booming, SDS was hurtling toward self-destruction. The June 1969 convention of SDS was to be its last. It was the scene of the final showdown between the organization's rival factions, all of them speaking in Marxist-Leninist tongues because, as Oglesby put it, there was "no other coherent, integrative, and explicit philosophy of revolution."[33] In opposition to the growing PL group, the Worker-Student Alliance, stood the newly constituted Revolutionary Youth Movement I, or Weathermen, so called after a line in a Bob Dylan song. They saw themselves as a "cadre organization" on the way to a "Marxist-Leninist party," committed to "armed struggle." Improvising from Chinese Defense Minister Lin Piao's 1965 polemic, the Weatherman sixteen-thousand-word position paper argued that, just as the Chinese revolutionaries had mobilized the peasantry and surrounded the cities, so revolutions in the Third World would surround the imperialist metropolis, the United States, and bring about its defeat. "The goal is the destruction of US imperialism and the achievement of a classless world: world communism."[34]

Fifteen hundred delegates convened in the Chicago Coliseum in June of 1969. About a third were controlled by the PL bloc, another third belonged to the Weathermen and their ally, the Revolutionary Youth Movement II (RYM II in the jargon of the time). The remaining third, writes Gitlin, "were baffled newcomers, dazed rank-and-filers, and other tendencies casting anathema on all the leading factions." For help the Weatherman–RYM II coalition brought in representatives of the Black Panthers, who delivered diatribes against the "armchair Marxists" of PL. At one point, a Black Panther spokesman read an ultimatum: the PLers had to change their line or "they will be considered as counterrevolutionary traitors and will be dealt with as such." The PL forces reacted by chanting "Smash redbaiting, *smash redbaiting*" and "Read Mao, *read Mao.*"

The climax came when the Weatherman–RYM II forces decided to expel PL and its allies for being "objectively anticommunist" and "counterrevolutionary." The expulsion question, it was determined, should not even be put to a vote of the plenary meeting, for it would have meant that "counterrevolutionaries" had the right to vote on their "counterrevolutionary nature." Instead, Bernardine Dohrn declared in a lengthy speech, the "Progressive Labor Party, because of its positions and practices, is objectively racist, anti-communist, and reactionary. . . . It has no place in SDS, an organization of revolutionary youth." This move led to a split in which each faction for a time claimed to be the real SDS.[35]

The end of SDS as an effective political organization had come. Many chapters collapsed, its members adopting a "plague on both your houses" attitude. SDS-PL continued to exist as a front for the Progressive Labor party until 1972, but it had lost its following and had become a mere shadow of its former self. In October of 1969, the Weathermen staged their "Four Days of Rage" in Chicago, in which two to three hundred people, equipped with helmets and armed with baseball bats and pipes, stormed through the streets of Chicago in order to "bring the war home." Cars and store windows were trashed, some seventy-five policemen were injured, and more than two hundred fifty of the self-styled revolutionaries were arrested.

During Christmas 1969, under the motto of bringing about "the disintegration of the pig order," the Weathermen convened a "national war council" in Flint, Michigan. John Jacobs, one of the leaders of the Columbia University uprising of 1968 and known as "JJ," declared: "We're against everything that's good and decent in honky America. We will burn and loot and destroy. We are the incubation of your mother's nightmare." Bernardine Dohrn praised Charles Manson and his "family," who had just been arrested for the murder of pregnant actress Sharon Tate and four others in Los Angeles, for understanding the wickedness of white America. "Dig it! First they killed those pigs, then they ate dinner in the same room with them, then they even shoved a fork into the victim's stomach. Wild!"[36]

Following this last public appearance, the Weathermen went underground and began a campaign of bombings. During the years 1969–70, there were 174 actual or attempted bombings associated with the white Left on the nation's campuses and at least 70 more off-campus.[37]

On March 6, 1970, several Weathermen were putting together antipersonnel bombs in a New York townhouse when one of them apparently misconnected a wire. Three of the bombers died in the blast that destroyed the house; several others staggered out of the rubble and disappeared into the night. The explosion not only killed three young lives; it marked the final and grotesque conclusion to the Port Huron dream of a new and better society. "We find violence to be abhorrent," the young idealists of 1962 had proclaimed, "because it requires generally the transformation of the target, be it a human being or a community of people, into a depersonalized object of hate."[38] Eight years later, one remnant of SDS had embraced hatred and a mindless campaign of systematic terrorism. Others drifted into revolutionary collectives or communes, described by Hayden as "closed enclaves with leadership worship, thought control, collective devouring of individual autonomy—totalitarian cells awaiting an apocalypse that never came."[39] Still others joined new, tiny and ever-splintering Marxist-Leninist groups.

Exclusionism, wrote Jack Newfield, one of the founders of SDS, in 1966, denies the root ideals of the radicalism of the New Left: "That human freedom and participation should be extended. That every individual is noble. That a new society based on love and trust must be created."[40] Whether a rejection of this highly idealistic view of human nature and the continued adherence to the principle of excluding undemocratic elements would have prevented the self-destruction of SDS none can say with assurance. The seemingly endless war in Vietnam had a strongly radicalizing effect, and SDS therefore might have embraced violence even if the organization had excluded totalitarians like PL. On the other hand, as we have seen earlier, the ideological competition with the PL forces was an important reason for the gradual drift of SDS into Marxism-Leninism and from there into revolutionary posturing and ultimately terrorism.

The unfortunate consequences of this contest have been acknowledged by some former members of SDS who for the longest time regarded the exclusion of Communists as an unprincipled concession to the spirit of the Cold War. SDS would have been a lot better off, conceded Maurice Isserman in 1983, "if it had been able to exclude the Stalinist Progressive Labor Party. In its early years S.D.S. was devoted to creating an indigenous, democratic radicalism; in its last years many of its activists wound up mimicking the language and style of the Progressive Labor Party cadre in a destructive 'more-revolutionary-than-thou' competition."[41] The issue, of course, goes beyond organizational provisions. Anti-anticommunism, the core of SDS's ideological independence, gradually became synonymous with sympathy for Third World Communist movements and regimes. Whether this abandonment of SDS's earlier commitment to democratic values was a logical and necessary outcome of the adoption of anti-

anticommunism is a question we need not speculate on here. The fact is that all organizations that have embraced anti-anticommunism have eventually ended up compromising their opposition to totalitarianism and have become apologists for Communist dictatorships in the Third World.

The anticommunism of liberals and democratic socialists was grounded in the recognition that the drive of Communists for the realization of heaven on earth, the classless and stateless society, had led to the widespread use of repression and the violation of elementary rules of human fairness and decency. Imbued with the belief that history is on their side and that communism is the necessary future of mankind, Communists employed coercive means that quickly turned their regimes into brutal tyrannies. In its early years, SDS rejected the totalitarian temptation, and many of its former leaders by now have affirmed the correctness of this position. Most of them have also acknowledged that the exclusion of Communists and others who defended repressive Communist regimes during SDS's early years was right on both prudential as well as moral grounds.

Yet the learning process has been limited and anticommunism is still suspect. Tom Hayden is one of several former SDSers who has admitted how mistaken he was in many of his political judgments about the Vietnamese in particular. "I was blind," he writes, "to the core of authoritarianism that, while crucial to military operations, led to the forced degradation of 're-education' camps, the horrifying exodus of the boat people, and the subordination of 'third-force' southerners and even former NLF cadres to the power and ideological interests of Hanoi after the war." Many of these flaws, Hayden concedes, "originated in the nature of Marxism-Leninism itself," and as a result of these experiences "revolution has lost much of its romantic quality for me."[42] Todd Gitlin, too, has taken note of "the injuries done to human freedom and dignity not only by the Soviet Union but by Castro's Cuba and the Chinese Cultural Revolution," and he has denounced the crimes and "the staggering carnage left by the Khmer Rouge."[43] At the same time, both Hayden and Gitlin affirm the need for "anti-interventionism" in Central America, a stance that could lead to the consolidation of new Communist regimes and more human tragedies of the kind that have overtaken Southeast Asia.

The Movement Against the Vietnam War Opts for Nonexclusion

When SDS organized the first major antiwar demonstration in Washington on April 17, 1965, it will be recalled, several prominent peace movement leaders including H. Stuart Hughes and Norman Thomas had issued a statement disavowing the policy of nonexclusion followed by the young radicals of SDS. The issue arose again during the SANE-sponsored march on Washington on November 27. But those old-timers upholding the exclusion of "kooks, Communists and draft dodgers" soon lost the argument for selectivity, and by the end of the year 1965 the unfolding antiwar movement had fully embraced the idea of nonexclusion. Increasingly, what became known as "The Movement" took on the character of a united front coalition in which various segments of the New and Old Left played a leadership role.

Ever since the beginning of the bombing of North Vietnam in February of 1965, various ad hoc committees opposing the growing American involvement had sprung up across the country. Seeking to reach a wide audience, these committees were nonexclusionary and included the National Coordinating Committee to End the War in Vietnam (NCC), which came into being in August. At the first national convention of the NCC held in Washington on November 25-28, attended by over one thousand delegates, almost half of those belonging to various "independent committees" were also members of the Young Socialist Alliance (YSA), the youth arm of the Trotskyist Socialist Workers party (SWP). Some SDSers, astonished by the systematic attempt of the "Trots" to take over, withdrew from the meeting, but the YSA soon made itself indispensable and consolidated its role in the antiwar movement. Before the NCC convention, recalls SWP leader Fred Halstead, the YSA "was generally considered the smallest and least influential of the three major radical youth groups (SDS, Du Bois Clubs, and YSA). After the convention it was recognized as a leading force in the immediate-withdrawal wing of the antiwar movement."[44]

The leaders of the antiwar coalition defended the principle of non-exclusion as a desirable political principle as well as a practical necessity in order to build a strong movement. It was upheld not only by Old Leftists who stood to benefit most from it but also by men such as A. J. Muste, who in earlier years had warned against the moral and political costs of cooperating with Communists. Now, in late 1966, Muste argued that the principle of nonexclusion was "necessary to the political health of the nation. People of the Left (Communists with or without quotation marks) should be permitted and expected to function normally in the political life of the country." One could not effectively combat the deep-rooted anticommunist psychology of the American people, on which toleration of the war was based, Muste maintained, if at the same time one excluded Communists from the antiwar movement. Finally, there was the pragmatic consideration that the Old and New Left represented the most activist core of the radical antiwar coalition. "What clinches the matter is that if we were to abandon the 'non-exclusion' principle we would quickly disintegrate."[45]

Nonexclusion soon came to mean not only the rejection of "red-baiting" and the granting of full citizenship to all prepared to oppose the war regardless of political affiliations and views but a deliberate attempt to bring Communists into leadership positions in the antiwar movement. At a gathering of antiwar activists in Cleveland, called by a faculty group at Western Reserve University in July 1966, a person was made a member of the group's steering committee because of his leading role in the Communist party. Similarly, the NCC chose Frank Emspak, a leader of the Communist Du Bois Clubs, as its national coordinator, and later added Arnold Johnson, an old-time national leader of the Communist party, to its steering committee.[46]

Also at work in creating sentiment for the principle of nonexclusion was the admiration felt by many members of the antiwar movement for the Communist revolutionaries who dared to stand up to the most powerful capitalist nation on earth. In a report on their visit to North Vietnam in early 1966, with stopovers in several Communist capitals, pacifist Staughton Lynd and SDS leader Tom Hayden related how they had discovered common elements with the Communists of Moscow, Prague, Peking, and Hanoi. "After all, we call ourselves in some sense revolutionaries. So do they. After all, we identify with the poor and oppressed. So do they. . . . One of the major tasks of the next generation if we are to have peace with justice, we think, will be to redefine America's interests, redefine Communism, redefine our place in the world, going beyond all conceptions inherited from the Cold War."[47] At a birthday dinner later that year for Herbert Aptheker, a leading functionary of the American Communist party, Lynd declared that the Old and the New Left had to maintain a dialogue and recognize their common interests. Both had to acknowledge their "historic responsibility to keep American imperialism from destroying the unprecedented upsurge of revolution in the Third World."[48] The Communists, it was felt by Lynd and Hayden as well as many of their contemporaries, had been maligned by American reactionaries. To overcome this heritage of McCarthyism it was necessary to practice nonexclusion.

While the idealistic young radicals of the New Left discovered common ideals with the Communists, the hard-nosed Old Left groups used the antiwar movement to enlarge their political influence and as a hunting ground for recruits to their organizations. The Trotskyist Socialist Workers party, in particular, recalled the radical pacifist Dave Dellinger several years later, "regularly packed meetings with delegates from exciting, new 'grass roots' Committees to End the War (the East Twenty-third Committee, the West Twenty-eighth Committee, the South Philadelphia Committee, the Morningside Housewives Committee), none of whom identified themselves as members of the SWP but all of whom were directed by an SWP floor leader."[49] Thus at the November 1966 organizing meeting of the Spring Mobilization Committee to End the War in Vietnam about half of the delegates were members of or sympathizers with the YSA. The Student Mobilization Committee, founded in December of the same year, was under the complete control of the YSA; SDS historian Sale calls it "a very successful front group" for the Trotskyists.[50]

As a result, the "Trots" were able to impose on what were then the two most active antiwar organizations their own line demanding an immediate and unconditional American withdrawal and rejecting any call for negotiations. Such a call, the SWP forces argued, carried the implication that the United States had a right to be in Vietnam. As a revolutionary socialist organization, its leader Fred Halstead later explained, the SWP "had an international obligation to do all it could to combat its own government's attempt to crush a colonial revolution" and to work for a victory of the Vietnamese Communists. In order to help bring this about the SWP avoided slogans like "Victory to the Vietnamese Revolution," which were considered inopportune from the point of view of gaining the support of the many Americans who sought peace and an end to the killing. Instead the Spring Mobilization worked at putting maximum pressure on the U.S. to get out of Vietnam. That, Halstead pointed out, "would help the Vietnamese revolution more than anything else we could possibly do."[51]

At the time, the dominant role of the SWP in the two mobilizations was clear only to the inner circle of the organizations. The Trotskyists' demand for an immediate and unconditional American withdrawal from Vietnam was presented as a policy that would bring peace and thus appealed to individuals and groups anxious to terminate a conflict with no apparent end. The rival policy of calling for negotiations between the warring parties had the backing of Arnold Johnson of the Communist party and of Cora Weiss of Women Strike for Peace, who argued for the need to bring in the "moderate groups."[52] This disagreement, of course, was purely tactical, for both Marxist-Leninist organizations were equally anxious to help the Vietnamese Communists. From early on, important segments of the movement against the American involvement in Southeast Asia were not so much antiwar as they were partisans of Hanoi, whose victory they sought to hasten through achieving an America withdrawal from Vietnam. Given the fragility of the Saigon government and the dependence of the South Vietnamese armed forces on American assistance, none could have any illusion about the effects of this policy. The New Left, too, soon came to favor a victory of Hanoi. A cover of *Ramparts,* the best-known magazine of the New Left, showed a picture of a child carrying a Viet Cong flag, with the caption: "Alienation is when your country is at war and you want the other side to win."

Not surprisingly, North Vietnam and the National Liberation Front went out of their way to support the activities of the antiwar movement. North Vietnamese officials, at meetings with radical antiwar activists held in Cuba, Hungary, and Czechoslovakia, provided tactical advice and helped coordinate worldwide antiwar demonstrations.[53] Communist propaganda regularly reported peace demonstrations as proof that the American people were weakening in their resolve. The North Vietnamese were convinced that, just as the Viet Minh had defeated France not only by skill on the battlefield but even more so by outlasting the patience of the French people for the war in Indochina, so North Vietnam and the Viet Cong would eventually triumph over the United States on account of their determination and the failure of the American people to last the course. This expectation proved all too accurate. American public opinion indeed turned out to be a crucial factor in the outcome of the war; it influenced military morale in the field, the long drawn-out negotiations in Paris, the settlement of 1973, and the cuts in aid to South Vietnam in 1974, a prelude to the final abandonment in 1975.

Communist influence in the antiwar movement was obvious to some lawmakers and government officials, though little of this information reached the wider public. At a private luncheon meeting with New York executives in October 1967, Secretary of State Dean Rusk related how FBI informants in the Communist apparatus had tipped him off to the exact wording of a peace telegram from an innocent antiwar group weeks before he officially received the same message. Rusk noted that, despite detailed intelligence information about Communist inroads in the antiwar movement, the administration had not shared most of this knowledge with the American people for fear of exposing information-gathering techniques as well as out of concern about setting off a new wave of McCarthyism.[54] The CIA's Operation CHAOS, started in 1967 at the request of President Johnson, as well as several other related CIA projects, found little evidence of foreign direction, control, or financing of the antiwar movement which went beyond consultation and coordination.[55] Information about the leadership role of the domestic radical left, on the other hand, was plentiful, even if the American public was told little about it.

A CIA report prepared in October 1967 noted that "both the individual peace groups and the coordinating organizations are well infiltrated with Communists of one stripe or another." The report stressed the great diversity that characterized the antiwar movement.

> Under the peace umbrella one finds pacifists and fighters, idealists and materialists, internationalists and isolationists, democrats and totalitarians, conservatives and revolutionaries, capitalists and socialists, patriots and subversives, lawyers and anarchists, Stalinists and Trotskyites, Moscovites and Pekingese, racists and universalists, zealots and nonbelievers, puritans and hippies, dogooders and evildoers, nonviolent and very violent.

Responsibility for coordinating this heterogeneous movement, the CIA reported, was in the hands of a small group of key leaders like Dellinger and Hayden, many of whom had close Communist connections, but who "do not appear to be under Communist direction. In any case, their purposes, as far as the war in Vietnam is concerned, coincide with those of the Communists." According to the CIA, the Communist role was "substantial," but Communists did not have a "controlling" influence. "Most of the Vietnam protest activity would be there with or without the Communist element." There was no evidence, the CIA concluded, that key activists were "under any direction other than their own. It should be noted that this probably would not be evident if they did, since their voluntary activities serve Communist and Chinese interests about as well as they could if they were controlled."[56]

Fearful that this CIA report might unleash a new outburst of McCarthyism, the Johnson administration did not make it public. In talking with his confidants, President Johnson often expressed his conviction that antiwar activities were controlled by the international Communist movement—a view which information gathered by the CIA at his request failed to substantiate—and there were occasional leaks to the media repeating these charges. The Senate Internal Security Subcommittee also sought to publicize the issue of Communist exploitation of the antiwar movement. But, on the whole, the American people heard little about this matter. Not that it would have made a difference. As the war dragged on with rising American casualties, Americans of all political persuasions increasingly began to question the prudence and wisdom of the American involvement in Southeast Asia. Fed up with the inconclusive conduct of the war and the seemingly endless bloodletting, they became the foot soldiers of the burgeoning antiwar movement. American disengagement from Vietnam was supported by a wide range of groups and individuals most of whom would have been surprised to learn that their desire for peace was being exploited by people with their own political agenda. In these circumstances, the fact that an unconditional

American withdrawal was pushed by the Left as a way of helping their Communist friends win the contest was largely irrelevant.

The march on the Pentagon in October 1967, the demonstrations at the time of the Democratic convention in August 1968, and the moratorium events of October 1969 were orchestrated by organizations with changing names but with essentially the same cast of leaders—radical pacifists and Old and New Leftists working in a coalition based on the principle of nonexclusion. For a time during 1968, moderate opponents of the war had taken comfort from the challenge to President Johnson's policies presented by the campaigns of Eugene McCarthy and Robert F. Kennedy. But the assassination of Kennedy in June by a disgruntled Palestinian ended any hope of uniting the Democratic party behind an antiwar candidate. The killing of Martin Luther King, Jr., in April of the same year contributed to the atmosphere of violence in the country. In September 1968, within a few days, three ROTC establishments were damaged by explosives or firebombs. During the same month, several Selective Service offices were also attacked. Hopes for a "new politics" were dashed and revolutionary rhetoric flourished. The mood of many of the demonstrations now turned ugly; overt resistance to the police, stone-throwing, and the building of street barricades were common occurrences. Viet Cong flags were flown regularly. All this was grist to the mill for revolutionary groups like the Weathermen and the Trotskyists, committed to what SWP leader Halstead called the Leninist "class struggle approach based on direct action by the masses against the regime."[57]

Operating with almost military discipline, the "Trots" were able to wield a disproportionate influence in the antiwar movement. "The paid cadre of young SWP workers," writes a historian of the movement, "were always able to stay late at meetings, long after others with the usual work and family obligations were gone."[58] These heavy-handed tactics did not pass uncriticized. At a meeting of the working committee of the Student Mobilization Committee held on May 8, 1968, radical pacifists and Communist party members accused YSA staffers of carrying out the policy of the Socialist Workers party rather than that of the committee. A similar criticism surfaced at the Youth Antiwar Conference called by the SMC in Cleveland in February of 1970. In each case, the YSAers were able to beat back the challenge by invoking the principle of nonexclusion, said to have overcome the Cold War and the witch-hunt atmosphere of earlier years. Ideas and individuals, it was argued, had to be judged on their merits and not on their political associations. The force of the idea of nonexclusion was so strong that even one of the opponents of YSA, SDS leader Clark Kissinger, felt obliged to state: "We don't want anyone voting for our proposal out of opposition to the Young Socialist Alliance. We are firmly opposed to anticommunism."[59]

The chief disagreement between the "Trots" and the other segments of the radical antiwar movement involved the question of whether the movement should concentrate just on mass action for immediate withdrawal from Vietnam or whether antiwar activities should be linked to other social and political problems such as racism, poverty, and political repression. The SWP forces argued that the Vietnam War was the focal point of "capitalist contradictions" and the key to the future development of American society. If the war could be ended by a popular movement, both capitalism and U.S. imperialism could be rolled back and the disintegration of the capitalist system might set in. Most of the people in the antiwar movement, the many thousands who joined demonstrations, they maintained, were simply against the war, and any stress on other social issues would alienate them and drive them away. The multi-issue advocates, on the other hand, argued that by emphasizing poverty and discrimination the antiwar movement would attract blacks and other minorities and thus broaden its reach. The controversy became interwoven with the decades-old feud between the Stalinist Communist party and the Trotskyist Socialist Workers Party. Each side accused the other of seeking to control the antiwar coalition and using it for its own political purpose.[60] The dispute festered for many months until it finally wrecked the New Mobilization to End the War, which had come into being in July of 1969.

In September 1970 those in favor of making the antiwar movement a multi-issue effort organized the National Coalition Against War, Racism and Repression, which in January 1971 changed its name to People's Coalition for Peace and Justice (PCPJ). The Communist party played a prominent role in this new umbrella group. The Trotskyists, meanwhile, set up the National Peace Action Coalition (NPAC). Both coalitions represented far fewer groups than the earlier mobilizations and often seemed far more interested in fighting each other than in combating the government's pursuance of the war.

More basically, with the withdrawal of American troops under way and a sharp decline in American casualties, the antiwar movement was rapidly becoming a sideshow. The large turnout for Vietnam Moratorium Day on October 15, 1969, endorsed by many respectable public figures, had been one of its last major successes. Public opinion sided with Nixon's policy of Vietnamization. The end of the draft helped pacify the nation's campuses. After the self-destruction of SDS, no national organization remained to keep an active student movement going. Far more damaging than the repressive measures of the Nixon administration, writes former SDS leader Todd Gitlin, was the degeneration of the movement "into everything idealists find alienating about politics as usual: cynicism, sloganeering, manipulation. The leadership groupings were giddy with their various styles of hopelessness. Far from being an inducement to political action, a consolation and reward for a thousand sacrifices, the organized movement, such as it was, had deliquesced into a swamp that only the most dedicated—or masochistic—would bother to try slogging through."[61]

Meanwhile the negotiations with the North Vietnamese conducted by Henry Kissinger were inching forward, and, after several false starts, a peace agreement was formally signed on January 27, 1973. The antiwar movement closed ranks once more in opposition to a continuation of aid to the Saigon government. In October of 1973 a meeting of antiwar activists in Germantown, Ohio, organized the Coalition to Stop Funding the War. This well-organized campaign circulated horror stories about the treatment of "political prisoners" in South Vietnam and sought to drive home the message that a regime guilty of massive political repression was not worthy of American support. The drive to deprive the Saigon government of essential military assistance and economic aid benefited from the Congress's war-weariness. Nguyen Van Thieu, wrote North Vietnam's Chief of Staff, General Van Tien Dung, in a retrospective on the final offensive of 1975, was now "forced to fight a poor man's war," his army suffering from serious shortages of ammunition and the mobility of his troops reduced by lack of aircraft, vehicles, and fuel.[62] Outgunned, demoralized, and ill-led, the South Vietnamese army collapsed. On April 30, 1975, North Vietnamese tanks entered Saigon, thus consummating the victory of the Vietnamese Communists for which the radical antiwar movement had worked so arduously.

The Effect of Nonexclusion on the Antiwar Movement

The fact that the American public gradually turned against the war in Vietnam was due primarily to the inordinate length of a seemingly inconclusive conflict and the rising level of American casualties rather than to the efforts of the antiwar movement. This today is the generally accepted view of social scientists who have studied the changes in American public opinion during these fateful years.[63] There is less agreement on the effect of the policy of nonexclusion. Antiwar leader Fred Halstead has attributed the success of the antiwar movement to its repudiation of anticommunism and its willingness to accept anyone willing to oppose the war. "The movement would not have grown as it did and drawn millions into activity unless it had abided by the principle of nonexclusion."[64] Others have argued that the antiwar movement gradually lost the support of middle America because, among other failings, it came to be perceived as a fifth column for the North Vietnamese Communists. One of the most stunning political facts of the Vietnam conflict, writes Gitlin, was that "as the war steadily lost popularity in the late sixties, *so did the antiwar movement.*"[65] According to another observer, the antiwar movement failed to gain the support of American workers because much of its leadership was "Stalinoid and neo-Stalinist," and many of its leading cadres were "enthusiastic supporters of Communist countries, above all Cuba, China and North Vietnam."[66] It is the latter view that appears to be supported by the evidence.

The war in Vietnam, fought in a faraway land few Americans had ever heard about and frustrating in its dearth of clear accomplishments, gave rise to an unprecedently acrimonious debate in the United States. Opposition to the American involvement in Indochina in the form of petitions, demonstrations, and organized attempts to end the war were far greater than in any previous American war, including the less than popular Korean conflict. Soon those in the forefront of this resistance came to see themselves not only as the conscience of America but also as articulating the feelings of a majority of the American people who were said to lack the opportunity to express their opposition to the war. And yet, evidence on the attitudes of the American people toward the Vietnam conflict, derived for the most part from public opinion polls, establishes conclusively that the central demand of the antiwar movement from 1968 on, the unilateral end of the American involvement and the complete and unconditional withdrawal of American troops from Vietnam, never commanded the support of a majority of the American people. This gulf between the highly visible and articulate groups protesting the war and the masses they claimed to represent grew as the antiwar movement became more disruptive and as instances of verbal and actual violence multiplied. While pacifists and others often sought to prevent violent outbursts such as flag-burning and attacks upon law enforcement officers, the acceptance of the principle of nonexclusion made it virtually impossible to control the conduct of the many diverse groups and individuals who were attracted to antiwar demonstrations. The result was a gradual but steady erosion of support for the antiwar movement.

By 1968, the protest movement against the war in Vietnam had managed to generate negative feelings among the American public to an all but unprecedented degree. A poll conducted by the University of

Michigan in 1968 asked the public to place various groups and personalities on a hundred-point scale. Fully one-third of the respondents gave
Vietnam protesters a zero and only 16 percent put them in the upper
half of the scale. Other studies show that popular reaction to the dis-
turbances surrounding the Democratic convention of 1968 was overwhelmingly favorable to the Chicago police and unfavorable to the demonstrators, all this despite the fact that press coverage was generally
biased in favor of the demonstrators. Even among those who supported
immediate withdrawal from Vietnam, 50 percent approved of the amount
of force used by the Chicago police and 25 percent thought that the
policemen had been too lenient.[67] "Opposition to the war," writes student of public opinion John Mueller, "came to be associated with violent
disruption, stink bombs, desecration of the flag, profanity, and contempt
for American values." These associations had a clearly negative effect
upon public opinion.[68]

The antiwar movement's resort to mass protests and the blockage of
streets and buildings, urged upon it by radicals in the antiwar coalition,
proved highly unpopular. The standing in the polls of Presidents Johnson and Nixon went up after each major large-scale demonstration in
Washington. Reaction to the wave of student strikes that followed President Nixon's decision in May 1970 to send American troops into Cambodia was similarly negative. According to the Gallup poll, 82 percent
of the American public rejected student strikes as a legitimate means of
protest. Even among young people, those between 20 and 29 years old,
73 percent condemned such strikes while only 25 percent approved. College graduates disapproved of them by 73 to 24 percent.[69]

The policy of nonexclusion guaranteed that the antiwar movement
came to be dominated by the most radical elements. In the climate of
bitterness and frustration created by the movement's inability to convert
the American public to its message, the apocalyptic elements had to
win out. The Marxist-Leninist cadres of the movement at times sought
to oppose the tactics of disruption pushed by SDSers and other enthusi-
asts of instant revolution, but they were usually outvoted or ignored.
Their contribution to the process of radicalization consisted in providing
the movement with the vocabulary of Marxism-Leninism. The war in
Vietnam, they argued, was not a mistake but the logical result of America's imperialist drive for world domination. All of this, in turn, increased
the American public's hostility to the antiwar movement. There is thus
reason to think that the antiwar movement contributed to the lengthen-
ing of the war not only because it encouraged Hanoi but also because
it frightened away "respectable" would-be opponents from joining the
cause. The fact that the American public eventually turned against the

war, writes another student of public opinion, Andrew M. Greeley, does not prove that the antiwar movement was responsible for the conversion. "In fact, a much better case can be made that the movement delayed the conversion and perhaps even prolonged the war."[70]

There is, of course, another side to the coin. Despite the small percentage of individuals who were actively involved in organized opposition to the war, the antiwar movement had a significant impact on both the Johnson and Nixon administrations. Not only does a small percentage of a country of 200 million constitute a sizable number of people, but the active and articulate few often can have an importance well beyond their proportion of the population. The increasingly wild antics of the antiwar movement, its attacks upon the basic values of American society, the expressions of solidarity with the Vietnamese Communists in the form of Viet Cong flags and slogans admiring Ho Chi Minh, as well as the trappings of the counterculture which accompanied all of this agitation—long hair, the widespread use of drugs, and the casual resort to obscenities—sharply antagonized the average American. At the same time, the antiwar movement's harsh rhetoric and tactics of confrontation contributed to the polarization of the country and gradually created a sense among lawmakers, the media, and other elite groups that the country was coming apart. This, of course, was precisely why from 1968 on antiwar activists such as Tom Hayden concentrated on the resort to disruption. The aim of this "cold calculation," Hayden argued, was to raise the price of continuing the war to the point where "heartless, cost-calculating decision-makers" would have to order a withdrawal from Vietnam.[71]

The tumultuous events of the spring of 1971 in Washington well illustrate this dual effect. The attempt of the May Day Tribe and its supporters in May of 1971 to "bring everything to a halt" by blocking traffic, harassing government employees, invading the meeting rooms of congressional committees, and resulting in thousands of arrests, gained the antiwar movement few friends. Yet it also reinforced a sense of urgency about terminating this highly divisive war for which no successful conclusion appeared to be in sight. Each new attempt of the radical antiwar movement to "bring the war home," note two students of the sixties, convinced "an ever-widening circle of influential and articulate Americans that if only for the sake of civil peace Vietnam must be ended."[72] Even many of those who for a long time had agreed with the basic rationale of the American involvement in Southeast Asia eventually came to feel that the social and political costs of the war, however just its goals, were too high and that the U.S. should cut its losses and get out.

The effect of the policy of nonexclusion upon the antiwar movement and upon the course of the war itself was thus complex. On one hand, nonexclusion contributed to the radicalization and political isolation of the antiwar movement. On the other hand, the increasingly confrontational tactics of the movement helped create a sense of chaos and disruption in the country which, coupled with a growing war-weariness, eventually led American lawmakers to call it quits. It was the Congress that finally enacted increasingly restrictive military and financial constraints upon the conduct of the war. Many Democrats, previously supportive of their President, turned against the war once it had become the burden of a Republican administration, and, supported by some war-weary Republicans, they forced President Nixon to sign a less than promising peace accord in 1973. By that time, the antiwar movement had long since ceased to exist as a street phenomenon. The movement's contribution to the tragic denouement of the Vietnam conflict had been made over the course of many years prior to the final abandonment of South Vietnam.

III

American Communism Today

The Old Left-New Left Nexus

From the Old to the New Left

As a result of the new and more hospitable political climate of the last two decades, the American Communist party recently has allowed several former secret Communists to come out of the closet. Victor Perlo, an economist in the New Deal administration, was named by both Whittaker Chambers and Elizabeth Bentley as a provider of classified information, but when questioned in 1948 about his activities and associations he invoked the Fifth Amendment. In 1981 the Party's theoretical journal *Political Affairs* identified him as "chairman of the Economic Section of the CPUSA."[1] Two members of the Hollywood Ten, Lester Cole and Ring Lardner, have openly talked and written about their earlier membership in the Communist party. Cole became film critic of the *People's World* in 1974 and continues to be a party loyalist. Lardner, who let his membership in the Party lapse in the early 1950s, nevertheless remains committed to the idea of communism. "I have never regretted my association with Communism," he told Philip Taubman of the *New York Times* during a visit to Russia in 1987. "I still think that some form of socialism is a more rational way of organizing a society, but I recognize it hasn't worked anywhere yet."[2]

Lardner's continuing loyalty to the idea of communism even though he is no longer a member of the Party is not at all unusual. He is part of a very large group of ex-Communists, numbering many thousands, who left the Party for one reason or another but who remained members in their hearts. Film director Elia Kazan has related that after he resigned from the Party in 1935 because of the Communists' bullying of artists he for many years "continued to think like a Communist."[3]

Probably the largest contingent of such unaffiliated Communists formed during the 1950s out of fear of government persecution or as a result of Khrushchev's revelations of the crimes of Stalin. Former SDS leader Todd Gitlin came to know these men and women, imbued with "a rosy memory of the Party, the Popular Front and 'progressive' politics generally," in the antiwar movement of the 1960s. "Many, perhaps the majority, never thought through what had gone so catastrophically wrong in the Soviet Union, or even in their own subservient Party. They were no longer Communists, but they were not exactly anticommunist."[4] Indeed, to be anticommunist was the worst of all possible options, for it meant being on the same side as the world's reactionaries. As Lionel Trilling described this mentality, although "for the moment at least, one need not be actually for Communism, one was morally compromised, turned toward evil and away from good, if one was against it."[5] These ex-Communists had given up their friends, but they had kept all their old enemies.

During the unfolding civil rights and peace movements of the late 1950s and early 1960s, a good number of these former Communists became once again politically active. The movement against the war in Vietnam, in particular, galvanized many of these people into action. Until that time, the mother of journalist Carl Bernstein told her son composing a memoir about his Communist parents, "it had all blown up. There was nothing to rally around."[6] Many of those who had been in or near the Party's orbit, noted Irving Howe in a perceptive article published in 1965, "continued to keep in touch with one another, forming a kind of reserve apparatus based on common opinions, feelings, memories. As soon as some ferment began a few years ago in the Civil Rights movement and the peace groups, these people were present, ready and eager; they needed no directives from the CP to which, in any case, they no longer (or may never have) belonged; they were quite capable of working on their own *as if they were working together.*" These were people, Howe wrote, "who could offer political advice, raise money, write leaflets, sit patiently at meetings, put up in a pleasant New York apartment visitors from a distant state."[7]

Author Jessica Mitford was one of those former Communists whose basic political outlook did not change despite her lack of a formal affiliation with the Party. The American Communist party, she conceded in her autobiography, had made "some abysmal mistakes," but she felt gratitude for all it taught her." She had resigned from the Party in 1958 in order to "better serve the cause by devoting the time we spent doing Party work to outside movements for radical change (harbingers, as it later turned out, of the sixties) that were springing up in the black community, in campuses, among white liberals."[8] In his study of Philadelphia Communists, Paul Lyons found former Communists active "in virtually every significant progressive organizing effort in the Philadelphia area." Most continued to believe in socialism and Marxism and used their skills as organizers and fundraisers in support of new radical causes.[9] These, then, were the people who served as a bridge between the Old and New Left and whose children—"red diaper babies" as they came to be called—often took a leading role in organizations like SDS. "Veterans of the radical movements of the 1950s," writes historian Maurice Isserman, "provided a political language in which those swept up in the new movements of the 1960s could begin to make sense of their own discontents and desires."[10]

Typifying the thinking of those members of the Old Left who sought to build bridges to the New Left was the *National Guardian,* a weekly paper edited by two avowed Communist fellow travelers, Cedric Belfrage and James Aronson. Both men had developed misgivings about the Soviet Union as a result of the show trials in Eastern Europe during the 1950s and the suppression of the Hungarian revolution. Yet despite the absence of an ideal foreign model, the editors of the *National Guardian,* according to their recollections published in 1978, "continued to believe that socialism was the only alternative to genocide of the human species. The fact that the struggle for it would be more agonizing than we once thought couldn't alter its inevitability."

The appearance of the New Left in the early 1960s was warmly welcomed by the *National Guardian.* An editorial on November 7, 1964, declared: "We hold with the movers of the New Left in America that the need of the hour is the development of a movement radical in content and form, which must set about to shake the foundations of the power structure." At times, Belfrage and Aronson were unhappy with the New Left's lack of firm structure. Unorganized confrontation, they felt, "was not enough, and the endless debates in the inner circles (one was not permitted to say 'leadership') in the name of participatory democracy produced fatigue, anger and indecision—and little continuing activity." They also criticized what they regarded as the New Left's unrealistic "romantic rhetoric of revolution." But on the whole, the *National Guardian* was supportive of the young radicals. The paper's role, as stated at its eighteenth anniversary dinner, held in November 1966, was to "encourage the emergent radicalism toward a unified, nonsectarian goal of socialism; to expose the chief obstacle to this goal—U.S. monopoly capitalism and imperialism." Differences with the Communist party were downplayed. "We insisted that we had no enemies on the left, however great the disagreement about certain tactics or policies."[11]

The early New Left, especially SDS, was characterized by a conscious disdain for rigid ideological systems. Some called it "a mood in search of a movement." And yet under the radicalizing impact of the Vietnam War, the Old and the New Left eventually came to have much in common. Both were alienated from the basic values of American society and demanded the radical transformation of what they saw as a repressive political system. Both movements considered socialism superior to capitalism and were in full sympathy with Communist regimes in the Third World led by the likes of Fidel Castro and Ho Chi Minh. Both the Old and the New Left praised the Soviet Union's support of national liberation movements in the Third World, while the United States was castigated as a bastion of reaction and imperialism. Both agreed on the "myth of the Soviet threat" and the need to oppose anticommunism.

The bitterness created by the seemingly endless Vietnam conflict solidified the alliance between Old and New Left. The psychological principle "My enemy's enemy is my friend" benefited the Soviet Union and its local representative, the American Communist party. Following the policy of nonexclusion, the antiwar movement had no hesitation in including among its leaders prominent members of the Old Left such as Arnold Johnson of the Communist party and Fred Halstead of the Socialist Workers party. Men like Sidney Peck, a sociologist and former Communist functionary in Wisconsin, and Sidney Lens, earlier connected with the pro-Trotskyist Workers party, assumed key roles and stressed the importance of fighting anticommunism. Much as I disagreed with the Stalinists, Lens recalled in his autobiography, it was wrong to read the Communists out of the radical movement "and inimical to any hopes of building an antiwar movement."[12]

By the end of 1967, the radical political landscape had undergone a significant change. "Under the heat of the Vietnam war," noted Donald Keys, just resigned from his post as executive director of SANE, "the Old Left and the New Left have coalesced, the latter providing the dynamism and numbers, the former attempting to channel the newly available energies to its own ends to the service of its own analysis of our society."[13] Communist organizations now were an integral part of the antiwar movement. As we have seen, during the early seventies, both the American Communist party and the Trotskyist Socialist Workers party were successful in leading antiwar coalitions. When the war ended, close relations between Old and New Left organizations had become firmly established, and this pattern of cooperation has continued to the present day.

A Case Study of Old Left/New Left Fusion

The amalgamation of Old and New Left that characterizes some segments of contemporary American radicalism is well exemplified by the recent history of the National Lawyers Guild (NLG). Indeed, the Guild is probably the only organization that has survived changes of both membership and leadership from the Depression of the 1930s to the present day and has prospered as a result of these changes.

The NLG was founded in 1937 as an association of progressive lawyers, a coalition of liberal and radical attorneys seeking an alternative to the highly conservative American Bar Association. The Guild's preamble, reflecting its roots in both the New Deal and the Popular Front, included a commitment "to function as a social force in the service of the people to the end that human rights shall be regarded as more sacred than property rights." Among the group's founders were two federal judges, justices of two state supreme courts, two members of Congress, two state governors, and five law professors. From the beginning, the NLG included a substantial number of Communist attorneys.[14]

By 1939, some of the Guild's liberal members had become concerned over the influence of Communists in the organization. The perception that the NLG was not fully committed to democracy, they felt, was a serious obstacle to its growth. At the 1939 convention, therefore, Morris L. Ernst, a founding member, proposed the adoption of an amendment to the constitution that would make clear the Guild's opposition "to dictatorship of any kind, whether Left or Right, whether Fascist, Nazi, or Communistic." The proposed amendment led to a lively debate. "Lawyers who were in or near the Communist Party," writes a historian of the NLG, opposed Ernst's proposal "as divisive because it would require people to define their attitudes toward Fascism and Communism at a time when the important task of New Dealers and all democratic forces was to join together to oppose Fascism."[15] Ernst's motion failed.

The Communist issue was revived a few months later, after the Hitler-Stalin Pact. Led by Securities Exchange Commissioner Jerome Frank, former Assistant Secretary of State Adolf A. Berle, Morris Ernst, and Abe Fortas, an influential group of liberals sought a reorganization of the Guild's national board. When their efforts failed, the liberals resigned in May of 1940, leaving the organization in a badly weakened condition. By the early 1950s only a handful of non-Communists including Osmond K. Fraenkel and Thomas I. Emerson were left. In September 1950, the House Committee on Un-American Activities called the Guild "the legal bulwark of the Communist party." In August 1953, Attorney General Brownell sought to place the group on the list of subversive organizations. The NLG's low point came in 1956, following Khrushchev's speech and the Soviet invasion of Hungary, when it was reduced to about 600 members.

The fortunes of the NLG were revived during the mid-1960s. There took place a large infusion of young law students and lawyers anxious to provide legal aid to the civil rights movement and, a little later, to represent Vietnam War draft resisters. Many of these newcomers were members of SDS. Relations between them and the old guard of the NLG at first were often strained. As Victor Rabinowitz, president of the Guild in 1967 and 1968, recalled: "To many of us, these 25- to 30-year-olds seemed undignified, contentious, noisy, undisciplined. The generational differences were startling and deep."[16] Gradually, however, the differences between Old and New Left were resolved, and the old-timers came to appreciate the revolutionary zeal of the new radicals. "Those of us who are Marxists," Rabinowitz wrote in the spring of 1968, should welcome the young militants' destruction of "oppressive institutions" even if they do not have a blueprint of what better institutions will look like. "In their emphasis on the freedom of the individual, perhaps the young are looking to the ultimate goal of Communism rather than to the intermediate station of Socialism."[17]

During the following years, the young radicals increasingly came to dominate the NLG, which saw itself as the legal arm of "The Movement." In 1970, law students were admitted to full membership; a year later, legal workers and "jailhouse lawyers" were given the same status. The proportion of active older members declined sharply as a new generation took over the helm. "In this period," write two historians of the Guild, "some older Guild members got in the habit of taking Lenin's *Left-Wing Communism: An Infantile Disorder*, or its equivalent, to read on the plane to prepare them for the meetings that lay ahead."[18]

Some of the clashes were bitter and intense; others had comic qualities. At the Guild's 1970 convention in Washington, members of a radical caucus provoked what became known as the "Banquet Dinner Riot." Unable to afford the traditional banquet, some fifty of them waited outside the chandeliered hall for the three hundred diners to finish their meal so that the program of the evening could begin. Impatient and hungry, someone crept inside and returned with a large plate of dinner rolls. This led to the posting of a group of lawyers to stand guard at the door so that the members without tickets would not rush in and get the Guild into serious trouble with the management of the hotel. At that, William Kunstler came outside, gave a rabble-rousing speech, and then burned his meal ticket. Before the beginning of the formal program, a spokesperson for the fifty was given the microphone and called for "future Guild conventions to be conducted in a place and style in conformity with the new membership." His speech was cheered by all.[19]

By the early 1970s, Old and New Left elements in the Guild had come to terms, for they shared basic goals, the most immediate of which was the victory of the Vietnamese Communists. "Our politics," wrote Guild president Paul Harris in 1980, looking back on the group's Vietnam strategy, "moved the Guild in 1965 to attack U.S. actions in Vietnam as an illegal war. Our left analysis then moved us in 1973 to a point where we supported the NLF, correctly viewing their efforts as an anti-imperialist war."[20] Marxist-Leninist terminology, previously shunned, now was used openly in Guild proceedings and publications. The 1973 convention, as described by two chroniclers of the Guild, was the scene of "the cataclysmic merger of old and new left politics," based on four key slogans: "Anti-Racism, Anti-Sexism, Anti-Capitalism, and Anti-Imperialism."[21]

By December 1979, the NLG had reached a membership of 6,000, organized in 86 chapters. Lawyers made up 55 percent, 35 percent were law students, 6 percent legal workers, and 4 percent jailhouse lawyers. Domestically, the Guild sought to use legal struggle as a contribution to the coming revolution of the working class. The radical lawyer, argued Arthur Kinoy, a professor at the Rutgers University School of Law, "must assist in the increasing and exploding radicalization of masses of people learning from their own political experience."[22] He should help the masses go beyond the "formal rights" guaranteed by bourgeois law under bourgeois democracy in order to win "real equality and social rights," two other NLG members affirmed.[23] In its international work, the NLG emphasized the struggle against "U.S. imperialism." In the words of Guild president Paul Harris in December 1979: "The role of U.S. multinational corporations, the action of the U.S. government abroad—these are our responsibilities, as we live in what Che Guevara accurately called 'the belly of the beast.' "[24] Harris, thirty-six years old, described himself as coming "from an old left background and new left experience."[25]

The NLG has a Theoretical Studies Committee, and members of the NLG are active in the Conference on Critical Legal Studies. But some Guild members have done more than undertake a Marxist analysis of the law or represent revolutionaries and terrorists in court. Weatherman leader Bernardine Dohrn started out as the NLG student organizer in 1967. Russ Neufield, editor of *Midnight Special*, an NLG journal for prisoners, was a member of the Weather Underground organization. Another staff member was Judith Clark, now serving a lengthy prison term for participating in the Brinks robbery-murder in Nyack, New York, in 1981.[26] Most NLG members avoid such violent activities, though the

endorsement of armed struggle by oppressed groups or national liberation movements is official NLG doctrine.

As of 1986, the NLG had 7,000 members, a more than ten-fold increase from the group's nadir in the late 1950s. The membership was
organized in 83 lawyer chapters, 102 law student chapters, and 12 jailhouse chapters. There was also an organization of Guild professors
teaching in law schools. The influence of members of the Communist
party is said to have increased in recent years. The NLG continues to
be affiliated with the Soviet-run International Association of Democratic
Lawyers (IADL). Organized in 1946, the IADL was expelled from France
in 1949 and is since headquartered in Brussels. It claims 64 national
affiliates. In October 1949, after the break between Stalin and Tito, the
IADL expelled the Yugoslav delegation. The NLG representatives at
the IADL meeting voted for this expulsion, but the Guild repudiated
this step and urged that the Yugoslav section be restored to membership.
In the years since, the IADL has continued to be a faithful supporter of
Soviet foreign policy, including the invasions of Hungary, Czechoslovakia, and Afghanistan, but the NLG no longer dissociates itself from
these positions.[27]

The NLG's stands on foreign policy issues such as nuclear testing,
the first use of nuclear weapons, the Strategic Defense Initiative, and
Central America faithfully echo the Soviet line. Its concern with the
observance of human rights has always stopped at the borders of the
Socialist bloc. In 1978, then vice president John Quigley affirmed that
"the Guild is not Amnesty International. Its aim is not to ferret out
human rights violations wherever they exist. As an anti-imperialist organization, its aim is to aid national liberation struggles."[28]

The leadership of the Guild has sought to steer clear of controversial
international issues that could split the organization, yet from time to
time divisive subjects have arisen. Jewish members have objected to the
Guild's support for the PLO; Maoists have been unhappy about its
pro-Soviet bias. In 1977 an open letter written by two Philadelphia members called for the formation of a Democratic caucus and charged that
"the leadership has conducted Guild affairs as though we were a committed Marxist-Leninist entity."[29] Also in 1977, an Anti-Imperialist Caucus organized around the slogans "Oppose the Two Super Powers!" and
"Oppose the CPUSA!" Composed of Maoists, this faction controlled
several chapters and perhaps as much as 15 percent of the NLG's membership. Only by being more even-handed, argued the dissenters, would
it be possible to recruit additional members from the ACLU and liberals
in state bar associations.

Then president William Goodman rejected the arguments of this opposition group. "We will not be able to organize into the Guild, and in fact we will lose much of our membership, if we promote slogans of opposing the Soviet Union and opposing the Communist Party. These are slogans which perhaps could organize George Meany, Daniel Moynihan, Henry Jackson, or Albert Shanker into the Guild, but are not likely to see us move forward. Those amongst us who view themselves as revolutionaries or Marxist-Leninists have a responsibility to act in a disciplined (as opposed to infantile) fashion if what we desire is a stronger and healthier Guild."[30]

In recent years, some leading members of the Guild have openly acknowledged their ties to the Communist party. At a dinner in her honor held by the Guild's San Francisco chapter in July of 1981, Doris Brin Walker, a member since 1941 and president of the NLG in 1970, stated that it had been the struggle of the working class that "has been both the keystone of my adult beliefs and the touchstone of my professional and organizational life. It is this commitment which makes me so proud to be a member of the Communist Party."[31]

Writing in 1984, Gerald Horne, an attorney and historian, noted with pride that the Guild was "as strong as it has been in a long time. Not the least reason for its revitalization has been its ability to maintain unity and to tolerate a diversity of viewpoints while adhering to principle."[32] The principle that has united the various ideological components of the NLG is, of course, Marxism-Leninism. This is the set of principles that is adhered to by both Old and New Left elements in the organization. It is this agreement on basic ideological precepts which makes the old categories of Old and New Left so much less meaningful in analyzing today's radical Left.

Results of the Policy of Nonexclusion

The American Left today is not a monolith. Some elements are caught in a stultefying "Third Worldism"; others resist the notion that the United States is the root cause of all the world's problems. The Left includes socialists committed to democracy as well as elements enamored of totalitarian schemes. Of course, the near-complete fusion of Old and New Left observed in the case of the National Lawyers Guild does not exist everywhere. Nevertheless, the Communist party has achieved a secure foothold in today's radical Left and thus is able to reach a sizable constituency.

Until the emergence of the New Left in the 1960s, in order to extend its political influence the Communist party had to establish front organizations or infiltrate and take over established political groups. Today such tactics are much less necessary, for Communists are welcome in the radical movement and can freely participate in its activities. More important, the goals of Old and New Left groups are largely identical. Both work for an end to American "interventionism" in the Third World and for dismantling of what they call the "national security state."

The most important New Left organization of the sixties, SDS, no longer exists today, but many of the groups who were active in the anti-war movement have managed to reconstitute themselves under new names and continue their efforts to hamstring the role of the United States in the world. During the late 1970s, the same forces that had pushed for the unconditional withdrawal of the U.S. from Vietnam and had successfully labored to cut American aid to the Saigon government now teamed up for the second time—to halt "U.S. intervention" in Central America. Some of the activists were old-timers. For example, Fred Branfman, formerly co-director of the Indochina Resource Center (with much justification called "the Hanoi Lobby" by many in Washington), now emerged as director of the Commission on U.S.–Central American Relations. The Commission included among its constituent organizations the Coalition for a New Foreign and Military Policy, the new name of the Coalition to Stop Funding the [Vietnam] War, and the Institute for Policy Studies. These organizations today are part of a large network of groups with overlapping leaders and supporters, called by Suzanne Garment the American left's new cottage industry, which "uses the language of human rights and social justice to delegitimize our imperfect efforts" to nurture democratic regimes in Central America.[33] In addition to the Commission on U.S.–Central American Relations, this network includes the North American Congress on Latin America, the Washington Office on Latin America, the Council on Hemispheric Affairs, and the Central American Historical Institute. Many of these organizations are supported financially by mainline Protestant churches through the National Council of Churches' Latin American Division.[34] All of these groups, with varying degrees of militancy, oppose U.S. aid to the government of El Salvador, while at the same time they minimize or deny Soviet-bloc support for the insurgents. All of them also fight American support for the Nicaraguan resistance and oppose the Reagan doctrine of aid to anticommunist resistance groups generally.

Another contemporary New Left umbrella organization, mentioned earlier in our discussion of the peace movement, is Mobilization for Survival (MfS), created in 1977 as a result of efforts by former antiwar activists Sidney Peck and Sidney Lens, both with roots in the Old Left. Looking back in 1987 on the first ten years of MfS, Peck expressed the hope that the American people eventually would reach an appreciation of the need for far-reaching social change in this country.[35] Many of these groups maintain links to the Soviet-run World Peace Council and its American affiliate, the U.S. Peace Council. In 1985, the Reverend Tony Watkins, disarmament coordinator for Clergy and Laity Concerned (CALC), earlier called Clergy and Laity Concerned About Vietnam, also served as Religious Circles Coordinator for the U.S. Peace Council. CALC has participated in all mobilizations and rallies against U.S. policy in Central America and continues to call for reconsidering the "validity of 'anticommunism' as the cornerstone of our military policy."[36]

In the case of some organizations it is difficult to decide whether to categorize them as Old or New Left. The Committee in Solidarity with the People of El Salvador (CISPES) was established in 1980 and functions as a support group for the Marxist-Leninist guerrillas fighting the elected government of El Salvador. Brought into being with the aid of the late Sandy Pollack, a member of the central committee of the American Communist party, and Cuban intelligence officers operating out of the United Nations, CISPES today operates without an open connection to the Communist party, though it has close ties to the U.S. Peace Council, which is represented on its steering committee. As in the case of the radical segments of the movement against the war in Vietnam, discussed in an earlier chapter, actual Communist control probably would not change the policies of CISPES in any important way. Many of CISPES's activists appear to be people drawn to the revolutionaries of Central America in the same way as an earlier generation of New Leftists was attracted to the National Liberation Front of Vietnam. CISPES has succeeded in developing links to mainstream churches and other respectable organizations.[37]

The same ambiguity characterizes the position of men such as Jack O'Dell, formerly a district organizer for the Communist party in the South, and today director of international affairs of Jesse Jackson's National Rainbow Coalition. O'Dell served as an editor of *Freedomways*, a journal that until its recent demise closely followed the Communist party line. He has been active in the World Peace Council. At a meeting held in Berkeley, California, in November 1985 to celebrate the sixty-eighth anniversary of the Bolshevik revolution, O'Dell charged that opposition to Communism served U.S. corporations and militarists, and he commended the Soviet Union for its peace policy and assistance to liberation struggles around the world. In a 1984 interview, O'Dell defined the goal of the Rainbow Coalition as "fundamental change" and suggested that it struggled against the same force as the rest of the world—capitalism.[38] As noted earlier, given Jack O'Dell's steadfast procommunist views and activities, the question of whether he is also a card-carrying member of the Communist party is essentially irrelevant.

Today a host of organizations, not formally linked to the Communist party and in many cases defying the categories of Old and New Left, carry on an energetic agitation for a radical transformation of American society, push for drastic cuts in the American defense budget if not for unilateral disarmament, and lobby for Communist guerrillas and regimes. The political outlook of these groups provides Communists with a perfect cover and allows them to ply their trade with little need to seize actual control. They cooperate with and function freely in these new organizations and coalitions which share most of the Party's aims even as their goals are said to be nothing more than the furthering of "peace and justice." Such alliances provide the Communist party with valuable political legitimacy and respectability.

Some young people of today's Left are said to be impatient with the sectarian language of Marxist-Leninist groups. At a meeting of student activists held at Rutgers University in February 1988, some advocates of militant direct action considered the Marxist-Leninists in attendance as too stodgy. As Lynda Sargent of Z magazine put it: "There seems to be a disdain for the sects, and this new generation's not going to put up with their stuff. I remember listening to speeches for half an hour in the old days. I'm happy not to have to listen to the sects now."[39] It is difficult to know how widespread this sentiment is. Whatever its strength, it has not prevented the acceptance of the Communists and their fronts in the radical Left's activities and public demonstrations.

Old and New Left met in harmony at a three-day conference on "Anti-communism in the U.S.: History and Consequences," that was held at Harvard University in November 1988. We have mentioned this gathering in our discussion of contemporary anti-anticommunism in Chapter 7. Among the 1200 participants were Communist functionaries Gus Hall and Angela Davis and former New Left leaders Carl Oglesby and Richard Flacks. A slightly discordant note was struck by journalist Carl Bernstein, who warned against the tendency of the Left to borrow from the struggle of the Soviet Union rather than the American experience. This tendency, said Bernstein, had "left many people with an arsenal of rather disdainful attitudes towards this country, its system, and how we go about solving our problems." But this comment appeared not to trouble anyone. Speaking to the same point at another panel, Gus Hall declared that a socialist USA will be "unique, different from any other." Because of this country's high level of industrial, scientific, and technological development, Hall argued, "a socialist USA will be much more democratic. It will not be a one-party system. In many ways it will be a Bill of Rights socialism." In a report on the conference, historian William Preston, Jr., noted with satisfaction that the gathering had been characterized by "lack of sectarian divisiveness" and "intergenerational unity." It promised to "restore a pluralistic dialogue and an intellectual freedom which anticommunism had largely extinguished."[40]

Similar Tactics

The New Left of the late 1960s embraced Marxism-Leninism, but its members were candid about their political agenda and proudly called themselves revolutionary Communists. They would have been embarrassed by being accused of concealing their radical beliefs or, even more, by being seen as anything but revolutionaries. By contrast, many segments of today's radical Left deceitfully present themselves as defenders of international morality and peace and hide their true political agenda. Indeed, much of the effectiveness of these groups is due to the fact that they pass themselves off as "progressives," champions of human rights and social justice. The Communist party itself continues to rely extensively on secret cadres. As reported at a recent Communist party conference and mentioned earlier, a full 80 percent of the Party's membership is secret; only 20 percent are allowed to appear openly as Communists. "The Party makes important contributions for which it cannot take credit," noted its organizational secretary in July 1989. "Often Communist trade union leaders, elected officials and cultural figures express their frustration about not being able [read: allowed] to be more open."[41] Both Old and New Left thus continue the tactics of secrecy and duplicity used by the Communists during the days of the Popular Front in particular.

The damaging consequences of the tactics of dissembling engaged in by the Communists have been recognized by some of today's intellectuals who generally defend the sincerity of the Communists, avow their opposition to liberal anticommunism, and are in sympathy with the contemporary Left. "The liberal perception of the Reds as duplicitous, opportunistic, cynical, untrustworthy," write Ceplair and Englund in their history of Communism in Hollywood, was "not hopelessly wide of the mark." In line with the dictates of the Party, Hollywood Communists on occasion "undermined their credibility, misserved their cause, and misled their contemporaries with their behavior, their attitude, and their words." American Communists generally, they note, "left themselves open to the justifiable suspicion that they not only approved of everything they were defending [in the Soviet Union], but would themselves act in the same way if they were in the same position." To this day, Ceplair and Englund complain, Communists and former Communists "have occasionally assumed stands of extreme incommunicability and exclusivity, and even outright dishonesty or intentional self-blindness, in their felt need to protect themselves, their movement, and their memories."[42]

Despite such occasional insights, the similarity between the deceitful tactics practiced by the American Communist party for much of its history and those of key elements of the contemporary radical Left, clothing themselves in the mantle of the struggle for "peace and justice," has received little attention or comment. The country's large and able corps of investigative journalists, always ready to pounce on even the slightest suspicion of wrongdoing on the part of the establishment, has not shown any eagerness to look into the duplicitous activities common among the radical Left.[43] Only very seldom does one find an acknowledgment of the real political agenda of these groups or their publications. Thus in their history of the *National Guardian*, published in 1978, editors Belfrage and Aronson, in a rare instance of candor, recalled that when they established the paper in 1948 they "decided against commitment to socialism, for we hoped to win a public beyond the 'converted,' 'starting where they are' and leading them by subversively rational steps to where we were."[44] In different circles, one calls such tactics of persuasion intellectual dishonesty.

Another similarity between the Communist party and much of today's radical Left involves the use of strong-arm methods against political opponents. During the twenties and early thirties, the Communists frequently broke up meetings of their Socialist and Trotskyist adversaries. The best known of these violent episodes was the disruption of the large Socialist rally in New York's Madison Square Garden on February 16, 1934.[45] The New Left of the sixties accepted the notion of its guru Herbert Marcuse that the forces of the right, promoting armaments, chauvinism, and aggressive foreign policies, were not entitled to benefit from toleration and freedom of speech and assembly. Consequently, on the nation's elite campuses, where SDS and other radical student groups were strong, defenders of the Vietnam War found it practically impossible to receive a hearing. The situation today is only slightly better. At its 1984 national conference, CISPES called for "creative harassment" of supporters of President Reagan's policies in Central America. In line with this directive, CISPES chapters have organized disruptions of speakers they deem "unacceptable," including former Secretary of State Henry

Kissinger.[46] Other groups have used the same tactic. Members of the Nicaraguan resistance, in particular, have frequently encountered efforts to prevent them from speaking. Here, then, is another manifestation of the fundamental likeness of Old and New Left that has emerged during the last twenty years.

14

Retrospect and Outlook

Sources of Strength and Weakness

The American Communist party reached its greatest strength and influence just before World War II. As a result of the Depression and the Communists' moderate course during the days of the Popular Front, the Party succeeded in drawing into its ranks many sympathizers and fellow travelers and by 1939 had almost 100,000 members. But this upsurge did not lead to lasting gains. Unlike in Europe, the Party never achieved a mass base among the working class. It refused to understand that American capitalism is a dynamic social system with little class-consciousness, an open society which Marx himself had feared as a solvent of European-bred socialist beliefs. In the footnotes to *Capital*, the prophet of scientific socialism had expressed his amazement at the number of people in America who could move about freely and change their occupations "much as a man could change his shirt, egad."[1] The American Communist party, on the other hand, for most of its history, persisted in seeing the American worker as a downtrodden slave of capitalism who sooner or later would embrace the gospel of communism. It failed to recognize that in this vast and wealthy land even the most exploited elements had reason to expect more from the capitalist system and the regular processes of democracy than the Communists could ever deliver them.

During the Popular Front era, the Party for a short time did appreciate the idea of "American exceptionalism" and consequently experienced expansion. Under the leadership of Earl Browder, American Communists realized that, in order to make headway among the American working class, they had to change not only the form of their revolutionary message but the message itself. The Party also managed to attract a good number of intellectuals, many of them Jewish. It is estimated that during the 1930s and 1940s, about half of the Party's membership was composed of Jews, many with an East European socialist background, who were drawn to communism as a way of overcoming their marginality. By attaching themselves to a universalist ideology that promised to abolish the distinction between Jews and Christians, Jews hoped to overcome the very categories that defined them as marginal.[2]

But even the successes of the thirties proved transitory. Turnover of membership was always high; the only truly safe generalization that can be made about American Communists is that most of them became ex-Communists. The Party's subservience to its Russian masters prevented enduring success. A basically self-satisfied nation did not provide a fertile soil for revolutionaries guided by a foreign power. The secretive and manipulative character of the Communist party led to distrust and hostility. Disabilities imposed upon the Party by unions, employers, and government, in turn, provided excuses for more secrecy, thus establishing a vicious cycle that increased lack of confidence in the Communists and contributed to their political isolation and lack of acceptance. The crisis in leadership following the ouster of Browder in 1946 and the impact of the Smith Act prosecutions severely weakened the Party. The denunciation of Stalin's crimes in Khrushchev's speech of 1956 and the suppression of the Hungarian revolution provided the final blow to an organization in a state of serious crisis. By 1957, the American Communist party had been reduced to a paid membership of just above 3000.

The war in Vietnam and the political radicalization caused by it helped the Old Left. The New Left's adherence to a policy of nonexclusion and its willingness to work with Communists provided the Party with new respectability. The Communists here and there criticized the New Left's "sectarianism" and "adventurism," but at the same time sought a common front. "In coordinated efforts," the 1966 draft program of the Communist party declared, "in the exchange of views and experiences, in the discussion of differences, the basis can be found for a unity that will become ever firmer."[3] During the 1970s, recalls former New Leftist Peter Collier, there developed a new tolerance for the Communist party among the New Left. The Communists, previously castigated as too moderate, now were seen as "good old warriors who might have been a bit obtuse ideologically but who had nonetheless fought the good fight."[4] This new political climate enabled the Party to break out of its political isolation and to show a moderate but steady growth in membership and influence. In his report to the twenty-second convention of the Communist party in August 1979, General Secretary Gus Hall noted the decrease in anticommunism and he welcomed the fact that Communists no longer had to fight to participate in various progressive movements. "In fact, we not only do not have to fight to participate, in most cases we are asked to join and help out."[5]

During the last few years, the Communists have also benefited from the more conciliatory policies of Soviet leader Mikhail S. Gorbachev. In late 1988, Gus Hall claimed a membership of 20,000 and half a million supporters. The Party, he told the *New York Times* in an interview, has been "a factor in changing the atmosphere from anti-Communist to a more leisurely, down-to-earth policy toward our party and to the idea that the Soviet Union is not an enemy or a military threat."[6]

Hall's figures are probably somewhat inflated, but knowledgeable outside observers agree that the Party has experienced growth. Harvey Klehr estimates that the Communist party today has around 15,000 paid members. About a third of the delegates to the Party's 1983 convention were between the ages of 18 and 34, indicating some success in attracting young people. Twenty-one percent had been Party members for less than five years.[7] The Party's *People's Daily World,* started in May of 1986, a little over a year later was said to have attained a weekend circulation of 70,000. By early 1990, on the other hand, in the wake of the epidemic of anticommunism sweeping the world from Bucharest to Managua, the Communist newspaper had begun to experience severe financial difficulties and had been forced to cut back publication from five days to four.

On the whole, the Communist party remains an unpopular sect. In the presidential election of 1984, the last time the Party ran candidates for the offices of President and Vice President, it received 36,386 votes, or 0.04 percent of the total of 92,652,793 votes cast. Because of the possibility of harassment and economic pressures, the Party has been exempted from reporting individual contributions to its political campaigns as required by federal law.[8] A recruiting brochure issued in 1984 assured prospective members that the Party tries "to guarantee the full privacy and security of every worker" to protect members from reprisals from employers.[9] Many members conceal their membership for the same reason or because they can be more effective politically without revealing their affiliation with the Party. In her report to a party conference held in July 1989, Judith LeBlanc, national organizational secretary, noted that because of the continuing strength of anticommunist sentiments "only 20 percent of the Party membership is public."[10] It is thus difficult to know the real size and political influence of the Party.

As in the past, much of the Communist party's influence today derives from the work of its front groups that enable it to reach a larger audience. The active role of the U.S. Peace Council in the peace movement has been discussed in an earlier chapter. The Party has also scored gains in the labor movement, once fiercely anticommunist, and among black politicians and civil rights leaders. For example, in December 1982, the Labor Research Association (LRA), a front organization founded by the Party in 1927 and for much of its existence shunned by organized labor, held a banquet to honor the Congressional Black Caucus. The affair was attended by eight hundred people, including six congressmen, six members of the New York State legislature, and representatives of thirty unions.[11] Sponsors of conferences organized by the LRA have included prominent trade union officials. Among the "distinguished warriors" in the struggle for civil rights honored by the Detroit Urban League at its annual dinner in February 1985 was Carl Winter, the retired editor of the Communist party's *Daily World* and a member of its central committee.[12]

Another front organization successful in attracting non-Communist support has been the National Alliance Against Racist and Political Repression (NAARPR), founded in 1972. A march in Raleigh, North Carolina, held on July 4, 1974, and attended by five to ten thousand people, was addressed by Ralph Abernathy of the Southern Christian Leadership Conference. Black Communist leader Angela Davis appealed for "a new popular front of the political left." At the Alliance's tenth anniversary conference in 1983, Congressman Charles Hayes served as chairman and John Conyers was the major speaker. The organization's concern with repression has been concentrated on the United States, Israel, and South Africa. Needless to say, it does not include the Soviet Union and the other socialist countries.[13]

The Outlook

For most of their history, American Communists have been, in Supreme Court Justice William O. Douglas's phrase in the *Dennis* case, "miserable merchants of unwanted ideas." Despite some recent gains, the Communist party today is no closer to its goal of a Communist United States of America. At a time when the bankruptcy of a centrally planned economy has been openly acknowledged in most of the Eastern bloc countries, American Communists continue to affirm the superiority of socialism over capitalism. Doctrinaire as ever, the Party closes its eyes to the demonstrated achievements of capitalism, probably the most efficient system for producing wealth and satisfying man's earthly needs the world has yet known. In view of these and other long-standing liabilities, the likelihood that the Party will ever succeed in winning the support of a majority of the American people is next to zero. The notion, nourished by some segments of the Right, that the Communist party would attempt, let alone succeed, by force to overthrow the government of the United States, has always been a paranoid fantasy.

Today the Communists play a political role less in their own right, but as a result of the fact that so many of their goals have also become the goals of the more numerous and more influential free-floating Left. This amalgam of often fluid political groups, forswearing the forbidding sectarian jargon of the Old Left, has gained a significant foothold among the churches and church-related social action organizations in particular. Many of its members are today tenured professors or journalists, successfully implementing what the German radical Rudi Dutschke during the 1960s had called "the long march through the institutions." At least some of the difficulties which the Reagan administration experienced in regard to its policy in Central America can be traced to the highly effective campaign of disinformation waged by this well-organized grassroots network, which portrayed the Sandinistas of Nicaragua as social reformers and the Nicaraguan resistance as mercenaries guilty of systematic violations of human rights. This network has been able to mobilize substantial voter sentiment. Since 1979, an estimated 40,000 Americans have visited Nicaragua to learn about the "progress" made by the Sandinista regime. Many more have been persuaded by "peace and justice" groups to send food, medicine, and money to the Sandinistas and their Marxist-Leninist allies in Central America. Some 100,000 Americans have signed the "Pledge of Resistance," committing themselves to be "on call" to engage in nonviolent direct action in the event of a U.S. military escalation in Central America.

In a free society, all voices have a right to be heard. The radical Left, like any other political group, is entitled to criticize American foreign policy and to propose alternative courses of action. What distinguishes the politics of much of the radical Left from those of the country's mainstream political forces is their hidden agenda. Rather than acknowledge their deep anticapitalist animus or their solidarity with Marxist-Leninists in Central America and the rest of the Third World, these groups pretend to defend the interests of the oppressed and talk of seeking a progressive social and economic order. The question of what policy the U.S. should adopt toward Nicaragua is one that can be the subject of reasonable disagreement. Yet when some radical groups allege that the Sandinistas are nonaligned, democratic socialists dedicated to Christianity, they are not staking out another legitimate political position but are manipulating a falsehood that can be shown to be a lie by the

Sandinistas' own pronouncements and well-documented deeds. Some speak of using a Marxist paradigm though in fact they are fully committed to Communism (or Marxism-Leninism, the currently fashionable term that appears to sound more benign).

In an open market of opinion, forced out from their deceptive covers, groups committed to Communist schemes are unlikely to find very many adherents. This point was addressed in 1947 by the President's Committee on Civil Rights. Its report, *To Secure These Rights,* criticized the "totalitarians of both left and right" who "have in common . . . a reluctance to come before the people honestly and say who they are, what they work for, and who supports them." The principle of disclosure, the committee argued, was the appropriate means to deal with those harboring subversive designs. "Our purpose is not to constrict anyone's freedom to speak; it is rather to enable the people better to judge the true motives of those who try to sway them."[14]

Five years later, in 1952, the noted civil libertarian Morris L. Ernst repeated these suggestions. "Our freedoms are based on the principle that in the marketplace of thought, truth and justice win out. But that holds true only if there is free trade in the market. We think the rules of free trade should carry protection for society by accurate labels on the package." Ideas entering the market, Ernst argued, should be properly identified as to support and financial backing. There was ample protection in the law against overt acts of treason, sabotage, and violent overthrow. The real danger to America's free institutions stemmed from stealth and deception.[15] Or as the philosopher Sidney Hook put it, what we have to fear "is not heresy but conspiracy. . . . The signs of conspiracy are secrecy, anonymity, the use of false names and labels, and the calculated lie."[16] As the French publicist Jean François Revel has observed, it is difficult to defend a democratic society by democratic means. "To totalitarianism, an opponent is by definition subversive; democracy treats subversives as mere opponents for fear of betraying its principles."[17]

The crisis of Communist ideology under way in the Soviet Union will change the constellation of forces in the world as well as the parameters of the contest of ideas. Official admissions of the bankruptcy of the Soviet economy and acknowledgments of the enormity of Stalin's crimes like the recent disclosure in a Soviet weekly that some 20 million died in labor camps, or as a result of forced collectivization, famine, and executions[18] are unlikely to raise the prestige of American Communism. Many of these admissions go beyond what even the harshest Western critics of the Soviet system have said in the past. Yet the New Left never regarded the Soviet Union as a model and these revelations therefore are unlikely to change its infatuation with "authentic" and "indigenous" revolutionary regimes like the Sandinistas of Nicaragua.

World Communism today is in a state of disintegration and turmoil that bodes ill for its future. Unprecedented free elections in Poland and East Germany and Hungary, and the toppling of Communist rule in East Germany, Czechoslovakia, Bulgaria, and Rumania coexist with the resolute suppression of the prodemocracy movement in China. Indirectly, the bloody events in China in early June 1989 have hurt the entire Communist world and have made many West European Communists distance themselves from the Communist East. "We are not part of an international Communist movement," declared Italian Party Secretary Achille Occhetto in a newspaper interview after the crackdown of Tiananmen Square. "There is absolutely nothing left of communism as a unitary and organic system."[19] On the other hand and not surprisingly, the American Communist party, one of the most Stalinist parties in the entire world Communist movement, has failed to condemn the repression of the Chinese student movement.[20]

The contest of ideas has certainly entered a decisive new phase. In those countries where Marxism-Leninism is the official creed, disillusionment and cynicism about this state-imposed system of thought are rampant. In much of the democratic world, Communist parties seek to turn away from their ideological origins. At the 1989 congress of the Communist party of Great Britain, keynoter Martin Jacques declared that "Stalinism is dead, and Leninism—its theory of the state, its concept of the party, the absence of civil society, its notion of revolution—has also had its day."[21] Several other European Communist parties are now being shaken by soul-searching and infighting over how to respond to the collapse of Communism in Eastern Europe.

The American Communist party, on the other hand, appears to be predominantly hostile to the new intellectual currents flowing in the world Communist movement. The reasons for this state of affairs are probably related to the American party's political isolation. Unlike many of their European counterparts, American Communists, for most of their past, have lacked a mass base and a chance to win electoral contests; they therefore had little incentive to abandon ideological purity and to adjust their programs to political realities. The Party's recent pronouncements against the Soviet Union's *glasnost* continue the tradition of hard-line orthodoxy that has characterized all but a few years of the Party's seventy-year history.

In a discussion published in the *World Marxist Review*, the coordinating organ of the world Communist movement, Jim West, a member of the American Party's national executive committee, expressed his con-

cern about the anti-Marxist-Leninist statements published in Soviet publications such as *Moscow News* and *New Times* without being subjected
to "a militant polemic against them." He also cautioned against confusing
perestroika with the "so-called Prague Spring of 1968 which was in fact
a counter-revoluntionary attempt."[22] About a year later, in December
1989, the Czech Communist party and the members of the Warsaw Pact
collectively pronounced the Soviet-led invasion that choked the Prague
Spring as unjustified.

At a special "Ideological Conference" convened in Chicago in July
1989, national chairman Gus Hall warned against the corrupting influence of bourgeois ideas and he recalled earlier heresies like Browderism,
"the 'new thinking' of the Teheran days." It was valid to criticize mistakes of the past, Hall acknowledged, but at the same time it was imperative "to defend and recommend socialism, rather than criticize in a
way that is destructive of socialism's image." The "fact that there are
some, even in socialist countries, who spend their time searching the
archives to find dirt to spread on front pages does not in any way negate
the correctness of our approach."[23] On the other hand, there are those
such as the Californian Communist David Engelstein, who decries the
Party's "dogmatism, the remnants of the Stalinist heritage" and who
acknowledges that "We need Glasnost."[24] If, as appears likely, the forces
of orthodoxy were once again to come out on top, the Party's fortunes
would continue to deteriorate. Together with the widely recognized
bankruptcy of the Communist ideology, such doctrinal rigidity would
further decrease the Party's attractiveness to intellectuals.

As of this writing, the Soviet Union under Gorbachev is trying to shed
many of its totalitarian features. As columnist Charles Krauthammer has
noted in a recent article, the search of so many Western intellectuals
for a more humane Communism has now come full circle.

> First Beatrice Webb and Lincoln Steffens and Paul Robeson and a hundred
> other gentle souls lodged their hopes in the Soviet Union. When these hopes
> were dashed, the next generation of innocents looked to the communist
> hinterland for the new dawn: first Mao's China, then Castro's Cuba, then
> the Vietcong and Uncle Ho, then Sandinista Nicaragua. Each hope ex-
> ploded in turn. Political pilgrimage, eternally in search of a communism
> to love, seemed to have reached its final dead end in the present-day ruins
> of Managua. Then along comes Gorbachev and gives the world a new
> shrine, the old shrine, at which to worship—Moscow.[25]

Gorbachev's reforms occasionally are indeed generating new illusions.
Apologists for Stalin's crimes like Paul Robeson are now celebrated

by some as prophets. The Communism they defended, it is argued, turned out to be not so bad after all. A press release for the recent Washington revival of the play *Paul Robeson* described him as "one of the most heroic figures of the 20th century." Even an honest biographer like Martin Bauml Duberman, who painstakingly documents Robeson's abject fealty to Stalinism and does not fail to criticize Robeson's political deviousness, calls him a "militant spokesman for the world's oppressed."[26] The fact that the well-informed Robeson had no tears and never found it necessary to speak up for the millions imprisoned and murdered in Stalin's gulag, in the eyes of his admirers does not detract from the famous singer's alleged concern for the oppressed of this world.

When Communists behave like Communists one encounters exculpatory explanations which serve to conceal the harsh essence of the Communist ideology. During the 1930s, some regarded the repression of all dissent in the Soviet Union a logical result of the Russian tradition of autocracy. Following the suppression of the pro-democracy movement in China in June 1989, many attributed these unfortunate events to the absence of a humane and democratic tradition in Chinese history. While historical factors such as these need not be entirely discounted, neither can they fully explain the scope and ferocity of the repressive practices involved. As the writer and critic Su Wei, who managed to escape from China, has argued, China's present circumstances are not so much the result of Chinese tradition as they are the product of a "Communist culture" that has consistently "suppressed free thought and is sustained by lies, by threats and by a requirement to forget."[27]

A new recognition of the repressive potential of Marxism-Leninism has manifested itself whenever the process of change in the Communist world has shown signs of slowing down or reversing itself. Thus, for example, after the mass killings in and around Tiananmen Square, voices were heard reminding Americans that perhaps the leopard had not changed his spots after all. A journalist connected with National Public Radio acknowledged that until shortly before these bloody events he had "thought the Chinese leadership was different from other communist dictatorships," but, alas, "Marxist logic" appeared to have triumphed over "Chinese pragmatism."[28] In the words of Charles Krauthammer, a "generation—too young to remember Budapest 1956, too distracted to notice Prague 1968, too far removed to fully absorb the Vietnamese gulag and the Cambodian genocide of the '70s—has finally been directly exposed to the meaning of Marxist-Leninism."[29]

The final outcome of the diverse developments in the Communist world cannot be foreseen nor can we foretell how American elites will respond to them. We do know that the relationship of the American

Communist party and many prominent members of this country's intellectual community over the past seven decades, examined in the preceding pages, was often characterized by a profound lack of moral integrity. The support given by many important people to the Party despite Stalin's reign of terror during the 1930s, the widespread infatuation with all things Russian during World War II, the often unreasonable reaction to the Communist problem at the time of McCarthyism, and, finally, the recent fad of anti-anticommunism demonstrate that the political and moral judgment of all too many American intellectuals has been less than keen.

Intellectuals, it appears, are especially vulnerable to the totalitarian temptation. They see themselves as the moral conscience of society and therefore find it easy to justify the use of the coercive power of the state in order to free ordinary folks from "false consciousness." Intellectuals are fond of social engineering and, to use Rousseau's classic phrase, they have little difficulty countenancing schemes that "force people to be free." Many American intellectuals, like their counterparts elsewhere, were misled by their yearning for utopia and seduced by wishful thinking about the Soviet Union. Communist ideology provided both explanation and emotional assurance. It claimed to explain the working of capitalism, which most intellectuals scorned as a vulgar and exploitative social system, while at the same time it promised the eventual victory of a new and just society. Politically and morally disoriented by their alienation from American society, a considerable number of American intellectuals became ensnared by a closed system in which the whole of history as well as their own person could find their place and meaning. All too willing to suspend their own judgment, they became part of an organization that exploited their idealism for its own nefarious ends.

And idealists, even if unduly naïve, most rank-and-file Communists indeed were. The Communist party included many different types of people, but, according to Aileen S. Kraditor, a party member for eleven years and a shrewd observer, two kinds stood out. There were those driven by hostility. These Communists affirmed their love for the people and praised the future society of peace and brotherhood, but it was not love of individual human beings but zealotry for a cause that dominated their lives. Others were generous and kind and had genuine concern and pity for the suffering of the underprivileged and exploited. Both types, Kraditor stresses, were sincere idealists, albeit within their own narrow ideological framework. They fervently believed in justice, equality, and the ending of poverty and discrimination, and they associated these noble ends with socialism and the kind of society being built in the Soviet Union. Mistakes in Soviet policies, if acknowledged at all, were dismissed as temporary abberations or inevitable excesses in the difficult tasks of creating a new society; they in no way called into question the overall thrust and superiority of the first socialist state. Ideological self-delusion and misperceptions of the real world were helped by the conviction that the class enemy's "facts" and arguments were self-evidently false, that the Party alone knew and told the truth, and by the rigid censorship of reading which members of the Party imposed upon themselves. Some, Kraditor recalls, had "unbeknownst to themselves, kept a corner of their minds independent of the Party's worldview, a private plot of soil in which a seed of reality could grow."[30] Many of those eventually returned to their liberal origins. Others, and especially the leading cadres, acquired the hardened political cynicism of the apparatchik who privately knew everything but publicly knew nothing. The 1930s in particular, as Philip Rahv noted in a retrospective comment made in 1964, were "a period of ideological vulgarity and opportunism, of double-think and power worship, sustained throughout by a mean and unthinking kind of secular religiosity."[31]

How difficult was it to withstand the totalitarian temptation? Edward Shils has argued that it did not take "any exceptional intelligence, or imagination, or erudition, or strength of character. . . . One just had to be intelligent and self-respecting enough to withstand prevailing opinions. . . . It took nothing more than a sober eye to size up the brutality and the moral shadiness of Communists, both in the Soviet Union and in Western countries."[32] Shils's appraisal, though basically correct, in perhaps a bit too uncharitable. The years of the Great Depression, in particular, were extremely trying, and it was easy to succumb to the siren song of a radical ideology like communism that in an hour of desperation promised a "new heaven and a new earth," the salvation of mankind. This observation is not meant to excuse but rather is put forth in order to help us understand why so many failed to achieve the qualities of character necessary to make a successful stand against a powerful utopian creed.

Perhaps the past will not be prologue. In looking at yesteryear and trying to discern what it holds for the future, one must also beware of hasty and unfair generalizations. Among American intellectuals of these eventful years we find repugnant types such as Joseph Freeman or Malcolm Cowley but also truly impressive figures such as John Dewey and Sidney Hook. Earlier than most of their contemporaries, these men recognized that a true opponent of tyranny had to be both antifascist and anticommunist. Some, like the Socialist leader Norman Thomas, learned in the hard school of experience that the exclusion of Communists was the only effective way of protecting an organization against the Communists' manipulative activities. During the 1950s, men and women of this persuasion knew that in order to oppose Senator McCarthy and his demagoguery one did not have to take a defensive stand on the Communist party and its tactics of deceit. With insights still applicable today, they maintained that it was possible to oppose the distorted political perceptions and deeply flawed moral values of the Communists while at the same time defend their civil rights and liberties. In short, anticommunism was a moral imperative and not a necessary prelude or accessory to McCarthyism and other forms of political repression. Just as a person had a right not to be smeared as Communist, they argued, because the Communists shared this or that of his political positions, so anticommunists were entitled not to be called reactionaries just because members of the far Right also defended the political stance of anticommunism.

The historical record thus reveals intellectual dishonesty and cowardice but also moral probity, courage, and principled dedication to the truth. These qualities, we can be sure, will be needed again in the days ahead. The fact that Communist totalitarianism today is losing ground almost everywhere may help us learn the lessons of the past. The decisiveness with which the people of Eastern Europe in recent months have expressed their hatred of Communism should serve as a reminder, for those who need it, that anticommunism is not "Cold War rhetoric" but an expression of man's yearning for freedom and human dignity.

Appendix

Communist Party Membership, 1919–1988

There exist few accurate figures on Communist party membership and for some years no information at all is available. Claims by party officials have often been exaggerated and they have frequently failed to distinguish between recruited, registered, and dues-paying members, the last category being the smallest. In at least one instance, the members of the Young Communist League appear to have been included in the total number of members claimed by the Party. Within these limitations, the figures given below provide a rough picture of the fluctuations in Communist party membership.

Date	Membership	Source
1919	40,000	Report to 8th Convention (1934)
May 1920	11,000	Claim of United Communist party
Nov. 1922	8,000	Report to Communist International
1923	11,000	Report to 4th Convention (1925)
1924	13,000	Report to 4th Convention (1925)
Early 1925	12,000	Report to 4th Convention (1925)
Late 1925	7,200	Report to 6th Convention (1929)
1926	7,500	Report to 8th Convention (1934)
1927	9,500	Report to 8th Convention (1934)
1928	9,500	Report to 8th Convention (1934)
1929	9,500	Report to 8th Convention (1934)
1930	7,545	Report to 8th Convention (1934)
1931	9,219	Report to 8th Convention (1934)
1932	14,474	Report to 8th Convention (1934)
June 1933	14,937	Report to 8th Convention (1934)
1934	24,500	Report to Communist International
1935	24,074	*Communist,* July 1935
1936	41,000	Report to 9th Convention (1936)
Dec. 1937	62,000	*Communist,* March 1938
Late 1938	82,000	Browder pamphlet
Sept. 1939	100,000	*Communist,* September 1939
April 1942	44,000	Report to National Committee
Spring 1944	79,000	*Worker,* July 16, 1944
Jan. 1945	65,000	Report to National Committee

Date	Membership	Source
Jan. 1946	52,500	Report by Party official
August 1948	60,000	Report to 14th Convention (1948)
Late 1949	54,174	Michael R. Belknap
Early 1953	24,796	Michael R. Belknap
Late 1955	22,663	Michael R. Belknap
Summer 1957	10,000	David A. Shannon
December 1957	3,474	Richard Gid Powers
1966	12,000	*Worker,* March 1, 1966
July 1968	13,000	Richard F. Staar
Feb. 1971	15,000	Richard F. Staar
Oct. 1972	16,500	*Daily World,* October 10, 1972
1976	15,000	Communist party claim
1976	4,200	FBI estimate
1981	20,000	Gus Hall claim
1985	17,500	Gus Hall claim
1988	15,000	Harvey Klehr
Late 1988	20,000	Communist party claim

In the preparation of the table above, I have drawn on the following works:

Michael R. Belknap, *Cold War Political Justice: The Smith Act, the Communist Party, and American Civil Liberties* (Westport, Conn.: Greenwood Press, 1977).

Milorad M. Drachkovitch, ed., *Yearbook of International Communist Affairs 1966* (Stanford, Calif.: Hoover Institution, 1967).

Theodore Draper, *American Communism and Soviet Russia: The Formative Period* (New York: Vintage Books, 1986).

Nathan Glazer, *The Social Basis of American Communism* (New York: Harcourt, Brace and World, 1961).

Irving Howe and Lewis Coser, *The American Communist Party: A Critical History* (New York: Frederick A. Praeger, 1962).

Maurice Isserman, *Which Side Were You On? The American Communist Party During the Second World War* (Middletown, Conn.: Wesleyan University Press, 1982).

Harvey Klehr, *The Heyday of American Communism: The Depression Decade* (New York: Basic Books, 1984).

Harvey Klehr, *Far Left of Center: The American Radical Left Today* (New Brunswick, N.J.: Transaction Books, 1988).

Richard Gid Powers, *Secrecy and Power: The Life of J. Edgar Hoover* (New York: Free Press, 1987).

David A. Shannon, *The Decline of American Communism: A History of the Communist Party of the United States* (Chatham, N.J.: Chatham Bookseller, 1971).

Richard F. Staar, ed., *Yearbook on International Communist Affairs, 1969–1987* (Stanford, Calif.: Hoover Institution Press, 1970–87).

Notes

Chapter 1. Early Years: Isolation and Internal Strife

1. Cf. Irving Howe and Lewis Coser, *The American Communist Party: A Critical History* (New York: Frederick A. Praeger, 1962), 1–17.

2. Quoted in Theodore Draper, *The Roots of American Communism* (New York: Viking, 1957), 110.

3. *The Worker*, November 4, 1922, cited by Draper, *Roots of American Communism*, 97.

4. Howe and Coser, *The American Communist Party*, 27.

5. Draper, *Roots of American Communism*, 158.

6. "Report upon the Illegal Practices of the United States Department of Justice," quoted in *ibid.*, 203, 226.

7. Bertram D. Wolfe, *A Life in Two Centuries: An Autobiography* (New York: Stein & Day, 1981), 386.

8. Nathan Glazer, *The Social Basis of American Communism* (New York: Brace and World, 1961), 41, 52–53; Theodore Draper, *American Communism and Soviet Russia: The Formative Period* (New York: Viking, 1968), 188–89.

9. Joseph R. Starobin, *American Communism in Crisis: 1943–1957* (Cambridge, Mass.: Harvard Univ. Press, 1972), 23.

10. Philip J. Jaffe, *The Rise and Fall of American Communism* (New York: Horizon, 1975), 12.

11. Draper, *American Communism and Soviet Russia*, 125.

12. Earl Browder, "The American Communist Party in the Thirties," in Rita James Simon, ed., *As We Saw the Thirties: Essays on Social and Political Movements of the Decade* (Urbana: Univ. of Illinois Press, 1967), 218. See also James Weinstein, *The Decline of Socialism in America: 1912–1925* (New York: Monthly Review Press, 1967).

13. For a more detailed discussion of these splits see Howe and Coser, *The American Communist Party*, ch. 4.

14. Max Eastman, "An Opinion on Tactics," *Liberator*, IV (Oct. 1921), 5–6, quoted in Eastman's autobiography *Love and Revolution: My Journey through an Epoch* (New York: Random House, 1964), 257.

15. *Daily Worker*, Jan. 8, 1930, p. 4, cited by Robert W. Iversen, *The Communists and the Schools* (New York: Harcourt, Brace, 1959), 77; Earl Browder, "A 'Fellow Traveler' Looks at Imperialism," *Communist* (June 1930), 568, cited by Harvey Klehr, *The Heyday of American Communism: The Depression Decade*

(New York: Basic Books, 1984), 70. See also Scott Nearing, *The Making of a Radical: A Political Autobiography* (New York: Harper & Row, 1972).

16. Joseph Freeman, *An American Testament: A Narrative of Rebels and Romantics* (New York: Farrar, Straus and Giroux, 1973), 323.

17. Richard Crossman, ed., *The God That Failed* (London: Hamish Hamilton, 1950), 133, 154.

18. Klehr, *Heyday of American Communism*, 74–76.

19. Quoted in *ibid.*, 75.

20. Edmund Wilson, "An Appeal to Progressives," *New Republic,* Jan. 14, 1931, pp. 234–38, reprinted in Edmund Wilson, *The Shores of Light: A Literary Chronicle of the Twenties and Thirties* (New York: Farrar, Straus and Young, 1952), 518–33.

21. John Dos Passos, "Whither the American Writer," *Modern Quarterly,* vol. VI, no. 2 (Summer 1932), 11.

Chapter 2. Problems of the United Front

1. Quoted in Philip J. Jaffe, *The Rise and Fall of American Communism* (New York: Horizon, 1975), 35.

2. Theodore Draper, *American Communism and Soviet Russia: The Formative Period* (New York: Viking, 1968), 31.

3. *Ibid.,* 44–47.

4. Quoted in *ibid.,* 75.

5. *Ibid.,* 90.

6. Alexander Bittelman in the *Daily Worker,* magazine supplement, Aug. 29, 1925, quoted in *ibid.,* 113.

7. *Daily Worker,* Dec. 4, 1924, quoted in *ibid.,* 121.

8. Jane Degras, "United Front Tactics in the Comintern 1921–1928," in David Footman, ed., *International Communism* (St. Anthony's Papers no. 9) (Carbondale: Southern Illinois Univ. Press, 1960), 15. See also Theodore Draper, *The Roots of American Communism* (New York: Viking, 1957), 327–30.

9. Earl Browder, *Communism in the United States* (New York: International Publishers, 1935), 149, 264.

10. Bertram D. Wolfe, *What Is the Communist Opposition?* (New York: Communist Party (Opposition), 1933), 28–29.

11. *Daily Worker,* Nov. 29, 1928, quoted in Draper, *American Communism and Soviet Russia,* 381.

12. T. Gusev, "Basic Tasks of the British and American Sections of the C. I." *Communist International,* Oct. 15, 1932, p. 674, quoted in Hillman M. Bishop, *The American League Against War and Fascism* (New York: pub. by the author, 1936), 4.

13. Norman Thomas, *The Choice Before Us: Mankind at the Crossroads* (New York: AMS, 1970), 80–81, 153, 155. See also Murray B. Seidler, *Norman Thomas: Respectable Rebel,* 2nd ed. (Syracuse: Syracuse Univ. Press, 1967), 123; W. A. Swanberg, *Norman Thomas: The Last Idealist* (New York: Charles Scribner's Sons, 1976), 141.

14. For examples of Communist disruptive tactics see Harvey Klehr, *The Heyday of American Communism: The Depression Decade* (New York: Basic

Books, 1984), 112–13; Benjamin Gitlow, *I Confess: The Truth about American Communism* (New York: E. P. Dutton, 1940), 221.

15. Frank A. Warren, *An Alternative Vision: The Socialist Party in the 1930s* (Bloomington, Ind.: Indiana Univ. Press, 1974), 239, n. 20.

16. Cited by Seidler, *Norman Thomas*, 155.

17. *New York Times*, Dec. 2, 1935, cited by Seidler, *Norman Thomas*, 156.

18. Haim Kantorovitch, "Notes on the United Front Problem," *American Socialist Monthly*, vol. V, no. 3 (May 1936), 8–9.

19. Browder, *Communism in the United States*, 31; Klehr, *Heyday of American Communism*, 178–79, 211, 220.

20. *Socialist Call*, Aug. 18, 1936, p. 12, quoted in Seidler, *Norman Thomas*, 179.

21. Norman Thomas, *Socialism on the Defensive* (New York: Harper and Brothers, 1938), 145.

22. *Ibid.*, 181.

23. *Ibid.*, 246.

24. Swanberg, *Norman Thomas*, 233.

25. *Socialist Call*, Sept. 2, 1939, quoted in Seidler, *Norman Thomas*, 187.

26. Swanberg, *Norman Thomas*, 149.

Chapter 3. Theory and Practice of Front Organizations

1. Irving Howe and Lewis Coser, *The American Communist Party: A Critical History (1919–1957)* (New York: Frederick A. Praeger, 1962), 386.

2. This often quoted phrase was apparently coined by Lenin, though it is not found in any of his writings. Both the Menshevik Rafael Abramovich and Angellica Balabanova, onetime secretary of the Comintern, have said that it was one of Lenin's favorite terms. Balabanova told John P. Roche that Lenin's manipulation of "useful idiots" contributed to her disillusionment with Communism (John P. Roche to the author, June 13, 1985).

3. Suzanne Labin, *The Techniques of Soviet Propaganda*, 10. This study, presented at a meeting of the Atlantic Treaty Association in Boston in September 1959, is reprinted in U.S. Senate, Committee of the Judiciary, Subcommittee to Investigate the Administration of the Internal Security Act and Other Internal Security Laws, 86th Congress, 2nd sess., 1960.

4. Theodore Draper, *American Communism and Soviet Russia: The Formative Period* (New York: Viking, 1968), 182.

5. *Ibid.*, 185.

6. C. Roselle, "How to Stabilize Finances in the Districts," *Party Organizer*, June 1931, p. 9, quoted in Harvey Klehr, *The Heyday of American Communism: The Depression Decade* (New York: Basic Books, 1984), 106.

7. Photostatic copies of the committee's checks were published in the newspapers. Cf. Sidney Hook, *Political Power and Personal Freedom: Critical Studies in Democracy, Communism and Civil Rights* (New York: Collier Books, 1962), 317.

8. For a good discussion of Party finances see Klehr, *Heyday of American Communism*, 374–78. Former highly placed Communist leaders such as Earl Browder and Bertram D. Wolfe have confirmed that the Soviet Union and the

Comintern provided the Party with large sums of money. Cf. Bertram D. Wolfe, *A Life in Two Centuries: An Autobiography* (New York: Stein & Day, 1981), and Draper, *American Communism and Soviet Russia*, 208. The story of Jack and Morris Childs, who by the early 1950s were instrumental in channeling $1 million in Soviet funds a year to the CPUSA, is told in David J. Garrow, *The FBI and Martin Luther King, Jr.: From "Solo" to Memphis* (New York: W. W. Norton, 1981), 37. On February 7, 1989, Alan C. Thomson, executive director of the National Council of American-Soviet Friendship, a front organization established by the Party in 1943, was arrested by the FBI for smuggling into the U.S. from the Soviet Union $17,000 (*Washington Times,* Feb. 8, 1989).

9. V. I. Lenin, "Theses on the Fundamental Tasks of the Second Congress of the Communist International," *Selected Works* (New York: International Publishers, 1938), vol. X, p. 169.

10. V. I. Lenin, *"Left-Wing" Communism, an Infantile Disorder, Selected Works in Two Volumes* (Moscow: Foreign Languages Publishing House, 1951), vol. II, part 2, p. 379.

11. V. I. Lenin, "The Tasks of the Youth League," in *ibid.,* 485, 483.

12. Cited by Clarence A. Hathaway, "On the Use of Transmission Belts in Our Struggle for the Masses," *Communist,* X (March 1931), 413.

13. From a resolution adopted on March 8, 1926, quoted in Jane Degras, ed., *The Communist International 1919–1943: Documents, Vol. II: 1923–1928* (London: Oxford Univ. Press, 1960), 267.

14. R. N. Carew Hunt, "Willi Muenzenberg," in David Footman, ed., *International Communism* (St. Anthony's Papers, no. 9) (Carbondale: Southern Illinois Univ. Press, 1960), 87.

15. Hathaway, "On the Use of Transmission Belts," 412–13.

16. Josef Peters, *The Communist Party: A Manual on Organization* (New York: Workers Library, 1935), 101–2.

17. Joseph R. Starobin, *American Communism in Crisis: 1943–1957* (Cambridge, Mass.: Harvard Univ. Press, 1972), 39.

18. Klehr, *Heyday of American Communism,* 413–14.

19. John C. Clews, *Communist Propaganda Techniques* (New York: Praeger, 1964), 94–95.

20. Bert Cochran, *Labor and Communism: The Conflict That Shaped American Unions* (Princeton, N.J.: Princeton Univ. Press, 1977), 81.

21. Howe and Coser, *The American Communist Party,* 348.

22. David A. Shannon, *The Decline of American Communism: A History of the Communist Party of the United States Since 1945* (Chatham, N.J.: Chatham Bookseller, 1971), 83; Klehr, *Heyday of American Communism,* 373.

23. Quoted in Hillman M. Bishop, *The American League Against War and Fascism* (New York: pub. by the author, 1936), 25.

24. Viola Ilma, *The Political Virgin* (New York: Duell, Sloan and Peace, 1958), 79.

25. James A. Wechsler, *The Age of Suspicion* (New York: Random House, 1953), 70.

26. Howe and Coser, *The American Communist Party,* 359.

27. Earl Browder, "The Struggle for the United Front," *Communist* (Oct. 1934), 958, cited by Klehr, *Heyday of American Communism,* 320.

28. Quoted in Ralph Lord Roy, *Communism and the Churches* (New York: Harcourt, Brace and World, 1960), 102.

29. Quoted in Klehr, *Heyday of American Communism*, 321.

30. Eleanor Roosevelt, *This I Remember* (New York, 1949), quoted in Howe and Coser, *The American Communist Party*, 360.

31. Howe and Coser, *The American Communist Party*, 360.

32. John Gates, *The Story of an American Communist* (New York: Thomas Nelson, 1958), 71.

33. Roy, *Communism and the Churches*, 106.

34. William Foster, "Seven Years of Roosevelt," *Communist* (March 1940), 246, quoted in Klehr, *Heyday of American Communism*, 397.

35. Lovett Fort-Whiteman, "American Negro Labor Congress," *International Press Correspondence*, Aug. 27, 1925, p. 983, quoted in Draper, *American Communism and the Soviet Union*, 331.

36. Wilson Record, *Race and Radicalism: The NAACP and the Communist Party in Conflict* (Ithaca, N.Y.: Cornell Univ. Press, 1964), 60.

37. W. I. Patterson, "The I.L.D. Faces the Future," *Communist* (July 1934), 718, quoted in Bishop, *The American League Against War and Fascism*, 24.

38. Harry Haywood, "The Scottsboro Decision: Victory of Revolutionary Struggle over Reformist Betrayal," *Communist*, vol. XI (1932), 1068, cited by Dan Carter, *Scottsboro: A Tragedy of the American South*, rev. ed. (Baton Rouge: Louisiana State Univ. Press), 1979, p. 138; *Daily Worker*, June 1, 1932, quoted in *ibid.*, 160.

39. Carter, *Scottsboro*, 167.

40. *New York Times*, Sept. 8, 1935. Cf. Wilson Record, *The Negro and the Communist Party* (Chapel Hill: Univ. of North Carolina Press, 1951), 138–39.

41. Klehr, *Heyday of American Communism*, 346–47.

42. Howe and Coser, *The American Communist Party*, 356 (italics in original).

43. Gunnar Myrdal, *An American Dilemma* (New York, 1944), quoted in *ibid.*, 357.

44. Roy, *Communism and the Churches*, 149.

45. Mark Naison, *Communism and Harlem During the Depression* (Urbana: Univ. of Illinois Press, 1983), 310–11.

46. Record, *Race and Radicalism*, 151–55, 162–63.

47. F. J. Baumgardner to W. C. Sullivan, Aug. 22–23, 1963, quoted in William W. Keller, *The Liberals and J. Edgar Hoover: Rise and Fall of a Domestic Intelligence State* (Princeton, N.J.: Princeton Univ. Press, 1989), 104.

48. Cf. Garrow, *The FBI and Martin Luther King, Jr.*, passim.

49. Larry Ceplair and Steven Englund, *The Inquisition in Hollywood: Politics in the Film Community 1930–1960* (Garden City, N.Y.: Doubleday, 1980), 111–12.

50. Ellen W. Schrecker, *No Ivory Tower: McCarthyism and the Universities* (New York: Oxford Univ. Press, 1986), 51.

51. Harvey A. Levenstein, *Communism, Anticommunism, and the CIO* (Westport, Conn.: Greenwood, 1981), 44.

52. Carl Bernstein, *Loyalties: A Son's Memoirs* (New York: Simon and Schuster, 1989), 80–81.

53. *Ibid.*, 43.

54. Quoted in Howe and Coser, *The American Communist Party*, 505.

55. Quoted in Maurice Isserman, *If I Had a Hammer: The Death of the Old Left and the Birth of the New Left* (New York: Basic Books, 1987), 23.

56. George Charney, *A Long Journey* (Chicago: Quadrangle Books, 1968), 117.

57. Levenstein, *Communism, Anticommunism and the CIO,* 45.

Chapter 4. The "Red Decade"

1. Lincoln Steffens, *Lincoln Steffens Speaking* (New York: Harcourt, Brace, 1936), 210.

2. Daniel Aaron, *Writers on the Left: Episodes in American Literary Communism* (New York: Harcourt, Brace and World, 1961), 151.

3. Sidney Hook, *Out of Step: An Unquiet Life in the 20th Century* (New York: Harper and Row, 1987), 158.

4. Granville Hicks, *Where We Came Out* (Westport, Conn.: Greenwood, 1973), 35. The book was originally published in 1954.

5. Quoted in Harvey Klehr, *The Heyday of American Communism: The Depression Decade* (New York: Basic Books, 1984), 81.

6. *Ibid.,* 82–83.

7. Hicks, *Where We Came Out,* 36–37.

8. *Ibid.,* 38, 33, 36.

9. Granville Hicks, "Communism and the American Intellectuals," in Irving D. Talmadge, ed., *Whose Revolution? A Study of the Future Course of Liberalism in the United States* (New York: Howell, Soskin, 1941), 95.

10. Henry Hart, ed., *American Writers' Congress* (New York: International Publishers, 1935), 12.

11. *Ibid.,* 66–70.

12. *Ibid.,* 71, 169–70, 59–65, 192.

13. *Ibid.,* 80–81.

14. Hicks, *Where We Came Out,* 45–46. See also William Phillips, *A Partisan View: Five Decades of the Literary Life* (New York: Stein and Day, 1983), 50–51.

15. Henry Hart, ed., *The Writer in a Changing World* (n.p.: Equinox Cooperative, 1937), 48–49, 52.

16. Dwight MacDonald, "The American Writers' Congress," letter to *The Nation,* June 19, 1937, p. 714.

17. Klehr, *Heyday of American Communism,* 356.

18. Matthew Baigell and Julia Williams, eds., *Artists Against War and Fascism: Papers of the First American Artists' Congress* (New Brunswick, N.J.: Rutgers Univ. Press, 1986), 62.

19. *Ibid.,* 71, 14. See also Klehr, *Heyday of American Communism,* 354.

20. Baigell and Williams, *Artists Against War and Fascism,* 29–32.

21. Diana Trilling, "A Memorandum on the Hiss Case," *Partisan Review,* vol. XVII (1950), 491.

22. Joseph Wood Krutch, *Was Europe a Success?* (New York: Farrar & Rinehart, 1934), 29.

23. Morris R. Cohen, "Why I Am Not a Communist," *Modern Monthly,* vol. VIII, no. 3 (April 1934), 141–42. See also Frank A. Warren, *Liberals and Com-*

munism: The "Red Decade" Revisited (Bloomington: Indiana Univ. Press, 1966), passim.

24. "A People's Front," *New Republic,* Jan. 8, 1936, p. 241.

25. Klehr, *Heyday of American Communism,* 360.

26. Lionel Abel, *The Intellectual Follies: A Memoir of the Literary Venture in New York and Paris* (New York: Norton, 1984), 63.

27. *Ibid.,* 360.

28. The full list can be found in Eugene Lyons, *The Red Decade* (New York: Bobbs-Merrill, 1941), 248–49.

29. Sidney Hook, "John Dewey Resigns," *Freedom at Issue,* Nov./Dec. 1986, pp. 15–18; Hook, *Out of Step,* 232.

30. The full text of the statement and the list of signers is reproduced in Lyons, *Red Decade,* 344–45.

31. Freda Kirchwey, " 'Red Totalitarianism,' " *Nation,* May 27, 1939, p. 605.

32. "Liberty and Common Sense," *New Republic,* May 31, 1939, p. 89.

33. Letter to the Editor, *New Republic,* June 28, 1939, pp. 217–18.

34. Edmund Wilson, *Letters on Literature and Politics* (New York: Farrar, Straus and Giroux, 1977), 357–58, cited by Hook, *Out of Step,* 233.

35. David Seideman, *The New Republic: A Voice of Modern Liberalism* (New York: Praeger, 1986), 149, 148, 146, 159.

36. Malcolm Cowley, *The Dream of the Golden Mountain: Remembering the 1930s* (New York: Viking, 1980), 117.

37. Malcolm Cowley, *And I Worked at the Writer's Trade: Chapters of Literary History 1918–1978* (New York: Viking, 1978), 139. The essay in question first appeared in *The Kenyon Review,* Spring 1965.

38. Philip Rahv in a review of Isaac Deutscher's *The Prophet Outcast* in *New York Review of Books,* Jan. 23, 1964, quoted in Cowley, *And I Worked at the Writer's Trade,* 144.

39. For this paragraph I have drawn mainly on the thoughtful discussion of Terry A. Cooney, *The Rise of the New York Intellectuals: Partisan Review and Its Critics* (Madison: Univ. of Wisconsin Press, 1986).

40. *Ibid.,* 120; Phillips, *A Partisan View,* 47–52.

41. Philip Rahv, "Two Years of Progress—From Waldo Frank to Donald Ogden Stewart," *Partisan Review,* VI (Feb. 1938), 22–30, cited by Cooney, *Rise of the New York Intellectuals,* 136.

42. Philip Rahv, *Essays on Literature and Politics: 1932–1972,* edited by Arabel J. Porter and Andrew J. Dvosin (Boston: Houghton Mifflin, 1978), 292. The quoted excerpt is from an essay, "Trials of the Mind," published in *Partisan Review* in 1938.

43. Sidney Hook, "Why I Am a Communist: Communism without Dogmas," *Modern Monthly,* vol. VIII, no. 3 (April 1934), 165.

44. A. J. Muste, "An American Revolutionary Party," *Modern Monthly,* vol. VII, no. 12 (Jan. 1934), 715–16.

45. Hook, *Out of Step,* 196.

46. David A. Shannon, *The Decline of American Communism: A History of the Communist Party of the United States Since 1945* (Chatham, N.J.: Chatham Bookseller, 1971), 124.

47. Lyons, *The Red Decade,* 324–25.

48. Philip Rahv, "Where the News Ends," *New Leader*, Dec. 10, 1938, p. 8.

49. Phillips, *A Partisan View*, 173.

50. Max Eastman, *Love and Revolution: My Journey Through an Epoch* (New York: Random House, 1964), 608–9.

51. The full list of the signatories is given by Lyons, *The Red Decade*, 349–51. See also Hook, *Out of Step*, 264–69.

52. Hicks, *Where We Came Out*, 56.

53. Granville Hicks, "How Red Was the Red Decade," *Harper's*, July 1953, pp. 53–61.

54. Aaron, *Writers on the Left*, 232.

55. Howe and Coser, *The American Communist Party*, 128–29.

Chapter 5. Demise and Rebirth of the Popular Front

1. *Sovietskaia Kultura*, May 18, 1988, quoted in Walter Laqueur, *The Long Road to Freedom: Russia and Glasnost* (New York: Charles Scribner's Sons, 1989), 73, n. 47.

2. Gordon A. Craig, "Dangerous Liaisons," *New York Review of Books*, March 30, 1989, p. 18. See also Anthony Read and David Fisher, *The Deadly Embrace: Hitler, Stalin and the Nazi-Soviet Pact, 1939–1941* (New York: Norton, 1988).

3. S. Fredrick Starr, "Was Hitler Stalin's Fault? With Glasnost, the Great Myth of World War II Is Unraveling," *Washington Post*, Sept. 18, 1988.

4. Francis X. Clines, "Soviets Print Report Saying Stalin Agreed to Split Poland with Hitler," *New York Times*, May 26, 1989.

5. Esther B. Fein, "Soviets Confirm Nazi Pacts Dividing Europe," *New York Times*, Aug. 19, 1989.

6. Browder before the Institute of Public Affairs, Charlottesville, Virginia, quoted in Irving Howe and Lewis Coser, *The American Communist Party: A Critical History* (New York: Frederick A. Praeger, 1962), 387.

7. The two messages in their entirety received by Browder on a short-wave radio receiver, were made available by him to his friend Philip J. Jaffe, who reprints them in his book *The Rise and Fall of American Communism* (New York: Horizon, 1975), 44–47.

8. *Communist*, XVII (Oct. 1939), 904, quoted in Maurice Isserman, *Which Side Were You On? The American Communist Party During the Second World War* (Middletown, Conn.: Wesleyan Univ. Press, 1982), 43.

9. Quoted in Jaffe, *Rise and Fall of American Communism*, 41.

10. Mark Naison, *Communism and Harlem During the Depression* (Urbana: Univ. of Illinois Press, 1983), 292.

11. This letter, probably written in mid-September, is quoted in Isserman, *Which Side Were You On?*, 38.

12. Malcolm Cowley, "In Memoriam," *New Republic*, Aug. 12, 1940, pp. 219–20.

13. David Seideman, *The New Republic: A Voice of Modern Liberalism* (New York: Praeger, 1986), 155.

14. Daniel Bell, "Bruce Bliven—Don Quixote of Liberalism," *New Leader*,

March 4, 1944, p. 4, quoted in William L. O'Neill, *A Better World: The Great Schism—Stalinism and the American Intellectuals* (New York: Simon & Schuster, 1982), 106.

15. Reprinted in Granville Hicks, *Part of the Truth* (New York: Harcourt, Brace and World, 1965), 185.

16. Granville, Hicks, *Where We Came Out* (Westport, Conn.: Greenwood, 1973), 49.

17. Lester Cole, *Hollywood Red: The Autobiography of Lester Cole* (Palo Alto, Calif.: Ramparts, 1981), 171.

18. Quoted in Jaffe, *Rise and Fall of American Communism*, 43.

19. *People's World*, April 10, 1940, quoted in Isserman, *Which Side Were You On?*, 65.

20. *Jewish Voice*, I (March–April 1941), 2, quoted in *ibid.*, 63.

21. Howe and Coser, *The American Communist Party*, 402–4.

22. Michael Gold, *The Hollow Men* (New York: International Publishers, 1941), 67, quoted in Howe and Coser, *The American Communist Party*, 400.

23. 54 Stat. 670, 18 U.S.C. 2385. For further details of the "red scare" of 1940 see Michael R. Belknap, *Cold War Political Justice: The Smith Act, the Communist Party, and American Civil Liberties* (Westport, Conn.: Greenwood, 1977), 23–24.

24. 54 Stat. 1201, 18 U.S.C. 2386.

25. Freda Kirchwey, "Communists and Democracy," *Nation*, Oct. 14, 1939, p. 400.

26. Jaffe, *Rise and Fall of American Communism*, 49.

27. Isserman, *Which Side Were You On?*, 111.

28. Quoted in *ibid.*, 110.

29. Howe and Coser, *The American Communist Party*, 419.

30. Bella Dodd, *School of Darkness* (New York: P. J. Kennedy & Sons, 1954), 138, quoted in Howe and Coser, *The American Communist Party*, 420.

31. Joseph Starobin in the *New Masses*, LXII (Jan. 13, 1942), 20, quoted in Isserman, *Which Side Were You On?*, 128.

32. Quoted in Howe and Coser, *The American Communist Party*, 433–34.

33. Quoted in O'Neill, *A Better World*, 60.

34. Howe and Coser, *The American Communist Party*, 431–32.

35. Quoted in *ibid.*, 433. For other examples of pro-Russian euphoria see Paul Willen, "Who 'Collaborated' with Russia," *Antioch Review*, Sept. 1954, pp. 259–83.

36. *Daily Worker*, April 7, 1944, p. 1, quoted in Ralph Lord Roy, *Communism and the Churches* (New York: Harcourt, Brace and World, 1960), 165.

37. John Patrick Diggins, *Up from Communism: Conservative Odysseys in American Intellectual History* (New York: Harper & Row, 1975), 208.

38. *New Republic*, March 15 and April 12, 1943, quoted in Isserman, *Which Side Were You On?*, 159–61.

39. Quoted in Diggins, *Up from Communism*, 207.

40. Hook, *Out of Step*, 313.

41. John L. Childs and George S. Counts, *America, Russia, and the Communist Party in the Postwar World* (New York: John Day, 1943), 70–71.

42. *New Masses*, Oct. 19, 1943, pp. 16–17, quoted in Isserman, *Which Side Were You On?*, 177.

43. *New York Times,* April 29, 1943, quoted in Isserman, *Which Side Were You On?,* 175.

44. Quoted in Jaffe, *Rise and Fall of American Communism,* 67.

45. Eugene Lyons, *The Red Decade* (New York: Bobbs-Merrill, 1941), 394–95.

46. Bert Cochran, *Labor and Communism: The Conflict That Shaped American Unions* (Princeton, N.J.: Princeton Univ. Press, 1977), 165; Harvey Klehr, *The Heyday of American Communism: The Depression Decade* (New York: Basic Books, 1984), 404.

47. Foster in the *Daily Worker,* June 17 and Dec. 8, 1941; Earl Browder, "The Strike Wave Conspiracy," *Communist,* June 1943, quoted in Howe and Coser, *The American Communist Party,* 398, 409.

48. Quoted in Jaffe, *Rise and Fall of American Communism,* 50.

49. Quoted in *ibid.,* 51.

50. John Gates, *The Story of an American Communist* (New York: Thomas Nelson, 1958), 127.

51. *Communist,* XXI (Jan. 1942), 52, quoted in Isserman, *Which Side Were You On?,* 142.

52. Howe and Coser, *The American Communist Party,* 415.

53. *CIO News,* V (May 2, 1942), quoted in Isserman, *Which Side Were You On?,* 144–45.

54. Quoted in Howe and Coser, *The American Communist Party,* 437.

55. The full text of the Duclos article, translated into English, can be found in *Political Affairs,* XXIV (July 1945), 656–72. My summary follows Isserman, *Which Side Were You On?,* 217–18.

56. Cf. Jaffe, *Rise and Fall of American Communism,* 84.

57. Editorial, *Nation,* June 6, 1945, p. 614.

58. Editorial, *New Republic,* Aug. 6, 1945, p. 150.

Chapter 6. Liberal Anticommunism During the Cold War

1. David A. Shannon, *The Decline of American Communism: A History of the Communist Party of the United States Since 1945* (Chatham, N.J.: Chatham Bookseller, 1971), 125.

2. Quoted in Ralph Lord Roy, *Communism and the Churches* (New York: Harcourt, Brace and World, 1960), 258.

3. Muhlen's article, published in the October 12, 1946, issue of the *New Leader,* is discussed in William L. O'Neill, *A Better World: The Great Schism— Stalinism and the American Intellectuals* (New York: Simon & Schuster, 1982), 135.

4. Gallup poll data, cited by Harvey A. Levenstein, *Communism, Anticommunism, and the CIO* (Westport, Conn.: Greenwood, 1981), 234.

5. "Address of the President in Oklahoma City," Sept. 28, 1948, quoted in Michael R. Belknap, *Cold War Political Justice: The Smith Act, the Communist Party, and American Civil Liberties* (Westport, Conn.: Greenwood, 1977), 44–45.

6. Richard M. Fried, *Men Against McCarthy* (New York: Columbia Univ. Press, 1976), 28.

7. Norman Podhoretz, *Breaking Ranks: A Political Memoir* (New York: Harper & Row, 1979), 21, quoted in O'Neill, *A Better World,* 161.

8. EO 9835 of March 21, 1947, 16 F.R. 3690.

9. James A. Wechsler, *The Age of Suspicion* (New York: Random House, 1953), 234.

10. *Ibid.*, 234–35.

11. Quoted in Philip J. Jaffe, *The Rise and Fall of American Communism* (New York: Horizon, 1975), 184.

12. Hope Hale Davis, "Looking Back at My Years in the Party," *New Leader*, Feb. 11, 1980, p. 18.

13. Irving Howe and Lewis Coser, *The American Communist Party: A Critical History (1919–1957)* (New York: Frederick A. Praeger, 1962), 361–62.

14. John P. Roche, *The Quest for the Dream* (New York: Macmillan, 1963), 221.

15. 64 Stat. 987, 50 U.S.C. 783.

16. 68 Stat. 775, 50 U.S.C. 783(a).

17. Cf. David Fellman, *The Constitutional Right of Association* (Chicago: Univ. of Chicago Press, 1963), 40–41.

18. William F. Buckley, Jr., and L. Brent Bozell, *McCarthy and His Enemies: The Record and Its Meaning* (New Rochelle, N.Y.: Arlington House, 1961), 277, 329, 331, 314.

19. Norbert Muhlen, "The Phantom of McCarthyism," *New Leader*, May 21, 1951, quoted in O'Neill, *A Better World*, 308–9.

20. Wechsler, *The Age of Suspicion*, 324–25.

21. Granville Hicks, *Where We Came Out* (Westport, Conn.: Greenwood, 1973), 175.

22. Norman Thomas, *A Socialist's Faith* (Port Washington, N.Y.: Kennikat, 1971), 220. (This autobiography was originally published in 1951.)

23. Sidney Hook, *Heresy, Yes—Conspiracy, No!* (New York: American Committee for Cultural Freedom, n.d.), 5. (This pamphlet reprinted two essays originally published in the *New York Times* magazine of July 9, 1950, and Sept. 30, 1951.)

24. *Barenblatt v. U.S.*, 360 U.S. 109, at 128–29 (1959).

25. *Communist Party v. Subversive Activities Control Board*, 367 U.S. 1, at 102–3 (1961).

26. Hubert H. Humphrey to Marvin Rosenberg, Aug. 27, 1954, quoted in William W. Keller, *The Liberals and J. Edgar Hoover: Rise and Fall of a Domestic Intelligence State* (Princeton: Princeton Univ. Press, 1989), 87, n. 44.

27. Thomas I. Cook, *Democratic Rights Versus Communist Activity* (Garden City, N.Y.: Doubleday, 1954), 35.

28. Beatrice Bishop Berle and Travis Beal Jacobs, eds., *Navigating the Rapids: 1918–1971. From the Papers of Adolf A. Berle* (New York: Harcourt Brace Jovanovich, 1973), 581.

29. *Washington Post*, June 6, 1951.

30. Morris Ernst, "Liberals and the Communist Threat," and Roger Baldwin, "Liberals and the Communist Trial," *New Republic*, Jan. 31, 1949, pp. 7–8.

31. Sidney Hook, *Political Power and Personal Freedom: Critical Studies in Democracy, Communism and Civil Rights* (New York: Collier Books, 1962), 248. (The essays in this collection had all been published before 1959.)

32. Thomas, *A Socialist's Faith*, 223.

33. Hook, *Heresy, Yes—Conspiracy, No!*, 21.

34. Sidney Hook, *Heresy, Yes—Conspiracy, No* (New York: John Day, 1953), 118. (This book is an enlarged version of the pamphlet carrying the same title.)

35. Alan Barth, *The Loyalty of Free Men* (New York: Pocket Books, 1952), 110, 138.

36. Hook, *Heresy, Yes—Conspiracy, No!* (pamphlet), 28; Hook, *Heresy Yes, Conspiracy No* (book), 28.

37. *Hansard,* March 15, 1948, quoted in H. H. Wilson and Harvey Glickman, *The Problem of Internal Security in Great Britain: 1948–1953* (Garden City, N.Y.: Doubleday, 1954), 17.

38. Arthur M. Schlesinger, Jr., "What Is Loyalty? A Difficult Question," in John C. Wahlke, ed., *Loyalty in a Democratic Society* (Boston: D. C. Heath, 1952), 16–17.

39. Robert J. Goldstein, *Political Repression in Modern America* (Boston: G. K. Hall, 1979), 374.

40. For some suggestions on how to adapt the security program to the conditions of the 1980s see Guenter Lewy, *The Federal Loyalty-Security Program: The Need for Reform* (Washington, D.C.: American Enterprise Institute, 1983).

41. Robert K. Carr, *The House Committee on Un-American Activities* (Ithaca, N.Y.: Cornell Univ. Press, 1952), 456–57.

42. *Barsky, et al. v. United States,* 167 F. 2d 241, at 246–47 (1948), quoted in Carr, *The House Committee on Un-American Activities,* 428–29, n. 38.

43. *Barenblatt v. United States,* 360 U.S. 109, at 131–32 (1950). See also the discussion in Charles E. Rice, *Freedom of Association* (New York: New York Univ. Press, 1962), 172.

44. Cf. Erwin N. Griswold, *The 5th Amendment Today* (Cambridge, Mass.: Harvard Univ. Press, 1955), 18–19.

45. Philip Dunne, *Take Two: A Life in Movies and Politics* (New York: McGraw-Hill, 1980), 197–200.

46. Dore Schary, *Heyday: An Autobiography* (Boston, 1979), 163, quoted in O'Neill, *A Better World,* 224.

47. Larry Ceplair and Steven Englund, *The Inquisition in Hollywood: Politics in the Film Community 1930–1960* (Garden City, N.Y.: Doubleday, 1980), 270.

48. *Lawson v. United States,* 176 F.2d 49, at 53 (1949).

49. Ceplair and Englund, *The Inquisition in Hollywood,* 68.

50. Lester Cole, *Hollywood Red: The Autobiography of Lester Cole* (Palo Alto, Calif.: Ramparts, 1981), 163.

51. Dalton Trumbo, *Additional Dialogue: Letters of Dalton Trumbo 1942–62* (New York: M. Evans, 1970), 44.

52. Edward Dmytryk, *It's a Hell of a Life but Not a Bad Living* (New York: Times Books, 1978), 71–72, 126.

53. Cole, *Hollywood Red,* 201.

54. *Ibid.,* 159.

55. Ceplair and Englund, *The Inquisition in Hollywood,* 311, 320.

56. O'Neill, *A Better World,* 225.

57. *New York Times,* April 12, 1952, quoted in Victor S. Navasky, *Naming Names* (New York: Viking, 1980), 204–5.

58. Laurent Frantz and Norman Redlich, "Does Silence Mean Guilt," *Nation,* June 6, 1953, pp. 471–77.

59. Alan F. Westin, "Do Silent Witnesses Defend Civil Liberties: The Course of 'Profoundest Wisdom,' " *Commentary*, June 1953, pp. 541, 544.

60. Quoted in *ibid.*, 542.

61. Irving Kristol, "Civil Liberties 1952: A Study in Confusion," *Commentary*, vol. XIII (March 1952), reprinted in Allen Guttmann and Benjamin M. Ziegler, eds. *Communism, the Courts and the Constitution* (Boston: D. C. Heath, 1964), 86.

62. *Ibid.*, 82, 85.

63. Carr, *The House Committee on Un-American Activities*, 449–59.

64. *Ibid.*, 462.

65. Morris L. Ernst and David Loth, *Report on the American Communist* (New York: Capricorn Books, 1962), 227. (Originally published in 1952.) See also Herbert L. Packer, *Ex-Communist Witnesses: Four Studies in Fact Finding* (Stanford, Calif.: Stanford Univ. Press, 1962), 246.

66. National Education Association of the United States, *Proceedings of the 87th Annual Meeting Held at Boston, Massachusetts, July 3–8, 1949* (Washington, D.C.: NEA, n.d.), 157.

67. Quoted in Sidney Hook, *Common Sense and the Fifth Amendment* (New York: Criterion Books, 1957), 74.

68. Quoted in Anthony Heilbut, *"Exiled in Paradise": German Refugee Artists and Intellectuals in America from the 1930s to the Present* (New York: Viking, 1983), 384.

69. Academic Freedom Committee of the American Civil Liberties Union, *The 1953 Statement of the Association of American Universities, "The Rights and Responsibilities of Universities and Their Faculties"* (New York: ACLU, 1958), 10.

70. American Civil Liberties Union, *Academic Freedom and Academic Responsibility: Their Meaning to Students, Teachers, Administrators and the Community* (New York: ACLU, 1952), 13–14.

71. "Report of Committee A," *AAUP Bulletin*, vol. XXXIV, no. 1 (Spring 1948), 126.

72. Cf. Ellen Schrecker, *No Ivory Tower: McCarthyism and the Universities* (New York: Oxford Univ. Press, 1986), 218.

73. For a succinct summary of Hook's views on this issue see his article, "Should Communists be Permitted to Teach?," *New York Times* magazine, Feb. 27, 1949.

74. Richard Frank, "The School and the People's Front," *Communist*, vol. XVI, no. 5 (May 1937), 440, 445.

75. Schrecker, *No Ivory Tower*, 43, 108.

76. Theodore Draper, "The Class Struggle: The Myth of the Communist Professors," *New Republic*, Jan. 26, 1987, pp. 29–30.

77. Schrecker, *No Ivory Tower*, 348.

78. *Ibid.*, 44.

79. Bertell Ollman, "On Teaching Marxism," in Theodor Mills Norton and Bertell Ollman, eds., *Studies in Socialist Pedagogy* (New York: Monthly Review Press, 1978), 248.

80. Quoted in Robert W. Iversen, *The Communists and the Schools* (New York: Harcourt, Brace, 1959), 165.

81. Granville Hicks, "How Red Was the Red Decade?" *Harper's*, July 1953, p. 60.

82. Robert Morris, *No Wonder We Are Losing* (New York: Bookmailer, 1958), 142.

83. Dean Jaros, *Socialization to Politics* (New York: Praeger, 1973), 128.

84. Schrecker, *No Ivory Tower*, 65, 41.

85. *Ibid.*, 309, 44.

86. Lionel S. Lewis, *Cold War on Campus: A Study of the Politics of Organized Control* (New Brunswick, N.J.: Transaction Books, 1988), 267, 272.

87. *Ibid.*, 277–82.

88. Raymond Aron, *The Opium of the Intellectuals*, trans. Terence Kilmartin (New York: W. W. Norton, 1962), 232.

89. William L. O'Neill, *American High: The Years of Confidence 1945–1960* (New York: Free Press, 1986), 167.

90. Sidney Hook, *Out of Step: An Unquiet Life in the 20th Century* (New York: Harper & Row, 1987), 498.

91. Lionel S. Lewis in *Academe*, Jan.–Feb. 1987, p. 50.

92. Nathan Glazer, "The Professors and the Party," *New Republic*, Oct. 8, 1986, p. 42.

93. Hook, "Should Communists Be Permitted to Teach," *New York Times* magazine, Feb. 27, 1949.

94. Hook, *Out of Step*, 420.

95. Christopher Lasch, *The Agony of the American Left* (New York: Vintage, 1969), 94, 80.

96. *New York Times*, March 25, 1955, quoted in *ibid.*, 431.

97. O'Neill, *A Better World*, 298–300.

98. Richard Crossman, *The God That Failed: Six Studies in Communism* (London: Hamish Hamilton, 1950), 16.

99. Cf. John Patrick Diggins, *Up from Communism: Conservative Odysseys in American Intellectual History* (New York: Harper & Row, 1975), 218, 328–30.

100. James Rorty and Moshe Decter, *McCarthy and the Communists* (Boston: Beacon, 1954), 16, 103, 105, 110, 125.

101. Irving Howe, *A Margin of Hope: An Intellectual Autobiography* (New York: Harcourt Brace Jovanovich, 1982), 217.

102. Hook, *Out of Step*, 423.

103. George F. Kennan to Nicolas Nabokov, June 19, 1959, CCF Archives, quoted in Peter Coleman, *The Liberal Conspiracy: The Congress for Cultural Freedom and the Struggle for the Mind of Postwar Europe* (New York: Free Press, 1989), 9.

104. Carey McWilliams, *The Education of Carey McWilliams* (New York: Simon & Schuster, 1979), 155.

105. Lasch, *Agony of the American Left*, 94, 98.

106. Hook, *Out of Step*, 453.

107. *Ibid.*, 455.

108. Howe, *A Margin of Hope*, 208.

109. Arthur Schlesinger, Jr., "Liberal Anti-Communism Revisited: A Symposium," *Commentary*, Sept. 1967, p. 70.

110. Stephen Spender in *ibid.*, 73.

111. Mary Sperling McAuliffe, *Crisis on the Left: Cold War Politics and American Liberals 1947–1954* (Amherst: Univ. of Massachusetts Press, 1978), 129.

Chapter 7. The Revival of Anti-Anticommunism

1. Cf. Joseph R. Starobin, *American Communism in Crisis: 1943–1957* (Cambridge, Mass.: Harvard Univ. Press, 1972), 220–23; Michael R. Belknap, *Cold War Political Justice: The Smith Act, the Communist Party, and American Civil Liberties* (Westport, Conn.: Greenwood, 1977), 190–92.

2. George Charney, *A Long Journey* (Chicago: Quadrangle Books, 1968), 250.

3. David A. Shannon, *The Decline of American Communism: A History of the Communist Party of the United States Since 1945* (Chatham, N.J.: Chatham Bookseller, 1971), 360.

4. John Gates, *The Story of an American Communist* (New York: Thomas Nelson, 1958), 5.

5. J. Edgar Hoover, *Masters of Deceit: The Story of Communism in America and How to Fight It* (New York: Holt, Rinehart and Winston, 1958), 78.

6. Cf. Richard Gid Powers, *Secrecy and Power: The Life of J. Edgar Hoover* (New York: Free Press, 1987), 339–41.

7. Arthur Schlesinger, Jr., in the *New York Post*, May 4, 1952, quoted in Victor S. Navasky, *Naming Names* (New York: Viking, 1980), 54.

8. Norman Thomas quoted in Nat Hentoff, *Peace Agitator: The Story of A. J. Muste* (New York: Macmillan, 1963), 166.

9. Jason Epstein, "The CIA and the Intellectuals," *New York Review of Books,* April 20, 1967, p. 18, quoted in William L. O'Neill, *A Better World: The Great Schism—Stalinism and the American Intellectuals* (New York: Simon & Schuster, 1982), 352.

10. James William Fulbright, *The Arrogance of Power* (New York: Random House, 1966), 106–7, 81.

11. Martin Luther King, Jr., "Honoring Dr. Du Bois," *Freedomways,* Spring 1968, p. 109.

12. American Friends Service Committee, *Anatomy of Anti-Communism* (New York: Hill & Wang, 1969), xv, 58.

13. Michael Parenti, *The Anti-Communist Impulse* (New York: Random House, 1969), 7–8.

14. "Liberal Anti-Communism Revisited," *Commentary,* Sept. 1967, pp. 70, 76, 37.

15. Irving Howe in *ibid.,* 49.

16. Arthur Schlesinger, Jr., in *ibid.,* 68–71.

17. *Ibid.,* 52, 57, 64.

18. Terry A. Cooney, *The Rise of the New York Intellectuals: Partisan Review and Its Circle* (Madison: Univ. of Wisconsin Press, 1986), 251.

19. Larry Ceplair and Steven Englund, *The Inquisition in Hollywood: Politics in the Film Community 1930–1960* (Garden City, N.Y.: Doubleday, 1980), 205, 204.

20. Mary Sperling McAuliffe, *Crisis on the Left: Cold War Politics and American Liberals 1947–1954* (Amherst: Univ. of Massachusetts Press, 1978), 147.

21. Kenneth O'Reilly, *Hoover and the Un-Americans: The FBI, HUAC and the Red Menace* (Philadelphia, Pa.: Temple Univ. Press, 1983), 179.

22. Ceplair and Englund, *The Inquisition in Hollywood*, 150.

23. O'Neill, *A Better World*, 355.

24. See most recently Athan G. Theoharis and John Stuart Cox, *The Boss: J. Edgar Hoover and the Great American Inquisition* (Phila., Pa.: Temple Univ. Press, 1988).

25. Theodore Draper, "The Class Struggle: The Myth of the Communist Professors," *New Republic*, Jan. 26, 1987, p. 29. The other quotations are from a 1983 article by Ellen W. Schrecker and are cited by Draper.

26. Peter Collier and David Horowitz, "McCarthyism: The Last Refuge of the Left," *Commentary*, Jan. 1988, p. 40.

27. Kenneth Waltzer, "The New History of American Communism," *Reviews in American History*, June 1983, p. 259.

28. Ellen W. Schrecker, *No Ivory Tower: McCarthyism and the Universities* (New York: Oxford Univ. Press, 1986), 25.

29. Paul Lyons, *Philadelphia Communists, 1936–1956* (Philadelphia, Pa.: Temple Univ. Press, 1982), 18, 189.

30. *Ibid.*, 238.

31. Theodore Draper, "American Communism Revisited," *New York Review of Books*, May 9, 1985, pp. 33, 37. The authors belonging to the "new history" school whose work is discussed in this essay are: Maurice Isserman, Gary Gerstle, Roy Rosenzweig, Norman Markowitz, Kenneth Waltzer, and Paul Lyons.

32. Theodore Draper, "The Popular Front Revisited," *New York Review of Books*, May 30, 1985, p. 46.

33. *Ibid.*, 47.

34. Draper, "The Class Struggle," 35.

35. *Ibid.*, 34.

36. Draper, "The Popular Front Revisited," 50.

37. O'Neill, *A Better World*, 370.

38. Helen Manfull, ed., *Additional Dialogue: Letters of Dalton Trumbo 1942–1962* (New York: M. Evans, 1970), 16–17.

39. Philip Dunne, *Take Two: A Life in Movies and Politics* (New York: McGraw-Hill, 1980), 205–6.

40. O'Neill, *A Better World*, 360. Hellman's attack upon anticommunist liberals is found in the third volume of her autobiography, *Scoundrel Time* (Boston: Little, Brown, 1976).

41. Elia Kazan, *A Life* (New York: Knopf, 1988), 462, 465.

42. Richard H. Pells, *The Liberal Mind in a Conservative Age: American Intellectuals in the 1940s and 1950s* (New York: Harper & Row, 1985), 262–63.

43. Robert Griffith, *The Politics of Fear: Joseph R. McCarthy and the Senate* (Lexington: Univ. Press of Kentucky, 1970), 30–31.

44. David Caute, *The Great Fear: The Anti-Communist Purge under Truman and Eisenhower* (New York: Simon & Schuster, 1978), 11–12.

45. Schrecker, *No Ivory Tower*, 339–40, 336.

46. Irving Howe, *A Margin of Hope: An Intellectual Autobiography* (New York: Harcourt Brace Jovanovich, 1982), 223.

47. Sidney Hook, *Political Power and Personal Freedom: Critical Studies in*

Democracy, Communism and Civil Rights (New York: Collier Books, 1962), 285.

48. Cord Meyer, *Facing Reality: From World Federalism to the CIA* (New York: Harper & Row, 1980), 81.

49. Collier and Horowitz, "McCarthyism," 39.

50. U.S. President, *Public Papers of the Presidents of the United States: Jimmy Carter,* vol. I (Washington, D.C.: Government Printing Office, 1977), 956.

51. On IPS generally, see the discussion in Harvey Klehr, *Far Left of Center: The American Radical Left Today* (New Brunswick, N.J.: Transaction Books, 1988), ch. 12. S. Steven Powell's *Covert Cadre: Inside the Institute for Policy Studies* (Ottawa, Ill.: Green Hill, 1987) includes some interesting new materials but is marred by factual errors and speculative inferences.

52. *New York Times,* Nov. 1, 1983.

53. The references are given by Klehr, *Far Left of Center,* 186, n. 12.

54. Cf. Hilton Kramer, "Anti-Communism and the Sontag Circle," *New Criterion,* Sept. 1986, pp. 1–7.

55. John Trinkl, "Socialists Confer and Differ," *Guardian,* May 2, 1984, p. 2.

56. John Trinkl, "Socialists Beyond Fragments?," *Guardian,* Dec. 18, 1985, p. 5.

57. *Guardian,* May 1, 1985, p. 18.

58. Joel Kovel, "The Victims of Anticommunism," *Zeta Magazine,* Jan. 1988, pp. 84–89.

59. Transcript of panel 4, "Are There New Opportunities for Independent Politics," available from the Institute for Media Analysis, 145 W. 4 St., New York, N.Y. 10012. See also the report on the conference in the first issue of *Friends of IMA,* Feb. 1989.

60. For a report on the conference see also David Evanier and Harvey Klehr, "Anticommunism and Mental Health," *American Spectator,* Feb. 1989, pp. 28–30.

61. Collier and Horowitz, "McCarthyism: The Last Refuge of the Left," 41.

62. Eric Breindel, "Joe McCarthy's Don't-Say-It Legacy," *New York Post,* May 9, 1987.

63. William F. Buckley, Jr., "Dartmouth Hears from Angela Davis," *Washington Post,* Oct. 19, 1988.

64. Klehr, *Far Left of Center,* 41; see also David Horowitz, "Angela Davis and Academic Freedom at Dartmouth," *Policy Forum* (National Forum Foundation), vol. V, no. 1 (Jan. 1989).

65. Angela Y. Davis, *Women, Culture and Politics* (New York: Random House, 1989).

66. William F. Buckley, Jr., "Learning History at Harvard," *National Review,* Sept. 21, 1984, p. 63.

67. A detailed report of Handal's U.S. trip was found in a Salvadoran safe house used by the guerrillas and was subsequently published by the State Department in its white paper *Communist Interference in El Salvador,* Special Report #80 (Washington, D.C.: Government Printing Office, 1981).

68. Philip Shenon, "FBI Papers Show Wide Surveillance of Reagan Critics," *New York Times,* Jan. 28, 1988.

69. Scott McConnell, "The Liberal Abdication," *National Interest,* Winter 1988/89, pp. 127–28.

70. Anthony Lewis, "Law and Ideology," *New York Times,* Feb. 18, 1988.

71. Paul Hollander, *The Survival of the Adversary Culture: Social Criticism and Political Escapism in American Society* (New Brunswick, N.J.: Transaction Books, 1988), 24.

72. Quoted in Georgi A. Arbatov, *The War of Ideas in Contemporary International Relations,* trans. David Skvirsky (Moscow: Progress Publishers, 1973), 130.

73. Y. Nalin, *Detente and Anti-Communism,* trans. Barry Costello-Jones (Moscow: Progress Publishers, 1978), 152, 154–55.

74. Henry Winston at the 23rd National Convention of the CPUSA, Nov. 10–13, 1983, *Daily World,* Nov. 17, 1983.

75. Joshua Muravchik, "What Is to Be Done? A Guide for Anti-Communists," *New Republic,* Nov. 30, 1987, pp. 16–17.

76. Samuel A. Stouffer, *Communism, Conformity and Civil Liberties: A Cross-section of the Nation Speaks Its Mind* (New York: Doubleday, 1955), 44, 41.

77. Clyde Z. Nunn et al., *Tolerance for Nonconformity: A National Survey of Changing Commitment to Civil Liberties* (San Francisco: Jossey-Bass, 1978), 42–43.

78. Herbert McClosky and Alida Brill, *Dimensions of Tolerance: What Americans Believe about Civil Liberties* (New York: Russell Sage Foundation, 1983), 74.

79. Norman Ornstein et al., *The People, the Press and Politics: The Times Mirror Study of the American Electorate* (Reading, Mass.: Addison-Wesley, 1988), 113.

80. E. J. Dionne, Jr., "A Liberal's Liberal Tells Just What Went Wrong," *New York Times,* Dec. 22, 1988.

81. Meg Greenfield, "Anticommunism Redefined," *Washington Post,* May 6, 1989.

82. Klehr, *Far Left of Center,* xii.

Chapter 8. *The ACLU Through Changing Times*

1. ACLU Papers, Reel 1, vol. 120, cited by William A. Donohue, *The Politics of the American Civil Liberties Union* (New Brunswick, N.J.: Transaction Books, 1985), 31.

2. Annual Report 1, pp. 4, 18, quoted in *ibid.,* 35.

3. ACLU Papers, Reel 1, vol. 120, quoted in *ibid.,* 34.

4. Joseph Freeman, *An American Testament: A Narrative of Rebels and Romantics* (New York: Farrar, Straus and Giroux, 1973), 326–27, 331, 329. (Originally published in 1936.)

5. "The Union's First Decade," *Civil Liberties,* no. 176 (Jan. 1960), 1.

6. Roger N. Baldwin, *Liberty under the Soviets* (New York: Vanguard, 1928), 253, 270, 2, 4.

7. Roger N. Baldwin, "Freedom in the USA and the USSR," *Soviet Russia Today,* Sept. 1934, p. 11, cited by Peggy Lamson, *Roger Baldwin: Founder of the American Civil Liberties Union* (Boston: Houghton Mifflin, 1976), 191.

8. Quoted in Roger Baldwin, "Recollections of a Life in Civil Liberties. II: Russia, Communism, and United Fronts, 1920–1940," *Civil Liberties Review,* vol. II, no. 4 (Fall 1975), 27.

9. ACLU Committee on Labor Rights, Memorandum on Ford Case, Feb. 28, 1938, quoted in Jerold S. Auerbach, "The Depression Decade," in Alan Reitman, ed., *The Pulse of Freedom: American Liberties* (New York: W. W. Norton, 1975), 85.

10. *Ibid.*, 84–85.

11. Joseph Brown Matthews, *Odyssey of a Fellow Traveler* (New York: Mount Vernon Publishers, 1938), 119.

12. Baldwin, "Recollections of a Life," 25–26.

13. Lamson, *Roger Baldwin*, 195.

14. Baldwin, "Recollections of a Life," 38–39.

15. Lamson, *Roger Baldwin*, 214.

16. "Why We Defend Free Speech for Nazis, Fascists and Communists," statement adopted April 1939, reproduced in full in Corliss Lamont, ed., *The Trial of Elizabeth Gurley Flynn by the American Civil Liberties Union* (New York: Horizon, n.d.), 181–84.

17. Holmes Statement, Oct. 26, 1939; John Dos Passos to Baldwin, Nov. 20, 1939, both quoted in Auerbach, "The Depression Decade," 91.

18. W. A. Swanberg, *Norman Thomas: The Last Idealist* (New York: Charles Scribner's Sons, 1976), 238.

19. Norman Thomas, "Your World and Mine," *Socialist Call*, Dec. 16, 1939, reprinted in Lamont, *The Trial*, 145–50.

20. Lamont, *The Trial*, 270. See also Auerbach, "Depression Decade," 88–89.

21. The significance of this fact is stressed by Donohue, *Politics of the ACLU*, 143, and downplayed by Auerbach, "Depression Decade," 91.

22. American Civil Liberties Union, *Background Information and Summary of Position Papers on the 1949 Resolution and Other Constitutional Issues*, Dec. 8, 1966, pp. 2–3 (made available by Alan Reitman, associate director).

23. "A Statement to Members and Friends of the American Civil Liberties Union," Released to the Press by the A.C.L.U. on February 5, 1940, reprinted in Lamont, *The Trial*, 185–86.

24. "Civil Liberties for the Communists," *New Republic*, Feb. 12, 1940, p. 197; ACLU, *Background Information*, 3. According to Auerbach, who relies on a communication between Baldwin and Holmes, ACLU local chapters were "practically unanimous" in condemning the resolution ("Depression Decade," 94, n. 69).

25. Lamont, *The Trial*, 45–48, 98–104.

26. *Ibid.*, 124.

27. *Ibid.*, 176–77, 18. For another view of the Flynn "trial" see Lucille Milner, *Education of an American Liberal* (New York: Horizon, 1954), ch. 14.

28. Corliss Lamont, *Freedom Is as Freedom Does: Civil Liberties Today* (New York: Horizon, 1956), 277–78.

29. See, for example, Larry Ceplair and Steven Englund, *The Inquisition in Hollywood: Politics in the Film Community 1930–1960* (Garden City, N.Y.: Doubleday, 1980), 151.

30. Osmond K. Fraenkel in a statement to Alan Reitman, May 4, 1973, reproduced in Reitman, *Pulse of Freedom*, 292.

31. *Ibid.*, 291.

32. Lamson, *Roger Baldwin*, 232.

33. Donohue, *The Politics of the ACLU*, 154–55.

34. Corliss Lamont, *Yes to Life* (New York: Horizon, 1981), 141, quoted in *ibid.*, 187. See also Aryeh Neier, "Adhering to Principle," *Civil Liberties Review*, vol. IV, no. 4 (Nov./Dec. 1977), 26–32.

35. Harrison E. Salisbury, "The Strange Correspondence of Morris Ernst and John Edgar Hoover," *Nation*, Dec. 1, 1984, p. 582.

36. ACLU, *Background Information*, 3–4.

37. Mary S. McAuliffe, *Crisis on the Left: Cold War Politics and American Liberals 1947–1954* (Amherst: Univ. of Massachusetts Press, 1978), 97–98. McAuliffe's interpretations are often tendentious, but her description of events, based on the ACLU files, is generally reliable.

38. James Lawrence Fly, "Affirmative Arguments," Sept. 1953 (mimeographed statement in possession of author).

39. Osmond Fraenkel, "Negative Arguments," Sept. 1953 (mimeo in possession of author).

40. McAuliffe, *Crisis on the Left*, 99–100.

41. ACLU, *Background Information*, 4–5.

42. "A Statement of Principles," May 15, 1954, *Rights*, vol. I, no. 10 (June 1954), 11.

43. William L. O'Neill, *A Better World: The Great Schism—Stalinism and the American Intellectuals* (New York: Simon & Schuster, 1982), 302–3.

44. Quoted in Swanberg, *Norman Thomas*, 369.

45. Quoted in McAuliffe, *Crisis on the Left*, 120.

46. *Ibid.*, 118.

47. Proposal of the ACLU of Southern California, quoted in ACLU, *Background Information*, 8.

48. *Ibid.*, 8. My account of events in the following paragraphs is based on the same source.

49. *Ibid.*, 10.

50. *Ibid.*, 16.

51. ACLU, Minutes of the Plenary Meeting of the Board of Directors, March 18–19, 1967, pp. 13–14.

52. ACLU, Excerpts from Dec. 2–3, 1967, Plenary Board Meeting Concerning Proposed Amendments to ACLU Constitution, pp. 2–3, 9.

53. Lamson, *Roger Baldwin*, 229; Lamont, *The Trial*, 27–28.

54. Quoted in Donohue, *The Politics of the ACLU*, 191.

55. Quoted in *ibid.*, 190.

56. Osmond K. Fraenkel, Memo to Board of Directors re Elizabeth Gurley Flynn Matter, Jan. 28, 1974.

57. This memo, dated Feb. 1, 1974, in addition to Baldwin was signed by Stuart Chase, Henry Steele Commager, Robert F. Drinan, Milton Konvitz, and other well-known liberals.

58. ACLU, Minutes of the Meeting of the Board of Directors, Feb. 9–10, 1974, pp. 1–2.

59. ACLU, Minutes of the Meeting of the Board of Directors, April 20–21, 1974, p. 5.

60. Memo of George Slaff to the members of the ACLU Board of Directors, Nov. 14, 1975.

61. Frank Haiman memo to members of board of directors, April 1, 1976, pp. 2–3.

62. Paul R. Meyer memo to members of the board of directors, April 1, 1976, pp. 2–3.

63. ACLU, Minutes of the Meeting of the Board of Directors, April 10–11, 1976, pp. 12–14.

64. "Playboy Interview," *Playboy*, Oct. 1970, pp. 228, 232. For other examples of Kunstler's thoughts see Victor Navasky, "Right On! With Lawyer William Kunstler," *New York Times* magazine, April 19, 1970.

65. Richard and Susan Vigilante, "Taking Liberties: The ACLU Strays from Its Mission," *Policy Review*, no. 30 (Fall 1984), 37.

66. Richard E. Morgan, *Disabling America: The "Rights Industry" in Our Time* (New York: Basic Books, 1984), 205–6.

67. Joseph W. Bishop, Jr., "Politics and ACLU," *Commentary*, Dec. 1971, p. 56.

68. ACLU, *Policy Guides* (1986), cited in L. Gordon Crovitz, "A Primer on the ACLU," *Wall Street Journal*, Oct. 3, 1986.

69. Vigilante, "Taking Liberties," 35.

70. *First Principles*, Sept. 1989, p. 3.

71. Lamson, *Roger Baldwin*, viii.

Chapter 9. The Peace Movement

1. V. I. Lenin, "Farewell Letter to Swiss Workers," *Selected Works*, vol. VI (New York: International Publishers, 1943), 16.

2. V. I. Lenin, Letter to G. V. Chicherin, March 14, 1922, *Collected Works*, vol. LXV (Moscow: Progress Publishers, 1970), 507.

3. Babette Gross, *Willi Münzenberg: A Political Biography* (Lansing: Michigan State Univ. Press, 1974), 133.

4. Arthur Koestler, *The Invisible Writing* (New York: Macmillan, 1954), 314.

5. Roger Baldwin, "Recollections of a Life in Civil Liberties. II: Russia, Communism, and United Front, 1920–1940," *Civil Liberties Review*, vol. II, no. 4 (Fall 1975), 31.

6. Harvey Klehr, *The Heyday of American Communism: The Depression Decade* (New York: Basic Books, 1984), 108.

7. Hillman M. Bishop, *The American League Against War and Fascism* (New York: pub. by the author, 1936), 5.

8. American Committee for the Struggle Against War, *The World Congress Against War*, quoted in Ralph Lord Roy, *Communism and the Churches* (New York: Harcourt, Brace and World, 1960), 83.

9. Klehr, *Heyday of American Communism*, 110.

10. Bishop, *The American League*, 7.

11. Klehr, *Heyday of American Communism*, 111.

12. The ten-point manifesto is reprinted in Joseph Brown Matthews, *Odyssey of a Fellow Traveler* (New York: Mount Vernon Publishers, 1938), 154–55.

13. Earl Browder, *Communism in the United States* (New York: International Publishers, 1935), 184.

14. *Communist*, Nov. 1933, quoted in Bishop, *The American League*, 8.

15. *The World Tomorrow*, Oct. 12, 1933, p. 571, quoted in Roy, *Communism and the Churches*, 85–86.

16. *Christian Century*, Feb. 14, 1934, p. 218.

17. *The World Tomorrow*, Oct. 26, 1933, p. 588, quoted in Roy, *Communism and the Churches*, 86.

18. "Communists and the United Front," *The World Tomorrow*, March 1, 1934, p. 100.

19. Letter of resignation, quoted in Charles Chatfield, *For Peace and Justice: Pacifism in America 1914–1941* (Knoxville: Univ. of Tennessee Press, 1971), 259.

20. *Labor Action*, Oct. 1, 1934, quoted in Bishop, *The American League*, 30.

21. Baldwin, "Recollections of a Life in Civil Liberties," 33.

22. Roy, *Communism and the Churches*, 90.

23. Earl R. Browder, *The People's Front* (New York: International Publishers, 1938), 50.

24. Peggy Lamson, *Roger Baldwin: Founder of the American Civil Liberties Union* (Boston: Houghton Mifflin, 1976), 199.

25. Bishop, *The American League*, 9–11; Roy, *Communism and the Churches*, 91; Earl Latham, *The Communist Controversy in Washington: From the New Deal to McCarthy* (Cambridge, Mass.: Harvard Univ. Press, 1966), 69.

26. Earl Browder, "The People's Front Moves Forward!," *Communist*, Dec. 1937, p. 1098, quoted in Klehr, *Heyday of American Communism*, 373.

27. John P. Roche, *The Quest for the Dream* (New York: Macmillan, 1963), 213.

28. Irving Howe and Lewis Coser, *The American Communist Party: A Critical History (1919–1957)* (New York: Frederick A. Praeger, 1962), 354.

29. Kirby Page, "A Christian Revolution," *Christian Century*, Feb. 20, 1935, p. 236.

30. Dorothy Detzer, *Appointment on the Hill* (New York: Henry Holt, 1948), 192–93.

31. *Ibid.*, 352–54.

32. Roy, *Communism and the Churches*, 146.

33. Baldwin, "Recollections of a Life," 34.

34. Harry F. Ward, *Democracy and Social Change* (New York: Modern Age Books, 1940), 252, 249.

35. Baldwin, "Recollections of a Life," 34; Robert Morss Lovett, *All Our Years: The Autobiography of Robert Morss Lovett* (New York: Viking, 1948), 265–66.

36. Baldwin, "Recollections of a Life," 34.

37. *Student Review*, Dec. 12931, p. 2, quoted in Klehr, *Heyday of American Communism*, 310.

38. Matthews, *Odyssey*, 98.

39. *Student Outlook*, Nov.–Dec. 1934, quoted in *ibid.*, 101.

40. James A. Wechsler, *The Age of Suspicion* (New York: Random House, 1953), 77.

41. Patti McGill Peterson, "Student Organizations and the Antiwar Movement in America, 1900–1966," in Charles Chatfield, ed., *Peace Movements in America* (New York: Schocken Books, 1973), 124.

42. Klehr, *Heyday of American Communism*, 318.

43. *Ibid.*, 205, 318–19; Hal Draper, "The Student Movement of the Thirties: A Political History," in Rita James Simon, ed., *As We Saw the Thirties: Essays*

on Social and Political Movements of the Thirties (Urbana: Univ. of Illinois Press, 1967), 179–80.

44. Peterson, "Student Organizations and the Antiwar Movement," 125.

45. Draper, "The Student Movement of the Thirties," 181; Klehr, *Heyday of American Communism*, 403.

46. Howe and Coser, *The American Communist Party*, 392–94.

47. Roy, *Communism and the Churches*, 153.

48. Frederick Vanderbilt Field, *From Right to Left: An Autobiography* (Westport, Conn.: Lawrence Hill, 1983), 187–88.

49. Maurice Isserman, *Which Side Were You On? The American Communist Party During the Second World War* (Middletown, Conn.: Wesleyan Univ. Press, 1982), 84.

50. Philip J. Jaffe, *The Rise and Fall of American Communism* (New York: Horizon, 1975), 48.

51. Field, *From Right to Left*, 195–97; Isserman, *Which Side Were You On?*, 110.

52. Howe and Coser, *The American Communist Party*, 395.

53. *Daily Worker*, Feb. 14, 1944, quoted in Roy, *Communism and the Churches*, 164.

54. Sidney Hook, *Out of Step: An Unquiet Life in the 20th Century* (New York: Harper & Row, 1987), 386.

55. *Ibid.*, 384.

56. Dwight MacDonald, "The Waldorf Conference," *Politics*, vol. VI, no. 1 (Winter 1949), 32–A.

57. Clive Rose, *Campaigns Against Western Defense: NATO's Adversaries and Critics* (New York: St. Martin's, 1985), 64–65.

58. Joanne Omang, "U.S. Groups Counter Contra Aid with Private 'Quest for Peace,'" *Washington Post*, April 19, 1987.

59. Rose, *Campaigns Against Western Defense*, 59.

60. Roy, *Communism and the Churches*, 215.

61. Willard Uphaus, *Commitment* (New York: McGraw-Hill, 1963), 98.

62. *The Witness*, Jan. 29, 1953, p. 13, quoted in Roy, *Communism and the Churches*, 220.

63. Arnold Johnson, "Halt the Tests! For a Summit Meeting for Peace!," *Party Voice*, no. 2 (1958), quoted in U.S. Senate, Committee on the Judiciary, Subcommittee to Investigate the Administration of the Internal Security Act and Other Internal Security Laws, *Communist Infiltration in the Nuclear Test Ban Movement*, Hearings, 86th Cong., 2nd sess., Part II (1960), 47–48.

64. Gus Hall, "Our Lights to the Future," *Political Affairs*, Jan. 1960, p. 9.

65. FOR, "Peace Fronts Today," May 1951; John M. Swomley, Jr., to F. Siegmund Schultze, Dec. 3, 1953, both quoted in Lawrence S. Wittner, *Rebels Against War: The American Peace Movement, 1933–1983* (Philadelphia, Pa.: Temple Univ. Press, 1984), 205–6.

66. A. J. Muste, "Communism and Civil Liberties," *Fellowship*, Oct. 1949, p. 10; Muste quoted in Nat Hentoff, *Peace Agitator: The Story of A. J. Muste* (New York: Macmillan, 1963), 162.

67. See ch. 7, p. 117.

68. Alfred Hassler, "The World's Newest Peace Group," *Fellowship*, March 1, 1963, p. 26.

69. Arnold Johnson, "The American Peace Movement," *Political Affairs,* March 1963, pp. 7–9.

70. Cf. Guenter Lewy, *Peace and Revolution: The Moral Crisis of American Pacifism* (Grand Rapids, Mich.: W. B. Eerdmans, 1988), ch. 10.

71. Harvey Klehr, *Far Left of Center: The American Radical Left Today* (New Brunswick, N.J.: Transaction Books, 1988), 31.

72. Quoted in Ronald Radosh, "The 'Peace Council' and Peace: Red-baiting, No. Anti-Communism, Yes," *New Republic,* Jan. 31, 1983, p. 16.

73. Tom DeLuca, "The Cutting Edge of Survival: Mobe Looks at Mobe," *Mobilizer,* May 1982, p. 4.

74. Sidney Peck, "Mobilization for Survival: Growth of a Movement," *Mobilizer,* Spring 1987, p. 13.

75. Y. Molchanov, "Soviet Foreign Policy as a Factor Promoting the Revolutionary Transformation of the World," *International Affairs,* no. 12 (1972), quoted in Roberta Goren, *The Soviet Union and Terrorism* (Winchester, Mass.: George Allen and Unwin, 1984), 97.

76. Marilyn Bechtel, *The Soviet Peace Movement: From the Grass Roots* (New York: National Council for American-Soviet Friendship, 1984), 59.

77. A. S. Milovidov and V. G. Kozlov, eds., *The Philosophical Heritage of V. I. Lenin and Problems of Contemporary War,* trans. U.S. Air Force (Washington, D.C.: Government Printing Office, 1974), 33.

78. Isserman, *Which Side Were You On?,* 111.

79. Carl Marzani, "Introduction" to John Lewis, *The Case Against Pacifism* (London: George Allen and Unwin, 1973), 9.

80. James E. Jackson, "Reaganomics and the Fight for Peace," *Political Affairs,* June 1982, pp. 22–24.

81. *Ibid.,* 24.

82. Bruce Kimmel, "What Next in the Fight for Peace?," *Political Affairs,* Aug. 1982, p. 28.

83. Gus Hall, "Class Unity, All People's Unity—the Only Way," *Political Affairs,* Sept. 1987, p. 16.

84. Michael Myerson, "Dear Friend," *Peace and Solidarity,* Jan.–Feb. 1988, no pagination.

85. Norman Solomon, "Letter to E. P. Thompson," *Nation,* June 11, 1983, p. 720.

86. E. P. Thompson, "Sleepwalking into a Trap: END and the Soviet Peace Offensive," *Nation,* Feb. 23, 1983, pp. 232–36; "Peace Is a Third Way Street," *Nation,* April 16, 1983, pp. 473–81.

87. "Welcome to Our Readers," *Peace & Democracy News,* vol. I, no. 1 (Spring 1984), 1.

88. *New York Times,* Dec. 1, 1985.

89. "The Basis of Unity," *Peace Courier,* Oct. 1984, p. 1.

90. *World Economics and International Relations,* no. 1 (Jan. 1986), quoted in U.S. Department of State, *Soviet Antipacifism and the Suppression of the "Unofficial" Peace Movement in the U.S.S.R.* (Washington, D.C.: Foreign Affairs Note, 1988), 3.

91. "World Peace Council Launches International Discussion on Its Future," *Peace and Solidarity,* Nov./Dec. 1988, no pagination. See also the issues of

July/Aug. and Sept. 1988 of the *Peace Courier* for further airing of these internal differences in the WPC.

92. *Peace Courier,* July–Aug. 1989, p. 12, Jan. 1990, pp. 10–11.

93. "Shevardnadze Speech to July Conference Noted," *Foreign Broadcast Information Service,* Sept. 22, 1988, Annex, pp. 8–10.

94. Stanislav Kondrashov, "Disarmament in Europe: The View from Moscow," *Economist,* May 13, 1989, pp. 25–26.

95. Quoted in Jim Hoagland, "Gorbachev Fails to Bite the Bullet on Cuban, East-West Questions," *Washington Post,* April 8, 1989.

96. U.S. Department of State, Bureau of Public Affairs, Address of Secretary of State James A. Baker III, Oct. 16, 1989 (Current Policy No. 1213).

97. "Officials Call for Dialogue," *New York Times,* March 16, 1989. See also John F. Burns, "Soviets, in Shift, Press for Accord in South Africa," in the same issue.

98. Elombe Brath, "Perestroika Policy Plays into the Hands of Apartheid," *Guardian,* April 26, 1989, p. 19.

99. Southscan, "Communist Congress Unveils New Strategy," *Guardian,* July 19, 1989, p. 4.

Chapter 10. The Travail of Progressivism

1. Israel Amter, "The Elections in New York," *Communist,* Dec. 1936, p. 1152, quoted in Harvey Klehr, *The Heyday of American Communism: The Depression Decade* (New York: Basic Books, 1984), 266.

2. Warren Moscow, *Politics in the Empire State* (New York: Knopf, 1948), 110.

3. Louis Waldman, *Labor Lawyer* (New York: E. P. Dutton, 1944), 292.

4. Klehr, *Heyday of American Communism,* 234; Philip J. Jaffe, *The Rise and Fall of American Communism* (New York: Horizon, 1975), 145.

5. "The Labor Party Purge," *New Republic,* Nov. 1, 1939, p. 356.

6. Letter to the Editor, *New Republic,* Dec. 13, 1939, p. 233.

7. Moscow, *Politics in the Empire State,* 111.

8. Quoted in Maurice Isserman, *Which Side Were You On? The American Communist Party During the Second World War* (Middletown, Conn.: Wesleyan Univ. Press, 1982), 210.

9. Quoted in Karl M. Schmidt, *Henry A. Wallace: Quixotic Crusade 1948* (Syracuse, N.Y.: Syracuse Univ. Press, 1960), 106.

10. Quoted in Max M. Kampelman, *The Communist Party vs. the C.I.O.: A Study in Power Politics* (New York: Frederick A. Praeger, 1957), 147.

11. Norman D. Markowitz, *The Rise and Fall of the People's Century: Henry A. Wallace and American Liberalism, 1941–1948* (New York: Free Press, 1973), 166.

12. Dwight MacDonald, *Henry Wallace: The Man and the Myth* (New York: Vanguard, 1948), 24.

13. Markowitz, *Rise and Fall,* 184.

14. "Wallace—A World Leader," *New Republic,* Sept. 23, 1946, p. 340, quoted in William L. O'Neill, *A Better World: The Great Schism—Stalinism and the American Intellectuals* (New York: Simon & Schuster, 1982), 143.

15. David A. Shannon, *The Decline of American Communism: A History of the Communist Party Since 1945* (Chatham, N.J.: Chatham Bookseller, 1971), 142.

16. O'Neill, *A Better World*, 144–45; Markowitz, *Rise and Fall*, 221.

17. Arthur M. Schlesinger, Jr., *The Vital Center: The Politics of Freedom* (Boston: Houghton Mifflin, 1962), 117. (Originally published in 1949). LaFollette's statement appeared in the *New York Times* of May 29, 1924.

18. Shannon, *Decline of American Communism*, 127.

19. Quoted in *ibid.*, 142–43.

20. Markowitz, *Rise and Fall*, 232–39, 59–60.

21. Quoted in James A. Wechsler, *The Age of Suspicion* (New York: Random House, 1953), 219.

22. The best account of these events is given by Joseph R. Starobin, *American Communism in Crisis* (Cambridge, Mass.: Harvard Univ. Press, 1972), chs. 7–8, especially pp. 170–73, and Jaffe, *Rise and Fall*, 118–19.

23. Starobin, *American Communism in Crisis*, 174–5.

24. Quoted in Schlesinger, *The Vital Center*, 116.

25. Clifton Brock, *Americans for Democratic Action: Its Role in National Politics* (Washington, D.C.: Public Affairs Press, 1962), 66.

26. O'Neill, *A Better World*, 146.

27. Max Lerner, "The Lessons of the Czechoslovak Coup," *New York Star*, March 11, 1948, quoted in O'Neill, *A Better World*, 157.

28. Communist announcement of April 10, 1948, quoted in Curtis D. Mac-Dougall, *Gideon's Army* (New York: Marzani and Munsell, 1965), vol. II, p. 425.

29. Quoted in Shannon, *Decline of American Communism*, 144.

30. Quoted in Markowitz, *Rise and Fall*, 258.

31. MacDougall, *Gideon's Army*, vol. II, p. 423.

32. *Ibid.*, 426–27.

33. Shannon, *Decline of American Communism*, 129; O'Neill, *A Better World*, 138.

34. James Loeb, Jr., "Progressives and Communists," *New Republic*, May 13, 1946, p. 699.

35. Brock, *Americans for Democratic Action*, 52, 33.

36. Freda Kirchwey, "Mugwumps in Action," *Nation*, Jan. 18, 1947, p. 62.

37. James Loeb, Jr., "Letter of the Week," *New Republic*, Jan. 27, 1947, p. 46.

38. Philip Dunne, *Take Two: A Life in Movies and Politics* (New York: McGraw-Hill, 1980), 189.

39. Brock, *Americans for Democratic Action*, 74.

40. Robert Bendiner, "Civil Liberties and the Communists: Checking Subversion without Harm to Democratic Rights," *Commentary*, May 1948, pp. 425–27.

41. Quoted in Brock, *Americans for Democratic Action*, 76–77.

42. *Ibid.*, 78.

43. Irving Howe and Lewis Coser, *The American Communist Party: A Critical History (1919–1957)* (New York: Frederick A. Praeger, 1957), 475.

44. Wechsler, *Age of Suspicion*, 232.

45. O'Neill, *A Better World*, 149.

46. Howe and Coser, *The American Communist Party*, 475–76; Wechsler, *Age of Suspicion*, 231.

47. Quoted in Howe and Coser, *The American Communist Party*, 476.

48. Shannon, *Decline of American Communism*, 143–44.

49. Quoted in Starobin, *American Communism in Crisis*, 185.

50. Editorial, *Nation*, July 31, 1948, quoted in O'Neill, *A Better World*, 156.

51. Quoted in Richard J. Walton, *Henry Wallace, Harry Truman, and the Cold War* (New York: Viking, 1976), 346–47.

52. I. F. Stone, "What of the Communists in the Progressive Party?," *Compass*, Feb. 18, 1950, reprinted in I. F. Stone, *The Truman Era* (New York: Random House, 1972), 161.

53. Markowitz, *Rise and Fall*, 311.

54. Quoted in Starobin, *American Communism in Crisis*, 185.

55. Wechsler, *Age of Suspicion*, 238.

56. Walton, *Henry Wallace*, 352–55, 249–52.

57. Cf. Schmidt, *Henry A. Wallace*, 274–78.

58. Howe and Coser, *The American Communist Party*, 459.

59. Kampelman, *The Communist Party vs. the C.I.O.*, 47.

60. Shannon, *Decline of American Communism*, 128–29; Kampelman, *The Communist Party vs. the C.I.O.*, 102.

61. Quoted in Brock, *Americans for Democratic Action*, 59.

62. *Ibid.*, 73.

63. CIO Proceedings, May 17-19, 1948, p. 813, quoted in Mary Sperling McAuliffe, *Crisis on the Left: Cold War Politics and American Liberals 1947–1954* (Amherst: Univ. of Massachusetts Press, 1978), 45.

64. *Ibid.*, 55.

65. Quoted in Harvey A. Levenstein, *Communism, Anticommunism, and the CIO* (Westport, Conn.: Greenwood, 1981), 298–99.

66. *Ibid.*, 299.

67. Resolution no. 58, quoted in Kampelman, *The Communist Party vs. the C.I.O.*, 159–60.

68. Shannon, *Decline of American Communism*, 216–17.

69. Kampelman, *The Communist Party vs. the C.I.O.*, 167.

70. CIO Proceedings, Aug. 29, 1950, p. 74, quoted in McAuliffe, *Crisis on the Left*, 58.

71. Kampelman, *The Communist Party vs. the C.I.O.*, 249.

72. McAuliffe, *Crisis on the Left*, 59.

73. Howe and Coser, *The American Communist Party*, 468.

74. Wechsler, *Age of Suspicion*, 170–71.

75. James A. Wechsler, *Reflections of an Angry Middle-Aged Editor* (New York: Random House, 1960), 55.

76. This chronicle of events is based on *ADA World* of May 1967, Feb. 1968, March/April 1968, July 1969, April 1971, May/June 1971, and June 1972. On the origins and political character of the National Peace Action Coalition see Nancy Zaroulis and Gerald Sullivan, *Who Spoke Up? American Protest Against the War in Vietnam 1963–1975* (Garden City, N.Y.: Doubleday, 1984), 336; Bradford Lyttle, *The Chicago Anti-Vietnam War Movement* (Chicago: Midwest Pacifist Center, 1988), 149.

77. *ADA World*, Jan. 1973, Jan./Feb. 1978, Spring 1982, Jan. 1983.

78. Bruce Cameron, "Foreign and Military Policy," *ADA World*, Winter 1980, p. 10.

79. Robert F. Drinan, "The Injustice of U.S. Intervention: The Reagan War in Central America," *ADA World*, July 1983.

80. J. Michael Waller and Joseph Sobran, "Congress's Red Army," *National Review*, July 31, 1987, p. 25.

81. A facsimile copy of this letter, written on congressional stationary and dated April 28, 1982, is reproduced by Allan C. Brownfeld and J. Michael Waller, *The Revolution Lobby* (Washington, D.C.: Council on Inter-American Security, 1985), 116–17.

Chapter 11. SANE: From Center to Left

1. Milton S. Katz, *Ban the Bomb: A History of SANE, the Committee for a Sane Nuclear Policy* (New York: Praeger, 1987), 21–24.

2. A facsimile copy of the ad is reproduced in *ibid.*, 27.

3. Sanford Gottlieb, "National Committee for a Sane Nuclear Policy," *New University Thought*, Spring 1962, p. 156, quoted in Katz, *Ban the Bomb*, 29–30.

4. "Statement Adopted by the Conference of the National Committee for a Sane Nuclear Policy," Sept. 29, 1958. (Materials not otherwise identified are in the possession of the author.)

5. Lawrence Scott, "Memo One—Shared Thinking," Swarthmore College Peace Collection (hereafter cited as SCPC), DG 58, Series A, quoted in Katz, *Ban the Bomb*, 46.

6. "How Sane the SANE?," *Time*, April 21, 1958, quoted in Katz, *Ban the Bomb*, 32.

7. Norman Cousins to Trevor Thomas, June 13, 1958, SCPC, DG 58, Series B, quoted in Katz, *Ban the Bomb*, 46–47.

8. FBI, Office Memorandum, July 30, 1958, quoted in Katz, *Ban the Bomb*, 47.

9. SAC, New York, to Director of FBI, Dec. 29, 1959, and Director of FBI to SAC, New York, Jan. 8, 1960, SCPC, DG 58, Series G, Box 30, Greater New York SANE.

10. Norman Thomas to Norman Cousins, Jan. 11, 1960, SCPC, DG 58, Series B, Box 20, SANE Cousins correspondence 1959–60. See also Katz, *Ban the Bomb*, 47–48.

11. Homer A. Jack to Norman Cousins et al., Jan. 27, 1960, SCPC, DG 58, Series A, Box 4, Statements 1959–60.

12. U.S. Senate, Committee on the Judiciary, Subcommittee to Investigate the Administration of the Internal Security Act and Other Internal Security Laws, *Communist Infiltration in the Nuclear Test Ban Movement*, Hearings, 86th Cong., 2nd sess., Part 1, May 13, 1960; Norman Cousins to Edmund C. Berkeley, June 30, 1960, SCPC, DG 58, Series B, Box 20, Communist Infiltration.

13. Lawrence S. Wittner, *Rebels Against War: The American Peace Movement 1933–1960*, rev. ed. (Philadelphia, Pa.: Temple Univ. Press, 1984), 259; Katz, *Ban the Bomb*, 45, 49–50.

14. The text of Dodd's speech is reproduced in *Communist Infiltration in the Nuclear Test Ban Movement*, 35–40.

15. Minutes of the National Board Meeting, May 26, 1960, SCPC, DG 58, Series A, quoted in Katz, *Ban the Bomb,* 50.

16. "Standards for Sane Leadership," Statement of Policy Passed by the Board of Directors of the National Committee for a Sane Nuclear Policy, May 26, 1960.

17. Memo of Donald Keys, "For Your Information," May 27, 1960, p. 2.

18. Robert Gilmore to Board of Directors, June 27, 1960, SCPC, DG 58, Series 5, Box 11, quoted in Wittner, *Rebels Against War,* 260.

19. The communications of the Long Island and Skokie committees are dated July 25 and Aug. 1, 1960, respectively. SCPC, DG 58, Series B, Box 20, Communist Infiltration.

20. Norman Cousins and Clarence Pickett to all SANE local committee chairmen, July 29, 1960, *ibid.,* SANE Cousins Correspondence 1959–60.

21. Norman Cousins and Clarence Pickett to Local Committee Chairmen, Sept. 29, 1960.

22. Minutes of the meeting of the board of directors, Oct. 24, 1960, p. 2, SCPC, DG 58, Series A, Box 4, Minutes-Resolutions 1959–61.

23. Hugh C. Wolfe to Walter Lear, SCPC, DG 58, Series I, Box 3, Correspondence 1960 Walter Lear.

24. Resolution passed by the Board of Directors, Nov. 7, 1960, *ibid.,* Correspondence Walter Lear.

25. Nathan Glazer, "The Peace Movement in America—1961," *Commentary,* April 1961, p. 292.

26. A. J. Muste, "The Crisis in SANE: Act II," *Liberation,* Nov. 1960, p. 7.

27. Letter to the Editor by Homer A. Jack, "The SANE Controversy," *Fellowship,* May 1961, p. 35.

28. Cf. Katz, *Ban the Bomb,* 55, 61; Maurice Isserman, *If I Had a Hammer: The Death of the Old Left and the Birth of the New Left* (New York: Basic Books, 1987), 185.

29. SANE, "Statement Adopted by the National Board on April 17, 1961," p. 1.

30. *SANE World,* Dec. 15, 1962, no pagination.

31. "What SANE Is and Is Not," *ibid.,* no pagination.

32. "Convincing the U.S. Public," *SANE World,* April 1, 1963, no pagination.

33. Michael Harrington, *Fragments of the Century* (New York: Saturday Review Press, 1973), 159; Fred Halstead, *Out Now! A Participant's Account of the American Movement Against the Vietnam War* (New York: Monad, 1978), 81 and 94.

34. Robert Wolfe, "American Imperialism and the Peace Movement," *Studies on the Left,* May–June 1966, p. 41, quoted in Katz, *Ban the Bomb,* 99–100.

35. Benjamin H. Spock, "Why Do We Betray Peace and Justice?," speech given June 8, 1965, SCPC, Series E, Box 5, Washington Office, Charters-by-laws 1965.

36. Quoted in Katz, *Ban the Bomb,* 101–2.

37. "April 15 Demonstrations of Spring Mobilization Committee," resolution adopted Feb. 12, 1967, and "Peace Demonstrations: General Recommendations," issued by national board June 17, 1963, SCPC, Series A, Box 4, Minutes of Board 1965–67.

38. SCPC, DG 58, Series C, Box 1, National SANE, 1967, Internal; Katz, *Ban the Bomb,* 103.

39. Donald F. Keys to Benjamin Spock, Feb. 20, 1967, SCPC, DG 58, Series C, Box 1, National SANE, 1966–67.

40. "Statement of National SANE Regarding the Spring Mobilization," April 14, 1967, SCPC, DG 58, Series A, quoted in Katz, *Ban the Bomb*, 103.

41. Nancy Zaroulis and Gerald Sullivan, *Who Spoke Up? American Protest Against the War in Vietnam: 1963–1975* (Garden City, N.Y.: Doubleday, 1984), 111.

42. Resolutions adopted by the national board on April 27, 1967, SCPC, DG 58, Series A, Box 4, Minutes-Resolutions 1965–67.

43. Members of the corporation to the national board, May 15, 1967, SCPC, DG 58, Series C, Box 1, National SANE, 1966–67.

44. Homer A. Jack, "An Old Alumnus Looks at the New Left," SCPC, DG 58, Series C, Box 1, National SANE 1967, "Internal," p. 4.

45. *Ibid.*, National SANE, 1966–67.

46. "A Statement of Concern," Feb. 27, 1967, SCPC, DG 58, Series C, Box 1, Chicago SANE, 1966–67.

47. Minutes of the June 28, 1967, meeting of the Chicago SANE Committee to review the by-laws, *ibid.*

48. Donald F. Keys to H. Stuart et al., Aug. 2, 1967, *ibid.*, National SANE, 1967.

49. Minutes of the meeting of the national board, Sept. 14, 1967, SCPC, Series A, Box 4, Board minutes 1965–67.

50. Minutes of the national board meeting, Sept. 14, 1967, SCPC, DG 58, Series A; "A Message from Dr. Spock," Sept. 1967, quoted in Katz, *Ban the Bomb*, 106.

51. Officers of the SANE regional office, San Francisco, to members of the SANE corporation and executive board, Sept. 20, 1967, SCPC, DG 58, Series C, Box 1, National SANE, 1966–67.

52. "Letter of Resignation," Oct. 10, 1967, *ibid.*

53. Minutes of the meeting of the national board, Oct. 19, 1967, SCPC, Series A, Box 4, Board minutes 1965–67.

54. Minutes of the meeting of the national board, Oct. 19, 1967, *ibid.*

55. Clarence Heller and Robert Pickus to Donald Keys, Oct. 21, 1967, *ibid.*

56. Donald Keys to members of the board, Nov. 13, 1967, *ibid.*

57. Donald Keys, "SANE's Wayward Drift to the Left," *War/Peace Report*, Jan. 1968, pp. 14–16.

58. "A Sane World Begins at Home: Demilitarizing American Society," approved by the SANE board on Jan. 16, 1971, SCPC, DG 58, Series G, Box 7, National office, Statements 1971.

59. Cf. *SANE World*, Oct. 1969, April 1975, Oct. 1981, Nov./Dec. 1985.

60. *SANE World*, Jan. 1976; Marcus Raskin, "SANE's Commitment," *SANE World*, Summer 1981, p. 2; Ed Glennon, "U.S. Plays Dominoes in Central America," *SANE World*, April 1981, pp. 1–3.

61. Duane Shank, "Nicaragua: The Struggle for Peace," *SANE World*, Nov. 1982, p. 2; *SANE World*, Nov./Dec. 1984; Dan Halberstein, "Nicaragua Since the Revolution," *SANE World*, Jan./Feb. 1986, p. 4; "SANE at Forefront of Lybian Raid Protest," *SANE World*, May/June 1986.

62. Minutes of the meeting of the national board, Nov. 17, 1966, SCPC, DG 58, Series A, Box 4, National board minutes 1965–67.

63. David Cortright, *Soldiers in Revolt* (New York: Doubleday, 1975), xi.

64. Winpisinger's name appears on the letterhead of the Committee for a Dialogue on Disarmament and Detente, formed by two American members of the World Peace Council presidential committee, which sponsored the dialogue. See also John Barron, *KGB Today: The Hidden Hand* (New York: Readers Digest Press, 1983), 245.

65. *New Republic,* Nov. 28, 1983, p. 10. In the face of allegations that O'Dell had not abandoned his ties to the Communist party, Martin Luther King, Jr., in late 1962 relieved O'Dell from his post in the Southern Christian Leadership Conference. Cf. David J. Garrow, *The FBI and Martin Luther King, Jr.: From "Solo" to Memphis* (New York: W. W. Norton, 1981), 46–50, 61–62.

66. Cf. Arch Puddington, "The New Soviet Apologists," *Commentary,* Nov. 1983, pp. 25–31; Harvey Klehr, *Far Left of Center: The American Radical Left Today* (New Brunswick, N.J.: Transaction Books, 1988), 145, 172.

67. *Peace and Solidarity* (Newsletter of the U.S. Peace Council), Jan. 1983, no pagination.

68. Carolyn Cottom, "Divining the Path to Peace," *SANE World/Freeze Focus,* Spring 1988, p. 2.

69. *SANE World,* Oct. 1980, p. 2.

70. "Those for Whom 'Peace Dividend' Means Deficit," *New York Times,* Feb. 12, 1990.

71. Katz, *Ban the Bomb,* xiii, 169.

72. "Peacework's Lesson: Peace Can Win," *SANE World,* May/June 1986, p. 1.

73. Homer A. Jack, *Nuclear Politics After Hiroshima/Nagasaki: Unitarian Universalist and Other Responses* (Swarthmore, Pa.: 1987 Minns Lectures, 1987), 75.

Chapter 12. SDS and the Movement Against the Vietnam War

1. Tom Hayden, *Reunion: A Memoir* (New York: Random House, 1988), 78.

2. Maurice Isserman, *If I Had a Hammer: The Death of the Old Left and the Birth of the New Left* (New York: Basic Books, 1987), 173–202.

3. Peter Collier and David Horowitz, *Destructive Generation: Second Thoughts about the Sixties* (New York: Summit Books, 1989), 144.

4. Norman Podhoretz, *Breaking Ranks: A Political Memoir* (New York: Harper & Row, 1979), 253, quoted in *ibid.,* 243, n. 65.

5. Quoted in James Miller, *"Democracy Is in the Streets": From Port Huron to the Siege of Chicago* (New York: Simon & Schuster, 1987), 337–38, 350. The entire Port Huron Statement is reproduced by Miller on pp. 329–74.

6. Constitution of the Students for a Democratic Society, Article III, section 2, quoted in Kirkpatrick Sale, *SDS* (New York: Random House, 1973), 665.

7. Michael Harrington, *Fragments of the Century* (New York: Saturday Review Press, 1973), 144–45.

8. Todd Gitlin, *The Sixties: Years of Hope, Days of Rage* (New York: Bantam Books, 1987), 120. For a description of the events preceding the settlement of the dispute see also Miller, *"Democracy Is in the Streets,"* 131–35.

9. Gitlin, *The Sixties,* 124.

10. Miller, *"Democracy Is in the Streets,"* 138.

11. Quoted in Edward J. Bacciocco, *The New Left in America: Reform to Revolution 1956 to 1970* (Stanford, Calif.: Hoover Institution Press, 1974), 161.

12. Sale, *SDS*, 177.

13. Thomas Powers, *The War at Home: Vietnam and the American People, 1964–1968* (New York: Grossman, 1973), 75–76.

14. Nancy Zaroulis and Gerald Sullivan, *Who Spoke Up? American Protest Against the War in Vietnam: 1963–1975* (Garden City, N.Y.: Doubleday, 1984), 40.

15. Harrington, *Fragments of the Century*, 158.

16. Gitlin, *The Sixties*, 191.

17. *Ibid.*, 191.

18. Alan Haber, "Nonexclusionism: The New Left and the Democratic Left," reproduced, with some omissions, in Massimo Teodori, ed., *The New Left: A Documentary History* (Indianapolis: Bobbs-Merrill, 1969), 218–28.

19. Quoted in Sale, *SDS*, 237.

20. *Ibid.*, 264.

21. Bacciocco, *The New Left*, 176; William Tulio Divale, *I Lived Inside the Campus Revolution* (New York: Cowles, 1970), 97–98.

22. Sale, *SDS*, 286.

23. Hayden, *Reunion*, 201–3.

24. Paul Jacobs and Saul Landau, *The New Radicals: A Report with Documents* (New York: Vintage, 1966), 193.

25. Sale, *SDS*, 398.

26. Quoted in *ibid.*, 465.

27. *Ibid.*, 466.

28. Miller, *"Democracy Is in the Streets,"* 285.

29. Gitlin, *The Sixties*, 386.

30. Jeff Gordon in *PL*, Oct. 1968, quoted in Sale, *SDS*, 467.

31. Gitlin, *The Sixties*, 329–30. On the attempted alliance with the Communists see Sale, *SDS*, 494.

32. "Handwriting on the Wall," #1, quoted in David Farber, *Chicago '68* (Chicago: Univ. of Chicago Press, 1988), 234.

33. Quoted in Gitlin, *The Sixties*, 384.

34. "You Don't Need a Weatherman to Know Which Way the Wind Blows," reproduced in Harold Jacobs, ed., *Weatherman* (San Francisco: Ramparts, 1970), 51–90 (the quotation is on p. 53).

35. Gitlin, *The Sixties*, 388–89; Sale, *SDS*, 572–75.

36. Quoted in Gitlin, *The Sixties*, 400.

37. Sale, *SDS*, 632.

38. The Port Huron Statement, quoted in Miller, *"Democracy Is in the Streets,"* 333.

39. Hayden, *Reunion*, 465.

40. Jack Newfield, *A Prophetic Minority* (New York: New American Library, 1966), 194.

41. Maurice Isserman, Letter to the Editor, *New Republic*, March 7, 1983, p. 6.

42. Hayden, *Reunion*, 244.

43. Gitlin, *The Sixties*, 437.

44. Fred Halstead, *Out Now! A Participant's Account of the American Movement Against the Vietnam War* (New York: Monad, 1978), 119.

45. A. J. Muste, "Mobilize for Peace," *Liberation*, Dec. 1966, p. 25.

46. Guenter Lewy, *Peace and Revolution: The Moral Crisis of American Pacifism* (Grand Rapids, Mich.: Wm. B. Eerdmans, 1988), 33; Halstead, *Out Now!*, 74 and 103.

47. Staughton Lynd and Thomas Hayden, *The Other Side* (New York: Signet, 1967), 18.

48. *Liberation*, July 1966, p. 37.

49. Dave Dellinger, *More Power Than We Know: The People's Movement Toward Democracy* (Garden City, N.Y.: Doubleday, 1975), 113–14.

50. Sale, *SDS*, 622.

51. Halstead, *Out Now!*, 724, 80.

52. Confidential report by a SANE member on Spring Mobilization National Committee meeting in New York, March 4, 1967, SCPC, DG 58, Series E, Box 3, Staff Reports 1967.

53. Cf. Guenter Lewy, *America in Vietnam* (New York: Oxford Univ. Press, 1978), 436 and the sources cited there.

54. This luncheon address was reported somewhat inaccurately by Rowland Evans and Robert Novak in their column in the *Washington Post* of Oct. 11, 1967. The summary of Rusk's remarks given by me is based on a letter of Rusk to me dated July 16, 1976.

55. U.S. Senate, Select Committee to Study Governmental Operations with Respect to Intelligence Activities, *Foreign and Military Intelligence*, Final Report, 94th Cong., 2nd sess., April 23–26, 1976, Book 3, pp. 692–93.

56. CIA, "International Connections of U.S. Peace Movement," reprinted in part in Charles DeBenedetti, "A CIA Analysis of the Anti-Vietnam War Movement: October 1967," *Peace and Change,* vol. IX, no. 1 (Spring 1983), 35–39.

57. Halstead, *Out Now!*, 724.

58. Zaroulis and Sullivan, *Who Spoke Up?*, 216.

59. *Ibid.*, 529.

60. Cf. Bradford Lyttle, *The Chicago Anti-Vietnam War Movement* (Chicago: Midwest Pacifist Center, 1988), 130–31.

61. Gitlin, *The Sixties*, 416–17.

62. Cf. Lewy, *America in Vietnam*, 207–8.

63. Cf. E. M. Schreiber, "Anti-war Demonstrations and American Public Opinion on the War in Vietnam," *British Journal of Sociology*, XXVII (1976), 225–36. See also William R. Berkowitz, "The Impact of Anti-Vietnam Demonstrations upon Public Opinion and Military Indicators," *Social Science Research,* vol. II, no. 1 (March 1973), 1–14.

64. Halstead, *Out Now!*, 715.

65. Gitlin, *The Sixties*, 262.

66. Julius Jacobson, "Neo-Stalinism: The Achilles Heel of the Peace Movement and the American Left," *New Politics*, vol. XI, no. 3 (Summer 1976), 50–51.

67. John Mueller, "Reflections on the Vietnam Antiwar Movement and on the Curious Calm at the War's End," in Peter Braestrup, ed., *Vietnam as History: Ten Years After the Paris Peace Accords* (Washington, D.C.: Univ. Press of America, 1984), 152; Andrew M. Greeley, "Antiwar Fictions," *New York Times*, Nov. 6, 1974.

68. Mueller, "Reflections," 152.

69. Milton J. Rosenberg et al., *Vietnam and the Silent Majority: The Dove's Guide* (New York: Harper & Row, 1970), 44.

70. Greeley, "Antiwar Fictions."

71. Cf. Gitlin, *The Sixties*, 289.

72. Irving and Debi Unger, *Turning Point 1968* (New York: Scribner's, 1988), 327.

Chapter 13. The Old Left–New Left Nexus

1. Victor Perlo, "Reagonomics—Rationale and Reality," *Political Affairs*, May 1981, p. 4. On Perlo's earlier activities see Joseph P. Lash, *Dealers and Dreamers: A New Look at the New Deal* (Garden City, N.Y.: Doubleday, 1988), 440, 443; Allen Weinstein, *Perjury: The Hiss-Chambers Case* (New York: Knopf, 1978), 22.

2. Philip Taubman, "One of Hollywood 10 Revisits Moscow," *New York Times*, Jan. 13, 1987; Lester Cole, *Hollywood Red: The Autobiography of Lester Cole* (Palo Alto, Calif.: Ramparts, 1981), 404.

3. Elia Kazan, *A Life* (New York: Knopf, 1988), 132.

4. Todd Gitlin, *The Sixties: Years of Hope, Days of Rage* (New York: Bantam, 1987), 72.

5. Lionel Trilling, Introduction to 1975 edition of *The Middle of the Journey* (New York: Harcourt Brace, 1975), xxi.

6. Carl Bernstein, *Loyalties: A Son's Memoirs* (New York: Simon and Schuster, 1989), 161.

7. Irving Howe, "New Styles in Leftism," *Dissent*, Summer 1965, 300–301, quoted in Maurice Isserman, *If I Had a Hammer: The Death of the Old Left and the Birth of the New Left* (New York: Basic Books, 1987), 33.

8. Jessica Mitford, *A Fine Old Conflict* (New York: Knopf, 1977), 319, 279–80.

9. Paul Lyons, *Philadelphia Communists, 1936–1956* (Philadelphia, Pa.: Temple Univ. Press, 1982), 174–75.

10. Isserman, *If I Had a Hammer*, xvii.

11. Cedric Belfrage and James Aronson, *Something to Guard: The Stormy Life of the National Guardian, 1948–1967* (New York: Columbia Univ. Press, 1978), 230, 315, 318–19, 331, 345.

12. Sidney Lens, *Unrepentant Radical: An American Activist's Account of Five Turbulent Decades* (Boston: Beacon, 1980), 222.

13. Donald Keys, "SANE's Wayward Drift to the Left," *War/Peace Report*, Jan. 1968, p. 14.

14. Ann Fagen Ginger and Eugene M. Tobin, eds., *The National Lawyers Guild: From Roosevelt Through Reagan* (Philadelphia, Pa.: Temple Univ. Press, 1988), 9; Harvey Klehr, *The Heyday of American Communism: The Depression Decade* (New York: Basic Books, 1984), 379.

15. Ginger and Tobin, *National Lawyers Guild*, 32.

16. Quoted in Jessica Mitford, "Lawyers of the Left: Their Embattled Guild Has Survived to Fight Again," *Washington Post*, May 24, 1987.

17. Victor Rabinowitz, "The President's Column," *Guild Newsletter*, May–June 1968, quoted in Ginger and Tobin, *National Lawyers Guild*, 258–59.

18. *Ibid.*, 305.

19. Dan Lund, "The 1979 Convention in Washington," in *ibid.*, 301.

20. "State of the Guild Speech by President Paul Harris," *Guild Newsletter,* April 1980, in *ibid.*, 244.

21. Ginger and Tobin, *National Lawyers Guild,* 315 and 342.

22. Arthur Kinoy, "The Role of the Radical Lawyer and Teacher of Law: Some Reflections," *NLG Practitioner,* Winter 1970, quoted in Ginger and Tobin, *National Lawyers Guild,* 274.

23. Barbara Wolvovitz and Jules Lobel, "The Right to Equality: A Marxist Analysis," *NLG Practitioner,* Jan. 1979, quoted in *ibid.,* Ginger and Tobin, *National Lawyers Guild,* 332–35.

24. Quoted in *ibid.,* Ginger and Tobin, *National Lawyers Guild,* 341.

25. *Congressional Record,* May 9, 1979, p. 10522.

26. Harvey Klehr, *Far Left of Center: The American Radical Left Today* (New Brunswick, N.J.: Transaction Books, 1988), 162.

27. Clive Rose, *Campaigns Against Western Defense: NATO's Adversaries and Critics* (New York: St. Martin's, 1985), 262.

28. *Congressional Record,* March 3, 1978, p. 5548.

29. *Ibid.,* 5546.

30. William Goodman, "Internal Struggles," *Guild Notes,* May 1977, quoted in Ginger and Tobin, *National Lawyers Guild,* 323.

31. Quoted in *ibid.,* 359.

32. Gerald Horne, "Our Common Struggles—Past, Present and Future," in *ibid.,* 357.

33. Suzanne Garment, *Wall Street Journal,* Dec. 3, 1982.

34. Cf. the Institute for Religion and Democracy, *A Time for Candor: Mainline Churches and Radical Social Witness* (Washington, D.C.: IRD, 1983), 35.

35. The full statement is cited in ch. 9 (p. 189).

36. Klehr, *Far Left of Center,* 145–47.

37. *Ibid.,* 135–42.

38. *Ibid.,* 172.

39. George Katsiaficas, "Report from National Student Convention: Cooperation and Movement-Building Emphasized," *Peacework,* March 1988, no pagination.

40. William Preston, Jr., "A Brilliant Beginning," *Friends of IMA,* no. 1 (Feb. 1989), 5. The comments of Carl Bernstein and Gus Hall were made at panels 16 and 4 respectively. Transcripts of the panel discussions are available from the Institute for Media Analysis (IMA) in New York.

41. Judith LeBlanc, "The Communist Party and Its Ideology," *Political Affairs,* Aug. 1989, p. 17.

42. Larry Ceplair and Steven Englund, *The Inquisition in Hollywood: Politics in the Film Community 1930–1960* (Garden City, N.Y.: Doubleday, 1980), 241, 428.

43. For an exception see Peter Collier and David Horowitz, "Another 'Low Dishonest Decade' on the Left," *Commentary,* Jan. 1987, pp. 17–24.

44. Belfrage and Aronson, *Something to Guard,* 12.

45. Harvey Klehr, *The Heyday of American Communism: The Depression Decade* (New York: Basic Books, 1984), 112–15.

46. Cf. Klehr, *Far Left of Center,* 140–41.

Chapter 14. Retrospect and Outlook

1. Quoted in Daniel Bell, " 'American Exceptionalism' Revisited: The Role of Civil Society," *Public Interest*, no. 95 (Spring 1989), 49.

2. Cf. Stanley Rothman and S. Robert Lichter, *Roots of Radicalism: Jews, Christians, and the New Left* (New York: Oxford Univ. Press, 1982), ch. 3.

3. Quoted in Milorad M. Drachkovitch, ed., *Yearbook on International Communist Affairs 1966* (Stanford, Calif.: Hoover Institution, 1967), 116.

4. Peter Collier, "Looking Backward: Memories of the Sixties Left," in John H. Bunzel, ed., *Political Passages: Journeys of Change Through Two Decades 1968–1988* (New York: Free Press, 1988), 177.

5. Gus Hall, "Class Struggle Is the Pivot," *Political Affairs*, Oct. 1979, p. 7.

6. Sam Roberts, "Top Communist in U.S. is Taking 'Fever' in Stride," *New York Times*, Dec. 8, 1988.

7. Harvey Klehr, *Far Left of Center: The American Radical Left Today* (New Brunswick, N.J.: Transaction Books, 1988), 10.

8. Cf. *Socialist Workers 1974 National Campaign Committee et al. v. Federal Election Commission and Common Cause*, Fed. Election Camp. Fin. Guide (CCH) § 9068, at 50,564 (D.C. Jan. 2, 1979) (summary of unpublished case).

9. *Join Us to Build a Better USA*, cited by Klehr, *Far Left of Center*, 9–13. See also Richard F. Staar, ed., *Yearbook of International Communist Affairs: 1987* (Stanford, Calif.: Hoover Institution Press, 1987), 147–48.

10. Judith LeBlanc, "The Communist Party and Its Ideology," *Political Affairs*, Aug. 1989, p. 17.

11. Klehr, *Far Left of Center*, 19.

12. *Daily World*, Feb. 28, 1985.

13. Klehr, *Far Left of Center*, 41–43.

14. President's Committee on Civil Rights, *To Secure These Rights* (Washington, D.C.: Government Printing Office, 1947), 51–53.

15. Morris L. Ernst and David Loth, *Report on the American Communist* (New York: Capricorn, 1962), 223–24.

16. Sidney Hook, *Heresy, Yes—Conspiracy, No!* (New York: Committee for Cultural Freedom, 1951), 4–5. I have made some suggestions for implementing such a program of disclosure in my article "Does America Need a *Verfassungsschutzbericht?*," *Orbis*, vol. XXXI, no. 3 (Fall 1987), 275–92.

17. Jean François Revel, "Can Democracies Survive?," *Commentary*, June 1984, p. 4.

18. Bill Keller, "Major Soviet Paper Says 20 Million Died as Victims of Stalin," *New York Times*, Feb. 4, 1989.

19. Clyde Haberman, "Chinese Upheaval Shakes Italy's Communists," *New York Times*, June 9, 1989.

20. John Trinkl, "Left Condemns Chinese Massacre of Students," *Guardian*, June 21, 1989, p. 7.

21. "Will 'End of Leninism' Bring a 'New Birth of Socialism'?" *Guardian*, Dec. 20, 1989, p. 18.

22. Jose Riva, et al., "Perestroika in the USSR and the International Communist Movement," *World Marxist Review*, Sept. 1988, pp. 94, 102.

23. Keynote speech of Gus Hall at Ideological Conference, July 14–16, 1989, *Political Affairs*, Aug. 1989, pp. 3, 11–12.

24. David Engelstein, "What Does the New Thinking Mean for Us?," *Political Affairs*, July 1989, p. 38.

25. Charles Krauthammer, "Seeing the Soviets as Victims," *Washington Post*, Feb. 17, 1989.

26. Martin Bauml Duberman, *Paul Robeson* (New York: Knopf, 1988), xiii.

27. Richard Bernstein, "To Be Young and in China: A Colloquy," *New York Times*, Oct. 7, 1989.

28. Warren Kozak, ". . . Not Technology," *Washington Post*, June 18, 1989.

29. Charles Krauthammer, "Communist Imperative," *Washington Post*, June 23, 1989.

30. Aileen S. Kraditor, *"Jimmy Higgins": The Mental World of the Rank-and-File Communist, 1930–1958* (Westport, Conn.: Greenwood, 1988), 41–42, 271.

31. Philip Rahv in a review of Isaac Deutscher's *The Prophet Outcast* in *New York Review of Books*, Jan. 23, 1964, quoted in Malcolm Cowley, *And I Worked at the Writer's Trade: Chapters of Literary History 1918–1978* (New York: Viking, 1978), 144.

32. Edward Shils, "Totalitarians and Antinomians," in Bunzel, ed., *Political Passages*, 12–13.

Index

Aaron, Daniel, 42, 58
Abel, Lionel, 50
Abernathy, Ralph, 297
Abrams, Henry, 227–28
Abzug, Bella, 223
Academic freedom, 101–8, 154; and
  Communist teachers, 101–2; impact of
  McCarthyism upon, 106–7; and indoc-
  trination, 103–4; and scholarly objec-
  tivity, 104–5
Addams, Jane, 177
Afghanistan, Soviet invasion of, 129, 191–
  93, 286
African National Congress (ANC), 197
Age of Suspicion, The, 84
Albaum, Henry, 105
Alien Registration Act. See Smith Act
Allen, Devere, 44, 170–71
Alsop, Stewart, 209
Alter, Victor, 68–69
Amalgamated Clothing Workers of
  America, 199
America First Committee, 180
American Artists' Congress, 47–48
American Association of University Pro-
  fessors (AAUP), 102
American Bar Association, 283
American Civil Liberties Union (ACLU),
  20, 73; and academic freedom, 102; and
  capitalism, 142–43; Chicago affiliate,
  153; and congressional investigations,
  155; constitution of, 159–60; criteria
  for membership, 158–60; and Dies Com-
  mittee, 148–49; expulsion of Elizabeth
  Gurley Flynn, 150–52, 161–63; founding
  of, 141; politicization of, 164–65; relations with FBI, 153; removal of ban on

Communists, 159–60; resolution against
  totalitarians, 149, 152–53, 158–60, 162–
  63; and rights of Communists, 154; role
  of Roger Baldwin, 145
American Committee for Cultural Free-
  dom (ACCF), 108–14, 157. See also
  Congress for Cultural Freedom
American Committee for Loyalist Spain,
  145
American Committee for Struggle Against
  War, 168
American Committee for the Defense of
  Leon Trotsky, 49–50
"American exceptionalism," 294
American Federation of Labor (AFL), 3,
  38, 217, 220
American Federation of Teachers (AFT),
  101
American Forum for Socialist Education,
  117, 186
American Friends Service Committee
  (AFSC), 118, 191, 248
American Intellectuals for Freedom, 108
American Labor party (ALP), 66, 198–201
American League Against War and
  Fascism, 26, 64, 145, 168, 170–74, 176–77
American League for Peace and
  Democracy, 147, 173, 175
American Legion, 28
American Nazi party, 165
American Negro Labor Congress (ANLC),
  33
American Peace Crusade, 184
American Peace Mobilization (APM), 64,
  66, 179–80
American People's Mobilization (APM),
  66, 180

Americans for Democratic Action (ADA), 56, 121, 217; change in leadership, 223; clash with Progressive party, 209–11; Communists barred from membership in, 209; origins of, 208–9; and Vietnam War, 222
Americans for Intellectual Freedom, 182
American Slav Congress, 25, 66
American Student Union (ASU), 177–78
American Union Against Militarism, 141
American Workers party, 55, 130, 171
American Writers' Congress, 45–48
American Youth Congress (AYC), 26, 29–32, 36–37
Amery, Julian, 111
Amnesty International, 287
Amsterdam Congress. *See* World Congress Against Imperialist War
Amter, Israel, 7, 180, 199
Anatomy of Anti-Communism, 118
Anderson, Sherwood, 168
Andropov, Yuri, 129
Angell, Ernest, 159
Angola, 191, 246
Anti-anticommunism, 116–17, 120, 124, 129, 134, 136, 164, 187, 215, 251, 253, 256, 263, 302
Anticommunism, 77, 80, 116, 118–20, 124, 126, 129–32, 136–37, 160, 241, 253, 256, 263; 1988 conference on, 131, 290–91
Anti-Communist Impulse, The, 118
Antifascism, antifascists, 59, 147, 174
Anti-Fascist Refugee Committee, 26
Appeasement policy, 60
Aptheker, Herbert, 266
Arbatov, Georgi A., 134
Arms control, 196
Aron, Raymond, 107
Aronson, James, 281, 292
Arvin, Newton, 42–44, 50
Association of American Universities (AAU), 101–2
Atomic bomb, 78, 183–84
Attlee, Clement Richard, 88
Auden, W. H., 62, 108

Baker, James A., III, 196
Baldwin, C. B. ("Beanie"), 202
Baldwin, Roger, 86, 141–44, 146, 149, 151–52, 158, 160–61, 165, 167, 169, 171–72, 175–76, 243
Baltic countries, annexation of, 60, 62
Barbusse, Henri, 64, 168–69, 176
Barnet, Richard, 194
Barth, Alan, 87
Bates-Batchellor, Tryphosa Duncan, 67
Batovrin, Sergei, 194
Bayh, Birch, 129
Bay of Pigs invasion, 252
Beard, Charles, 49

Becker, Carl, 49
Belfrage, Cedric, 281, 292
Bell, Daniel, 63, 70, 108, 119
Bell, Tom, 259
Bendiner, Robert, 210
Beneš, Edvard, 47, 206
Bentley, Elizabeth, 78, 279
Berle, Adolf A., 86, 283
Berlin: airlift, 212; blockade of, 77, 206
Bernstein, Carl, 38, 280, 290
Bernstein, Carl Milton, 38
Bernstein, Leonard, 181, 243
Bill of Rights, 70, 148, 152, 156, 165
Bingham, Alfred, 49
Bishop, Joseph W., Jr., 165
Bishop, Maurice, 223
Bittelman, Alexander, 16, 18
Black, Algernon, 158
"Black Belt," 33–34
Black churches, 33
Blacklisting, 92, 95
Black Panthers, 261
Blum, Leon, 173
Boas, Franz, 10, 179
Boat people, 118
Bok, Derek, 133
Bolshevik Revolution, 4
Bowman, LeRoy E., 175
Branfman, Fred, 288
Brecht, Bertold, 38
Breindel, Eric, 132
Brezhnev Doctrine, 193–94
Brinks robbery (1981), 285
Bromley, Dorothy Dunbar, 150
Brooklyn College, 105
Brotherhood of Sleeping Car Porters, 35
Browder, Earl, 7, 9, 18, 20, 22, 30–31, 50, 61, 65, 169, 172–73, 180, 201, 294–95; on Communist espionage, 81; and Communist Political Association, 70–71; at Congress of American Writers, 45–47; ouster of, 75, 204; and Teheran Declaration, 74–75
Brown, John, 44
Brownell, Herbert, 283
Buckley, William F., 83–84, 133
Budenz, Louis F., 141
Bukharin, Nikolai, 8, 50
Bulgaria, 300
Bund, Socialist Jewish, 68
Burnham, James, 110
Bush, George, 165
Butler, William, 232
Byrnes, James F., 202

Cahiers du Communisme, 74
Caldwell, Erskine, 42, 45
California, University of, 107
Calverton, V. F., 49

Cameron, Bruce, 222–23
Campaign for Peace and Democracy/East and West, 193–94
Campaign for Peace with Justice in Central America, 248
Camus, Albert, 258
Cannon, James P., 7, 55
Capital, 294
Capitalism, 11, 41, 54–55, 294, 297
Carr, Robert K., 89, 99–100
Carter, Jimmy, 128–29, 248
Castro, Fidel, 129, 188, 196, 253, 260, 263, 282, 301
Caute, David, 127
Central American Historical Institute, 288
Central Intelligence Agency (CIA), 112–14, 119, 268–69
Ceplair, Larry, 93, 125, 291
Chaffee, Zechariah, Jr., 5
Chamberlain, John, 49
Chambers, Whittaker, 78, 80, 279
Chandra, Romesh, 183, 195
Chaplin, Charlie, 109
Chapman, Abraham, 68
Charney, George, 39, 115
Chase, Stuart, 43
Chicago: Days of Rage, 262; Democratic convention riot, 260, 274
Chicherin, G. V., 166
Childs, John, 70
China, People's Republic of, 78, 82, 197, 258
Choice Before Us, The, 19
Chomsky, Noam, 194
Chou En-lai, 78
Church, Frank, 129
Church Council of Greater Seattle, 137
Churchill, Winston, 66, 71, 75
CIA. *See* Central Intelligence Agency
CISPES. *See* Committee in Solidarity with the People of El Salvador
City College of New York, 106
Civil Liberties Bureau, 141
Civil Rights Congress, 25, 29, 36
Civil-rights movement, 157, 280
Clark, Judith, 285
Clark, Tom C., 80, 204
Clear and Present Danger Doctrine, 90
Clergy and Laity Concerned (CLAC), 289
Coalition for a New Foreign and Military Policy, 188, 288
Coalition to Stop Funding the War, 272, 288
Codman, John, 142
Coffin, William Sloane, 188
Cohen, Morris, 49, 54
COINTELPRO (Counterintelligence Program), 116
Cold War, 75–76, 78, 130, 157, 187, 192, 215, 249, 266

"Cold War liberalism," 117, 120–21, 127, 215, 249
Cole, Lester, 94, 279
Collective security, 23, 31, 54, 59, 174, 178
Collectivization, 299
Collier, Peter, 128, 132, 250, 295
Cominform. *See* Communist Information Bureau
Comintern, 5–6, 12, 17, 26–27, 39, 44, 54–55, 61, 65, 167, 170, 173, 177; dissolution of, 69; influence of, on CPUSA, 7, 123; and Popular Front, 22; in Third Period, 18–19; and united front, 7, 13–16, 18–19
Commager, Henry Steele, 87
Commentary, 79, 119
Commission on U.S.–Central American Relations, 288
Committee for a Sane Nuclear Policy (SANE), 186; change in political outlook, 245–48; Chicago SANE, 239; Communist infiltration of, 226–28; criteria for leadership, 229–30, 247; and FBI, 226; Greater New York SANE, 226, 231–32, 234; merger with nuclear-freeze movement, 249; origins of, 185, 224; and Senate Internal Security Subcommittee, 227–28, 231; and Vietnam War, 235, 242, 255
Committee for Cultural Freedom (1939), 50–51, 58
Committee for the Defense of Trotsky, 23
Committee for the First Amendment, 91
Committee in Solidarity with the People of El Salvador (CISPES), 133–34, 223, 245–46, 248, 289, 292
Communist Control Act, 83
Communist Information Bureau (Cominform), 204, 219
Communist International. *See* Comintern
Communist Labor Party of America, 5
Communist League of America, 55
Communist Party of America, 5
Communist Party of the United States (CPUSA): and American exceptionalism, 294; appeal of, 41–42; blacks in, 33–36; Comintern influence on, 7, 123; dissolution of, 70–71; and election of 1924, 17; and election of 1932, 42; and election of 1984, 296; and espionage, 81–82; expulsions from, 9; factional struggles in, 7–8; finances of, 26, 309–10 n.8; and Gorbachev's reforms, 300–301; and Hitler-Stalin Pact; 62, 175; and intellectuals, 10, 12, 43–44; Jews in, 64, 295; membership of, 25, 29–30, 56, 63, 66, 71, 77, 115, 294, 306–7; and movement against war in Vietnam, 266, 268–71; new history of, 120–24; origins of, 3–5; outlawry of, 79–80, 83, 86; and Progressive party, 204–5, 214–16; reestab-

Communist Party of the United States
(*Cont.*)
lishment of, 75; and secrecy, 6, 28, 37–39,
81, 85, 93, 106, 291–92; and teachers,
101–8; and trade unions, 71–72, 216–21;
violent tactics of, 20, 292
Communist Political Association, 70
Comparable worth, 165
Conference for Progressive Political Action
(CPPA), 14, 16–17
Conference on Critical Legal Studies, 285
Congress for Cultural Freedom (CCF),
111–14. *See also* American Committee
for Cultural Freedom
Congressional Black Caucus, 297
Congressional investigations, 82, 90–100,
111, 155, 324; abuses of, 96, 99–100; legal
status of, 90–91, 95
Congress of Industrial Organizations
(CIO), 71–72, 124; expulsion of Com-
munist unions from, 216–21; and Henry
Wallace campaign, 205; merger with
AFL, 220
Contras, 193
Conyers, John, 223, 297
Cook, Thomas I., 86
Coolidge, Calvin, 17
Coombe, William M., 81
Cooney, Terry A., 121
Copland, Aaron, 181
Corey, Lewis, 42
Cortright, David, 246–47
Coser, Lewis, 4, 29, 31, 35, 58, 82, 111,
216, 220
Council on Hemispheric Affairs, 288
Counterculture, 275
Counts, George, 70, 108
Cousins, Norman, 182, 224, 226–27, 230–32,
236–38, 240–41, 243
Cowley, Malcolm, 10, 42, 45–46 48, 50, 52,
63, 304
Craig, Gordon, 61
Crockett, George, 223
Croly, Herbert, 48
Cromwell, Oliver, 44
Cross, Samuel, 68
Crossman, Richard, 110
Cruise missiles, deployment of, 193, 246
Cuba missile crisis of 1962, 235
Cuban Revolution, 258
Cultural and Scientific Conference for
World Peace, 108, 181–83
Cultural Revolution in China, 264
Culture and Crisis, 42
Czechoslovakia, 77, 206, 286, 300

Dallin, David, 54
Darkness at Noon, 94
Dartmouth College, 132
Dashichev, V., 60

Daughters of the American Revolution
(DAR), 28, 67
Davies, Joseph E., 67
Davis, Angela, 132–33, 290, 297
Davis, Elmer, 43, 49, 209
Davis, Hope Hale, 81
Davis, Jerome, 50
Davis, Robert Gorham, 97, 105
Davis, Stuart, 47
Dean, James, 250
Debs, Eugene Victor, 3–4
DeCaux, Len, 217
Decter, Moshe, 110–11
Dellinger, Dave, 269
Dellums, Ronald V., 223, 248
Dennis v. United States, 86, 297
Detzer, Dorothy, 174
Dewey, John, 43–44, 49–50, 58, 69, 73, 304
Dies, Martin, 91, 121, 148–49. *See also*
Special Committee for the Investigation
of Un-American Activities
Dimitroff, Georgi, 22, 61
Disarmament and Common Security by
the Year 2000, 248
Dissent, 119
Dmytryk, Edward, 94
Dodd, Christopher, 129
Dodd, Thomas J., 227–29, 231
Dohrn, Bernadine, 259–60, 262, 285
Dollar Diplomacy, 8
Dollfus, Engelbert, 20
Dos Passos, John, 10–11, 42, 45–46, 58,
110, 147, 169
Douglas, Paul, 211
Douglas, William O., 297
Draft, 165
Draper, Theodore, 7, 26, 104, 122–24
Dreiser, Theodore, 10, 11, 41–42, 45, 50,
168–69, 179
Drinan, Robert F., 223
Dual responsibility, theory of, 195
Duberman, Martin Bauml, 301
Dubinsky, David, 24, 199–200, 202, 209
Du Bois, W. E. B., 118
Du Bois Clubs of America, 257, 265–66
Duclos, Jacques, 74–75
Duffey, Joseph, 222
Dukakis, Michael, 136
Dung, Van Tien, 272
Dunne, Philip, 92, 125, 210
Dupee, Fred, 53
Dutschke, Rudi, 298
Dylan, Bob, 261

Eastern Europe, 77, 305
Eastman, Max, 8, 52, 57–58, 69, 108–11,
182
Einstein, Albert, 157
Eisenhower, Dwight D., 76
Eisler, Gerhard, 26

Elks, 175
Ellison, Ralph, 108
Ellsberg, Daniel, 194
El Salvador, 134, 165, 191, 222–23, 246, 288
Emergency Civil Liberties Committee
  (ECLC), 156
Emergency Committee for Southern
  Political Prisoners, 10
Emergency Peace Campaign, 174
Emergency Peace Mobilization, 179
Emerson, Thomas I., 156, 283
Emspak, Frank, 266
Encounter, 112, 119
Engels, Friedrich, 44
Engelstein, David, 301
Englund, Steven, 93, 125, 291
Epstein, Jason, 118
Epstein, Judith, 174
"Equal responsibility," theory of, 194
Erlich, Henryk, 68–69
Ernst, Morris L., 65, 86, 148–49, 154, 209,
  283, 299
Espionage, 78, 81–82, 85, 88–89, 100, 121
Espionage Act of 1917, 4
Ethiopia, Italian invasion of, 34, 173
European Nuclear Disarmament (END),
  193, 195
Exclusionary policy. *See* American Civil
  Liberties Union; Americans for Demo-
  cratic Action; Committee for a Sane
  Nuclear Policy; Students for a Demo-
  cratic Society
Ex-Communists, phenomenon of, 233,
  279–81

Fadayev, A. A., 182
Falk, Richard, 194
False consciousness, 189, 303
Fanon, Frantz, 258
Farabundi Marti National Liberation
  Front (FMLN), 134
Farfield Foundation, 114
Farmer-Labor party, 7, 14–17, 26
Fascism, 21, 23, 49, 95
Fast, Howard, 181
FBI, 36, 68, 115, 127, 133, 153, 226
Federal Bureau of Investigation. *See* FBI
Federated Farmer-Labor party (FFLP), 15
Federation of Modern Painters and
  Sculptors, 48
Fellowship of Reconciliation (FOR), 170,
  186, 188
Fellow travelers, concept of, 29
Field, Frederick Vanderbilt, 179–80
Fifth Amendment, 91, 95–97, 101, 125,
  155, 231
Finerty, John F., 151
Finland, Soviet invasion of, 60, 62–63, 147,
  176, 178
First Amendment, 90, 92, 97, 125

Fisher, Louis, 50
Fitzpatrick, John, 14–15
Flacks, Richard, 290
Fly, James L., 154–55
Flynn, Elizabeth Gurley, 150, 152, 161–63
Ford, James W., 42
Ford Motor Company, 144
Foreign-language federations, 4–7
Foreman, Clark, 156
Fortas, Abe, 125, 283
Fort-Whiteman, Lovett, 33
Foster, William Z., 6–7, 17, 42, 70, 72,
  74–75
Fractions, use of, 27–28
Fraenkel, Osmond K., 147, 152, 154–55,
  161, 163, 283
France, 60
Frank, Barney, 136–37
Frank, Jerome, 283
Frank, Lewis, Jr., 213
Frank, Waldo, 42, 45–47
Frankfurter, Felix, 5, 85
Frantz, Laurentz, 96
Freedom House, 182
Freedomways, 289
Freeman, Joseph, 9, 46, 142, 304
Freiheit, 64
Friends of the Soviet Union, 10, 26, 143,
  168
Front, The, 124
Front organizations, 25, 28, 36–40, 82, 167,
  287–88, 296. *See also specific*
  organizations
Fuchs, Klaus, 78
Fulbright, James W., 118, 129

Galbraith, John Kenneth, 131, 209
Gandhi, Mohandas, 167
Garment, Suzanne, 288
Gates, John, 32, 73, 116
Gellhorn, Walter, 154
Genoa Conference of 1922, 166
German-American *Volksbund*, 39
German Democratic Republic, 300
Gilmore, Robert, 224, 228–29, 233
Gitlin, Todd, 253, 255, 260–61, 263, 272–
  73, 280
Glasnost, 61, 301
Glazer, Nathan, 107, 233, 243
God That Failed, The, 10, 110
Gold, Mike, 9–10, 64–65
Goldman, Emma, 143
Goodman, William, 286–87
Gorbachev, Mikhail S., 50, 61, 194–96, 296,
  301
Gordon, Jeff, 260
Gorki, Maxim, 168
Gornick, Vivian, 124
Great Britain, 60
Great Depression, 11, 29, 32, 41, 44, 95,

Great Depression (*Cont.*)
120, 177, 294, 304
Great Fear, The, 127
Greece, 77
Greeley, Andrew M., 275
Greenfield, Meg, 137
Grenada, 223
Griffith, Robert, 126
Gropper, William, 181
Group for the Establishment of Trust
Between the USSR and USA, 192
Guardian, 130
Guevara, Che, 285
Guilt by association, 88, 154, 158
Gulag, 54, 301
Gulf of Tonkin resolution, 254

Haber, Al, 253, 256–57
Haiman, Frank, 162
Hall, Gus, 129, 131, 185, 192, 290, 296
Halstead, Fred, 265, 267, 270, 272–73, 282
Handal, Farid, 134
Harlan, John Marshall, 85
Harlan County, 11
Harrington, Donald, 241
Harrington, Michael, 251–52, 255
Harris, Paul, 285
Hart, Gary, 129
Harvard University, 101, 105
Hassler, Alfred, 186, 188
Hatfield, Mark, 129
Hathaway, Clarence A., 27, 45
Hayden, Tom, 250–53, 258, 263–64, 266, 269, 275
Hayes, Charles, 297
Hayford, James, 212
Hays, Arthur Garfield, 145, 148–49, 151, 154
Hazlitt, Henry, 43
Healey, Dorothy, 39
Hearst, William Randolph, 56
Heller, Clarence, 243
Hellman, Lillian, 50, 125, 164, 181
Helms, Jesse, 129
Henderson, Donald, 169
Henderson, Leon, 209
Hicks, Granville, 42–46, 50, 63, 84, 97, 105
Hillman, Sidney, 24, 68, 72, 199–200, 202
Hillquit, Morris, 19, 24
Hiss, Alger, 78, 80–82, 85, 98, 121, 126
Hitler, Adolf, 18–19, 21, 60, 62, 66–67, 95
Hitler-Stalin Pact, 24, 32, 35, 37, 48, 60–65, 67, 71, 117, 146–47, 152, 175–76, 178, 197, 199, 283
Ho Chi Minh, 275, 282, 301
Hollander, Paul, 134
Hollow Men, The, 65
Hollywood Ten, 91–94, 125, 279
Holmes, John Haynes, 145, 147, 151

Hook, Sidney, 42, 50, 54–55, 85–88, 102–3, 105, 107–8, 111–13, 127, 168, 182, 299, 304
Hoover, J. Edgar, 36, 116, 127, 226
Horne, Gerald, 287
Horowitz, David, 128, 132, 250
House Un-American Activities Committee
(HUAC), 36, 79, 80, 85, 91–92, 95, 99–100, 105, 125, 187, 234, 283
Howe Irving, 4, 29, 31, 58, 82, 111, 113, 119, 127, 216, 220, 240–41, 247–48, 280
HUAC. *See* House Un-American Activities
Committee
Hughes, H. Stuart, 242, 254, 265
Humphrey, Hubert Horatio, 83, 86, 211
Hungarian Revolution of 1956, 115, 117, 186, 252, 281, 284, 286, 295
Hungary, 300
Hutchins, Robert M., 107

Ickes, Harold, 174
Illinois Self-Advancement Club, 17
Ilma, Viola, 30
Independent Citizens' Committee for the
Arts, Sciences and Professions, 181, 202
Indochina Resource Center, 288
Indoctrination, 103, 105
Industrial Workers of the World
(IWW), 3
In Fact, 76
INF Treaty, 192–93
"Innocents," 27–28, 167
Institute for Media Analysis, 131
Institute for Policy Studies (IPS), 129, 194, 246–47, 288
Intercollegiate Socialist Society, 250
Internal Security Act, 83, 86, 109, 185
Internal Security Subcommittee of the
U.S. Senate, 100, 105, 227, 231–32, 234, 269
International Association of Democratic
Lawyers (IADL), 286
International Institute for Peace, 183.
See also World Peace Council
International Labor Defense (ILD), 33–34
International Ladies Garment Workers
Union (ILGWU), 64, 170, 199
International Workers Order, 25, 168
Iran, 77
Israel, 40
Isserman, Maurice, 263, 281

Jack, Homer A., 187, 227, 233, 239, 247, 249
Jackson, Andrew, 70
Jackson, George, 133
Jackson, Henry, 287
Jackson, James E., 190–91
Jackson, Jesse, 248, 289
Jacobs, John ("JJ"), 262
Jacobs, Paul, 258

Jacques, Martin, 300
Japanese-Americans, relocation of, 73–74
Jefferson, Thomas, 22, 70
Jewish Anti-Fascist Committee, 68
Jewish Voice, 64
Jews: in Communist party, 295; and
  Hitler-Stalin Pact, 64
Jim Crow, 73
John Birch Society, 132
Johnny Got His Gun, 64
John Reed Clubs, 9–10, 44, 46, 53, 168
Johnson, Arnold, 185, 187, 266–67, 282
Johnson, Lyndon Baynes, 222, 254, 269–70,
  274–75
Josephson, Matthew, 41–52, 62
Judd, Walter, 174

Kahn, Tom, 255
Kallen, Horace, 49
Kamenev, Lev, 16, 47, 50
Kampelman, Max, 220
Kantorovitch, Haim, 21
Katz, Milton R., 249
Kazan, Elia, 95, 126, 279
Kempton, Murray, 120
Kennan, George F., 112
Kennedy, Robert, 260, 270
Kent, Rockwell, 47
Keys, Donald, 229, 237–40, 243–45, 282
Khmer Rouge, 124, 264, 302
Khrushchev, Nikita, 39, 115, 117, 280,
  284, 295
Killing Fields, The, 124
King, Martin Luther, Jr., 36, 118, 129, 236,
  260, 270
Kingdom, Frank, 205
Kinoy, Arthur, 285
Kirchwey, Freda, 51, 65, 83, 202, 209, 213
Kissinger, Clark, 270–71
Kissinger, Henry, 272, 292–93
Klare, Michael, 248
Klehr, Harvey, 43, 296
Koestler, Arthur, 94, 108, 167
Kohn, Hans, 108
Kondrashov, Stanislav, 196
Konrad, Gyorgy, 194
Korea, 191, 246
Korean War, 82, 107, 116, 156, 183–85, 273
Kovel, Joel, 131
Kraditor, Aileen S., 303
Krauthammer, Charles, 301–2
Kristol, Irving, 97–98, 118
Krutch, Joseph Wood, 43, 49
Kuhn, Fritz, 39
Ku Klux Klan (KKK), 154, 160
Kulish, V. M., 61
Kunstler, William, 158, 164, 284
Kuusinen, Ottomar V., 27

Labor party, British, 88

Labor Research Association (LRA), 297
Ladejinsky, Wolf, 109
LaFollette, Robert M., 7, 15–17, 203
LaFollette, Suzanne, 10, 69
Lahey, Edwin A., 215
Lamont, Corliss, 66, 147–48, 152–53, 156,
  160
Lamson, Peggy, 146
Landau, Saul, 258
Lardner, Ring, 94, 279
LaRocque, Gene, 223
Lash, Christopher, 108–9, 112
Lash, Joseph, 177–79
Lattimore, Owen, 98
Lawrence, Bill, 212
Lawson, John Howard, 92–93
League Against Fascism and Dictatorship,
  64
League Against Imperialism, 145, 167
League for Industrial Democracy (LID),
  39, 171, 251, 253, 255
League of American Writers, 45–46, 62
League of Nations, 22, 173
League of Professional Groups for Foster
  and Ford, 42–43
League of Struggle for Negro Rights, 33
Lear, Walter, 232
LeBlanc, Judith, 296
*Left-Wing Communism: An Infantile
  Disorder*, 284
Lend-Lease Act, 180
Lenin, V. I., 16, 26–27, 38, 40, 44, 166,
  261, 284
Lens, Sidney, 130, 188, 282, 288
Lerner, Max, 50, 58, 206, 209
Levenstein, Harvey, 39
Levitas, Sol, 54
Levy, Herbert Monte, 153
Lewis, Anthony, 134
Lewis, John L., 71
Lewis, Lionel S., 107
Liberals, liberalism, 48–53, 62, 76, 82–84,
  88, 96, 98, 121, 127, 210, 235, 263
Liberal party, 56, 201
Liberator, 8
Libertarians, 133
Liberty under the Soviets, 143
Life, 67
Little, Brown and Company, 57
Lincoln, Abraham, 70
Lin Piao, 261
Lithuanian Workers' Literature Society,
  15
Litvinov, Maxim, 21
Loeb, James, Jr., 208–11
Lombardi, Franco, 111
London, Jack, 3
Lore, Ludwig, 7
Lovestone, Jay, 8, 169–70
Lovett, Robert Morss, 176, 179

Lowell, Robert, 108
Loyalty oaths, 87, 107
Loyalty-Security Program, 80, 87–89, 111
Lundberg, Ferdinand, 51
Lybia, 246
Lynd, Staughton, 266
Lyons, Eugene, 56, 58, 72
Lyons, Paul, 122–23, 281
Lysenkoism, 182

McAuliffe, Mary S., 220
McCarran, Pat, 82, 97
McCarthy, Eugene, 129, 222, 270
McCarthy, Joseph R., 82, 87, 91, 97–100, 107, 109–11, 116, 121, 128, 137, 154, 304
McCarthy, Mary, 53
McCarthy and the Communists, 110–11
McCarthyism, 79, 83, 84, 98, 106–7, 111, 114, 116–17, 121, 124, 126–28, 132, 134–35, 152, 157, 187, 233, 239, 250–51, 253, 256, 269, 302, 304
McConnell, Scott, 134
MacDonald, Dwight, 47, 53, 70, 108, 182, 201
Macedonian independence, resolution on, 212
Machiavelli, Nicolò, 38
MacIver, Robert, 107
MacLeish, Archibald, 62
McReynolds, David, 194
McWilliams, Carey, 112
Madison Square Garden riot (1934), 20, 171, 292
Mahoney, William, 16–17
Mailer, Norman, 181
Malta summit, 196
Managua, 301, *See also* Nicaragua; Sandinistas
Manchuria, 77
Mangold, William, 174
Mann, Thomas, 47, 62, 181
Manson, Charles, 262
Mao Tse-tung, 78, 261, 301
Marat, Jean-Paul, 44
March on Washington (1941), 35–36
Marcuse, Herbert, 258, 292
Markowitz, Norman D., 216
Marshall, George, 77
Marshall, Margaret, 57
Marshall Plan, 77, 113, 204–5, 211, 217–19
Marx, Karl, 44–45, 294
Marxism, Marxists, 41, 44, 54–55, 70, 104, 298
Marxism-Leninism, 103, 259, 261, 263–64, 274, 285, 287, 291, 299, 302
Massnahme, Die, 38
Mathiessen, F. O., 58
Matthews, J. B., 145, 169, 177
Maurer, James Hudson, 43

May, Alan Nunn, 78
May Day Tribe, 275
May Second Committee, 254–55, 257
Meacham, Stewart, 228, 232–33
Meany, George, 287
Meiklejohn, Alexander, 70
Meyer, Cord, 128
Meyer, Lawrence, 241
Meyer, Paul, 162–63
Midnight Special, 185
Miller, Arthur, 181
Miller, James, 259
Mills, C. Wright, 250
Milner, Lucille B., 141
Milosz, Czeslaw, 109
Minimum consensus, concept of, 191
Minnesota Farmer-Labor party, 15
Minor, Robert, 73, 169
Miracle, The, 109
Mission to Moscow, 67, 69, 91, 94
Mitford, Jessica, 280–81
Mobilization for Survival (MfS), 188, 288
Modern Monthly, 49, 54
Monat, Der, 112
Mooney, Tom, 125
Mortimer, Wyndham, 38
Moscow News, 300
Moscow purge trials, 48–50, 53, 98
Motion picture industry: blacklisting in, 92; Communists in, 93; HUAC investigation of, 91–92; pro-Soviet films in, 94. *See also* Hollywood Ten
Moynihan, Daniel, 287
Mueller, John, 274
Münzenberg, Willi, 27, 167–68
Muhammad, 44
Muhlen, Norbert, 77, 83–84
Muller, A. J., 111, 182
Mumford, Lewis, 47
Munich Pact, 24
Muravchik, Joshua, 135
Murray, Philip, 68, 217–20
Murrow, Edward R., 207
Mussolini, Benito, 34, 173
Muste, A. J., 55, 108, 117, 130, 170–71, 181–82, 186, 224, 233, 236, 254, 265
MX missile, 222, 246
Myerson, Michael, 188, 192
Myrdal, Gunnar, 35

Nabokov, Nicolas, 112
Nalin, Y., 135
Naming Names, 125
Nation, 5, 57, 65–66, 75–76, 79, 83–84, 130, 201, 213
National Alliance Against Racist and Political Repression (NAARPR), 297
National Association for the Advancement of Colored People (NAACP), 34–36, 171

National Citizens' Political Action Committee (NCPAC), 202
National Civil Rights Mobilization (1950), 36
National Coalition Against War, Racism and Repression, 271
National Committee for the Defense of Political Prisoners, 10
National Conference for New Politics, 240
National Coordinating Committee to End the War in Vietnam (NCC), 265
National Council of American-Soviet Friendship, 66, 76, 190
National Council of Churches, 188, 288
National Council of Jewish Communists, 64
National Council of the Arts, Sciences and Professions, 181
National Education Association (NEA), 101
National Endowment for Democracy, 114
National Guardian, 257, 281–82, 292
National Labor Relations Board (NLRB), 144
National Lawyers Guild (NLG), 223, 283–87
National Liberation Front (NLF), 235, 244, 254, 263, 268, 289
National liberation movements, 190–91, 244, 282
National Mobilization Committee to End the War in Vietnam, 243
National Negro Congress (NCC), 35–36
National Office faction (NO), 258, 261
National Peace Action Coalition (NPAC), 222, 271
National Rainbow Coalition, 289
National Scottsboro Action Committee, 29
National States Rights party, 165
National Student League, 30, 106, 176
Navasky, Victor, 125–26, 130
Nazi party, 132
Nazi-Soviet Pact. *See* Hitler-Stalin Pact
Nearing, Scott, 8
Needle trade unions, 199
Negro Self-Determination, doctrine of, 33–34
Neier, Aryeh, 164
Neufield, Russ, 285
Neuhaus, Richard J., 239
Neutrality Act of 1935, 48
Neutron bomb, 222, 246
New Deal, 22–23, 31–32, 82, 144, 178, 279, 283
Newfield, Jack, 263
New Leader, 54, 56, 69, 77, 83–84, 199
New Left, 117, 120, 160, 187, 222, 235, 239, 244, 249–50, 256, 265–66, 268, 270, 281–82, 284–85, 288, 290, 292–93, 295, 299

Newman, Henry, 10
New Masses, 9–10, 45, 52, 66
New Mobilization to End the War in Vietnam, 271
New Republic, 11, 48–52, 63, 66, 68, 75–76, 79, 150, 173, 200–202
New School for Social Research, 101
"New thinking," 194–95, 197
New Times, 300
New York Communist, 4
New York Review of Books, 117
Nicaragua, 130, 165, 193, 196, 223, 246, 298–99. *See also* Sandinistas
Nicolayevsky, Boris, 54
Niebuhr, Reinhold, 43, 170, 208–9
Nixon, Richard M., 165, 271–72, 274–75
NKVD, 68
North American Congress on Latin America (NACLA), 288
North Atlantic Treaty Organization (NATO), 77–78, 181, 218
North Korea, 78, 183
North Star, The, 68, 94
Norway, fall of, 64
Nuclear Disarmament, Campaign for (CND), 192
Nuclear-freeze movement, 164, 193, 246
Nuclear pacifism, 185
Nuclear weapons, testing of, 224–25
Nunn, Alan, 78

Occhetto, Achille, 300
O'Dell, Jack, 248, 289, 337 n.65
Oglesby, Carl, 256–57, 261, 290
"Old Guard" of Socialist party, 19, 20–24, 49, 198–99
Old Left, 122, 265–66, 270, 281–82, 284–85, 288, 290, 293, 295
Ollman, Bertell, 104–5
O'Neill, William, 95, 107, 121, 124–25
Operation CHAOS, 268
Oppenheimer, J. Robert, 109
Oxford Pledge, 178

Pacifists, pacifism, 166, 170, 174, 189–90
Page, Kirby, 171, 174
Paine, Thomas, 70
Pakashlahti, Johannes, 195
Palestine, 64
Palestine Liberation Organization (PLO), 286
Palmer, A. Mitchell, 5
Pardun, Robert, 258–59
Parenti, Michael, 118, 129
Parker, Dorothy, 50
Participatory democracy, 263, 281
Partisan Review, 52–54, 70, 120

Pauling, Linus, 226, 232–33
Peace and Democracy News, 193
Peaceful coexistence, concept of, 189, 195–96
Pearl Harbor, 66
Peck, Sidney, 188–89, 282, 288
Pell, Orly, 241
Pells, Richard H., 126
Pentagon, march on (1967), 243, 270
People's Coalition for Peace and Justice (PCPJ), 271
People's Daily World, 296
People's Voice Culture Club, 17
People's war, Chinese theory of, 261
Perestroika, 300
Perjury: The Hiss-Chambers Case, 81
Perlo, Victor, 279
Pershing II missiles, deployment of, 193, 246
Peters, Josef, 28
Philadelphia Communists, 123
Philip, André, 111
Phillips, William, 53, 57, 120
Phillipson, Ilene, 130
Pickett, Clarence, 224, 228, 230–31
Pickus, Robert, 243
PL. *See* Progressive Labor party
Pledge of Resistance, 248, 298
PM, 201
Podhoretz, Norman, 79–80, 251
Poland, 60–61, 300
Polish Peace Coalition, 194
Political Affairs, 129
Politics, 70
Pollack, Sandy, 134, 188, 289
Pol Pot, 124
Popular Front, 19, 22–25, 28–29, 32, 35, 37, 44, 47–48, 51, 53–54, 56, 58–59, 62–63, 65–66, 70–71, 76, 80, 93–94, 106, 116, 123, 173, 177, 206–8, 214, 280, 283, 294
Porter, Fairfield, 48
Porter, Paul A., 209
Pound, Dean Roscoe, 5
Powell, Adam Clayton, 62
Power Elite, The, 250
Powers, Thomas, 254
Prague coup of 1948, 77
Prague Spring, 300
President's Committee on Civil Rights, 299
Pressman, Lee, 201, 211–12, 217–18
Preston, William, Jr., 291
Progressive, 130
Progressive Citizens of America (PCA), 202–4, 209, 217
Progressive Labor party (PL), 254–55, 257, 258–63
Progressive party, 79, 156; demise of, 215; origins of, 204, 208; role of Communists in, 216; Vermont resolution rejected by,

212–13. *See also* Wallace, Henry
Proletarian internationalism, 197
Proletarian literature, 9, 46, 53

Quarantine speech, 178
Quemoy and Matsu, 185
Quigley, John, 286
Quill, Mike, 200–201, 204, 221

Rabinowitz, Victor, 284
Radek, Karl, 13, 50
Radosh, Ronald, 121
Rahv, Philip, 52–54, 57, 120, 304
Ramparts, 268
Randolph, A. Philip, 35–36, 228
Raskin, Marcus, 246–48
Rasmussen, Ralph, 39
Razin, Stenka, 44
Reader's Digest, 67, 69
Reagan, Ronald, 131, 137, 248, 292, 298
Reagan Doctrine, 288
Red Army, 67
Red-baiting, 38, 76, 116, 134, 147, 163–64, 191–92, 208, 210, 251, 259, 262, 266
Red Channels, 95
Red Decade, The, 56
"Red-diaper babies," 251, 253, 281
Red Eye Farmers Club, 17
Redlich, Norman, 96
Red Scare (1920), 5
Reed, John, 4, 8
Reitman, Alan, 152
Reporter, 79
Republican party, 79
Reserve Officers Training Corps. *See* ROTC
Reuther, Victor, 241
Reuther, Walter, 209, 216, 228
Revel, Jean François, 299
Revolutionary Youth Movement I. *See* Weathermen
Revolutionary Youth Movement II (RYM II), 261–62
Richardson, Thomas, 184
Rickenbacker, Edward V., 67
Riesman, David, 110
Robeson, Paul, 211, 301
Roche, John P., 173, 222
Rogge, O. John, 204
Rolland, Romain, 168
Romains, Jules, 111
Romance of American Communism, The, 124
Roosevelt, Eleanor, 31–32, 209, 217, 228
Roosevelt, Franklin D., 22, 32, 35, 47, 62, 64, 66, 68, 71–72, 75, 173, 178–80, 198, 200
Rorty, James, 42, 110–11
Rose, Alex, 199–200
Rosenberg, Julius, 78, 85, 121, 126

ROTC, attacks on, 164, 260, 270
Roth, Henry, 50
Rousseau, Jean-Jacques, 303
Royal Commission, 100
Rumanian Progressive Club, 15
Rusk, Dean, 268
Russian Revolution of 1917, 4
Russian War Relief, 66
Rustin, Bayard, 224, 254
Ruthenberg, Charles E., 4

Sacco-Vanzetti case, 69
Sale, Kirkpatrick, 258, 267
Sandburg, Karl, 179
Sandinistas, 130, 194, 246, 298–99, 301.
    See also Nicaragua
SANE. *See* Committee for a Sane Nuclear
    Policy
SANE/FREEZE, 249
Sargent, Linda, 290
Sartre, Jean-Paul, 258
Schary, Dore, 92
Schlesinger, Arthur M., Jr., 88, 108–11,
    113, 116, 119–20, 182, 203, 209
Schmidt, Carlo, 111
Schrecker, Ellen, 37, 103–7, 127
Schulberg, Budd, 181
Schuyler, George S., 109
Scopes case, 143
Scott, Carlottia A., 223
Scott, Lawrence, 224, 226
Scottsboro boys case, 33–34, 125
Screen Writers Guild, 91, 93
SDS. *See* Students for a Democratic Society
Seabury, Paul, 222
Security and Terrorism Subcommittee of
    the U.S. Senate, 100
*Seeing Red: Stories of American Com-
    munists,* 124
Seldes, George, 50, 58, 76
Serge, Victor, 70
Shachtman, Max, 7, 55
Shanker, Albert, 287
Shapiro, Meyer, 47–48
Shapley, Harlow, 181
Shaw, Irving, 50
Sheen, Fulton, 68
Shevardnadze, E. A., 195–96
Shils, Edward, 304
Silone, Ignazio, 111
Sinclair, Upton, 3, 142, 169, 250
Slaff, George, 158, 161–63
Slovo, Joe, 197
Smith Act, 65, 72–73, 80, 86–87, 295
Social Democratic Federation (SDF), 22–
    23, 198–99
Social fascists, 19
Socialist party, 11, 14, 18, 20, 39, 43, 169,
    171–72; and election of 1932, 43, mem-
    bership, 5; "Militants," 19; "Old

Guard," 19–20, 49; origins of, 3; split of,
    22; in World War I, 3–4. *See also*
    Thomas, Norman
Socialist Review, 130
Socialist Scholars Conference, 130
Socialist Workers party, 55, 222, 235, 265–
    67, 270–71, 282
Solidarity (Poland), 192
Soll, George, 159
Solomon, Norman, 192
Somoza, Anastasio, 131, 194
Song of Russia, 68, 94
Sontag, Susan, 129–30
South Africa, 197
Southern Christian Leadership Con-
    ference, 297
Soviet Russia Today, 143
Soviet Union: attraction of, 11, 44, 50, 67,
    303; constitution of, 151; crisis of
    ideology in, 299; foreign policy of, 19,
    22, 34, 61; German invasion of, 32, 65,
    67, 179–80; and nuclear testing, 225;
    "thaw," 157. *See also* Moscow purge
    trials
Spanish Civil War (1936–1939), 24, 47–48,
    52, 173
Special Committee for the Investigation
    of Un-American Activities, 91, 148, 175
Spender, Stephen, 113
Spock, Benjamin, 236–41, 244–45
Spring Mobilization to End the War in
    Vietnam, 236–38, 267
SS-20 rockets, 193
Stalin, Joseph, 8, 16, 63, 67, 69, 71, 75, 77,
    115, 148, 151, 157, 185, 196, 261, 280,
    286, 299
*Stalin: An Appraisal of the Man and His
    Influence,* 68
Stalinists, Stalinism, 51–52, 54, 58, 84,
    113–14, 119, 253
Steffens, Lincoln, 3, 8, 41, 301
Steinberg, William, 219
Stewart, Donald Ogden, 181
Stockholm Peace Appeal, 183–84
Stolberg, Ben, 58
Stone, I. F., 58, 214
Stop the U.S. War in El Salvador, 248
Stouffer, Samuel A., 135
Strategic Defense Initiative (SDI), 246, 286
Strontium-90, 225
Student League for Industrial Democracy
    (SLID), 23, 177, 250–51
Student Mobilization Committee to End
    the War in Vietnam, 267, 270
Student Peace Union, 250
Students for a Democratic Society (SDS),
    117, 264–65, 282, 284, 288, 292; and
    anticommunism, 251, 253; distrust of
    ideology, 282; and Marxism-Leninism,
    259–61; membership, 261; and move-

Students for a Democratic Society (SDS) (*Continued*)
ment against war in Vietnam, 254–55, 259–61; origins of, 250; and participatory democracy, 259, 281; and policy of nonexclusion, 251, 255–56, 263; Port Huron statement, 251–53, 263; and Progressive Labor party, 257–62; self-destruction of, 371; and Third World, 253, 260–61, 264; and use of violence, 262–63
Students for a Sane Nuclear Policy, 250
"Submarines," 28
Subversion, 134
Subversive organizations, list of, 87
Supreme Court of the United States, 85, 93
Su Wei, 302
Swomley, John M., 186
Syndicalists, 3

Tammany Hall, 198
Tate, Sharon, 262
Taubman, Philip, 279
Taylor, Glenn, 213
Teheran conference, 74–75
Terrorism, 263
"Thaw," Soviet, 117
Thieu, Nguyen Van, 272
Third Period, 18
Third World, 190, 253–61, 263–64, 266, 282, 287, 298
Thomas, J. Parnell, 121
Thomas, Norman, 11, 44, 77, 85–86, 108, 117, 142, 157, 172, 186, 200, 253, 304; and ACLU, 147–49, 154, 158; Communist attacks on, 20; in election of 1932, 43; on Socialist-Community unity, 19–22; and Soviet Union, 21, 23–24; and Vietnam war, 235–38, 254, 265
Thomas, Trevor, 226–27
Thompson, E. P., 192–94
Thomson, Alan C., 190
Thurmond, Strom, 213
Tiananmen Square, 300, 302
Tito, Josip, 286
To Secure These Rights, 299
Totalitarianism, temptation of, 302–3
Trachtenberg, Alexander, 45
"Transmission belts," 25, 27
Transport Workers Union (TWU), 200
Trevor-Roper, Hugh, 111
Tribunal of Inquiry, 100
Trident submarine, 222, 246
Trilling, Diana, 48, 108–9
Trilling, Lionel, 119, 280
Trotsky, Leon, 16, 47, 49–50, 54, 68
Trotskyists, Trotskyism, 7, 9, 55, 72, 267, 269–71
Truman Doctrine, 77, 203, 205

Truman, Harry S, 77, 79–80, 82–83, 88–89, 205, 213, 215, 217
Trumbo, Dalton, 64, 93–94, 125
Tugwell, Rexford, 211–12, 216
Turkey, 77
Turn Toward Peace, 255
Twenty-one Point Statement of Principles, 6
Twilight of Empire, The, 8

Under Fire, 64
Union for Democratic Action (UDA), 208–9
Union of American Hebrew Congregations, 188
United Automobile Workers (UAW), 38, 216
United Electrical Workers (UE), 38, 218–19
United front, 13–15, 18, 20
United Nations, employment practices of, 155
United Office and Professional Workers of America, 219
United Public Workers of America, 38
United States Congress Against War, 169
United States Peace Council (USPC), 188, 245, 248, 289, 296
United Workingmen Singers, 15
University of California, 107
Uphaus, William, 185
Urban League of Detroit, 297
"Useful idiots," 25, 309 n.2
USSR Society for Friendship and Cultural Relations with Foreign Countries, 190

Veterans of the Abraham Lincoln Brigade, 29
Viet Cong, 236, 268, 301
Vietnam Moratorium Day (1969), 271
Vietnam War, 117–20, 125, 165, 185, 187–88, 259; and American public opinion, 273–74; casualties, 260; movement against, 264–76, 280; 1973 peace accord, 272; Vietnamization, 271
Village Voice, 130
Voorhis, Jerry, 65, 148
Voorhis Registration Act, 65

Waldman, Louis, 4, 21, 199–200
Waldorf-Astoria Peace Conference. *See* Cultural and Scientific Conference for World Peace
Walker, Doris Brin, 287
Wallace, Henry, 76, 79, 203, 206; attitude toward Communists, 207–8, 214–15; Madison Square Garden speech, 202; 1948 campaign, 181, 205–8, 212–13; and Soviet Union, 201–3, 215. *See also* Progressive party
Walton, Richard J., 215

Ward, Harry F., 141, 145, 147, 150, 171–72, 175–76
Warnke, Paul, 129
Warren, Earl, 116
War Resisters League (WRL), 188–89
Washington, George, 70
Washington Office on Latin America, 288
Washington Post, 86
Watergate scandal, 125
Watkins, Tony, 289
Weathermen, 164, 260–62, 270, 285. *See also* Students for a Democratic Society
Webb, Beatrice, 301
Weber, Alfred, 111
Wechsler, James, 30, 80, 84, 97, 177, 212, 215, 221
Weinstein, Allen, 81, 121
Weiss, Cora, 248, 267
West, Jim, 300
Westin, Alan F., 96–97
Wheeler, Burton K., 17
Wilder, Thornton, 169
Williams, G. Mennen, 228
Williamson, John, 74
Wilson, Dagmar, 187
Wilson, Edmund, 11–12, 42, 52, 73
Wilson, J. Finley, 174
Winchell, Walter, 109
Winpisinger, William, 247–48, 337 n.64
Winston, Henry, 135
Winter, Carl, 297
Wolfe, Bertram D., 18
Wolfe, Hugh C., 232
Wolfe, Robert Paul, 235–36
Womack, John, 133
Women's International League for Peace and Freedom (WILPF), 174, 177, 187–88, 248
Women Strike for Peace, 187, 234
Workers Alliance, 23
Worker-Student Alliance (WSA), 258, 261. *See also* Students for a Democratic Society
World Committee of the Partisans for Peace, 183
World Congress Against Imperialist War, 168, 176
World Congress of Intellectuals, 181
World Federation of Trade Unions, 218
World Marxist Review, 300
World Peace Council (WPC), 183–84, 188, 192, 195, 247–48, 289
World War I, 3, 5, 13
World War II, 60, 77, 302
Wright, Richard, 10

Yalta conference, 75
Yanks Are Not Coming, The, 63
Yoneda, Karl, 74
Young Communist League (YCL), 30–31, 72
Young People's Socialist League (YPSL), 30, 177, 250
Young Socialist Alliance (YSA), 265, 267, 270–71
Yukalov, Yuri, 197

Zeta, 131, 290
Zhdanov, Andrei, 111, 182, 204
Zimmerman, Charles, 170
Zinoviev, Grigori, 16, 47, 50